New Criticism and Pedagogical Directions for Contemporary Black Women Writers

New Criticism and Pedagogical Directions for Contemporary Black Women Writers

Edited by
LaToya Jefferson-James

LEXINGTON BOOKS
Lanham • Boulder • New York • London

Published by Lexington Books
An imprint of The Rowman & Littlefield Publishing Group, Inc.
4501 Forbes Boulevard, Suite 200, Lanham, Maryland 20706
www.rowman.com

86-90 Paul Street, London EC2A 4NE

Copyright © 2022 by The Rowman & Littlefield Publishing Group, Inc.

excerpts from Black Girl in Paris by Shay Youngblood © Riverhead Books, 2000

All rights reserved. No part of this book may be reproduced in any form or by any electronic or mechanical means, including information storage and retrieval systems, without written permission from the publisher, except by a reviewer who may quote passages in a review.

British Library Cataloguing in Publication Information Available

Library of Congress Cataloging-in-Publication Data

Names: Jefferson-James, LaToya, 1981- editor.
Title: New criticism and pedagogical directions for contemporary Black women writers / edited by LaToya Jefferson-James.
Description: Lanham : Lexington Books, [2022] | Includes bibliographical references and index. | Summary: "New Criticism and Pedagogical Directions for Contemporary Black Women Writers spans the contemporary era into the AfroFuture. It begins with Ann Petry, who has been forcibly mashed into masculinized critical paradigms, and ends by introducing audiences to Black speculative and Science Fiction writers"— Provided by publisher.
Identifiers: LCCN 2021056402 (print) | LCCN 2021056403 (ebook) | ISBN 9781793606709 (cloth) | ISBN 9781793606723 (paperback) | ISBN 9781793606716 (ebook)
Subjects: LCSH: American literature—African American authors—History and criticism. | American literature—Women authors—History and criticism. | American literature—African American authors—Study and teaching (Higher) | American literature—Women authors—Study and teaching (Higher)
Classification: LCC PS153.B53 N49 2022 (print) | LCC PS153.B53 (ebook) | DDC 810.9/896073—dc23/eng/20220118
LC record available at https://lccn.loc.gov/2021056402
LC ebook record available at https://lccn.loc.gov/2021056403

Contents

Acknowledgments		vii
Preface: From the Present to the Afro-Future		ix
Introduction: Eschewing Social Science and Defying Categorization: An Introduction to Contemporary Black Women Writers *LaToya Jefferson-James*		xv
1	"You Can't Run from the Street": Failed Escapes in Ann Petry's *The Street* (1947) and Shay Youngblood's *Black Girl in Paris* (2000) *Shahara'Tova V. Dente*	1
2	You Can't Shut Me Up: Using Gwendolyn Brooks to Help Students Be Seen and Heard *Carissa McCray*	27
3	Kathleen Collins: BAM Filmmaker and Fiction Writer *Cynthia Davis*	47
4	Closed in Silence and Clothed in Heteronormativity and the (Anti-)Lesbian Embrace: The Woman's Plight in Gayl Jones' *Eva's Man* and "The Women" *Georgene Bess Montgomery*	57
5	Grange's Grapple and Brownfield's Battle: Redefining Manhood in Alice Walker's *Third Life of Grange Copeland* *Lana N. Lockhart*	75

6	Reconnections to Gendered Black Identities in Alice Walker's *The World Will Follow Joy* Linda Mustafa	95
7	Womanist Freedom Dreams: "Stay on the Battlefield" by Sonia Sanchez and Sweet Honey in the Rock Michael C. Montesano	111
8	Mothers Incognito in Toni Morrison's *Paradise* Linda Mustafa	127
9	Love in a Time of Pretentiousness: The Social and Personal Consequences of Romance in Chimamanda Ngozi Adichie's *Americanah* Anna E. Schmidt	147
10	Endless Love: The Evolution of Healers in Octavia Butler's *Patternist* Series Ebony Gibson	163
11	"I Would Restore What Could Be Restored": Reclaiming Identity in Octavia Butler's *Fledgling* Rashell Smith-Spears	181
12	Audre Lorde's *Zami* as a Speculative Womanist Guide to Self-Actualization in Octavia Butler's *Dawn* Roslyn Nicole Smith	197
13	Arc of Memory in Natasha Trethewey's Works Nagueyalti Warren	217
14	Seen and Unseen: The Role of the Venus in N. K. Jemisin's *The Fifth Season* Jasmine H. Wade	237
15	Eco-Justice as Womanist Practice in Contemporary Black Women's Poetry Marta Werbanowska	251
16	*Who Fears Death*: Necropolitics, Gender, and Radical Ontology in Africanfuturist Literature Venise N. Adjibodou	279
Conclusion		299
Index of Authors and Topics		309
About the Editor and Contributors		315

Acknowledgments

I would like to thank my mother, Mrs. Virginia Jefferson Gibson, for the gift of reading; Mrs. Debra Brown, "my other mother," for the many books, stories, and support over the years; and my paternal grandmother, the late Mrs. Annie G. Vaughn, for a legacy of teaching and a genuine love of learning and education. I would also like to thank all of the mothers of Centreville, Mississippi, who prayed for me and kept me on the straight and narrow. You all taught me the meaning of womanism before I had ever heard of the term! A special thanks to two colleagues Verner Mitchell of the University of Memphis and Alison Ligon of Morehouse University—your support and open ears mean more to me than you could ever imagine. I want to thank all of the contributors. In this time of pandemic, simply combing the archives has been extremely difficult. Thank you for your contributions and your patience.

A special thanks to each and every student who sat for my lectures—your contributions in class, the many, many discussions, and journals that you painstakingly handwrote in the digital age, and the papers that you turned in helped to inspire this work. I would especially like to thank those English and English Education majors of Rust College who were there for the duration of my time there. This book was born as I prepared for their American Literature I and American Literature II classes. And though the students testify that I was a top-notch instructor and advisor, they underestimate how much they helped me grow professionally. We worked very hard together.

I would like to thank Mr. Nedrick Patrick, an instructor at Jackson State University and a PhD candidate. As a PhD student and later candidate, Mr. Patrick introduced me to still more American writers of color, was generous when sharing instructional material, and never hesitated to answer my phone call (and I mean at all hours of the day), and for crazy discussions of pedagogy and theory. I am glad that I am not too arrogant to learn from others: knowledge is ever-growing, ever-changing.

Finally, I would like to thank the library staff at the University of Mississippi and Mississippi Valley State University (MVSU). The library staff at MVSU has always been there whenever I needed them. A researcher cannot ask for a more professional and all-around nice staff.

Preface: From the Present to the Afro-Future

While an assistant professor of composition and world literature some time ago at Rust College in Holly Springs, Mississippi, I received an assignment from my chair to teach American literatures I and II. To this day, I truly believe that these classes were given to me with a bit of malignant intent. Anyone who has ever had the displeasure of enduring any of my professional complaints and venting sessions knows that early American literature is an anathema to me. It vexes my very soul just thinking about reading and discussing it with colleagues, and the thought of teaching it increases the likelihood of an excruciating migraine attack. Even typing about it on my laptop is giving me headache symptoms. One of my former graduate school professors is still discouraged by my lack of progress with *Moby Dick* (I began the Transcendental tome a full decade ago, and only the current environmental crisis has truly compelled me to complete it this summer at last). It took me seven years to complete *The Scarlet Letter* (that Rev. Dimsdale and the society that produced and supported his brand of misogyny were the pond scum of Western humanity, by the way), and *Sister Carrie* with its arid tone and the protagonist's worship of material acquisition and stardom is insomnia reading only. Perhaps, since our current generation is in danger of never achieving the American Dream, whatever that may be, I shall finish it.

As a woman from the Pine Belt of South Mississippi, I have managed to break all of the arbitrary rules of academia and have suffered for it. And I suppose that it began innocently enough. My paternal grandmother, Mrs. Annie G. Vaughn, educated at Mississippi Industrial College, then at Jackson State College (now Jackson State University), was an elementary school teacher at Finch Elementary School in my hometown for many decades, and I benefited from that. I honestly do not know when I began to read—only that I read voraciously and was encouraged to do so by this grandmother and my mother. As a reader, my reading interests gravitated between British literature and African American writers. In one school year, I remember quite clearly reading *The Strange Case of Dr. Jekyll and Mr. Hyde* and my mother literally handing me the book that made me fall in love with African American literature: Margaret Walker's *Jubilee*. I was in the third grade and stayed up quite late into the night crying at Hetta's passing and then at other misfortunes that Vyry suffers throughout her life as an ex-slave with a blended family. To this day, I tend to purchase a copy of this text whenever a new edition is published. As an opinionated, rambunctious third grader who hated math but also loved history, science, and social studies, I could not have known then that my reading habits—which continue today—would have any bearing on my career (I wanted to be a medical doctor as an undergraduate, but even the hard "C"s that I viewed in science classes that I once labeled as "useless" as I pursued an English doctorate have helped me to teach Afrofuturism effectively) as a practicing professor and writer.

As I sat across from my chair at the time explaining my teaching preferences, I thought back to the many years that I had labored on the adjunct field in pursuit of an education and financial support. I had never received British literature in any era as a teaching assignment, though I was often overloaded with classes, overwhelmed with student numbers, and never acknowledged for advising. Each time that I requested it, I was rather flippantly dismissed, though I was "allowed" to teach African American literature and those classes were used to increase enrollment on several occasions. Even in graduate school, when I chose to take a British Romanticism class that began with the perpetually enigmatic William Blake rather than slog through those early American literature classes with their Puritanical sermons, many of my African Americans cohorts chose to distance themselves from me, because they accused me of being the contrarian rebel who desired to upset the status quo in order to dispel myths about Black intellectual inferiority. They did not take me seriously until I became a teaching assistant for a Medievalist so that I may deliver texts like *Beowulf* more effectively to undergraduates who may no longer even read the King James Version of the Bible routinely. I am not sure why I thought being at a Historically Black College/University would make a difference. I am not sure why I thought that employment at an HBCU meant an escape into British Literature once more. I explained all of this, in addition to my hatred of early American literature to deaf ears. My chair sat there stone-faced.

Needless to say, that assignment did not change. I was stuck with American literature I and II. To compound my frustration, we were teaching on an accelerated schedule, and I had very little time to prepare a syllabus for either section of the class. Nevertheless, being a good teacher is as much a source of pride for me as research and publication. I have never fully believed in the "publish or perish" mantra that we were all fed in graduate school. I find that mantra disdainful and even dangerous in that it can be misinterpreted by *some* to mean that effective teaching in higher education is a mundane, inert pursuit in the race for almighty tenure and an appointment as an endowed professor at an R1 institution. Yes, tenure is desirable and a noble pursuit. But as a Black woman, I have had to walk, chew bubble gum, mentally balance a check book, and remember to pick up somebody's prescription before the pharmacy closes for a very long time. To live life is a delicate balancing act and academia is no different. I research, write, and publish as it infuses my teaching. My teaching inspires my researching, writing, and publishing almost every semester. Almost every semester that I teach, I find something that needs academic interrogation. It is very rewarding, even when things are challenging or unpleasant, and all professors, particularly those of us in general education, have those challenging semesters.

At the time, Rust College was using the textbooks, *The Bedford Anthology of American Literature vols. 1 & 2* (2008). As I flipped through the table of contents for each one, I noticed that the second volume contained a short story by Toni Morrison that was totally new to me, "Recitatif." After many years of graduate school, I thought I had read all of Morrison's creative works and most of her nonfiction essays. When I read the introductory piece, I found that this story was written for an anthology coedited by Amiri and Amina Baraka, *Confirmation* (1983). Immediately, I tracked this book down at the University of Mississippi (Ole Miss) library. In it were 49 Black women writers—most of them familiar to me—some of them were not. They contributed poetry, plays, prose, and nonfiction. I encountered many works by familiar authors for the first time. For example, I read Alice Walker as a poet of amazing range that gave the genre a plasticity that one encounters with sculpture rather than words. I found a more militantly womanist Margaret Walker with her poem, "My Truth and My Flame," and was introduced to Michele Wallace the prose writer with the short story, "The Envelope." Heretofore, I had only read her as a fierce Black womanist with the book, *Black Macho and the Myth of the Superwoman* (1978). In addition, the anthology contained a piece by Vertamae Smart-Grosvenor, "Skillet Blond." Having read the piece no less than five times, classification of it as a genre remains elusive. Only its power to move me as a non-myth remains. The story is as linguistically devastating as Morrison's *The Bluest Eye* (1970) and is as deserving of attention from trauma theory specialists as Danticat's *Breath, Eyes, Memory* (2003), and it is with urgent and ardent desire that I hope someone gives it due diligence upon reading this preface.

As a practicing academic, I remained dedicated to my craft and allowing my teaching to infuse my research, I discovered that the unpleasant semester that I spent slogging hurriedly through American literature proved no different (our modules were only eight weeks long, so we covered both sections of the class in one semester). First, through the textbook, I found a tangible anthology of 49 Black women writes coedited by Amiri Baraka. Had not conventional criticism accused him and other Black male writers of the Black Arts Movement of rampant misogyny and homophobia? He, along with his wife, states in the introduction that the "purpose of this volume is to draw attention to the existence and excellence of black women writers." In graduate school, it was stated repeatedly that the misogyny of Baraka and his cohorts directly contributed to the Black womanist writers' backlash of the 1980s. Here was tangible evidence that he was participating in it. Second, presented with material that I thought was familiar to me in preparation for class forced me to analyze it with fresh eyes and to realize that I had accepted metanarratives that obscured the literature that it supposedly explicated. Was Phillis Wheatley as apolitical as traditional pedagogical strategy suggests? Her poems, "Liberty and Peace, A Poem," and "To His Excellency General Washington," both included in the anthology, show a woman who was acutely aware of Revolutionary-era politics transnationally. She was unafraid to speak publicly about slavery, comparing colonization to servitude, publicly to political figures as a woman. Third, in all of my years as a scholar, why had I not read a solitary reference to *Confirmation*? Yes, tenure is wonderful when it is earned for research and service well-done, but class preparation should never be underestimated. Had I not taken class preparation seriously, I may have never heard of this anthology. In preparing for a class that I continue to detest, I "discovered" the material that led to a project that has been more than five years in the making: an edited collection of critical and pedagogical essays on Black women writers that has now grown to two volumes!

As stated by Baraka, Black women writers are concerned with history, can be pan-Africanist in scope, and focus on community uplift rather than individual socioeconomic advancement. Since Wheatley, Black women writers have read and continue to read and support one another's work. And if *Confirmation* was offered as an anthology of the diverse talent and rich tapestry of Black women's viewpoints and voices rather than a political stance or a gendered dialectic between Black women and Black men, the collection offered here in two parts is a glimpse at how academics critique and teach Black women writers from across the globe. Though many of us do rely upon anthologies such as the aforementioned one, many of us are realizing the value of reaching deeper into this tradition of womanist writing and thinking, seeking Black women writers who are not included in anthologies or those works that may not be as heavily anthologized or critiqued and reading canonized authors through new lenses of critique as recovered knowledge of the historical conditions that informed their texts have been made available. Presented in two parts, the aim of this collection is to increase and enhance students' and professors' access to the richness of Black women writers' voices in America, the Caribbean, and the Afrofuture. The first part, which you now hold in your hands or are reading digitally, covers Black women writers of the contemporary era and into the Afro-future. The second part (and I know that this is backwards), covers Black women writers from the earliest beginning of the tradition to the Caribbean. In presenting it this way, I hope to achieve something as an editor: to situate current, exceptional Black women writers within a tradition of Black women writers who never failed to use their pens to speak truth to oppressive power—no matter the artistic (and sometimes personal) risk.

WORKS CITED

Baraka, Amiri. "Introduction." *Confirmation*. Edited by Amiri Baraka (LeRoi Jones) and Amina Baraka, William Morrow and Company, 1983, pp. 15–26.

Introduction
Eschewing Social Science and Defying Categorization: An Introduction to Contemporary Black Women Writers

LaToya Jefferson-James

This chapter is meant to be an introduction to the first half of a collection on the criticism and pedagogy of Black women writers. As such, it is a poor rhetorical example, for I fear that you are being plunged media res into this project, Reader. This half of the collection, focuses on Black women writers who published roughly around the World War II era and those who are currently writing into the Afrofuture. I must say that this half of the collection has given me the most difficulty. The beginning date has been the most troubling. Indubitably, I had the most difficulty placing Margaret Walker, a poet and prose writer, editor, a professor at Jackson State College (now Jackson State University), and a producer of the culture that she often wrote! While I could have easily placed her chronologically with the earlier writers (soon to follow), she appears in *Confirmation* (1983) alongside women who are decades younger, but her contributions for the volume are as fiercely womanist and transnationalist as that of the younger authors. Her earlier writing spans genres and defies categorization. Her cultural activities unified generations of Black women writers and reinforced the idea that Black women, from the very beginning of the Black belletristic tradition, wrote in communities and supported one another's works.

In 1973, Dr. Margaret Walker Alexander hosted the Phillis Wheatley festival at Jackson State College (now University) at the Institute for the Study and Culture of Black People in order to celebrate the 200th birthday of Wheatley. (When Dr. Alexander founded the center in 1968, it was the first of its kind to advocate Black Studies at a Historically Black College or University complete with an archive in the state of Mississippi. And to date, still the only one at an HBCU with archival capacity, unfortunately. It is now the Margaret Walker Alexander Center.) There were over 20 poets in attendance—including Nikki Giovanni, Carolyn Rodgers, Mari Evans, and June Jordan. The four-day festival also included a play based upon Wheatley's life by playwright Vinie Burrows and a bronze sculpture of Wheatley by Elizabeth Catlett. In an article in the *New York Times*, dated November 9, 1973, Walker Alexander gave her reason for hosting the festival, " 'Black women,' Dr. Walker said, 'have always been tokens in the publishing world. The textbooks haven't included them, no matter how received or critically acclaimed they were. And this is one of the reasons we're having this festival.' "[1] Using the facility that she created (with profits from her book sales), Walker Alexander created visibility for writerly communities of Black women.

Furthermore, the poems that she submitted to *Confirmation* were womanist and transnationalist in nature, two stances not traditionally associated with Alexander. The first stanza of "My Truth and My Flame" boldly declares the poet's identity as a Black woman, but the rest of the poem identifies her as someone who sides with the globally oppressed:

for I rise with the masses of mankind . . .
with the peoples of the earth; . . .
against the systems of oppression. . .[2]

Notice that the speaker uses the plural form, "systems," in recognition that racism colludes and intersects with class and caste in so-called meritocratic capitalist economic societies. This speaker, who openly confesses her Black womanity at the beginning of the poem, is not interested in the rise of one individual but with the advancement of oppressed people. She is not concerned with an individualistic, Hegelian showdown with a white man or men for control of or unlimited access to resources and power, either. True liberation comes in changing collusive systems and not changing the color of the faces who control the system.

That aforementioned analysis seemingly belongs to a poet of the Black Arts Movement—perhaps Mari Evans or Sonia Sanchez or even Nikki Giovanni—and not a poet who was first published in 1934 and who won the Yale Younger Poets Award in 1942. For that reason, it was difficult for me to place Walker, so I decided to write about her in this introduction *as an introduction* to the ways that Black women writers in the contemporary era write about themselves, their communities, and communities throughout the world. Black women writers link the struggle against oppression inside the United States to international struggles while never losing sight of the idiosyncrasies and personal dramas that define the interior lives of those they write about. It is a taut tight-rope to walk, but Walker's poetry typifies all of those things. The poem most students encounter by her is the heavily anthologized, "For My People." In fact, her reputation as a poet was established upon this collection, *For My People*, which portrays Black life, even the Southern agrarian portion of it, unabashedly. The poem repeats the phrase, "For my people . . ." for six stanzas. It breaks this pattern at the beginning of stanzas three, four, five, and ten, when she highlights, playmates, "bewildered years," "boys and girls," and the possibility of a "new earth." Each stanza is a snapshot of Black people in America living in spite of racism and oppression. There are action verbs, but no direct confrontations with white men. Instead, the people of "For My People" are "trying to fashion a better way from/ confusion, from hypocrisy and misunderstanding, trying to fashion/a world that will hold all the people, all the faces, all the adams/and eves and their countless generations" (lines 38–42). This is action without the reaction of literature that has been cycled through social science. In this sense, Margaret Walker Alexander, indeed most contemporary Black women writers, are literary daughters of Zora Neale Hurston who was a social scientist (an anthropologist) but chose humanity over objectivity and reactivity in her writing.

Albert Murray begins his essay, "The Clutch of Social Science Fiction Fiction" by stating, "Only a few American writers since the twenties have been able to create fiction with implications beyond the most obvious and tiresome of the cliches derived from social science" (106). On the contrary, contemporary Black women writers eschew the quantified stereotypes that define urban social science as applied to Black folk and ask tough questions of reading audiences. Sometimes, they tackle social science fiction fiction with the tenacity of a professional linebacker, burst through that critical defensive line, run the crucial groundbreaking yardage, then spike that fictional/creative nonfictional football in the in-zone with no compunction. They present and re-present the "stuff" of the interior: be it good, bad, or ugly. They give us what is scatological in rarified, beatific prose-poetry that is as inimitable as the metered hymns of a country church and as honest as a church mother's advice. Mostly, contemporary Black women writers ignore the politics of respectability and opt for what is both artistic and truthful.[3] Even if Black elders were well-meaning in trying to emotionally strengthen Black girls, was it always conducive to ostracize and harangue the "tender-hearted" among us? Can a relatively dark-skinned Black woman who lives in a kitchenette building on the South Side of Chicago find self-worth while married to a philandering, emotionally unavailable man? Can teenage pregnancy liberate a young woman from an abusive, two-parent home rather than entrap her in a cycle of single-parenthood, poverty, and public assistance? Can the practice of voodoo help a bisexual Black woman overcome the social prejudices instilled in other Black people by Christian teachings and fight for justice when she is falsely accused of child molestation?

In the aforementioned paragraph, I am referring to four different Black women writers, writing across four different genres in four different decades. The common threads holding these works together are how they address and discard "social science fiction fiction," and sometimes, even the convention of the genres in order to present the humanities of the speakers and shake the reader free of certain metanarratives of Black psychopathology. Published 11 years after *For My People*, Gwendolyn Brooks' *Maud Martha* represented a break with Black writers and the larger presses of New York. This collection was originally published by Harper & Brothers, but Brooks chose the independent, Black-owned Third World Press, located in Chicago to reprint it. Though well established as a poet, *Maud Martha* is Brooks' only novel. Though the novel is written in prose, the language has a poetic quality. In her description of Maud Martha Brown, the book opens with what the child likes and not what she looks like: "What she liked was candy buttons, and books, and painted music (deep blue, or delicate silver) and the west sky, so altering, viewed from the steps of the back porch; and dandelions" (1). This is not a novel of yearning for social acceptance from white America, but one of psychological exploration and growth despite the external pressures that life in a segregated, caste-based, white supremacist society brings. Maud Martha, as plain as the dandelions she loves, grows, loves, marries an unfaithful man, and has a child. She, a brown-skinned woman in a sexist society that does not value her for the human being that she is, has an epiphany with a mouse and learns to love herself in a kitchenette building. It is one of the most poetic epiphanies of self-love in all of American literature. In the chapter, "Maud Martha Spares the Mouse," the protagonist refuses to kill a trapped mouse in her kitchenette building and in sparing the life of the mouse, realizes that she has some agency and is worthy of love. Allow me to quote the scene at length here:

> Suddenly, she was conscious of a new cleanness in her. A wide air walked in her. A life had blundered its way into her power and it had been hers to preserve or destroy. She had not destroyed. In the center of that simple restraint was—creation. She had created a piece of life. It was wonderful.
> "Why," she thought, as her height doubled, "why, I'm good! I am *good*."
> So she ironed her aprons. Her back was straight. Her eyes were mild, and soft with godlike loving kindness. (70–71, emphasis Brooks')

Agency is the ability to choose or to act. Given even this teacup of power, Maud Martha chooses to allow a mouse to live. Brooks turns the sparing of a mouse's life into a moment of empowerment for a dark-skinned Black woman who does not live in the lap of luxury. Contrast that to the opening scene of

Native Son in which a rat invades the kitchenette building of the Thomas's, the sister becomes so frightened that she faints, and the mother uses Bigger's adolescent antics to verbally humiliate and castrate him. Everything about Wright's scene reeks of Black hopelessness and defeat and possibly insanity, with sexist stereotyping of women who cannot bear the sight of rodents in the house. While Wright's book ends with Bigger's destruction, Brooks' book ends with Martha's second pregnancy and the world, with all of the joys of motherhood and the daily creativity it brings, opening up to her. Though her marriage is no paradise, she refuses to be defeated by external forces that would crush her, including beauty standards circulated by the Black press. In a secret moment, Maud Martha had spared life; in the privacy of her home and without the help of a doctor and only two women to assist her, Martha had brought life into the world (a girl); and Martha, as plain as a dandelion, was about to give the world another life. She no longer cared that the Black presses presented her with its "usual representations of womanly Beauty, pale and pompadoured. . ." (179). *She* was a creator and a giver of life. To the protagonist, that was power. Plain Maud Martha Brown, who had once been overlooked by everyone, slowly and privately became her own hero—no other validation was needed.

Writing almost two decades later and for another independent press, June Jordan, another Black woman poet, published her novel *His Own Where* with The Feminist Press in 1971. It was the first novel to be published in total Black English, and it flew in the face of urban social science. It follows the story of Buddy and Angela. Buddy is from a single-parent home, but it is his mother who leaves the family and returns to her native island of Barbados. In conventional social science wisdom, the father leaves the mother to be a single parent. Later, his father is hit by a car and hospitalize where Buddy watches him die slowly. He meets Angela, the love of his life, at the hospital. By all of the conventions of social science, Angela's home life should have been more stable than Buddy's. She has a mother and father. However, the poverty of Brooklyn forces both parents to work several jobs, leaving Angela to be the real parent. The family's whole psychology is manifested by a language of commodification in which the children have been quantified into dollars and cents. Instead of valuing Angela for the domestic labor that she provides while the parents are out working, the mother refers to her as a "freeloader." When the mother wants to verbally abuse Angela to the father, it is in economic terms: "She making it impossible for decent people try to earn a living to go out with easy mind and earn they bread" (27). The language of religion has been bastardized by the prospect of money-getting; and this monism, coupled with overt malignant narcissism in the mother, is used to justify making an emotional and physical punching bag of the one person who is performing the adult duties of raising the children. The mother's verbal abuse is augmented by the father's molestation and physical abuse that lands Angela in the hospital. At the Catholic girls' home where social services place her after the hospital stay, she is exposed to lesbianism. Even after being called a prostitute and a whore, being beat to the point of hospitalization, being shipped upstate to a house of holy lesbians, and being told by her mother that she is an unwanted freeloader, Angela views her siblings as her family: "She miss her brothers and sister. Now she realize she have no home. Her family be parents beat you in the head or hate you. She mean the father mother family. Her sister and her brothers make another family where she love and care" (62–63). June Jordan, with this character, has changed the whole definition of what an American nuclear family even is. What is a family? Is a two-parent, dysfunctional family better than a single-parent family where there is love? Clearly, there is love between Buddy and his father. That is why the car accident is devastating to the young man. That car clipped away the only love and support the child had ever known. How could a distant mother in Barbados, who left without a single word of explanation to the child, meet the emotional needs of her son?

Buddy wants to rescue Angela from all of the noise and the loneliness that they each feel and the only place of respite that he finds is the cemetery. It is in the cemetery, looking out at a reservoir from an abandoned house where Buddy, 16, and Angela, 14, make love with the hopes that she becomes pregnant (it was not their first time making love). They do not refer to it as sex. They refer to it explicitly as "making love" (72). Among the silence of the dead and a city of tombstones, they want to create new life—a family of order in chaos and love without the hatred that Angela's parents have shown her. Now, Buddy and Angela are teenagers and they have not thought through the practical side of life, but there is nothing miscreant in Buddy's intentions to "liberate" (That is Buddy's word and not mine. He uses some form of it repeatedly throughout the narrative. See chapter 12 for an example.) Angela from parents who hate her and nuns who want to sexually prey upon her.

While most of us know VertaMae Smart-Grosvenor as a chef and a chef who writes (she referred to herself as a "culinary griot" throughout her career and in many interviews), she appears as a creative writer in 1983 in *Confirmation* with the short story, "Skillet Blond." First of all, the title of the story itself confronts chromatism within the African American community. "Skillet blond" is a clever way of calling someone "sooty black," an undesirable color. Aforementioned in *Maud Martha*, the representation of womanly beauty in the African American community was a woman of light skin with European or what was called "sharp" facial features (a thin nose and lips), with European-textured hair. Undesirable facial features were full lips, broad noses, and "nappy" hair (hair that curls and coils like African textured hair), and dark skin. Several skin lightening creams and straighteners were developed at the turn of the twentieth century, especially in the Northern United States, to help African Americans compete with European immigrants economically.[4] The author draws the reader's attention to her name and the italicized epigraph with heavy use of the diacritic and accent marks. An ordinary word becomes marked and demands the reader's attention. For example, the author's name, as we are accustomed to seeing it, is: "Vertamae Smart-Grosvenor." In this story, it is spelled as: "Vèrtàmàè Smart-Gròsvènòr" (124). This writer has something to say, even with a common word such as "note." It becomes, "nòté" (124). When the story begins, Smart-Grosvenor begins by challenging the "wisdom" of Black agrarian elders: "You're a kid and you believe everything they tell you. They are grown and grown folk know everything" (124). Some of the things that "grown folk" say hurt this child: "Specially when they tell you that you are entirely too dark to wear red. Red is your favorite color. You feel like crying when they predict that you will never be able to wear lipstick" (124). When she cries, they shame her by saying she is acting "tenderhearted" (125). The child waits for adulthood and hopes that it may relieve her of the harsh words that she encounters and is disheartened when she finds that it does not. Black folks are still overly-concerned with phenotype. Instead of crying, she writes. The narrator, now addressing the audience in the second person as a woman, says, "You will write from the heart on how it feels to be a skillet blond woman. A Myth. You can explore the curious way folks have of talking out of both sides of their mouths about myths; if she protests she is a ball-busting matriarchal bitch. If she keeps quiet she is a handkerchief head aunt jemima mammy bitch" (126). And these are the two constructions of Black women that social scientists, Black and white (and mainly male) have given the world of the matriarchal Black woman. Smart-Grovesnor, with this frame narrative, takes on the dual nature of how it feels to be a myth and a woman simultaneously.

Writing almost 30 years later for a press that specializes in speculative fiction, Nisi Shawl presents in the short story, "Pataki," a bisexual Black woman who has been accused of child molestation. To date, critics have had a difficult time classifying Shawl. Is she speculative fiction? Science fiction? Fantasy fiction? Or even marvelous realism fiction? Whatever Shawl produces, she uses the past to comment upon the present and enrich the lives of her reading audience. The word, "Pataki," is a Voodoo parable that is aimed to teach the hearer a lesson. The protagonist, Rianne, knows that she is a "strange woman. Rianne moved to the Bay Area of California looking for the freedom to be herself, not who others wanted to believe she was" (6). Like the speaker in "Skillet Blond," those of her own community in Detroit inflicted damage. They accused Rianne of child molestation. Rianne, who is a follower of the Voodoo goddess Osun, retaliated with a slander case, won, and moved to California against the wishes of the person who had inducted her into the priesthood. A child, Shinel, hires Rianne to find her father. Trouble begins again and Rianne wants to run again. It is only through a spiritual/psychological dream-like sex act with the dead King of Pop, Michael Jackson, that Rianne finds the strength to stay put and fight the prejudices that Black people harbor against any form of sexuality that is not heteronormative and religions that are not Christian. Oddly, an older family member, Shinel's grandmother, is the one character in the story who understands the syncretic nature of Black spiritual life in America. While Shinel's mother violently objects to the child's visits, the grandmother is supportive. The elder of the family, Big Mama, visits Rianne and brings her a lock of Rianne's father's hair. The elder said, "I ain't totally ignorant of how hoodoo done." The elder believes in Rianne's ability, and refers to her in Christian terms, " 'You are a good woman,' she added, already out on the porch. 'I see the angels sittin on your shoulders'" (19). Traditionally, Voodoo has been associated with black magic and witchcraft. Again, this is not the first time that a Black woman writer has mixed Voodoo with Christianity. One of Zora Neale Hurston's least critiqued/taught novels, *Moses, Man of the Mountain* (1939), mixes the Hebrew God scripture/Old Testament story of Exodus/figure of Moses with Voodoo. In this way, Shawl is also a literary daughter of Hurston. Second, Shawl's linking of the past to the present and future as commentary links her to Hurston. In fact, one of the most famous quotes circulating around the internet is one by Hurston that involves the continuity of time: "The present was an egg laid by the past that had the future in its shell."[5]

Throughout this introduction, I have discussed four Black women writers of the contemporary era who typify what this collection embodies. The works of Black women writers, even when they may seem familiar to us, continue to be mined for the richness of the perspectives they offer, because they are works of the interior that connect the local to the national to the international. The Civil Rights Movement is more than a parochial, hierarchal struggle for control of resources between men: it is part of a worldwide struggle against multiple, colluding systems of domination that work to oppress women, laborers, and all people of color globally. Defying categorization and eschewing social science fiction fiction, some Black women writers of the contemporary era present beatific art for art's sake that is nonetheless political in its content even if that was not the original intent. This collection contains analyses of those authors who appear on our syllabuses such as Ann Petry but read from a twenty-first-century perspective—away from the forced and accepted narrative that she is no more than Richard Wright's female counterpart. The woman-centered, Gothic nightmare that plays out on the streets of Harlem stands in its own right and does not need to be anchored to any male author. This collection reintroduces "lost" Black women writers to twenty-first-century audiences. Playwright Kathleen Collins, who wrote and

Introduction   xxiii

directed *Losing Ground* (1982), the first feature-length drama by an African American woman, is not being studied or written about as often as she should (and that may be due to her untimely death in 1988) be. Last, this collection features several articles on Black Afrofurism/speculative fiction, dispelling the myth that Black people just do not do science fiction. Black people have been producing science fiction since Sun-Ra's Arkestra told us to face the music and George Clinton and Parliament/P-Funk's Mothership landed, and Dr. Funkenstein, in all of his funky glory, waltzed down those steps to remind Black folk "that ain't nothing good unless you play with it."[6] Black women writers continue to write into the Afrofuture from Canada (Dionne Brand) to Africa (Nnedi Okorafor) and all points in between. And while I am ultimately proud of this collection, I know it is only just the beginning.

NOTES

1. Hunter, Charlayne. *New York Times*. https://www.nytimes.com/1973/11/09/archives/poets-extol-a-sisters-unfettered-soul-sold-to-boston-merchant.html Accessed November 14, 2020. I have tried to contact the Margaret Walker Alexander Center for a more complete picture of the program, but due to the COVID-19 crisis, I suspect that the staff is on reduced hours and I was not able to contact them by the date of this publication.

2. Walker, Margaret. "My Truth and My Flame" in *Confirmation*, edited by Amiri Baraka and Amina Baraka. This poem and four others were new to me, though I had read many as a graduate student.

3. The politics of respectability is defined in *Righteous Discontent: The Women's Movement in the Black Baptist Church, 1880–1920* by historian, Evelyn Brooks Higginbotham. Accordingly, the politics of respectability involved imbibing white, middle-class values and a disavowal of folk culture (which was considered negative) in the belief that this would remove the stigma of blackness and help Black people gain socioeconomic equality (if not tolerance) in the United States. Some of the negative behavior, especially when displayed in public, included: " 'gaudy' colors in dress, snuff dipping, baseball games on Sunday, and other forms of 'improper' decorum" (15).

4. For an example of these kits, which normally sold for $2, please see *Colored American Magazine*, an early precursor to *Ebony* and *Jet*. They were regular advertisements. *Colored American* is easily accessible via a Google search.

5. This quote can be found in numerous places. I happen to find it on AZ Quotes. https://www.azquotes.com/quote/139535. A quick Google search of "Hurston and time" yields roughly 960 results of this quote alone.

6. There is now a replica of the original Mothership in the Smithsonian. At this moment in Dr. Funkenstein's incarnation, he was reminding Black musical artists that all of Black musical genius is based upon improvisation and not formulas that would gain them "crossover appeal," or acceptance and more record sales from white

audiences. He encouraged the musicians behind him to engage in improvisation while the bass line held a steady note.

WORKS CITED

Brooks, Gwendolyn. *Maud Martha*. Chicago: Third World Press, 1953, 1993.

Higginbotham, Evelyn Brooks. *Righteous Discontent: The Women's Movement in the Black Baptist Church, 1880-1920*. Cambridge: Harvard UP, 1993.

Hunter, Charlayne. "Poets Extol a Sister's Unfettered Soul." *The New York Times*, 9 November 1973, https://www.nytimes.com/1973/11/09/archives/poets-extol-a-sisters-unfettered-soul-sold-to-boston-merchant.html. Accessed 14 November 2020.

Jordan, June. *His Own Where*. New York: The Feminist Press, 1971.

Murray, Albert. "A Clutch of Social Science Fiction Fiction," *Albert Murray Collected Essays and Memoirs*, Edited by Henry Louis Gates, Jr. and Paul Devlin, The Library of America, 2016, 106–144.

Shawl, Nisi. "Pataki." *Something More and More*. Edited by Nisi Shawl, Aqueduct Press, 2011, 3–29.

Smart-Grovesnor, Vertamae. "Skillet Blond." *Confirmation*. Edited by Amiri Baraka (LeRoi Jones) and Amina Baraka, William Morrow and Company, Inc., 1983, 124–131.

Walker, Margaret. "For My People." *The Norton Anthology of African American Literature*, Third Edition v.2. Edited by Henry Louis Gates, Jr. and Valerie A. Smith, W.W. Norton, 2014, 319–320.

———. "My Truth and My Flame." *Confirmation*. Edited by Amiri Baraka (LeRoi Jones) and Amina Baraka, William Morrow and Company, Inc., 1983, 361–362.

Chapter 1

"You Can't Run from the Street"

Failed Escapes in Ann Petry's The Street *(1947) and Shay Youngblood's* Black Girl in Paris *(2000)*

Shahara'Tova V. Dente

> I was living in two places, night and day. In the night place I ran but they never caught me, and in the morning brown angels kissed my face. I woke up with tears on my pillow.—Shay Youngblood's *Black Girl in Paris*

Ann Petry's *The Street* hails as a hallmark of Naturalist writing in the African American literary tradition. Its protagonist, Lutie Johnson, finds herself in an oppressive, bleak state in America's North. As Lutie seeks out upward economic mobility in the northern landscape, she has to confront its streets and the dangers they present. Petry crafts a narrative that employs the street as a character, with real social, economic, and racial implications for African American women. Similarly, Shay Youngblood's *Black Girl in Paris* is a contemporary rendering of the urban landscape, but one that extends far beyond the North. Set during the Civil Rights Movement, Youngblood's novel revisits the migration narrative by tracing Eden's journey from the American South to Paris, France. Her protagonist, Eden, an aspiring writer, journeys out of the South. For Eden, the American North is not far enough. She, like many African American writers and entertainers just a generation before her, escapes to Paris for a life free of the physical constraints of racism. Eden believes newfound freedom in Paris will empower her to become a writer. Though Lutie does not journey from South to North and abroad like Eden, Lutie does migrate across the northern landscape. Both Lutie and Eden take journeys in search of more amiable conditions; they navigate the streets, both in the Northern United States and in Paris, France, in an attempt to secure a life free of economic hardship and racial bigotry. Though the issues in American and Paris are not identical, there are some key similarities in how racism, sexism, and classism affect the decisions Lutie and Eden face. Though the cultural histories of racism differ in both environments, the constant is that Lutie and Eden must confront the street's urban landscape. What they discover is that sometimes you can't run from the streets.

The juxtaposition of these stories is important because they reveal how African American women writers engage not only feminism but also intersectionality and create a street literature that shows the way geographical and metaphysical spaces converge upon African American female bodies. These narratives reveal a trope in African American narratives in which the street is more than a place or a backdrop. For example, *The Street* takes place in a northern, industrial global city; Petry's setting is indispensable for several reasons. First, the timing of the narrative is important, because in some African American folklore, personal letters, and newspaper stories, the industrial North is represented as a veritable, racial utopia where war-time labor shortages promise economic success. Second, African Americans were encouraged to shake off the shackles of their agrarian past and to embrace all of the promises that northern city life had to offer. Essayists such as Alain Locke wrote about utopian, northern spaces. Third, the second migration, which occurred slightly before and during World War II, saw African Americans become a mostly urban people for the first time in the history of Africans in America. Unlike most immigrants who came to America's urban, industrial cities, African Americans were not allowed to choose their neighborhoods. By a series of methods such as redlining, African Americans were often locked into certain, dilapidated housing situations with little hope for improvement. Many African American writers, including Petry, James Baldwin, Richard Wright, and Ralph Ellison, began to describe the dismal condition of life in supposed racial utopias.[1] Lutie is a product of the North and must navigate the vagaries of its covert racism, sexism, and classism while she confronts the very real streets to which she is confined.

Similarly, Eden, a woman living in the urban South, in Atlanta, Georgia, post-Civil Rights Movement, also feels imprisoned in her environment, though there are no vestiges of the segregation that once characterized her Southern landscape. Eden escapes to Paris in an attempt to finally achieve her artistic goals. For Eden, this type of artistic freedom is neither accessible nor achievable in the United States because of continuous racism and sexism prevalent in American society. Eden escapes her environment, only to find that regardless of geographical positioning, the street whether in the United States or abroad poses similar issues for African American women. Like Lutie, her 1946 predecessor, who wanders the streets of Harlem looking to achieve the economic comfort of the American Dream, Eden finds that even in Paris, the dominant, Western culture inscribes certain notions upon her African American, female flesh, which limits her earning potential and imprisons her as an artist.

Even though they appear in different decades and are set in different countries, the stories of Lutie and Eden mirror one another. Geographical positioning does not afford the escape these women seek. I argue that when put in conversation with each other, *The Street* and *Black Girl in Paris* provide a trajectory of women who must navigate an urban landscape to find their place both in America and abroad, but who are unable to escape sexism, racism, and poverty because of respectability politics, socioeconomic politics, and sexual politics that prevent them from being comfortable in their own space.

CRITICAL ENGAGEMENTS WITH PETRY

There has been much scholarship devoted to Petry's works, particularly *The Street*, which is often considered *Native Son*'s feminine counterpart. Scholars have worked toward disentangling the book from these kinds of limiting labels. For example, Keith Clark, in "A Distaff Dream Deferred? Ann Petry and the Art of Subversion," contends that Petry

> recasts the Herculean quest for the American Dream in an unequivocally female context . . . the novel represents the "distaff" side of the African-American literary tradition, emerging as a groundbreaking work in its examination of the black woman's pursuit of happiness . . . she illustrates how black women subvert the quest for the American Dream and fulfill their own version of it. (495–497 Clark)

Twenty years later, Clark continues to argue for deeper explorations of Petry as an artist independent of Wright, in *The Radical Fiction of Ann Petry* (2013). He contends that *The Street* is, in fact, a Gothic novel that "moves beyond the realm of 'social' terror. The novel's catholicity marks Petry as a malleable gothic architectonics, the framework of which she manipulates and alters for manifold rhetorical ends" (Clark 97).[2] Though Clark does much to separate Petry from Wright, it is also necessary to continue to bring new insights to Petry's text. Clark's works point to different ways of engaging with Petry's text across different decades. While the Wright-Baldwin influence of subsequent male writers, such as Reed and Ellison, is widely studied, few African American women writers like Petry receive the same kind of critical treatment.[3] Wright is a mainstay in African American literary critical conversations, but placing Petry's texts in conversation with texts from other genres opens up more ways to engage her text.

Positioning Petry's text alongside Youngblood's *Black Girl in Paris* reveals a continuum of influence in African American women's writings and allows for diversification in conversation. One way to diversify the conversations around Petry's and Youngblood's texts is to think more broadly about how these works function when placed into conversation with texts with thematic/theoretical similarities. Specifically, this means examining how different women engage these works. Cheryl Wall, in "Nellie—Pioneer of Black Feminist Literary Criticism: Nellie McKay and Black Women's Studies" argues,

> Since 1988 our awareness of additional lenses through which to read and interpret has only grown. Critics now employ lens[es] that zoom in on differences of sexuality, ethnicity, national, and transnational identity. But as the awareness of difference continues to grow, the ability to negotiate shifts in perspective . . . becomes ever more necessary. (Wall 19)

Though Wall is specifically discussing a reading McKay does of Petry's *The Narrows* (1953), the sentiment can also be applied to contemporary readings of *The Street*. There is much to be gained from revisiting older, canonical works. Revisiting older works and putting them in conversation with comparable, contemporary texts allows for diversification of critical conversations with works like *The Street* and *Black Girl in Paris*. As Wall suggests, McKay recognized this need for newer critical lenses and shifts in perspective when applying criticism. When examining how both novels' main characters, Lutie and Eden, experience difficulties with systemic racism, classism, and gender disparities, it is clear that these women are subject to these difficulties regardless of the streets they frequent.

Historically, African American women were mostly decentered from white-dominated waves of the feminist movements throughout the United States and Europe. White women and white, female feminists are placed in a position of privilege above African American women. Battling against sexism can unite women. Classism can unite the poor. But, unity around race lacks, which leaves African American women alone. For them, these identities are intertwined and cannot be severed. Kimberle' Crenshaw, in "Demarginalizing the Intersection of Race and Sex," claims that "because the intersectional experience is greater than the sum of racism and sexism, any analysis that does not take intersectionality into account cannot sufficiently address the particular manner in which Black women are subordinated" (Crenshaw 24). Moreover, any discourse that attempts to engage in an accurate discussion of the oppression and discrimination that African American women face must discuss the two in tandem. Employing intersectionality as a means to analyze literature can only be beneficial to canon growth and expansion. In a later essay, "Mapping the Margins," Williams comments, "Through an awareness of intersectionality, we can better acknowledge and ground the differences among us and negotiate the means by which these differences will find expression in constructing group politics" (377). Intersectionality provides a framework that allows Lutie's and Eden's blackness and femaleness to be viewed through the same lens. After doing so, then the work can be done to apply different modes of thinking to the works.

Although critic Suzanne Jones, in her essay "*Black Girl in Paris*: Shay Youngblood's Escape from the 'Last Plantation,' " places Youngblood's text side by side with James Baldwin's *Another Country* (1962), *The Fire Next Time* (1961), *Giovanni's Room* (1956), and *Notes of a Native Son* (1955), the novel has not been placed into conversation with Petry's *The Street*. Both texts showcase other African American women who feel the urgency to escape their surroundings while they search for home, a safe space, and love that is otherwise unavailable to them in their previous or current environments. Jones' reading of Youngblood's text provides another lens through which to experience African American women's narratives. She invokes Thadious Davis' observations about African American authors and artists who migrate to Paris in pursuit of creative freedom and an escape from the racial and political landscape in the American South.[4] Jones argues that Eden "sees such a move as a step away from the safe, respectable work in a museum that she takes after disappointing her parents by majoring in English, rather than nursing. She believes that a sojourn in Paris will provide a necessary first step toward a career in writing" (44). Here, Jones reads Youngblood's Eden through the lens of her contemporaries like James Baldwin. Eden's purpose for going to Paris is twofold; she wants to escape the American Southern past from which she runs in her sleep, and she wants to experience artistic freedom like James Baldwin did almost 30 years before her. For Eden, there is no artistic opportunity for African American women writers, particularly during this violent period. In Eden's mind, she cannot achieve her goal of being a writer along the same vein as James Baldwin unless she follows in his footstep and sojourns in Paris.

In conducting an intertextual analysis of Petry's *The Street* and Youngblood's *Black Girl in Paris*, I shift the gaze toward a Black feminist reading of these texts, by employing Crenshaw's intersectionality as a lens through which the reader is more aptly able to engage both Lutie and Eden as they battle respectability politics, socioeconomic politics, and sexual politics. In this way, the reading of Youngblood's text reveals an opportunity to broaden critical conversations within African American letters, as African American women writers continue to engage feminist critiques (including intersectionality) to demonstrate the limiting forces that cripple their attempts to carve metaphysical spaces for themselves.

ESCAPING RESPECTABILITY POLITICS

The societal circumstances surrounding Lutie Johnson and other women in her position dictate the level of success that she may achieve. In 1940s Harlem, African American women work mostly as domestics; African American men are mostly out of work. Racial dynamics between African Americans and whites are strained, and there is a clear separation between the races and classes in urbanized ghettos. Women like Lutie navigate the urban landscape in search of work and economic stability to support their families. Oftentimes, this means women are the heads of the households. This is a stark contrast from prescriptive societal rules for women in general, particularly since women are often expected to be caregivers, wives, mothers, and domestics.

In *The Street*, Petry uses prescribed gender roles and notions of respectability politics to critique available modes for employability and economic stability for women. Evelyn Brooks Higginbotham coins the term "respectability politics" in her 1993 book, *Righteous Discontent: The Women's Movement in the Black Baptist Church, 1880–1920*. Broadly, respectability politics suggest that to receive equitable treatment from those in positions of power, one must act, dress, and speak in a way that is pleasing or considered acceptable to the dominant group. While Petry's text predates Higginbotham's work, it is a useful lens through which one can understand the politics and social implications Petry's characters face. Women like Lutie have been groomed to work as domestics outside and inside the home, even though Black men experience dismal unemployment opportunities. The men of the novel who are employed in some way use their positions as economic free agents in attempts to possess Lutie sexually.

Since Lutie is a domestic worker with limited options for advancement, Lutie is much like the other women in the street. Those women work in white women's homes to provide food and shelter for their families. Most times they receive little assistance from the men in their lives. Because of racial discrimination, African American women like Lutie are normally married to African American men who face either unemployment or underemployment. The aforementioned character, Mrs. Pizzini, though an immigrant who can barely speak English, is not African American and is therefore afforded certain privileges in America denied to Lutie and other African American women who are forced to work as domestics. Although Mrs. Pizzini is only mentioned once, her condemnation of working women permeates Lutie's narrative.

White society's expected gender roles are at play even on 116th Street where the physical street is a liminal space. It is the home for the overburdened and overworked, yet it can provide no real home or comfort to any of its inhabitants, particularly Lutie and her son Bub. Either the street is filled with overworked women or men who are out of work. On the one hand, Lutie cannot be more successful and harder working than her man because that destroys the myth that a woman's place is at home, not as the head of a household. On the other hand, the only jobs that Lutie can take are domestic work. Lutie ponders this problem, "And yet, she thought, what else is a woman to do when her man can't get a job?" (Petry 65). Her only option is to walk the streets of Harlem in search of better economic opportunities even if it means she cannot be a wife or a full-time mother. Those women who assume this position do so either because they are single mothers, like Lutie, or because their man is one of those poor, African American men on the street. These jobs do not pay enough for Lutie to support a household, hence the economic circumstances that bring her to the streets of Harlem in the first place. Even in the African American community, African American women are held to white society's impossible standards of what it means to be a wife, mother, and provider.

Additionally, Petry uses the elder women in Lutie's life to trace the origins of her struggle with society's respectability politics. Through another minor character, Lutie's grandmother is indicative of a lineage of African American women who are policed by ancient maternal figures who had little or no control over how they lived. Lutie remembers a conversation between herself and her Granny. Granny had "foreseen men like this Super. She had told Pop, 'let her get married, Grant. Lookin' like she do men goin' to chase her till they catches up. Better she get married" (Petry 76). Granny is that voice from the past that suggests though the world can be cold and evil, there are certain strategies African American women use to cope. In *The Street*, marriage is one of those strategies. Lutie does marry, but the marriage dissolves due to economic pressures. These are mainly Jim's unemployment and Lutie's employment as a domestic in Connecticut. Following the dissolution of the marriage, subsequent loss of employment, and a string of employment failures, Lutie can never save enough to divorce Jim, so that becomes less of a priority for Lutie. Here, marriage is one of those standards Lutie is expected to abide by even though Jim and Lutie do not have a strong, supportive, or healthy marriage. Granny views marriage as a means to an end; Lutie views her marriage as another bill that she can neither afford to keep nor eliminate.

Though Jim abandons Lutie for another woman, Lutie does not blame him for the dissolution of their marriage. He, too, is a victim of the racist environment in which they both live. The streets are filled with men who "lounged against the sides of the building, their hands in their pockets while they stared at the women who walked past, probably deciding which woman they should select to replace the wife who was out working all day" (Petry 65). Though it seems that an escape from marriage would be ideal, Lutie fashions it as one more thing she cannot afford. Divorcing Jim costs money and Lutie's economic situation prevents her from doing so. Additionally, this puts a strain on her ability to foster any healthy relationship. Lutie is very clear that she is not the type to use her body as a vehicle to obtain financial stability, though Boots Smith later tests this.

So, as Petry situates Lutie and other women in *The Street*, a woman's place is outside the home, on 116th Street, fighting to survive. Intraracial respectability politics demand that women like Lutie, those who are heading toward middle age with young children, stay at home. Racist economic policies force them outside the home to help support their families. Sometimes, in the case of Lutie Johnson, they are the sole breadwinners through no fault of their own.

Like Lutie in Harlem, Eden works as domestic in Paris, yet respectability politics still confront her, keeping her in subservient roles. Youngblood's Eden discovers that there is no escape from domestic work and poverty in Paris. Eden maneuvers a life around whites and negotiates a way to earn a living and work with the French. However, there are rules for working and living abroad. There are also consequences to being an American in Paris, and one of them is facing understated condescension. This condescension, while understated, is another way Eden is put in her "place." Though she is a foreigner, Eden is still an African American woman in Paris, and that means she must always remember her place: in a position of service, inferior to white women. Eden works as an *au pair*, to have food and a warm place to sleep.[5] This domestic job also gets Eden farther and farther away from becoming the writer she wants to be. Eden's confrontation with soft bigotry is most prominent in her conversations with Charlotte Rockefeller, a member of one of the most powerful family lineages in the United States. Though Eden never discloses the specifics of her writing to Charlotte, other than she wants to write like James Baldwin, it is her professed affection for Baldwin and his works that gives Charlotte pause. Charlotte has an interesting reading of Baldwin and his perceived experience in Paris. She says,

> Paris was a relief for him. He didn't have "colored only" signs to deal with, there weren't places off limits to him because of his color. He could relax here. I don't believe he was angry as he seemed. . . . He was preachy and very proper as if he were in church giving a sermon to the unconverted. . . . He made me want to burn down my father's house and dance around the flames. (Youngblood 84)

In a way, Charlotte seems to disregard Baldwin as a mentor or inspiration for Eden, instead of positioning herself in his place. Charlotte's opinion about the type of art she should produce is a thinly veiled attempt to subvert Eden's voice and remake her into someone respectable by white society, namely, the

Rockefellers', standards. Thus, Eden still finds no escape from racism and soft bigotry in Paris. About Charlotte Rockefeller, Eden comments, "She was trying to transform me into a black Rockefeller, and she was failing miserably. There were too many rules and restrictions in the life she was planning for me. This was not the kind of freedom I came to Paris for" (Youngblood 82). Thus, Eden, like Lutie, finds no escape from economic hardships and restrictions.

Charlotte, though nice, is another reminder of the unsustainable level of respectability that African American women are expected to maintain. As a member of such a prominent family, Charlotte has a level of privilege and wealth that prevents her from relating to Eden. While Charlotte means to be nice to Eden, the way she talks to her, specifically about her writing, is condescending and out of touch with Eden's reality. When Charlotte attempts to control Eden's writing, Eden decides to reject any type of friendship and association with Charlotte. Eden says, "She knew I wanted to be a writer. 'Write something happy, something gay. Your life is very interesting, but the sorrows of the poor angry, blacks, my dear, that has been done' " (Youngblood 83). Rockefeller's "advice" here is reminiscent of Richard Wright's essay, "Blueprint for Negro Writing."[6] While Wright champions inclusiveness and a link between art and social progress in African American writing, Charlotte expresses distaste for any future writings on the subject of the African American condition. With Charlotte, Youngblood points out the tendency for the white elite to constantly seek control of the type of writing that African Americans produce, even without knowing much about the art's content, context, or purpose.

ESCAPING SOCIOECONOMIC POLITICS

The social and economic barriers for African American women impede their ability to exist in their environment free of poverty and classism. In *The Street*, the implications of race, class, and gender are particularly relevant. In a reflective moment, Lutie considers the fact that her current circumstances mirror those of other women in a similar station in life. Additionally, Lutie recognizes the long tradition of African American women who have been forced to do domestic work for survival. Lutie says, "You see, colored people have been shining shoes and washing clothes and scrubbing floors for years and years. White people seem to think that's the only kind of work they're fit to do. The hard work. The dirty work. The work that pays the least" (Petry 70). Here, Lutie reflects on the circumstances to which she is resigned. Socioeconomic and racial politics lead to an existence for Lutie that impedes her advancement in society.

Petry uses Lutie's interactions with her son, Bub, to further highlight this point. Lutie discovers that Bub has taken an afterschool job of shining shoes, as many of the other children in the apartment building. Her response to such an innocent ambition to make money for the overall betterment of their family is both shocking and disheartening. Specifically, it is a cold splash of water to the face for readers:

> Her voice grew thick with rage. "I'm working to look after you and you out here in the street shining shoes just like the rest of these little niggers." And she thought, You know that isn't all there is involved. It's also that Little Henry Chandler is the same age as Bub, and you know Little Henry is wearing gray flannel suits and dark blue caps and long blue socks and fine dark brown leather shoes. He's doing his homework in that big warm library in front of the fireplace. And your kid is out in the street with a shoeshine box. (Petry 67)

There is nothing worse for Lutie than seeing her son succumb to the same socioeconomic situation from which she is working so desperately to rescue them. Bub's youth and naiveté do not allow him to understand why Lutie does not want him to work or spend too much time chasing money. Innocently, Bub thinks he is only doing what brings his mother less stress and more income. In reality, his working serves as a reminder for Lutie of their dire financial situation.

Lutie's desire for her son to have more out of life is a direct reflection of her awareness of the lack of societal advantage and opportunity for those who become trapped in a domestic work environment. This is more evident when Lutie thinks on Bub's potential life of subservience: Lutie knows that the only jobs available to Black men like Bub (when they are available) are window washing and elevator operating. While Lutie fights socioeconomic challenges in Harlem, Eden's socioeconomic challenges are more closely linked to ongoing violence as a result of French xenophobia. Eden is in Paris to be a writer because her circumstances at home prevent her from exploring this creative avenue; she looks for the type of freedom in Paris, which would allow her to do so. Instead, she is confronted with violent bombings, protests, work discrimination, and covert forms of racism. Although the violence and racism Eden runs from in Birmingham is not culturally the same as the violence Eden witnesses in Paris, those landscapes are filled with the same kinds of violence. The bombs dropping in Birmingham destroy churches; the bombs dropping in Paris destroy embassies. Because of these similarities, Eden learns first that there is no escape from the violent outburst of groups who seek social or economic reform or those who oppose it. Although Eden writes about the terror that plagues Birmingham in her youth, Paris is supposed to be an escape from that. She writes,

> When the four little girls were killed by a segregationist's bomb at church one Sunday morning in 1963, I had just started to write my name. I still remember writing theirs . . . Cynthia, Addie Mae, Carole, Denise . . . Our church sent letters of condolence to their families. We moved to Georgia, but I did not stop being afraid of being blown to pieces . . . on an ordinary day if God wasn't looking . . . for most of my childhood I woke up each morning tired from so much running in my dreams—from faceless men in starched white sheets, from policeman with dogs, from firemen with water hoses. (Youngblood 5)

Instead of being that safe place, the first day, and several days after she arrived in Paris, bombs are exploding. It is almost as if Birmingham, Alabama has been reincarnated abroad. Eden reflects on this violence while Indego takes her on a tour of Paris.[7] The inherent need for one group to control another with fear and violent tactics is the same in both places. The difference is that Eden is in the oppressed group in the United States. In Paris, Eden is not the target of that violence, yet she still experiences other forms of racism. She remarks, "Hotel de Ville . . . had recently been the site of a bombing that killed a female postal clerk and wounded eighteen others. . . . Lebanese terrorists had given the French government an ultimatum to release three jailed suspected terrorists. . . . Four more bombs went off in the next six days, killing a total of eight people and wounding nearly two hundred" (Youngblood 45). And later, "It is true that there are no places here that keep a black person out, no, the French are not racist in that way. But there is a condescension, a superiority, a patronizing attitude that comes through between most foreigners and the average French person" (Youngblood 52). Here, Youngblood reveals that there is a global problem with violence, governmental policies, xenophobia from French citizens, naturalization, and citizenship. Ultimately, these issues are not relegated specifically to African Americans, but are aimed at the larger African Diaspora, particularly Algerians, Haitians, and formerly colonized Africans; therefore, there is no racial sanctuary.

Jones, in her treatment of Youngblood's text, likens the text to Baldwin's works in which he details his experiences in Paris and the tensions between the warring nations. She argues,

> Youngblood calls attention to similarities between postcolonial tensions in France and violence during the civil rights era in the U.S. South. This comparison works to name southern white violence "terrorism" and to point up the similarities in racial and ethnic tensions that Youngblood herself experienced in France in the mid-1980s. Baldwin writes about tensions between the French and immigrants from Algeria . . . about tensions between the French and the Lebanese and the Haitians as well as the North Africans. (Jones 45)

While Petry writes about African Americans in urban epicenters like Harlem during and after the second migration, Youngblood mirrors her Parisian experiences through Eden. In Meri Nana-Ama Danquah's *Shaking the Tree: A Collection of New Fiction and Memoir by Black Women* (2003), an excerpt from Youngblood's text appears in which she prefaces her excerpt by inspiring her novel and an account of her voyage to Paris in 1986. This expedition led to the creation of *Black Girl in Paris*. Youngblood comments, "I explored the ways in which an individual could create identity, cross sexual and cultural boundaries. . . . Eden found that the writer's life was not so glamorous as she imagined, that freedom had a price and Paris was not without its own variety of racism" (Danquah 264). Youngblood inserts these experiences into Eden's Parisian exploits. While Eden is attempting to find work, she comments on some of the laws that prevent Americans from obtaining work permits. She says, "Working papers were difficult to get since stricter immigration rules were being enforced . . . officially the new laws were designed to contain the new wave of terrorism, unofficially they were created to keep out new immigrants. There are still many fascists in our society" (Youngblood 60). Again, while racism in the United States and Paris, France are not motivated by the same stimuli, there are some key similarities in how these conflicts affect Eden.

When Eden leaves the United States, she does so in an attempt to escape laws that legalize segregation and support systemic racism and oppression of African Americans. The racially motivated laws of the Jim Crow South did much to ensure that races were kept separately. However, in Paris, immigrants are the targeted groups of people. The dangers of terrorism that Parisian officials feared is similar to the propaganda spread about the dangers of African Americans coming to power in the United States. Eden does not understand the language very well, but she understands this concept. It does not occur to Eden that in her plan to escape an oppressive and dangerous environment in the United States, she runs to a similarly oppressive and dangerous environment for a different group of minorities. As much as socioeconomic status and legislation keep groups separate, racial politics also play a role in these tensions.

Malik, a French national from Haiti, further embodies a racialized, lived experience in Paris. He explains that his family has a long history of conflict with the law and their experiences are not unlike many of those violent incidents in the American South. Malik and his family were, "called dirty" stopped regularly by police and checked for drugs, turned down for jobs on the telephone when the interviewer asked his name" 80). This is the first indication that skin color is also a problem in Paris. Through this inclusion, Youngblood paints a picture of global tension that extends beyond the confines of home. Fleeing the American streets for Parisian streets does not free Eden from socioeconomic politics.

ESCAPING SEXUAL POLITICS

While Lutie and Eden fight to avoid political, racial, and social conflict, both women grapple with sexual politics. Instead of fighting against countries and nations, which seek to control a population politically and economically, African American women fight to maintain agency over their bodies. In *The Street*, Jones' (the superintendent) preoccupation with Lutie is dangerous. Jones watches Lutie and uses her son, Bub, to gain access to her apartment. His goal is to insert himself into her life as a way to make her want him. The closer he gets to Lutie—her lipstick, her clothes, her bathroom—the more his disgust for Min, his live-in girlfriend, is apparent. While in Lutie's apartment, Jones "began thinking of Min. He would throw her out tonight. He had to get rid of her. . . . He wouldn't be able to stand the thought of her any more after being close to Lutie like this" (Petry 109). Min is physically able to be the warm body that Jones sexually desires; yet, he is unable to find any sexual gratification or true satisfaction from her. Lutie, from the moment she entered the street apartments on 116th Street, is a symbol of unattainable sexual gratification for Jones. The aforementioned warnings from Granny to Lutie's father were a prelude to the type of sexualized experience a woman like Lutie would experience her entire life. Marriage, then, would be the only way to save Lutie from falling into a life of ill repute. Lutie also reflects on Mrs. Hedges' first comments were "You married, dearie?" (Petry 76). Lutie's response to Mrs. Hedges' assumption—that Bub was illegitimate since she was likely not married—earned a rebuff from. But, what does that suggest about how Lutie has been conditioned to think about unwed or "separated" mothers? Lutie's need to clarify that she is "separated" rather than single speaks to her prescribed notions of respectability. It is more acceptable to be separated from detrimental marriage, than to either ignore the question or to say "no," which would assuredly paint a negative image of Lutie for Mrs. Hedges. In this moment, Lutie cannot escape the sexual politics ascribed to women.

Lutie's failure to escape sexual politics makes the street a place of lost hopes and dreams. Lutie is forced to confront the harsh realities of the street and the urban landscape after her career as a singer fails to materialize, largely because she refused to barter her body to Junto for a singing career. For example, the entire house knows that Mr. Smith (who is African American) beats his wife when he is inebriated, but none of the women, including Lutie, offer to help Mrs. Smith. It also speaks to the commonality of violence against women's bodies in the small spaces where African American and white men take particular advantage of women and use their bodies, not for intimate or sensual exchanges, but for an area for power struggle dynamics. Lutie never mentions seeking out Mrs. Smith and coming to her rescue.

This is partly because Lutie is quite limited in how she can help. Her failure to help is more about accepting that she can offer little or no help for Mrs. Smith, so it is best that she refrains from intervening.

Normalized African American violence is commonplace in highly populated urban spaces. More troubling, though, is the hyper-normality of domestic violence in these spaces. Throughout *The Street*, there are several instances where Lutie hears a woman screaming and crying as she endures physical assault. The only person who steps in to aid a woman being assaulted is Mrs. Hedges. However, Mrs. Hedges' motivations for helping Lutie are questionable. She does not help her out of sheer concern for her safety, but out of concern for a potential investment. Though Mrs. Hedges is the most powerful woman in the novel, her power is a direct result of Junto and his influence. Mrs. Hedges and Junto work in tandem; his desire to sexually possess Lutie, and Mrs. Hedges' access to Lutie, only complicates the sexual politics at work against Lutie. Further, if Junto had been allowed access to Lutie, or if Lutie had relented to Junto's stealth-like advances, it is highly unlikely that Mrs. Hedges would have interfered in Lutie's near-rape encounter with Jones. As proof, there is never a discussion or mention of Mrs. Hedges going to aid the other women in the tenement whose partners assault them.

Moreover, Mrs. Hedges does not interfere in the physical assaults Jones makes against Min. Left to her own devices, Min shifts the power dynamic in the apartment with Jones. After consulting the root doctor, Prophet David, Min places a large, gold cross over the bed. When Jones sees it, he reacts in a defeated manner. Petry writes, "Almost immediately he started backing away from the sight of it, retreating toward the living room where he wouldn't be able to see it" (140). And later, the sight of the cross becomes too much for Jones to bear. It gives Min some sort of power and authority over Jones. It is also important to note that Min is left to stand up to Jones without the aid of any women in the novel; she is also the only woman who "escapes" the harshness of 116th Street. Power, then, becomes subjective; Min has the metaphysical power to stop Jones from physically abusing her until she can escape. However, Mrs. Hedges has the means and opportunity to use the women and Junto to her advantage.

Even when Mrs. Hedges understands Lutie's predicament with Bub, Mrs. Hedges still offers her no real assistance or guidance that will allow Lutie to maintain possession of her sexual autonomy.[8] After visiting the lawyer, Mrs. Hedges brings Lutie back to the stark reality that her socioeconomic status could be different if she only used her body as a bargaining chip. Instead of informing Lutie that she probably would not need a lawyer at all for such a minor offense, Mrs. Hedges uses the opportunity to talk about Junto again. More disturbing though is that Mrs. Hedges does not understand, or perhaps she understands too well, how this is part of the problem with women on the street. Those young girls who room at Mrs. Hedges' apartments are using their bodies for money, but ultimately Mrs. Hedges is the person who benefits. Those girls are Mrs. Hedges' escape because she is unable to use her body the way those men desire because she lacks youth and beauty.

Mrs. Hedges represents another facet of sexual politics in *The Street*. It is one thing to have the men, Jones, Junto, and Boots, sexually lusting after Lutie, covertly and overtly, but Mrs. Hedges also engages in and facilitates a kind of sexual exploitation. Sure, she provides a way for some girls to make money to survive the streets, but she also perpetuates an air of sexual impropriety and danger. There is no indication that any of Mrs. Hedges' girls are better off than Lutie. Instead of helping the girls succeed or save money, Mrs. Hedges is largely benefiting from their bodies much like the men who frequent Mrs. Hedges' girls and the men who lust after Lutie. To make matters worse, instead of offering Lutie help, Mrs. Hedges offers a direct entrée into prostitution. The only difference is that Mrs. Hedges would control Lutie instead of Boots or Jones. Junto would still benefit from Lutie's body. This realization disgusts Lutie and sends her into a rage.

Although Junto has never been formally introduced to Lutie until this moment, his presence has been following Lutie, haunting her, throughout the novel. Mrs. Hedges was the first to allude to Junto in her description of a "nice white gentleman" who would help Lutie and other young girls out who need extra money. Alone with Boots, Junto is being mentioned again. It was Junto all along, seemingly, controlling the mechanism of the street. Lutie is enraged and needs to strike something, "She thought, I would like to kill him, not just because he happens to be Junto, but because I can't even think straight about him or anybody else any more. It is as though he were a piece of that dirty street itself, tangible, close at hand, within reach" (Petry 422). Here, the reader experiences Lutie's rage first hand. While this is the only time she exhibits some control over her life, Lutie loses control over her body at the same time. While striking back at Boots, Lutie has an out-of-body experience in which she strikes back, almost robotically, at all of the things oppressing her. In her attempt to protect her body and reclaim agency over it, Petry does not allow Lutie agency. The rage that is festering inside her cannot be suppressed any longer. Boots' fleeting moment of control over Lutie slips away at the same time his life does. It is important that Petry's last glimpse into Boots' stream of consciousness mirrors his true intent and Junto's intent. Boots' and Junto's bartering and negotiations of Lutie as property are the most destructive relationships in the novel.

Though Clark argues that Lutie's "own obsession with exploiting [Boots Smith] financially positions her more closely to Jones as someone guided by wolfish impulses," (105) one must not reposition Lutie in a way that makes her the person in control. The circumstances that land Lutie at Boots' apartment are a direct reflection the male characters' preoccupation with usurping Lutie's authority and agency. Lutie's body is the prize, whether first or last, in Boots' eyes. This is clear when Petry writes, "Sure, Lutie would sleep with Junto, but he was going to have her first . . . he can have the leavings. After all he is white and this time a white man can have a black man's leavings" (422). Here, Lutie ponders how both Junto and Boots seek to possess her. Petry uses this moment of reflection to show how Lutie has been living under the control of two men and Mrs. Hedges since she moved to 116th Street. Their actions or inactions have dictated the majority of Lutie's life. These revelations cause Lutie's rage to climax when she murders Boots Smith. The vivid imagery and descriptions that Petry uses to describe the scene show that Lutie is finally striking back at her environment and its treatment of women, African Americans, and the poor.

> Even after he lay motionless, she kept striking him . . . she was venting her rage against the dirty, crowded street . . . dilapidated old houses . . . small dark rooms . . . narrow dingy hallways . . . the little lost girls in Mrs. Hedges' apartment . . . smashed homes where women did drudgery because their men had deserted them. She saw all these things and struck at them. (430)

Here, Lutie is striking against those things that brought her to 116th Street in the beginning of the novel. Here, Lutie is striking against all of the men who have recently tried to take advantage of her body. Boots ceases to become a person, but becomes a symbol of the consequences of violence against female bodies instead.

Lutie's sexual autonomy is the one thing that she never relinquishes throughout the novel. Regarding female bodies, Patricia Hill Collins, *In Black Sexual Politics: African Americans, Gender, and the New Racism* (2004), argues, "Sexuality was one of the few realms in which masses of African American women could exercise autonomy, and thus tangibly distinguish themselves as free women both from the sexual exploitation of slavery as well as the demands of having thirteen babies in insular Southern rural families" (72). Her attempts to advance economically are thwarted, not because she is a greedy opportunistic character, like Keith Clark's Gothic reading of Lutie would suggest, but because the men in Lutie's space, in her life, are Hell-bent on owning, or temporarily possessing, her body. It is this realization, at the novel's climax, that leads to Lutie's murderous strikes. She realizes that white society has long considered her body disposable. In essence, while Lutie's life and body are disposable in the novel, Bub's life is also cast aside. As Lutie visualizes Bub becoming a product of the racially segregated, classist hegemony that governs and polices African American lives, Bub is highly likely to become like Jones or Boots Smith. Lutie tells the reader early in the novel that she wants to get Bub away from Lil and Pop, but their escape from that life proves to be their undoing. Lutie and Bub never have a chance to thrive; they are always going to be casualties of the street. As the novel closes, the audience is left to envision Bub as he embarks on a life of uncertainty, poverty, and abandonment that, unfortunately, neither he nor Lutie ever have a chance to escape.

SEXUAL POLITICS IN *BLACK GIRL IN PARIS*

While economic inequality complicates sexuality in *The Street*, for Eden in *Black Girl in Paris*, terror often juxtaposes sexuality. In *Black Girl in Paris*, Eden, very early in her narrative, discusses her "touching games" as a young girl with childhood friend Rosaleen and her brother Anthony.[9]

> I was no stranger to terror. . . . When I was thirteen years old and living in Georgia I was in love with a girl in my class named Rosaleen and with her older brother, Anthony. Rosaleen and I played touching games in her bedroom, games she'd learned from her brother. Once when Anthony was home from college he sent Rosaleen downstairs to watch television, and he and I played the touching games. . . . My feelings about Rosaleen and Anthony created a confusion in me, a terror of choosing. (Youngblood 6)

Eden's choice to describe these "touching games" and the bombs that constantly explode in Birmingham, Alabama, as forms of terror is key to understanding her confusion about her sexuality and her inability to engage properly in meaningful relationships with either sex later in the novel. Youngblood alludes to child molestation between Anthony and Rosaleen, a blossoming bisexuality or sexual confusion, and a yearning for affection among all three parties. Though Eden seems sure that it is Rosaleen, in fact, whom she wants to touch her on the inside, it is not clear if this inside refers to her vagina, which would infer a sexual touching, or if Eden means touching her heart. Regardless, this is the first time Eden is aware of an attraction to women.

Later, Eden says, "After Rosaleen and Anthony I was terrified that no one would ever love me again, that desire was a bubble that would burst when I touched it. Years later I met Leo, who loved my body for a while, then left me when I felt I needed him most. A bomb can kill you instantly, love can make you wish you were dead" (Youngblood 6–7). Again, the reader is immediately presented with a violent image of bombs exploding, and Eden's relationship explodes in much the same way. This is another key difference between Petry's text and Youngblood's. The men in the text covet Lutie's body for sexual gratification. No man shows interest in having a meaningful relationship with Lutie. Meanwhile, Youngblood allows Eden to experience several relationships that defy the respectability and sexual politics that confine Lutie. Eden has a sexual interaction with Indego in exchange for his help. Though it is never an explicit request, Eden expects that Indego is so helpful to her and accommodating because he wants to be intimate with her. "I knew he wanted to make love, but he wanted me to make the first move. He spoke in metaphor and simile about the poetry of love, the passion and experience age brings to a union of love" (Youngblood 54). After this romantic entanglement, Eden is left alone and potentially homeless. Indego leaves Paris, sublets his apartment, and Eden is left once again, at the mercy of Paris. Arguably, Indego uses Eden for her body. Though Eden, too, uses Indego, this is one instance where this character differs from Petry's character. Lutie never allows the men to use her body or possess her. She briefly considers a relationship with Boots Smith before she realizes that her employment as a singer will bring no economic relief. Youngblood's Eden is already sexually confused and is less guarded about her body. Though Eden shows gratitude for Indego's help and his friendship, she gives in to his advances in the night because she longs for intimacy. An orphan who racial violence haunts, Eden often feels a lack of closeness to others. Whether this is an example of Eden's decision to barter her body or not is left up to interpretation.

Later, when Eden does use her body as a means of financial support, she becomes a modernized Venus Hottentot.[10] Since Paris is the place in which Sarah Baartman is on display as a scientific phenomenon—in life and death—it is important to examine Youngblood's employ of Eden similarly. In order to make money, Eden agrees to be a nude model. Though she detests the idea of posing for money, she sees no other alternative to survive and remain in Paris. Eden's naked body is on display for men to study and draw, but little to no humanity or regard for Eden's personality exudes from the pictures. Eden states, "The sketches I saw of myself made me feel good about my body . . . I was disappointed that the artists hardly ever put details in my face although they captured the density and curl of my pubic hairs, the exact shape of my hardened nipples, and weight of my breasts against gravity" (Youngblood 70). This is one of the first ways Eden's body is used as a form of artistic production. Although her goal is to produce art through words in the way that James Baldwin and Langston Hughes do, she must use her body as a means of financial support until she can write. So, while Eden does have some agency, there is no escape from the public consumption of her body. Baartman, too, is unable to escape the public prodding and degradation, even in death. While Eden is not displayed in the same fashion as Baartman, her African American body is still the subject of study; men and women study her body and draw its beauty, yet Eden is not the recipient of any of that affection. She is just a specimen.

Even though the majority of Eden's relationships and friendships are fleeting, each one teaches Eden something about herself and about navigating the Parisian landscape. Her relationship with Ving, a white musician, is the only one that works for Eden, but it too has a flaw. Eden is drawn to the sound of Ving's horn before knowing that he is a white man. His music reminds her of home in Georgia.[11] Speaking of which, Jones argues, "Ving is the only white person Eden encounters who produces this positive effect. White people, whether southern or not, negatively remind her of home, most especially of the South's racial history but also in the case of the British poet Elizabeth of its regional position as provincial Other to the nation" (48). Although Eden's relationship with Ving is promising, "Youngblood signals that emancipation will not be an easy one . . . Eden becomes rapidly romantically involved with Ving, and Youngblood makes their relationship seem like a perfect match—artistically, culturally, personally, even as regards both his and her androgynous appearance and possible bisexual orientation" (Jones 48). Here, Eden seems to finally be on track to accomplish her goals of finding love in Paris and finding Baldwin. Ving does not attempt to control Eden or subvert her voice into what society deems respectable writing. But, even in this relationship, the politics of race, class, and sexuality reemerge.

Eden gets a very harsh reminder from a street encounter while out walking with Ving one night. A group of men shouts at them, "Look at the queer walking his black dog. Salope. Putain. Bitch. Whore" (Youngblood 164). This encounter takes Eden back to that place of racist language that she wanted to escape initially. It also invades her new feeling of emotional and physical security in Paris. Jones writes that this encounter "frightens Eden out of her sexual desire and sends her back to the 'last plantation' out of a need for self-protection" (48). Here, the last plantation is an iteration of Baldwin's from his text *The Fire Next Time*, in which he discusses the social forces responsible for all of his fear and discomfort become internalized.[12] Once those terrors are internal, one carries them into every space, whether in the American South or Paris, France. Eden experiences the same kind of sexual frustration and societal fears that Baldwin experiences. The mind transforms into the last plantation because those exterior terrors are now mentally affecting how African Americans navigate the landscape. By escaping to the "last plantation," more so than any other place in Youngblood's text, Eden is reminded that there is no escape from the harsh realities of racism, sexual discrimination, respectability politics, and violence. Even though Eden is thousands of miles away from the American South, in the most romantic city in the world, she cannot escape this reality. Youngblood writes,

> Those men hadn't cared that I was American, college-educated, and Christian; all they saw was the color of my skin. Back home, I still wouldn't be able to

hold Ving's hand without inviting comment or threat. What made me think I could be free? He was a white man, yet he couldn't protect me here in Paris or any part of the world. What kind of future could we have together? What about our children, if we had any? . . . My sweet high was gone. (165)

This encounter is an abrupt reminder about the implications of being African American and violently thrust upon a white background. The harsh reality that he is both white and possibly queer usurps Eden's love for Ving. Until this point, Eden is only covertly aware of the racism that Paris has to offer her. However, a real relationship with Ving transports Eden back to the American South, where interracial relationships are unacceptable in many parts of society, whether African American or white. Youngblood also depicts Eden's horror at the thought of children being born out of their union. They, too, would be subject to this type of verbal abuse. This is not a life that Eden wants in the American South, hence her escape; however, she cannot escape this possibility on the streets of Paris, standing next to her white lover, Ving.

Ving's marriage proposal, after this incident, suggests that Eden's race and the opinions of his white peers are of no consequence to him. Jones argues, "Youngblood reminds readers that when black people attempt to flee that 'last plantation,' the likelihood is high that not just a white person, but a person of their own race may try to bring them back.[13] Even Haitian Olu-Christophe, allegedly Ving's best friend, objects to their interracial liaison" (49). Therefore, the novel ends with their relationship status unclear. Arguably, Ving is Eden's equal and her most healthy relationship throughout the novel; however, the implications of respectability, socioeconomic, and sexual polity will not allow this relationship to prosper. Eden abandons the streets of Paris for a small countryside village where she begins to write alone. Eden escapes the harsh American streets, with the hopes of finding her writerly voice and fulfilling relationships; she never finds that in the Parisian streets.

CONCLUSION

Petry's *The Street* presents Lutie Johnson as an empathetic character. The sexual politics she confronts as a resident of Harlem's 116th Street force her to make life-altering choices. Lutie is driven to murder because of the unending need for the men in the novel to possess her body. Even as Petry depicts Boots Smith as Lutie's best opportunity to escape the street and its dangers, it becomes another opportunity for Petry to showcase how patriarchal society largely determines a woman's freedom and economic progression. Though she never truly needs a lawyer to rescue her son, her failure to understand the justice system prevents Lutie from saving her son from the dangers of the street. Though Lutie never sees Bub again, she understands that he will become a system kid, and he will likely fall into the same lifestyle Lutie fights so hard to escape. Instead, Lutie is forced out of 116th Street without her son. This decision means that another African American youth is left at the mercy of the street, susceptible to the system of oppression from which Lutie desperately runs. Lutie attempts to escape the respectability politics, the sexual politics, and the socioeconomics politics that plague the street, but she never really escapes. Like Lutie, many women migrate from one street to the next, constantly searching for a freedom and liberation that will likely never come. The reader is left with the eerie feeling that when Lutie disembarks from the train in Chicago, she will live on a street similar to 116th Street.

Shay Youngblood's *Black Girl in Paris* depicts a different type of failed escape. Eden's street is America's street. America's street is littered not with trash and poverty, but with bombings and hate and the inability for African Americans to be artistically free. Eden's escape takes her not *just* north, but it takes her to Paris. Eden not only wants to be a writer, but she wants to write like James Baldwin. Though Eden has trouble escaping issues of race, class, and gender, one must also consider how Eden feels inclined to be a writer in the image of James Baldwin. She sacrifices so much to be like a male writer while having to confront several difficulties of African American womanhood. While Eden thinks about how men desire her, she ultimately casts those concerns to the side to write like Baldwin. In doing so, Eden does not succeed in meeting or becoming Baldwin. She also does not escape the intersections of race, class, and gender in the Parisian streets. In her mind, she can only be a great writer if she goes to Paris and finds him. In doing so, she will escape social, economic, and artistic confinement. Analyzing Eden's failed escape in terms of how Parisian streets mirror the American streets provides a space for comparative intertextual analysis. For Eden and Lutie, America cannot provide solidarity and separation of public and private space for African American women. In the same way Eden must confront issues of respectability politics, socioeconomics, and sexual politics in America, she must also confront these issues as an au pair in Paris. What Youngblood does with Eden is to show that despite being in a different country, there is no escape from issues of race, class, and gender. Eden and Lutie could be the same person in two different decades.

The same social conventions that hinder Lutie from prospering in her environment and orphan Bub are the same conventions that complicate Eden's Parisian escape. Though she eventually catches a glimpse of Baldwin on her last day in Paris, what she finds is that she has always been capable of becoming a writer. She did not need to seek out Baldwin to achieve that goal. It is only when Eden stops chasing Baldwin that she begins to understand how to be the best writer possible. She has a voice, and thanks to her experiences and failed escapes from America's street and Paris' street, Eden now has much lived experience from which to draw. Eden set out to escape racism, sexism, and economic struggles. Instead, Paris affords Eden a worldview of global concerns: civil rights in America, immigrant rights in Paris; socioeconomic difficulties in the American South, socioeconomic restrictions on foreigners and immigrants abroad; sexual tensions and confusions in her youth, sexual confusions, and relationship difficulties as an adult in Paris.

Finally, placing both Petry's and Youngblood's texts side by side reveals that there are striking similarities and differences between how these women navigate the urban landscape while searching for an escape from society's conventions. While *The Street* is frequently a part of academic and critical discussions, Shay Youngblood's *Black Girl in Paris* exists in the margins of critical inquiry and discussion. It is important to continue to engage older texts, while also opening up avenues for newer criticisms of them. At the same time, doing intertextual analyses provides a new method of engaging older texts and invites contemporary authors into critical spaces. Though Youngblood's text spans the late 1960s to the mid-1980s, she offers a fresh interpretation of street literature that forces the reader to take up texts by older authors like Petry or Baldwin and place them in conversation with the Shay Youngbloods in contemporary African American literature. This ensures that there are ample critical engagement and artistic production that will pull more texts from the periphery of academia and toward the center of critical examination. Thus, more diverse conversations occur with new textual pairings, which invites fresh critical study of Petry and others like her. Changing how street literature is classified makes way for texts like Youngblood's to gain more critical attention. More critical attention brings diverse perspectives to a text that adds a global perspective to issues of race, class, gender, and how these issues intersect for women on the street.

NOTES

1. Paul Laurence Dunbar is credited with having written the first migration narrative, *Sport of the Gods* (1902), in which the appalling effects of ghetto life are described fully.

2. Clark is reading critic Evie Shockley's essay, "Buried Alive: Gothic Homelessness, Black Women's Sexuality and (Living) Death in Ann Petry's *The Street*," and is evoking her reading of Petry's construction of social terror for poor, African American residents in Harlem.

3. Thanks to the pioneering work of Alice Walker, Zora Neale Hurston remains one of the few African American female writers of the Harlem Renaissance who remains widely taught and anthologized. Toni Morrison is the last American writer,

and the first African American, to win the Nobel Prize for literature. Though an octogenarian, she continues to write. Her last novel, *God Help the Child*, debuted in 2015.

4. Davis, Thadious M. "Sashaying through the South." *South to the Future: An American Region in the Twenty-First Century*. Ed. Fred Hobson. Athens: University of Georgia Press, 2002. Print.

5. *Au Pair* is French for baby sitter or nanny. As Youngblood describes Eden's responsibilities to the children, they align closely with the duties and responsibilities of American domestic workers who earn a living by taking care of white families, for little pay or room and board.

6. Wright's "Blueprint for Negro Writing" poses the question: "Shall Negro writing be for the Negro masses, moulding the lives and consciousness of those masses toward new goals, or shall it continue begging the question of the Negroes' humanity?" (99). Wright critiqued existing Negro writing for lacking a substantive concept to link the political and social change with the artistic and creative productions of Blacks.

7. Indego helps Eden out by giving her room and board until she can find a job. In the beginning, this allowed Eden to focus on her quest to find James Baldwin, but she very quickly realizes that Indego is being too nice to her and getting nothing in return. Though she knows he will eventually want more than her friendship, Eden takes odd jobs in order to support herself, but she is unable to do so without Indego's help. Eventually, she starts a sexual relationship with him, but she is not in love with Indego and he knows it. Eden has unfulfilling sex with Indego for survival. The sex is unfulfilling much like her relationship with Anthony. Eden stays with him until he leaves Paris and sublets his apartment to someone else.

8. Jones befriends Bub as a way to get close to Lutie. Since Lutie and Bub need money, Jones convinces Bub to conduct a mail scam that involves stealing mail and money from several buildings in Harlem. Once Bub is caught, Bub is taken to juvenile detention. Meanwhile Lutie has no money to pay for a lawyer and no other way to earn money except by either offering her body to Junto, per Mrs. Hedges' suggestion, or by submitting her body to Boots and then Junto. Either way, she chooses, Lutie loses.

9. Anthony is Eden's first male relationship. She has a sexual relationship with him, but yearns for his sister Rosaleen to whom she is more attracted. Rosaleen is Eden's first love, but she is confused by her feelings for both a man and a woman. This sexual confusion complicates Eden's future relationships.

10. "Sarah Baartman was the most popular and widely circulated stereotype of black female sexuality in early 19th century French culture. . . . Baartman went to England in 1810 for the specific purpose of displaying her near-nude 'Hottentot' body in early-nineteenth-century sideshows. . . . In 1814, Boer Peter Cexar took Baartman to Paris and sold her to an animal trainer. . . . Baartman became the subject of satirical cartoons, including a one-act vaudeville play, *Venus*, written by Suzan-Lori Parks, and most notably a scientific oddity for a panel of French scientists and zoologists in the Jardin du Roi for a three-day conference in March 1815. After her death, instead of burying her body, Georges Cuvier dissected Baartman's body and held the pieces on display for further scientific experimentation, for almost thirty years. After Nelson Mandela rose to the presidency of South Africa in 1994, he made a formal request to

repatriate Baartman's remains. Baartman's remains were returned to South Africa for formal burial in 2002" (Tillet 944).

11. Indego is the only other person who brings elements of the American South to Eden in a way that is not negative.

12. Jones is using a phrase that African American journalist and critical race theorist Njerio Itabari coined.

13. Suzanne Jones discusses "the last plantation" by stating, "through Eden's encounters with white southerners in Paris, Youngblood illustrates a phenomenon that Baldwin articulated in *The Fire Next Time*, when he wrote that 'the social forces which menaced me had become interior" (49–50). Black journalist and critical race theorist Njeri Itabori has recently named this interior space, the last plantation, arguing that "even as we are victimized by the ethos of slave masters and their descendants, we often define ourselves and operate in terms that speak to the psychological slavery that leaves the mind the last plantation" (Jones 50). The mere fact that Eden is in France, however, literally takes her out of her usual place in southern society, but also out of her black community as well, thereby putting her in a physical position to break the ideological bonds of both (Jones 46).

BIBLIOGRAPHY

Clark, Keith. "A Distaff Dream Deferred? Ann Petry and the Art of Subversion." *African American Review* 26, no. 3 (1992). 495–505. Web. 5 Dec 2013.

———. *The Radical Fiction of Ann Petry*. Baton Rouge: Louisiana State University Press, 2013. Print.

Collins, Patricia Hill. *Black Feminist Thought: Knowledge, Consciousness, and the Politics of Empowerment.* New York: Routledge, 2000. Print.

Crenshaw, Kimberle. "Demarginalizing the Intersection of Race and Sex: A Black Feminist Critique of Antidiscrimination Doctrine." *Feminist Theory and Antiracist Politics*. 46.3. (2000): 208–238. Web. 10 Nov 2013.

Davis, Thadious M. "Sashaying through the South." *South to the Future: An American Region in the Twenty-First Century.* Ed. Fred Hobson. University of Georgia Press, 2002.

Danquah, Meri Nana-Ama. *Shaking the Tree: A Collection of New Fiction and Memoir by Black Women.* W.W. Norton & Company, 2003.

Higginbotham, Evelyn Brooks. *Righteous Discontent: The Women's Movement in the Black Baptist Church, 1880–1920.* Harvard University Press, 1994.

Holladay, Hilary. *Ann Petry*. Twayne Publishers, 1996.

Jones, Suzanne. W "Black Girl in Paris: Shay Youngblood's Escape from the 'Last Plantation'." *South Atlantic Review* 73.3 (2008): 44–52. Academic OneFile. Web. 22 Nov. 2013.

Petry, Ann. *The Street*. Houghton Mifflin, 1946, 1974.

Shockley, Evie. "Buried Alive: Gothic Homelessness, Black Women's Sexuality, and (Living) Death in Ann Petry's *The Street*." *African American Review*. 40, no. 3 (2006): 439–460. Web. 18 Sept. 2015.

Tillet, Salamishah. "Black Girls in Paris: Sally Hemings, Sarah Baartman, and French Racial Dystopias." *Callaloo* 32, no. 3 (2009): 934–954. Project Muse. Web. 15 Oct. 2013.

Wall, Cheryl. "Nellie—Pioneer of Black Feminist Literary Criticism: Nellie McKay and Black Women's Studies." *Nellie McKay—A Memorial. African American Review* 40, no. 1 (2006): 17–19. Web. 8 Dec. 2013.

Williams, Kimberle Crenshaw. "Mapping the Margins: Intersectionality, Identity Politics, and Violence Against Women of Color." *Stanford Law Review* 43, no. 6 (1991): 1241–1299. Web. 10 Nov. 2013.

Wright, Richard. "Blueprint for Negro Writing (1937)." In *Within the Circle: An Anthology of African American Literary Criticism from the Harlem Renaissance to the Present*. Ed. Angelyn Mitchell, 97–106. Durham and London: Duke University Press, 1994. PDF file.

Youngblood, Shay. *Black Girl in Paris*. Riverhead Books, 2000.

Chapter 2

You Can't Shut Me Up

Using Gwendolyn Brooks to Help Students Be Seen and Heard

Carissa McCray

Teaching literature and living as Black must be activism. Gwendolyn Brooks understood her role as a Black woman born in 1917, living in Chicago as a published poet in the 1940s, and raising Black children. Her role included using her voice to write about what she saw, speaking powerfully to Black reality. However, in traditional classroom literature, Gwendolyn Brooks has been reduced to "We Real Cool," a poem of young Black boys and their untimely, or timely (depending on the readers' perspective) death. This is because, in traditional classroom literature, Black students are often neglected, prompting division, isolation, and discrimination among racial and ethnic groups. The need for Black literature has been discussed in academia for several decades; however, the implementation and incorporation have yet to manifest fully across educational programs, with stakeholders, or across districts. Black authors are silenced in pedagogical practices. Throughout this chapter, a brief history of Black women's silence and Gwendolyn Brooks' will be followed by how Gwendolyn Brooks used poetry and her only novel, *Maud Martha*, to both criticize and laud voicelessness and silence.

Developed, explored, and redefined throughout our lives, a sense of identity provides us with foundational fortitude. To understand the role schools have in the development of students of color identity more research is needed;[1] however, several scholars have concluded that multicultural curricula have had a positive impact on the academic, social, and cultural achievement of students.[2] Exploring diverse and complex voices should not just entail adding literature or briefly discussing the concepts—this strategy would not demonstrate the complexity or critical need of the literature. Multicultural literature as a form of critical literacy adds to the positive development of identity if there is a full exploration of themes, topics, and images that will empower Black students.[3]

DuBois' discussion of the American Black double consciousness during the late 1800s and early 1900s is still relevant today as Whaley addresses how non-white racial and ethnic groups judge themselves or are judged based on their assimilation into white culture. Black students struggle with race being the first indicator of who they are—people create narratives for a person of color before getting to know them.[4] Gender is then used to argue how someone fits into stereotypical norms. Internally, students may struggle with class identity, sexual identity, religious identity, family identity, or other social constructs that may limit their opportunities. When educators begin to incorporate critical multicultural literature, they should also understand identity conflict. Multicultural literature seeks to incorporate authentic texts with literature that moves beyond racial stereotypes and demonstrate complex, empowered, and humanistic characters, personas, and themes for full exploration.[5] If characters are not complex, empowered, or humanistic, there is little involvement, discussion, or change.

The Black female writing culture has expanded beyond country lines to explore diverse forms of Blackness throughout the world. Because Black female authors desire to create societies based on reality, religion, and meditation, the narratives allow identities to form while cultivating the uniqueness of women, relationships, and interactions across the world. Authors such as Zora Neale Hurston, Nnedi Okorafor, Chimamanda Ngozi Adichie, Bernice McFadden, and Toni Morrison have created Black female characters who are multifaceted, unique, and conquerors of their circumstances.

Representation is a powerful concept. By allowing little Black girls to see themselves represented outside the stereotypical sassy Black girl/woman, Black girls' futures will overflow with examples and goals for greatness that will expand their current standards. Not only does the Black female need diverse literature to create powerful identities, but Black female authors also allow Black females to engage in experiences that may surpass their current circumstances.

SILENCE IN LITERATURE

There are multiple dimensions of silence. These dimensions exist based on experiences, current situation, and the reactions of others. In literature when a woman is silent, especially a Black woman, the silence is louder than what is being said. Typically, women in literature, as reflective in the real world, are attempting to deconstruct the images of them as submissive, silent, and an object of pleasure or possession that stems from hegemonic patriarchal standards.⁶ For Black women, the demands of a patriarchal society are even more demeaning because Black women are at the intersection of race and gender. In 1989, Crenshaw published an analysis of the mistreatment and disparities of the legal system for Black women. While women and Blacks were receiving some form of legal justice, Crenshaw found that Black women were being treated as either/or rather than at the intersection of Black and female.⁷ From this, Crenshaw coined the term "intersectionality" to illuminate the injustices Black women were subjected to and reduce the silence. Additionally, silence becomes multidimensional, because it becomes an act of survival, protection from sociopolitical hostilities, a sign of love or hatred, or a visual representation of exhaustion because of the constant assault on Black women.⁸ The silence of Black women is why the exploration of literature through a Critical Race Theory and intersectionality lens is vital. Critical Race Theory and intersectionality allow voices of marginalized persons, individuals discriminated against, or those denied opportunities because of their race, ethnicity, gender, sexuality, and other intersections to have a voice, transforming their capacity for growth and accomplishment. Williams, one of the foundational scholars of Critical Race Theory, suggests that scholars of Critical Race Theory engage in the following: an understanding of laws and how Black people are impacted, realizing that racism is systematic, understanding situational context, realizing that neutrality and color-blindness are detrimental, and using various forms of writing to convey research and legal ideas.⁹ The pedagogical practices of Critical Race Theory and intersectionality provide the opportunity for those who have experienced discrimination to speak because they have the insight into oppression and how silences can be both destructive and uplifting. With knowledge, narratives, and foundational resources, Critical Race Theorists can prompt change within communities with little fear of having their perspectives and experiences dismissed.¹⁰

In Black literature, Black women move in silence. The silence is a form of censorship—to become demure to blend into a culture that asks her "tone down" her voice, hand gestures, hair, and other forms of policing. First, the act of silence is not always a cowardly form of silence but an empowering attitude. Because of silence, when a woman speaks (to some, finally), she is freer and is using her voice from a dominant perspective in a way to reject boundaries and walls that prevent her from being herself.¹¹ Black women have dealt with the misconception of their silence and voice. When silent, Black women are perceived as moody or unhappy. When vocal, Black women are seen as too boisterous and demanding. These two dichotomous ideas of Black woman's voice and silence create frustration that can lead to emotionlessness or feed into women becoming stereotyped as the strong Black woman who has to be independent, selfless, and a provider to all but herself creating a cycle of socialization, stress, and distress.¹² Because of the internal and external battles that present themselves when Black women are both vocal and silent, Gwendolyn Brooks' narratives provide a voice for those who are speaking and not heard and for those who are afraid to speak.

Gwendolyn Brooks speaks for those who may not have the capacity or strength to speak for themselves. Brooks used her poetry and novel to fight for and encourage the dignity of children; encourage humanity needed for adolescents moving toward adulthood, compassion, and understanding for the poor; and empathy for those old and forgotten, which made her literary genius accessible for all who were seeking to see themselves portrayed in unprejudiced and real presentations.[13] Brooks focuses on her audience and representation was not only through observations—she lived without lights on, even upon winning the Pulitzer Prize.[14] With both observation and experience of life as a Black woman living in poverty, Brooks' poetry was widely received; yet, her novel, *Maud Martha* was disregarded as just an extension of her poetry rather than a narrative of how Black women are silenced and must remain silent for their survival.[15] It is ironic how as Brooks wrote about women lacking the power and influence to speak, and her novel was received in the same light. Despite the disheartening reception of *Maud Martha*, Brooks' work has left an indelible mark on society's patriarchal and racist norms.

VOICES IN POETRY

Poetry has many purposes. For many, however, poetry is political. Poetry acts as a conduit to express how one feels without repercussions while holding a mirror to the outside world to illuminate concerns, provide answers, or ask more questions. Poetry opens the door for discussions that may be too difficult to begin by creating a lyrical, metaphorical, or imagery-filled portrait of current circumstances and ideas. With poetry, the audience has more capacity to remember and those memories then begin to reflect a change in their lives and possibly the community. For Gwendolyn Brooks, her poetry portrayed the multifaceted characters of Black—joy, torment, peace, fear, love, struggle, confidence, anxiety, and hope—even with the harsh realities of living in a world that hated Blackness. As Mathew states, Brooks wrote with "Black ideal [that] italicizes black identity, black solidarity, black self-possession and self-address" to call Blacks traditions that solidified Black strength, solidarity, and pride.[16] Gwendolyn Brooks' poetry provided realistic perspectives for those who were poor, abandoned or abused, dark-skinned, and were proud or even needed encouragement to be proud of Blackness.

Throughout Gwendolyn Brooks' catalog of poetry, there are many poems dedicated to the plight of the poor, underserved, and underprivileged. In poems like "kitchenette building," "The Children of the Poor," "The Lovers of the Poor," and "An Old Black Woman, Homeless, and Indistinct," Brooks urges her audience to be understanding, have empathy, and if possible, to transform the conditions that create these circumstances.

In 1945, "kitchenette building" was published that detailed the early morning lives of those who live in kitchenette buildings. Brooks' poem demonstrated the discriminatory housing practices that kept Black families cramped in buildings with poor conditions. Because of these poor conditions, "dreams" were dismissed because the priorities became "rent" and "feeding a wife" in times where laws enforced discriminatory employment practices as well.[17] The man's job, during this time (illustrated in this poem), was to ensure his family had a house over their head and food to eat, whereas the woman was responsible for "satisfying a man."[18] However, this existence—of providing for each other—is countered by trash, building smells, and a sense of failure as dreams are lifted up but immediately enraptured by defeat because of discrimination, and limited time. The struggle to keep a dream or dreams alive by those who are poor are demonstrated throughout "kitchenette building" with discrimination being the most significant obstacle and time being the biggest needed resource—"since Number Five is out of the bathroom" and there is an opportunity to engage in basic necessity.[19] Dreaming, for the poor, as Brooks illustrates, is not feasible. There are few opportunities and even fewer resources for Black people. By publishing this poem in her first collection of work, Brooks illuminates the plight of those much like herself, who lived in a kitchenette building with her husband, while serving as a model to continue dreaming. She begins the poem: "dream makes a giddy sound," it can be sent "up through onion fumes . . . flutter . . . down these rooms" and provide some type of hope for the future of the dreamer.[20] The semblance of hope allows the audience to become enamored with the poem and shows them that poor people do try to improve their lives. Brooks' contrasts of dreams with onions demonstrates how abstract dreams can always manifest, but the audience must understand that they may not come to fruition because of the challenges the poor face, including lack of resources.

Gwendolyn Brooks captures the same failings of society in "The Children of the Poor," published in 1949. In the opening sonnet/stanza, Brooks juxtaposes both positive and negative aspects of being a parent, as children "trap" women with their "softness" and "helplessness" that creates "in conditions of love."[21] Even while poor, a child has needs, and the mother and father are responsible for ensuring those needs are met. The society the parents live in does not allow for "velvety velour,"[22] but instead, love and basic necessities of food, shelter, and clothing are enough. The goal is that children of the poor are prepared for how to cope with the world. These children must understand that they cannot and will not have everything they desire, but must understand that their lives have meaning. For children, life has meaning when children know that those who love them also provide protection. Parents risk their lives protecting their children by not "paus[ing] in the fire" or "hesitat[ing] in the hurricane to guard" and protect their children.[23] Additionally, the parent tells their children that they have a purpose, must have "plentitude of plan" to achieve that purpose, and to "sew up belief if that should tear" so that nothing will deter the child from a meaningful and purpose-filled life.[24] As this parent continues to question how they can nurture their children, they begin to question religion.

Historically, religion has been a safe-haven for Black men, women, and their families; however, religious values have taught Blacks to hold out for better times rather than fight for better now. Because of this perception, the speaker asks the child to question religious practices before dogmatically following them by "revis[ing] the psalm if that should frighten you" to maintain growth from generation to generation.[25] This growth is evident in the fourth stanza/sonnet. Brooks writes "first fight" to suggest that productivity, strength, and self-dignity are necessary to survive as poor and necessary to climb out of poverty, to "win war."[26] As a parent living in poverty, death is a constant conversation. In stanza five, our speakers desire the children to achieve justice in their lifetimes to prepare for their generations. However, death looms, and questions of whether the children will be alive long enough to achieve economic, psychological, and political justice forces the parent to reconcile their fears and to just hope for improvement. To win this war against economic struggle and racial injustices, children of the poor must be "first to arms, to armor" and "carry hate in front of [them] and harmony behind" to ensure that the oppressors will have no choice but to give them equal rights and opportunities.[27] The speaker in Brooks' poetry is empowering the audience to act rather than settle for mistreatment and abuse.

Contrasting the joyous yet entrapping feelings of motherhood in "The Children of the Poor," Brooks analyzes the despair abortions in "the mother" that was published in 1945. As Brooks is known to lend her voice to the poor, she also provides a voice for those abandoned and abused. An initial reading of "the mother" may seem as if the speaker is regretful and guilty for having an abortion. However, further inspection and analysis illustrates that the woman is alone, possibly abandoned, and abortion/multiple abortions were performed for the children's sake, because now she will "never neglect or beat them" nor "leave them" because of the historical lack of employment opportunities, financial hardships, and segregation.[28] Less than 15 years after the publication of "the mother," Lorraine Hansberry writes and publishes *A Raisin in the Sun* where a wife, from the South Side of Chicago, puts a down payment on an abortion. Chicago's Black Belt had over 60,000 Blacks living in confined and poorly maintained units, kitchenette buildings, and overcrowded areas due to redlining from the banking industry and race restrictive covenants from home associations.[29] Often, families were faced with abortion for survival—mentally and financially. Even with little choice on how they were going to survive, families knew that grief, whether from getting an abortion and losing the baby or keeping the baby and struggling to feed the child, would engulf their lives.

This woman grieves for her lost children from abortions of what she will never be able to do. In the opening stanza, the repetition of "never" exacerbates the speaker's current situation. The audience questions if she will ever be able to have children or if a basement abortion took the opportunity away permanently. The guilt the speaker feels begins to evolve into internalized anger in which she feels that she has taken a future—marriage and even death—away from her potential children. This mother begins to deeply question her decision, feeling as if her plan was not thought out thoroughly; maybe there were other options. Nevertheless, at the end of the second stanza, it is almost as if the speaker has sobered up and come to the conclusion that she did what was necessary for survival—"the crime was other than mine."[30] Understanding the perspectives, Brooks wrote from and the experiences she used to create her poetry, it is possible that the "crime" can imply more than the pregnancy and abortion, but the means of how a pregnancy occurred. This woman, throughout the entirety of the poem, did not want an abortion, yet in 1945 or earlier, she had one. The "crime" can imply prostitution, rape, or an abusive relationship, especially as the speaker mentions that there were "children," and she "loved [them] all."[31] Toward the end of the poem, there is a tone of defeat; there is nothing she can do—"you were born; you had a body, you died," similar to how Black men and women felt having to fight for almost everything they had in their lives: a home, a job, respect, life.[32]

This motif of death is present in Gwendolyn Brooks' poetry of the abandoned and abused. In "The Boy Died in My Alley," published in 1975, Brooks investigates multiple relationships: male children and the adults, the police and the neighborhood, and male children and society. The first relationship between male children and adults illustrates how people in communities are aware of the negative lifestyle boys in the neighborhood commit to and that there is little-to-nothing anyone can do to change the trajectory of the boys in the neighborhood. The speaker acknowledges that "I heard the Thousand shots before"[33] to suggest that many boys have been lost to their lives in the street and alleyways. The speaker continues to say, "I joined the Wild and killed him with knowledgeable unknowing" to argue that we know the future of male children if they continue in the street life, yet there is nothing anyone can do.[34] As many boys who have died in the alley and as many times as the adults in the community have stepped forward to prevent premature death from occurring, the streets are beckoning the boys. The discussion of death also illustrates the hardened relationship between police and neighborhoods. Throughout the poem, the policeman is represented in a tone that is fearful and angry. The policeman is sarcastic, blaming those in the neighborhood while pounding on doors looking for someone to arrest for the murder of a running boy.

The relationship between the policeman and the neighborhood is sour, possibly due to interactions such as racial profiling and abuse of those within the community: these interactions may have also contributed to the untimely death of the boy. Additionally, "The Boy Died in My Alley," asks us to question the relationships between young boys and society. As Brooks continuously analyzes the economic and racial landscapes of communities, the young boy may have had no choice but to enter into street life. Society has led the young boy, and others like him, to fight the street and embrace death—aborting their futures. The poem is dedicated "to Running Boy," which causes the reader to question if the boy is running to safety or running to the streets.

As Brooks discusses the difficulties associated with being poor, abandoned, and abused, she delves into a challenging topic in the Black community: colorism. Research, history, and experiences have defined colorism as: economic, educational, marriage, housing, and employment privileges that light-skinned people of color receive.[35] Colorism infiltrated the Black community early during slavery and continues today. Much of it stems from the perceived desire that Black men have for white women, as illustrated in "Ballad of Pearl May Lee," published in 1945. In the "Ballad of Pearl May Lee," the speaker is excited, almost ecstatic, that someone she once loved is going to jail, laughing as this man is dragged away by the police. This division between Black men and women was created when the Black man "wanted white arms to enfold" him rather than be with women who were Black.[36] The laughter and excitement are almost hysterical because the woman feels as if this Black man is paying for the "white arms" and the "bright little girls," he desired so wantonly.[37] Throughout history, as Gwendolyn Brooks reports in her poetry, "yellow was to look at, black was for the famished to eat"—no one wanted dark-skinned women.[38] This lack of desire created animosity because he "grew up with bright skins on the brain" and often cut the darker-skinned woman "cold" but would allow her in his "bed," creating animosity, hatred, and belligerent attitudes.[39] Because of the negative ideas toward darker-skinned women, Black men tended to desire white women who, as Brooks described, would say rape occurred to see the demise of the Black man: "you raped me, nigger" while still in the bed and planning to "tell every white man in this town . . . [to] get your body tomorrow."[40] However, for our darker-skinned speaker, she still calls out to her "brother[s]" to understand that they have to pay with their "hide and [her] heart" to get a "taste of pink and white honey."[41] However, this continues as we the media portray some professional entertainers publicly saying that Black women are gorillas while they have white women or non-Black women on their arms (many Black professionals and entertainers marry Black women and women of color, but they are not portrayed as often in the media). This animosity created between Black men and women creates a community of self-loathing.

The self-loathing of Black men and women are discussed in several poems by Gwendolyn Brooks that include "The Ballad of Rudolph Reed," "The Life of Lincoln West," and "The Ballad of Chocolate Mabbie." In "the ballad of chocolate Mabbie," the audience encounters a dark-skinned grammar school girl who feels the sting of rejection from children her age because of the darkness of her skin. The opening stanzas discuss how Mabbie enjoyed life, was happy with whom she was and enjoyed being with Willie Boone in history class. However, as Mabbie waits for her friend outside of school, she is filled with happiness that quickly becomes anxiety when Willie Boone does not meet her. When Willie Boone finally leaves school, he is with a "lemon-hued lynx with sand-waves loving her brow."[42] Now Mabbie is alone and blames her dark skin for the reason people like Willie Boone do not want her. This feeling of abandonment and contempt at such a young age continues with Mabbie.

We see women like Mabbie in the "Ballad of Pearl May Lee" who may have grown up without anyone finding them attractive and become embittered and enraged by the lack of love given to them because they are darker than others. This idea of light-skinned women being better continues today when entertainment often portrays lighter-skinned women as the sensitive, weaker, damsels-in-distress, and innocent; whereas, the darker-skinned women are vindictive, angry, bitter, or violent. Choices in marriage also perpetuate the idea of lighter-skinned women are better than darker-skinned women. Often, we see Black men marry and date lighter-skinned women while disregarding darker-skinned women. Ironically, when the roles are reversed, and dark-skinned women date white men, they are often called bed-wenches or argued to be suffering from a slave mentality.

Gwendolyn Brooks, through her experiences and interactions with Black people, was able to craft her poetry to reflect their lives—trauma, happiness, economic woes, and love. This reflection allowed and continues to allow her audience to engage in her writing, to see themselves in the poetry, and to question how we can come together to create a positive community for each other and future generations. With the incorporation of Gwendolyn Brooks' poetry, Black students' voices will be heard and discussions can revolve around the multifaceted existence of Blackness. As Brooks' poetry addresses silently dealing with trauma, she ironically manifests the current pedagogical practices in classrooms across the United States: the silencing of those who are considered marginalized groups. Dealing with poverty, feelings of abandonment, and animosity directed toward one's skin color are echoed in Brooks' only novel, *Maud Martha*. Because Brooks sought to reflect her experiences and the experiences of Black men, women, and children in her poetry, her novel reflects the same experiences, hopes, and opportunities of Black people, with an emphasis on Black women.

VOICELESSNESS IN MAUD MARTHA

Throughout the literary world, *Maud Martha* has been disregarded, ignored, or given little attention while critiquing the text as "juvenile fiction."[43] However, many critics missed an opportunity to discuss the intersectional biases that Black women face. *Maud Martha*, published in 1953, presented a multidimensional female character; yet was met with criticisms that perceived the text as unilateral. Brooks' treatment of the Black female character is ladened with daily, realistic experiences, opportunities (or the lack thereof), and dismissive behavior that Black women faced during that time. While critics discussed the charm and delicacy of the text, they lacked the insight to discuss the suppressed fury and rage within *Maud Martha* that was created by her existence as a Black woman.[44] In 1953, society was not prepared for a Black woman to be filled with rage, fictional or real, whether emotions were hidden by silence, a mask of peacefulness, or spoken.[45] However, Brooks created this character to illustrate how silence does not mean happiness, and sometimes women have difficulty communicating their disdain, unhappiness, anger, and rage. In 1953, the world for Black women was changing, and they were moving outside of traditional roles established by patriarchal systems; yet, they remained silent to their desires and ambitions. Maud Martha's struggle to obtain and maintain her individuality was limited by her color, her poverty, and her gender and was met with resistance from family members and people in her community.[46] It is important to note that the silence of Maud Martha was not merely due to patriarchal systems, but also due to her dark skin and Eurocentric standards that rendered her unable to speak because of self-hatred and self-doubt.[47] This internalized anger and bitterness makes her silence vital because it becomes a reflection of the pain and turmoil many women face and their lack of capacity to articulate the rage that festers inside of them. The concealment of this anger sometimes renders Maud Martha as peaceful, timid, and loving; yet, the masks she wears are misinterpreted, sometimes purposefully.

Opening the novel, Brooks begins with "Description of Maud Martha." The first chapter of the novel describes flowers in their everyday and ordinary appeal as a metaphorical description of Maud Martha. This description of the flowers is threefold. One, the description is telling of Maud Martha's personality; she is ordinary, and she loves flowers because of their everyday beauty. Two, the description of the flowers introduces the reader to how Maud Martha wants to be treated—"cherished" like flowers because of their ordinariness.[48] Furthermore, third, when describing flowers as ordinary, Maud Martha references herself, yet when she describes them as having "heart-catching beauty," she references her sister, Helen.[49] Through this description of the flowers, the audience understands that Maud Martha sees herself as ordinary and desires to be cherished. As Maud Marth looks and compares herself to these flowers, she understands, at only seven years old, how she and her nine-year-old sister are stark contrasts: Helen with "height and weight and thickness . . . long lashes, the grace, the little ways with the hands and feet" and knows that her sister is at an advantage because of her beauty.[50]

At the age of sixteen, Maud Martha still has an idea of who she wanted to be and her contribution to the world. After going to a performance and witnessing a Black male singer give his all—"private identities; shake themselves about; be very foolish for a thousand eyes"—Maud Martha decided that she was going to live to give the world some good.[51] Maud Martha did not crave worship or money. Her craving stemmed from an innate feeling of wanting to feel good about herself and wanting those feelings to be reciprocated. This understanding of the world is not naïve for Maud Martha, throughout her life, found that pleasantries, loving the ordinary, and seeing the good in people were able to keep her alive and out of trouble. It is possible that when she viewed others attempting to break through obstacles or traditions, that they landed much further away from their goal than when they began.

Additionally, Maud Martha thrived in her silence. She was her companion, and she created an internal environment in which she could cultivate who she wanted to be without having to create a pretense, be center of attention, or alter another's life for her own. Analyzing the relationship with Maud Martha's parents and her sister illustrates how an individual does not have to seek attention to be disrespected and shot down for the things they do. Maud Martha was generally ignored by her parents, and when she would speak was either told to "shut up" or simply dismissed.[52] Nevertheless, powerfully, these interactions did little to deter Maud Martha from maintaining a sense of who she was and who she wanted to become. Maud Martha's possible ignorance of the disrespect she was given has a duplicitous outlook: (1) She is able to continue living life for herself without worrying about trying to please others; and (2) she is unable to have happiness because her goodness is rooted in how others perceive her. This dichotomous internal quarrel is what women face daily. Women strive to be independent, creative, vocal, and powerful human beings; however, their assurances of who they are and want to be are sometimes grounded within other's perceptions. Maud Martha continuously compares herself to Helen because she knows her mother respects Helen's voice and her father prefers Helen. When Maud Martha speaks, her mother "look[s] at her quickly, decid[ing if] the statement was . . . suspect."[53] When Helen eats, Maud Martha sees what her father sees: "daintily" eating, "gracefully" sitting in her chair, "how pure . . . and unwrinkled" her robe, and "how neatly arranged her hair," and understands why "their father preferred Helen . . . to Maud Martha."[54] Both her parents instill within Maud Martha that she is not enough. Her voice and appearance are rarely worth their effort to engage with or admire, further enhancing Maud Martha's insecurities.

At the age of seventeen, Maud Martha had a reckoning. She realized that her ordinariness and her darkness were a problem. Walking home with her sister, Helen, a boy of their age, about their age, approached them and asked "about a ride."[55] Maud Martha replied in her most sultry voice of hello and was meant with a sharp reproach, "I don't mean you, you old black gal" and her sister, without saying anything to Maud Martha, climbed in the vehicle and left.[56] This was when Maud Martha began questioning herself, and the audience gains a description of what Maud Martha looks like. She had long, thick hair, she was smart, she read books, and she was dark. At this point, Maud Martha reflected on those who treated her differently, her mother, her father, her brother, another family, and friends. However, she did not blame them for their biases and prejudices. Instead, Maud Martha justifies them and suggests that they are "enslaved" by their fascination. This enlightenment Maud Martha receives does alter her perspective into other relationships and adulthood—she feels as if she will never be considered beautiful and that she must settle for who wants to be with her. The realization of having to settle for whoever wants her because of the relationship with her parents, especially not receiving love and admiration from her father, and the relationship with her sister prompts Maud Martha to feel as if she is unworthy. Even though she has justified others' feelings and perceptions toward her, she feels the brunt of their dislike for her. Helen, who sees a decline in Maud Martha's self-confidence and possibly due to discussions with Maud Martha, suggests that she stop reading books if she wants a man. Here is another example of silencing women and illustrating why Maud Martha suggests that people are enslaved and, therefore, ignorant. Her sister, whom everyone adores because of her daintiness and light skin, knows that ignorance and silence appease men.

When married, Maud Martha and Paul, her husband, are a young couple in love who read with each other. The topics of leisurely reading are not what Maud Martha usually reads, but include sexually oriented books that she and her husband can enjoy and then enjoy each other. Maud Martha is in love, and Paul loves her, too. They cherish each other, flirt with each other, and Paul is a gentleman who opens doors and keeps Maud Martha safe. Paul offers Maud Martha what she desired in the opening chapter of the book—to be loved and cherished. Yet, through the course of their marriage, Maud Martha learns to love herself. This is evident when Maud Martha spares a mouse. After entrapping the mouse, the creature looked at Maud Martha and she believed "the little creature seemed to understand that there was no hope of mercy from the eternal enemy, no hope of reprieve or postponement—but a fine small dignity."[57] The mouse and Maud Martha were caught up in an exchange seemingly questioning the dignity of each other, their lives, hardships, whether there was "enough food in its larder" to feed "a puny child."[58] Maud Marth releases the mouse and has a "new cleanness in her" because she was given the option "to preserve or destroy" and "she had not destroyed."[59] Maud Martha's confidence, strength, and self-love increased and she opened up to receive love from all who were willing to love her.

However, when Paul is invited to the Annual Foxy Cats Dawn Ball, Maud Martha details her love for her "not too yellow" husband who had "that extraordinary quality of maleness" even though he was "not very handsome."[60] After two dances with Maud Martha, Paul led her to a bench and left her there to dance with another. This woman was "red-headed . . . and white as a white."[61] After several moments of solitude, Maud Martha was asked to dance by a man as dark as she to whom Maud Martha confesses that "it's [her] color that makes him mad . . . . What I am inside, what is really me, he likes okay. However, he keeps looking at my color, which is like a wall. He has to jump over it in order to meet and touch what I've got for him. He has to jump away up high in order to see it. He gets awful tired of all that jumping."[62]

Paul returns from the reception hall with the woman still attached to his arm. Here is when we are introduced to Maud Martha's rage, as she says to herself that she could "go over there and scratch her upsweep down. I could spit on her back . . . I could scream, 'I'm making a baby for this man and I mean to do it in peace.'"[63] Nevertheless, Maud Martha says nothing and allows her silence to overtake her in the continuation of the marriage. She has forgiven Paul for his contempt for her because it is not his fault that she is so dark. She allows these behaviors to occur because she feels as if this is the best she can get because of the darkness of her skin. Maud Martha believes that her skin is the root of the problem, and since there is no way to change that, there will be no way to change how people interact with her, including her husband.

When giving birth, Maud Martha no longer has the capability of being silent. Birthing has provided her the opportunity to scream all her sorrow, frustration, and pain. Maud Martha even gets the courage to tell her mother that she can leave if she decides to come in a fuss about her giving birth. Nevertheless, Maud Martha continued to attempt to silence herself through her pain by apologizing when she screamed—"I just can't help it. Excuse me."[64] Her mother, however, lets Maud Martha know that screaming is her privilege, which provides Maud Martha a brief and positive interaction that was not given during her childhood. During childbirth is one of the only times we hear Maud Martha express her concern regarding others and just merely screaming through her frustration. However, this outspoken Maud Martha does not last long. Within five minutes of giving birth, her mother seeks acceptance from her, and Maud Martha, to herself, admonishes her mother's behavior. Maud Martha continues to feel as if she has no one to lean on and "not the love of a single person."[65] Once again, she is contemplating her role in her marriage and with her child as she has no one to lean on, but she is the post for others to rely on. Becoming more exhausted with the life she had, Maud Martha desired something substantial to provide her support, encouragement, and a sounding board for her frustration.

Before the table of contents in Maud Martha, Brooks writes, "Maud Martha was born in 1917, she is still alive" to possibly demonstrate that Maud Martha's silence has kept her alive. This opening sentence is an allusion to the end of the novel in which Maud Martha and her daughter are out for a walk and Maud Martha comes to the conclusion that she is alive, Black people are being lynched, men are not coming back from wars, and poor economic experiences of Black people. She looks to the heavens and walks with her daughter and her unborn child to a place that would give her what she needs to both survive and be happy with her life. Maud Martha was able to realize that her words may not have meant much, but her actions were the true representation of who she wanted to become.

CONCLUSION

Gwendolyn Brooks established her poetry and writings to represent her community of Black women, men, children, lovers, those alone, disabled, poor, wealthy, Southern, Northern, and many other characteristics of being Black in America. Brooks was able to create narratives and prose that discussed the multidimensional aspects of Blacks while reaching out to society to assist in riding the world of institutional and structural racism. The institutional and structural racism, especially when exposing how Black poverty was a reflection of racist economic laws and routines, made Gwendolyn Brooks a poet of the people.

Using Gwendolyn Brooks' texts in educational settings does more than embracing the diverse aspects of different groups, but can act as a balance between the discussion of unity, diversity, equity, and inclusion.[66] The aim is to provide students, especially those of color, with resources, strategies, courage, and a robust foundational identity to impact the global society while allowing them to see themselves outside of stereotypical roles. Because of the diversity in Brooks' poetry and prose, she promotes the acquisition of breadth, depth, and application to impact global change in a world that would prefer for women, especially Black women, to remain silent.

NOTES

1. Adrianna Aldana and Christy M. Byrd, "School Ethnic-Racial Socialization: Learning about Race and Ethnicity among African American Students." *The Urban Review* 47, no. 3 (2015): 563–576. doi: 10.1007/s11256-014-0319-0

2. James A. Banks, "Teaching for Social Justice, Diversity, and Citizenship in a Global World," *The Educational Forum* 68, no. 4 (2004): 296–305, doi: 10.1080/00131720408984645.; Jonda C. McNair, "#WeNeedMirrorsAndWindows: Diverse Classroom Libraries for K–6 Students," *The Reading Teacher* 70, no. 3 (2016): 375–381. doi: 10.1002/trtr.1516.; Greg Wiggan and Marcia Watson, "Teaching the Whole Child: The Importance of Culturally Responsiveness, Community Engagement, and Character Development in High Achieving African American Students," *The Urban Review* 48, no. 5 (2016): 766–798. doi: 10.1007/s11256-016-0377-6.

3. Terry Meier, "The Brown Face of Hope," *The Reading Teacher* 68, no. 5 (2015): 335–343. doi: 10.1002/trtr.1310.

4. William E.B. DuBois, *The Souls of Black Folk* (Mineola: Dover Publications, 1994). Arthur L Whaley, "Identity Conflict in African Americans during Late Adolescence and Young Adulthood: Double Consciousness, Multicultural, and Africentric Perspectives," *Africology: The Journal of Pan African Studies* 9, no. 7 (2016).

5. Ramona F. Amthor and Kevin Roxas, "Multicultural Education and Newcomer Youth: Re-imagining a More Inclusive Vision for Immigrant and Refugee Students," *Educational Studies* 52, no. 2 (2016): 155–176. doi: 10.1080/00131946.2016.1142992; Gregory S. Jay, *American Literature and the Culture Wars* (Ithaca: Cornell University Press, 2018); Tiphany Phan, "To Kill a Stereotype: An Examination of Canonical Literature and Racial Representation in the Classroom," Honors Theses at the University of Iowa (2019). Retrieved from https://ir.uiowa.edu/honors_theses/254. in Black Families:

6. Lois P. Zamora, *Contemporary American Women Writers: Gender, Class, Ethnicity* (London: Routledge, 2017).

7. Kimberlè Crenshaw, "Demarginalizing the Intersection of Race and Sex: A Black Feminist Critique of Antidiscrimination Doctrine, Feminist Theory and Antiracist Politics," *University of Chicago Legal Forum*, 139 (1989)."

8. Sharde Davis, "Taking Back the Power: An Analysis of Black Women's Communicative Resistance," *Review of Communication* 18, no. 4 (2018). doi: 10.1080/15358593.2018.1461234; Chanequa Walker-Barnes, "When the Bough Breaks: The StrongBlackWoman and the Embodiment of Stress," In *Black Women's Mental Health: Balancing Strength and Vulnerability*, edited by Stephanie Y. Evans,

Kanika Bell, Nsenga K. Burton, and Linda Goler Blount, 43–55 (Albany: SUNY Press, 2017).

9. Patricia J. Williams, *The Alchemy of Race and Rights* (Cambridge, MA: Harvard University Press, 1992).

10. Austen C. Brown, *I'm Still Here: Black Dignity in a World Made for Whiteness* (New York: Convergent, 2018); Mari Matsuda, "Looking to the Bottom: Critical Legal Studies and Reparations," In *Critical Race Theory: The Key Writings that Formed the Movement*, edited by Kimberlè Crenshaw, Neil Gotanda, Gary Peller, and Kendall Thomas, 63–79 (New York: The New Press, 1995); Patricia J. Williams, "Metro Broadcasting, Inc. v. FCC: Regrouping in Singular Times," In *Critical Race Theory: The Key Writings that Formed the Movement*, edited by Kimberlè Crenshaw, Neil Gotanda, Gary Peller, and Kendall Thomas, 63–79 (New York: The New Press, 1995).

11. Lois P. Zamora, *Contemporary American Women Writers: Gender, Class, Ethnicity* (London: Routledge, 2017).

12. Chanequa, Walker-Barnes, "The Burden of the Strong Black Woman," *Journal of Pastoral Theology* 19 (2009): 1–21.

13. Angela Jackson, "A Diamond in Her Hands: The Poetry of Gwendolyn Brooks & Old Age," *Obsidian* 43, no. 2 (2017): 165–172; Nisha Mathew, "A Transcultural Re-reading of Black Experience in Poems of Gwendolyn Brooks and Benjamin Zephaniah," *Indian Journal of Postcolonial Literature* 17, no. 1 (2017): 22–30.

14. Major Jackson, "Anatomy of a Pulitzer Prize Letter: A Close Look at the Letter Recommending Gwendolyn Brooks as the Recipient of the Pulitzer Prize in 1950 Reveals more Than Just the Reigning Aesthetics of that Period," *Poets & Writers Magazine* 45 no. 3 (2017); Patricia Lattin and Vernon E. Lattin, "Dual Vision in Gwendolyn Brooks' *Maud Martha*," *Critique: Studies in Contemporary Fiction* 25, no. 4 (1984): 180–188. doi: 10.1080/00111619.1984.9937800; Jeni Rinner, "From Bronzeville to the Mecca and After: Gwendolyn Brooks and the Location of Black Identity," *MELUS* 40, no. 4 (2015): 150–172. doi: 10.1093/melus/mlv049.

15. Valerie Frazier, "Domestic Epic Warfare in *Maud Martha*," *African American Review* 39, no. 1/2 (2005): 133–141.

16. Mathew, "A Transcultural Re-reading of Black Experience," 23.

17. Gwendolyn Brooks, *The Essential Gwendolyn Brooks,* Edited by Elizabeth Alexander (New York: The Library of America, 2005), 1, lns. 2, 4.

18. Brooks, *The Essential Gwendolyn Brooks,* 1, ln. 4.

19. Brooks, *The Essential Gwendolyn Brooks,* 1, ln. 13

20. Brooks, *The Essential Gwendolyn Brooks,* 1, lns., 2, 5.

21. Brooks, *The Essential Gwendolyn Brooks*, 49, lns. 10, 12, 14.

22. Brooks, *The Essential Gwendolyn Brooks,* 50, ln. 18.

23. Brooks, *The Essential Gwendolyn Brooks,* 49, lns. 3, 4.

24. Brooks, *The Essential Gwendolyn Brooks,* 50, lns. 25, 39–40.

25. Brooks, *The Essential Gwendolyn Brooks,* 50, lns. 38–39.

26. Brooks, *The Essential Gwendolyn Brooks,* 51, lns. 43, 54.

27. Brooks, *The Essential Gwendolyn Brooks,* 51, lns. 51–52.

28. Brooks, *The Essential Gwendolyn Brooks,* 2, lns. 6, 10.

29. Michelle Gordon, "Somewhat like War: The Aesthetics of Segregation, Black Liberation, and *A Raisin in the Sun*," *African American Review* 42, no. 1 (2008): 121–133; Arnold R. Hirsch, *Making the Second Ghetto: Race and Housing in Chicago, 1940-1960* (Cambridge, MA: Cambridge University Press, 1983).
30. Brooks, *The Essential Gwendolyn Brooks,* 2, ln. 28.
31. Brooks, *The Essential Gwendolyn Brooks,* 3, lns. 36.
32. Brooks, *The Essential Gwendolyn Brooks,* 3, lns. 34.
33. Brooks, *The Essential Gwendolyn Brooks,* 114, ln. 9.
34. Brooks, *The Essential Gwendolyn Brooks,* 114, lns. 27–28.
35. Margaret Hunter, "The Persistent Problem of Colorism: Skin Tone, Status, and Inequality," *Sociology Compass* 1, no. 1 (2007): 237–254, doi: 10.1111/j.1751-9020.2007.00006.x; Taunya L. Banks, "Colorism: A Darker Shade of Pale," *University of California in Los Angeles Law Review* 47 (1999): 1705–1752; JeffriAnne Wilder and Colleen Cain, "Teaching and Learning Color Consciousness Exploring Family Processes and Women's Experiences with Colorism," *Journal of Family Issues* 32, no. 5 (2011): 577–604, doi: 10.1177/0192513X10390858.
36. Brooks, *The Essential Gwendolyn Brooks,* 19, lns. 18, 21.
37. Brooks, *The Essential Gwendolyn Brooks,* 19–20, lns. 22, 36.
38. Brooks, *The Essential Gwendolyn Brooks,* 20, lns. 38–39, 40–41.
39. Brooks, *The Essential Gwendolyn Brooks,* 20, lns. 43–44.
40. Brooks, *The Essential Gwendolyn Brooks,* 21, lns. 68, 70, 75, 78.
41. Brooks, *The Essential Gwendolyn Brooks,* 22, lns. 92, 99–100.
42. Brooks, *The Essential Gwendolyn Brooks,* 5, lns. 19–20.
43. Lattin and Lattin, "Dual Vision in Gwendolyn Brooks' *Maud Martha*"; Mary H. Washington, "Taming all that Anger Down": Range and Silence in Gwendolyn Brooks' *Maud Martha*," *The Massachusetts Review* 24, no. 2 (1983): 453.
44. Frazier, "Domestic Epic Warfare in *Maud Martha*."
45. Washington, "Taming all that Anger Down."
46. Bubikova, Sarka Bubikova, "Maud Martha and the Tradition of the Ethnic Female Bildungsroman," *Litteraria Pragensia* 21, no. 41 (2011): 7–21.; Frazier, "Domestic Epic Warfare in *Maud Martha*."
47. Harry B Shaw, "*Maud Martha*: The War with Beauty," In *A Life Distilled: Gwendolyn Brooks, Her Poetry, and Fiction*, edited by Maria K. Mootry and Gary Smith, 254–269 (Urbana: University of Illinois Press, 1987); Washington, "Taming all that Anger Down."
48. Gwendolyn Brooks, *Maud Martha* (Chicago: Third World Press, 1993), 2.
49. Gwendolyn Brooks, *Maud Martha*, 2.
50. Gwendolyn Brooks, *Maud Martha*, 3.
51. Gwendolyn Brooks, *Maud Martha*, 21.
52. Gwendolyn Brooks, *Maud Martha*, 10.
53. Gwendolyn Brooks, *Maud Martha*, 31.
54. Gwendolyn Brooks, *Maud Martha*, 37.
55. Gwendolyn Brooks, *Maud Martha*, 33.
56. Gwendolyn Brooks, *Maud Martha*, 34.
57. Gwendolyn Brooks, *Maud Martha*, 69–70.

58. Gwendolyn Brooks, *Maud Martha*, 70.
59. Gwendolyn Brooks, *Maud Martha*, 70–71.
60. Gwendolyn Brooks, *Maud Martha*, 83.
61. Gwendolyn Brooks, *Maud Martha*, 85.
62. Gwendolyn Brooks, *Maud Martha*, 87–88.
63. Gwendolyn Brooks, *Maud Martha*, 88.
64. Gwendolyn Brooks, *Maud Martha*, 95.
65. Gwendolyn Brooks, *Maud Martha*, 100.
66. Banks, "Teaching for Social Justice."

BIBLIOGRAPHY

Aldana, Adrianna and Christy M. Byrd. "School Ethnic-Racial Socialization: Learning about Race and Ethnicity among African American Students." *The Urban Review* 47, no. 3 (2015): 563–576. doi: 10.1007/s11256-014-0319-0

Amthor, Ramona F. and Kevin Roxas. "Multicultural Education and Newcomer Youth: Re-imagining a More Inclusive Vision for Immigrant and Refugee Students." *Educational Studies* 52, no. 2 (2016): 155–176. doi: 10.1080/00131946.2016.1142992

Banks, James A. "Teaching for Social Justice, Diversity, and Citizenship in a Global World." *The Educational Forum* 68, no. 4 (2004): 296–305. doi: 10.1080/00131720408984645

Banks, Taunya L. "Colorism: A Darker Shade of Pale." *University of California in Los Angeles Law Review* 47 (1999): 1705–1752.

Brooks, Gwendolyn. *Maud Martha*. Chicago: Third World Press, 1993.

Brooks, Gwendolyn. *The Essential Gwendolyn Brooks*. Edited by Elizabeth Alexander. New York: The Library of America, 2005.

Brown, Austen C. *I'm Still Here: Black Dignity in a World Made for Whiteness*. New York: Convergent, 2018.

Bubikova, Sarka. "Maud Martha and the Tradition of the Ethnic Female Bildungsroman." *Litteraria Pragensia* 21, no. 41 (2011): 7–21.

Crenshaw, Kimberlè. "Demarginalizing the Intersection of Race and Sex: A Black Feminist
 Critique of Antidiscrimination Doctrine, Feminist Theory and Antiracist Politics." *University of Chicago Legal Forum*, 139 (1989).

Davis, Sharde. "Taking Back the Power: An Analysis of Black Women's Communicative Resistance." *Review of Communication* 18, no. 4 (2018): 301–318. doi: 10.1080/15358593.2018.1461234

DuBois, William E.B. *The Souls of Black Folk*. Mineola: Dover Publications, 1994.

Frazier, Valerie. "Domestic Epic Warfare in *Maud Martha*." *African American Review* 39, no. 1/2 (2005): 133–141.

Gordon, Michelle. "Somewhat like War: The Aesthetics of Segregation, Black Liberation, and *A Raisin in the Sun*." *African American Review* 42, no. 1 (2008): 121–133.

Hirsch, Arnold R. *Making the Second Ghetto: Race and Housing in Chicago, 1940-1960*. Massachusetts: Cambridge University Press, 1983.
Hunter, Margaret. "The Persistent Problem of Colorism: Skin Tone, Status, and Inequality." *Sociology Compass* 1, no. 1 (2007): 237–254. doi: 10.1111/j.1751-9020.2007.00006.x
Jackson, Angela. "A Diamond in Her Hands: The Poetry of Gwendolyn Brooks & Old Age." *Obsidian* 43, no. 2 (2017): 165–172.
Jackson, Major. "Anatomy of a Pulitzer Prize Letter: An Close Look at the Letter Recommending Gwendolyn Brooks as the Recipient of the Pulitzer Prize in 1950 Reveals more Than Just the Reigning Aesthetics of that Period." *Poets & Writers Magazine* 45 no. 3 (2017): 37+.
Jay, Gregory S. *American Literature and the Culture Wars*. Ithaca: Cornell University Press, 2018.
Lattin, Patricia and Vernon E. Lattin. "Dual Vision in Gwendolyn Brooks' *Maud Martha*." *Critique: Studies in Contemporary Fiction* 25, no. 4 (1984): 180–188. doi: 10.1080/00111619.1984.9937800
McNair, Jonda C. "#WeNeedMirrorsAndWindows: Diverse Classroom Libraries for K–6 Students." *The Reading Teacher* 70, no. 3 (2016): 375–381. doi: 10.1002/trtr.1516
Mathew, Nisha. "A Transcultural Re-reading of Black Experience in Poems of Gwendolyn Brooks and Benjamin Zephaniah." *Indian Journal of Postcolonial Literature* 17, no. 1 (2017): 22–30.
Matsuda, Mari. "Looking to the Bottom: Critical Legal Studies and Reparations." In *Critical Race Theory: The Key Writings that Formed the Movement*, edited by Kimberle Crenshaw, Neil Gotanda, Gary Peller, and Kendall Thomas, 63–79. New York: The New Press, 1995.
Meier, Terry. "The Brown Face of Hope." *The Reading Teacher* 68, no. 5 (2015): 335–343. doi: 10.1002/trtr.1310
Phan, Tiphany. "To Kill a Stereotype: An Examination of Canonical Literature and Racial Representation in the Classroom." Honors Theses at the University of Iowa, 2019. Retrieved from https://ir.uiowa.edu/honors_theses/254
Rinner, Jeni. "From Bronzeville to the Mecca and After: Gwendolyn Brooks and the Location of Black Identity." *MELUS* 40, no. 4 (2015): 150–172. doi: 10.1093/melus/mlv049
Shaw, Harry B. "*Maud Martha*: The War with Beauty." In *A Life Distilled: Gwendolyn Brooks, Her Poetry, and Fiction*, edited by Maria K. Mootry and Gary Smith, 254–269. Urbana: University of Illinois Press, 1987.
Walker-Barnes, Chanequa. "The Burden of the Strong Black Woman." *Journal of Pastoral Theology* 19 (2009): 1–21.
Walker-Barnes, Chanequa. "When the Bough Breaks: The StrongBlackWoman and the Embodiment of Stress." In *Black Women's Mental Health: Balancing Strength and Vulnerability*, edited by Stephanie Y. Evans, Kanika Bell, Nsenga K Burton, and Linda Goler Blount, 43–55. Albany: SUNY Press, 2017.
Washington, Mary H. 1983. "Taming all that anger down": Range and Silence in Gwendolyn Brooks' *Maud Martha*." *The Massachusetts Review* 24, no. 2 (1983): 453–466.

Whaley, Arthur L. "Identity Conflict in African Americans during Late Adolescence and Young Adulthood: Double Consciousness, Multicultural, and Africentric Perspectives." *Africology: The Journal of Pan African Studies* 9, no. 7 (2016): 106–131.

Wiggan, Greg and Marcia Watson. "Teaching the Whole Child: The Importance of Culturally Responsiveness, Community Engagement, and Character Development in High Achieving African American Students." *The Urban Review* 48, no. 5 (2016): 766–798. doi: 10.1007/s11256-016-0377-6

Wilder, JeffriAnne and Colleen Cain. "Teaching and Learning Color Consciousness in Black Families: Exploring Family Processes and Women's Experiences with Colorism." *Journal of Family Issues* 32, no. 5 (2011): 577–604. doi: 10.1177/0192513X10390858

Williams, Patricia J. *The Alchemy of Race and Rights*. Cambridge, MA: Harvard University Press, 1992.

Williams, Patricia. "Metro Broadcasting, Inc. v. FCC: Regrouping in Singular Times." In *Critical Race Theory: The Key Writings that Formed the Movement*, edited by Kimberle
Crenshaw, Neil Gotanda, Gary Peller, and Kendall Thomas, 191–200. New York: The New Press, 1995.

Zamora, Lois P. *Contemporary American Women Writers: Gender, Class, Ethnicity*. London: Routledge, 2017.

Chapter 3

Kathleen Collins
BAM Filmmaker and Fiction Writer
Cynthia Davis

Kathleen Collins (1942–1988) not only contributed to and documented the Black Arts and Black Power Movements in her fiction but also wrote and directed two feature films. Her posthumously published collections *Whatever Happened to Interracial Love* (2016) and *Notes from a Black Woman's Diary* (2019), both edited by her daughter, Nina Lorez Collins, include short stories, letters, plays, and screenplays. Together, they form a sort of Portrait of the Artist as a Young Black Woman. Like James Joyce, Lorraine Hansberry, Jean Rhys, and Dorothy West, Collins grounded her work in her intense subjectivity, in the history of her complex and fascinating family, and in a scathing indictment of the irrational nature of race, gender, and class prejudice. Due perhaps to her untimely and early death, little critical analysis has been done on Collins' *oeuvre*; this essay seeks to address by exploring a selection of her short stories and plays and her two films *The Cruz Brothers and Miss Molloy* (1980) and *Losing Ground* (1982), starring actress Seret Scott.

Collins, raised in Jersey City, New Jersey, lived and wrote at the intersection of art and activism. In 1962, during her junior year at Skidmore College, she met Charles Sherrod and Charles Jones, two leaders of the Student Nonviolent Coordinating Committee (SNCC) and the Albany Movement; they recruited Collins to register voters in Southwest Georgia. Peggy Trotter Dammond, a student at Hunter College and a great-niece of Boston race activist William Monroe Trotter, met Collins when she accompanied Sherrod and Jones to Skidmore.[1] Collins became close to Peggy Dammond's family and described them in the poignant story of love and race, "The Happy Family." Charter members of W. E. B. DuBois' "Talented Tenth," the glamorous, intellectual Dammonds had been race people and activists for generations; in the early 1960s, they were in the vanguard of the Civil Rights

Movement, and through them, Collins met the movement's current leaders: Bayard Rustin, Julian Bond, and James Forman. Stokely Carmichael, then living in the Bronx, was a good friend of Peggy's brother Hank, and Collins often met him at the Dammond apartment in Harlem.[2]

In the summer of 1962, Dammond and Collins traveled to rural Georgia where they bravely "combed the hot dirt roads, pleading with folks to come out and vote, come out and be shot."[3] Collins was arrested twice for civil disobedience, but despite the vermin and the filthy jail conditions, she "used part of the time to teach other prisoners about civil rights and voter registration."[4] Collins and Dammond lived with the indomitable community organizer, "Mama" Dolly Raines. Raines, a 70-year-old farmer and midwife, sometimes sat up all night with a shotgun, guarding her interracial group of student volunteers. One night Raines told Charles Sherrod: "Baby, I brought a lot of these white folks into the world and I'll take them out if I have to."[5] However, Collins was terrified when, despite Raines' vigilance, "they shot holes all through Mama Dolly's farm and she came home."[6] Collins' short stories "Whatever Happened to Interracial Love," "The Happy Family," and "Conference Parts I and II," document the elation and terror of the Civil Rights Movement.

Perhaps because Collins knew firsthand the risks of speaking truth to power, and had experienced the cloak of critical and commercial invisibility that shrouded the work of African American artists in the 1970s, particularly women artists, she takes every opportunity to name and celebrate the artists and activists whom she knew. Sometimes, as in the case of SNCC leader Charles Jones, who appears as "Charlie Jones" in the story "Conference: Parts I and II," Collins does not even bother with pseudonyms. The "mug shots" taken of Jones in 1961 in Montgomery, Alabama, clearly reveal him as the "Freedom Rider [from] Johnson C. Smith University" with whom the story's protagonist Mildred Pierce (the real name of Collins' mother) becomes infatuated.[7] Mildred, emerging from her racially isolated existence at all-white Skidmore College, is "thrilled to have a real-life Negro coming into my rarefied atmosphere with real green eyes, freckles and extra-light skin."[8] Her classmates assure her: "He's so good-looking, he doesn't even look like a Negro," while her parents, equally enamored of his complexion, ignore his politics and find him "charming . . . 'Handsome boy,' said my father, 'looks just like one of the family.' "[9] Collins slyly exposes colorism among Blacks and whites when, despite social approbation and the couple's physical and intellectual attraction, the romance founders on sexual incompatibility. Their relationship is one of several in the Collins *oeuvre* that interrogates the fraught intersections of color, race, gender, and sexuality. Nevertheless, the story captures the cool demeanor and steely determination of the young SNCC leader.

Whatever Happened to Interracial Love, the book's title story, set in 1963, is an ironic send-up of the romantic illusions and naïve hypocrisies of the early Civil Rights Movement, as well as an eyewitness account of the Umbra Writers Workshop, "the nexus of what became known as the Black Arts Movement in the mid-1960s and 1970s."[10] In the story, the interracial group living in an Upper West Side apartment claims to be "color-blind, religion-blind," but Collins carefully labels each character in parentheses as ("white") or ("negro").[11] A historic moment in SNCC history is referenced as Collins contrasts the rhetoric of Bayard Rustin, Julian Bond and James Farmer (and their enthusiastic interracial audiences) with Stokely Carmichael who appears as "a tall, somber young man (West Indian, and West Indians are not "negroes") called Derek."[12] In Derek's "methodical, messianic mind there is a theory building that perhaps integration is just another form of imitation ... stultification ... impersonation ... and a year later he will shout from the podium "Black Power! Black Power! Black Power!" and the romance will go up in smoke."[13]

Collins' short story is one of the few that documents the Umbra Group, a gathering of African American poets who met weekly on New York's Lower East Side; they also made frequent forays to Harlem, where Langston Hughes kindly "organized a series of readings by young black poets at an art gallery on Seventh Avenue and 135th Street."[14] Collins notes the presence of Amiri Baraka and Ishmael Reed who "in later life will be counted the most illustrious members."[15] Other members included Tom Dent, David Henderson, Askia Muhammad Touré (then Rolland Snellings), and Calvin Hernton.[16] Loosely associated with the group were saxophonist Archie Shepp, drummer Max Roach, and illustrator Tom Feelings.[17] Dent described "the essential quality of Umbra as search, quest ... many individual quests woven together."[18] Their interests included collaborative projects, a newspaper and a journal, open poetry readings, civil rights activism, and an opposition to the commercialism of the "American Dream." The group proclaimed the poet as Afrocentric *griot* and validated vernacular culture, as epitomized in stories about a down-home character dubbed "Junebug" or "Junebug Jabba Jones." Shepp, for example, penned a one-act jazz play called *Junebug Graduates Tonight*. Much like Langston Hughes' Jesse B. Semple, the Junebug character also inspired stories by SNCC members who celebrated the wisdom and wit of the African American community.[19] Tom Dent, along with the actress Seret Scott, eventually left the Lower East Side of New York to establish the Free Southern Theatre (FST) in New Orleans; that organization currently exists as Junebug Productions.[20]

That Collins knew the Umbra poets well is clear from her references in her short story to poetry readings at St. Mark's on the Bowery and to two mentions of the protagonist's favorite poem, "Junebug." Equally clear is her rejection of a macho, phallocentric literary group that marginalized women. Although Brenda Walcott was involved with Umbra, her name appears in none of firsthand accounts of the period, and women poets are conspicuously absent from Collins' short story. Rather, the women in the story listen adoringly as the men declaim their work. Thus, while Collins testifies to the contribution of Umbra to African American literature, she does not hesitate to call out the members for their gendered discrimination.

Apart from the Umbra poets, Black women's voices were emerging in the 1960s and 1970s, although they "came mostly in the form of poetry, short stories and the novel . . . [such as] Toni Morrison, Alice Walker, Toni Cade Bambara, Gwendolyn Brooks, Sonia Sanchez and Lucille Clifton."[21] At this time, Collins was working as a film editor, while writing plays and film scripts. Filmmaker Haile Gerima introduced her to the work of Lorraine Hansberry, whose life and work became a major inspiration. "The older I get," Collins once said, "I have this feeling of being very connected with Lorraine Hansberry. I've never found another black writer who I felt was asking the same questions I was asking. . . . she was able to encompass this wide range of experience, from Jewish intellectuals to black middle class. . . . she had a really incredible sense of life."[22]

Meanwhile, Collins' close friend, the actress Seret Scott, had returned to New York, and became both a muse and an alter ego; Collins, who cast her in several plays, including *Remembrance*, a dramatic monologue about a woman artist struggling with the demands of motherhood and domesticity. In 1982, Scott starred in Collins' play *The Brothers*, at the experimental American Place Theatre, directed by Billie Allen. The play explores Collins' father's family, talented and ambitious men who were conflicted about race and constrained by racism. Interestingly, the "brothers" never appear; instead, their sister expresses both moral outrage at the ways in which race limited the men's lives and anger at the way she, as a Black woman, was forced to play a subordinate role to her brothers' neurotic and domineering personalities. Critic Frank Rich praised the play in *The New York Times*, citing Collins as "a promising writer . . . funny . . . [and] fond of the sound of words."[23] Both plays were highly autobiographical and reflected Collins' interests in the depredations of racism, neurosis, and colorism in the African American families. One sees clearly Hansberry's influence in these plays; like Hansberry, Collins exposes the veneer of familial harmony and the deep anger of the successful, Black middle class.

Along with her plays, Collins had long been engaged in the "development of an aesthetic for filmic works specifically by, for, and about black women."[24] Influenced by Julie Dash, Haile Gerima, and Charles Burnett, Collins was determined to make films; she had written her first screenplay in 1971 but "nobody would give any money to a black woman to direct a film. It was probably the most discouraging time of my life."[25] Nevertheless, she persisted, encouraged by one of her students at City College of New York (CCNY), where she taught film studies. Although her stories and plays had been intensely personal and subjective, Collins was concerned about achieving an artistic distance from the material in her films.

Perhaps for that reason she chose, for her first project, *The Cruz Chronicles*, a novel by Henry H. Roth, a colleague at CCNY with whom she was romantically involved. Collins' adaptation of a book by a Jewish writer about three orphaned Puerto Rican brothers, the ghost of their dead father, and a wealthy, elderly white woman, emerged in 1979 as *The Cruz Brothers and Miss Molloy*. The film, produced on a shoestring budget of $5,000, was, according to Collins, "terribly hard . . . it was like going down a terribly long tunnel . . . but we did it because [filmmaker] Ronald Gray and I . . . both have an incredible tenacity."[26]

Now divorced from her first husband, Collins had moved with her two young children to Piermont, a formerly grand but now decaying village in Rockland County on the Hudson River. Full of crumbling Victorian mansions set amid lush greenery and overgrown gardens, with romantic river views, the town was primarily occupied by Hispanic families seeking relief from high New York City rents. Collins set *Cruz Chronicles* in Piermont, and the lost-in-time, nostalgic setting became like a character in the film. Her daughter recalled that the project was "very much a local affair. The composer for the film, Michael D. Minard, was sharing Roth's house at the time and associate producer Eleanor Charles came from [nearby] Spring Valley."[27] Eleanor Charles, who scouted many of the Rockland County locations for the film, was the first to see the town's potential; later, Woody Allen set *The Purple Rose of Cairo* in Piermont.[28]

In terms of her film, aesthetic Collins, who had studied film at the Sorbonne in 1965 on a John Whitney Hay scholarship, is deeply influenced by the French directors of the Nouvelle Vague, including Francois Truffaut, Agnes Varda, and Jean Luc Goddard; however, according to her daughter, the strongest influence on her "talky, artsy films featuring all-black casts" is Eric Rohmer.[29] Rohmer "once described himself as being less interested in what people do, than with what is going on in their minds while they are doing it."[30] Collins' bohemian characters with their "palpably infinite inner lives" feature the same "erotics of thinking" as do Rohmer's characters, although they exist "entirely outside the white gaze."[31] Technically, Collins' films, like Rohmer's, feature "a strict fidelity to the reality of time and place, [the] use of natural light . . . and direct, non-dubbed sound";[32] one sees how the lush, dream-like landscape of Piermont is particularly suited to this approach.

Funding had always been a struggle for Collins, but her low-budget films made a virtue of necessity, utilizing inexpensive jump cuts, and relying on outdoor locations. Interiors were often shot in her own home or in residences begged and borrowed from friends; for example, the artist's loft and the protagonists' summer home in *Losing Ground* belonged to wealthy friends from Skidmore. According to her daughter, the movies were edited in Piermont, and she remembers "film swishing through the Steenbeck editing machine that sat in our dining room."[33] A comparison of her scripts with the actual films shows that, like Rohmer, she allowed her actors to improvise dialogue.

All of these techniques and approaches are apparent in Collins' second film *Losing Ground* (1982), starring Seret Scott. The long-delayed, posthumous release of *Losing Ground* to critical acclaim in 2016 has solidified Kathleen Collins' artistic reputation. "If there was ever a prototypic black woman filmmaker with a black feminist sensibility *avant la lettre*, it was Kathleen Collins," stated critic and novelist John A. Williams when the film's screenplay was published in 1994.[34] Although at first glance, the film seems very different from *The Cruz Brothers and Miss Molloy*, shot two years earlier, they demonstrate many commonalities. In addition to the Piermont location, and all of the Rohmer-inspired techniques, the films share a concern with racial and gendered marginalization, with cultural clashes leading to epiphany, with the search for identity and authentic self-expression, and with the quest for ecstatic or metaphysical experience despite the drudgery of daily life. In *Losing Ground*, the film's themes of "marital malaise, male dominance and impotence, and freedom of expression and intellectual pursuit" are delineated by the protagonist, a "self-reflective woman who moves from a state of subjugation to empowerment."[35]

These themes link Collins' films to the plays and her short stories that were inspired by her work with SNCC and her encounters with the Umbra poets. Throughout her writing, she "challenged stereotypes and explored the interlocking oppressions of gender, race and class."[36] Kathleen Collins' untimely death in September 1988 at the age of 46 occurred at the height of her artistic potential. However, thanks to the tireless efforts of her daughter, Nina Lorez Collins, who has overseen the distribution of her films and the publication of her fiction, we have not lost her voice. In an interview shortly before her death in which she clearly invokes her mentor Lorraine Hansberry, Collins states:

> My basic premise is that illness is psychic disconnection of some kind . . . the nature of illness and female success and the capacity of the female to acknowledge her own intelligence is a subject that interests me a lot. . . . I knew I had it, knew that I had the talent . . . knew that all the years of working quietly and quite alone, were beginning to pay off.[37]

NOTES

1. Nina Lorez Collins, "Extended Biography," 4.
2. Faith S. Holsaert et al., eds. *Hands on the Freedom Plough: Personal Accounts by Women in SNCC* (Urbana: University of Illinois Press, 2012), 166.
3. Kathleen Collins, *Whatever Happened to Interracial Love?* (New York: HarperCollins, 2016), 41.
4. Nina Lorez Collins, "Extended Biography," 4.
5. SNCC Digital Archives.
6. Kathleen Collins, *Whatever Happened to Interracial Love?*, 42.
7. Civil Rights Digital Library; Kathleen Collins, *Whatever Happened to Interracial Love?*, 59–60.
8. Kathleen Collins, *Whatever Happened to Interracial Love?*, 62.
9. Kathleen Collins, *Whatever Happened to Interracial Love?*, 63.
10. Lorenzo Thomas, "The Need to Speak: Tom Dent and the Shaping of a Black Aesthetic." *African American Review,* 40, no. 2 (2006): 327.
11. Kathleen Collins, *Whatever Happened to Interracial Love?*, 48.
12. Kathleen Collins, *Whatever Happened to Interracial Love?*, 49.
13. Kathleen Collins, *Whatever Happened to Interracial Love?*, 49.
14. Tom Dent, *Black American Literature Forum,* vol. 14, no. 3 (Autumn 1980): 105; Paul Breman, "Poetry into the 'Sixties." In *The Black American Writer, Vol. II,* edited by C.W.E. Bigsby (Baltimore: Everett/Edwards, 1969), 101.
15. Kathleen Collins, *Whatever Happened to Interracial Love?*, 33.
16. Tom Dent, "Umbra Days," 106.
17. Lorenzo Thomas, "The Need to Speak: Tom Dent and the Shaping of a Black Aesthetic," 325.
18. Tom Dent, "Umbra Days," 105.
19. Allison Considine, "Know a Theatre: Junebug Productions of New Orleans." https://www.americantheatre.org/2016/08/02/know-a-theatre-junebug-productions-of-new-orleans/
20. Allison Considine, "Know a Theatre: Junebug Productions of New Orleans."
21. Elizabeth Alexander "Forward." In *Whatever Happened to Interrracial Love,* edited by Kathleen Collins (New York: Harper Collins, 2016), xii.
22. Nina Lorez Collins, "Extended Biography," 4.
23. Frank Rich. "Theatre: Black Anguish in 'Brothers.'" *The New York Times* (April 6, 1982). https://www.nytimes.com/1982/04/06/theater/theater-black-anguish-in-brothers.html
24. John A. Williams, "Echoes from the Past: Screenplays of the African American Experience." *African American Review,* 28, no. 2 (Summer 1994): 318.
25. Nina Lorez Collins, "How Kathleen Collins's Daughter," 6.
26. Nina Lorez Collins, "Extended Biography," 6.
27. Nina Lorez Collins "Extended Biography," 6.
28. Nina Lorez Collins, "Extended Biography," 6.
29. Nina Lorez Collins, "Extended Biography," 6; and Personal Interview.
30. French New Wave.

31. Elizabeth Alexander, "Forward." In *Whatever Happened to Interrracial Love*, edited by Kathleen Collins (New York: Harper Collins, 2016), xiii.
32. French New Wave.
33. Nina Lorez Collins "How Kathleen Collins's Daughter," 3.
34. John A. Williams, Echoes from the Past: Screenplays of the African American Experience," 318.
35. Nina Lorez Collins "Extended Biography," 4.
36. Nina Lorez Collins, "Extended Biography," 6.
37. Nina Lorez Collins "Extended Biography," 4.

BIBLIOGRAPHY

Alexander, Elizabeth. "Forward." In *Whatever Happened to Interrracial Love*, edited by Kathleen Collins, xi–xv. New York: Harper Collins, 2016.
Arsenault, Raymond. *Freedom Riders: 1961 and the Struggle for Racial Justice*. New York: Oxford University Press, 2006.
Breman, Paul. "Poetry into the 'Sixties." In *The Black American Writer, Vol. II*, edited by C.W.E. Bigsby, 99–109. Baltimore: Everett/Edwards, 1969.
Civil Rights Digital Library. Charles Jones, Police Photograph. http://crdl.usg.edu/cgi/crdl?query=id%3Asmokinggun_hotcrm_1103052mmugs89&_cc=1
Collins, Kathleen. *Whatever Happened to Interracial Love?* New York: HarperCollins, 2016.
Collins, Nina Lorez. "Extended Biography." 2016. http://kathleencollins.org/about/
Collins, Nina Lorez. "How Kathleen Collins's Daughter Kept Her Late Mother's Career Alive." *Vogue* (September 5, 2016). https://www.vogue.com/article/kathleen-collins-filmmaker-career-daughter-nina-lorez-collins
Collins, Nina Lorez. Telephone Interview with Author, March 24, 2018.
Considine, Allison. "Know a Theatre: Junebug Productions of New Orleans." https://www.americantheatre.org/2016/08/02/know-a-theatre-junebug-productions-of-new-orleans/
"Daughter of African-American Filmmaker Asks, What Happened To Kathleen Collins?" *Weekend Edition Saturday*, 3 Dec. 2016. *Gale Literature Resource Center*, https://0-link-g alecom.libcat.sanjac.edu/apps/doc/A473651067/LitRC?u=txshracd2544 &sid=LitRC&xid=6ad41894. Accessed 19 Sept. 2020.
Dent, Tom. "Umbra Days." *Black American Literature Forum*, 14, no. 3 (Autumn 1980): 105–108.
French New Wave: Where to Start. http://www.newwavefilm.com/new-wave-cinema-guide/nouvelle-vague-where-to-start.shtml
Holsaert, Faith S, Martha Prescod Norman Noonan, Judy Richardson, Betty Garman Robinson, Jean Smith Young, and Dorothy M. Zellner, eds. *Hands on the Freedom Plough: Personal Accounts by Women in SNCC*. Urbana: University of Illinois Press, 2012.
Neal, Larry. "The Black Arts Movement." In *The Black American Writer, Vol. II*, edited by C.W.E. Bigsby, 187–202. Baltimore: Everett/Edwards, 1969.

Rich, Frank. "Theatre: Black Anguish in 'Brothers'." *The New York Times*, 6 April 1982. https://www.nytimes.com/1982/04/06/theater/theater-black-anguish-in-brothers.html

SNCC Digital Archive. https://snccdigital.org/people/mama-dolly-raines/

Thomas, Lorenzo. "The Need to Speak: Tom Dent and the Shaping of a Black Aesthetic." *African American Review,* 40, no. 2 (2006): 325–338.

Thomas, Lorenzo. "The Shadow World: New York's Umbra Workshop & Origins of The Black Arts Movement." *Callaloo,* 1, no. 4 (October 1978): 52–72.

Williams, John A. "Echoes from the Past: Screenplays of the African American Experience." *African American Review,* 28, no. 2 (Summer 1994): 317–320.

Chapter 4

Closed in Silence and Clothed in Heteronormativity and the (Anti-)Lesbian Embrace

The Woman's Plight in Gayl Jones' Eva's Man *and "The Women"*

Georgene Bess Montgomery

In a foreword to *Sula*, Morrison wrote, "Outlaw women are fascinating—not always for their behavior, but because historically women are seen as naturally disruptive and their status is an illegal one from birth if it is not under the rule of men."

Writing of "dark phrases of womanhood/ of never having been a girl" (Shange 17), Ntozake Shange, in her seminal choreopoem that gave voice to colored girls around the world, beseeched her listening, watching, and reading audience, "somebody/ anybody/ sing a black girl's song/ bring her out/ to know herself/ . . ./ sing her song of life" because she's "been dead so long/ closed in silence so long/ she doesn't know the sound/ of her own voice/ her infinite beauty" (18). Perhaps responding to Shange's call, Gayl Jones gives voice to the voiceless women who have been imprisoned by heterosexist silence and stereotyped-informed gender roles. Through her bitter and poignant novels, *Corregidora*, *Eva's Man*, and short story "The Women," Jones portrays Black women's quest for self: a self that has been too long submerged and lost in enforced gender roles and stereotypical heterosexist assumptions and effectively demonstrate how "myths or the ways in which men perceive women actually define their character" (Tate 97). Because of their often brutal and self-destructive relationships with men, the protagonists of the two novels are ripe for a lesbian experience, but because they are so steeped in heterosexist assumptions, they reject the lesbian embrace and even a nonsexual lesbian friendship. Living in a male-dominated, male-oriented society that regards women at best as mere vessels for male pleasure, at worst as whores and bitches, these women have been conditioned to accept a degrading view of themselves. These women are victims of sexist and heterosexist assumptions that force the lowest of stereotypical gender roles. They are women who need love but do not know where to find it.

Eva's Man, *Corregidora*, and the short story "The Women" represent Jones' working and reworking the problems of women held in ethical and psychological thrall to heterosexism and heterosexist assumptions and stereotypes, who have Othered and been Othered by society at large and other women. For Jones, this is a deliberate act that enables "marginal people [to] step from the margins into the center of their own worlds, of their own texts and fiction and re-invent themselves and begin to see themselves and not as subordinates" (Claybough 246–247). And by allowing these characters to tell their own stories, the beautiful and the ugly, the painful and the joyous, that reflect their real lives, sometimes hard and unrelenting, Jones decolonizes the text, freeing it from the control of the colonist, who would dictate:

> When patterns of stories and patterns of ideas in stories and how stories are made from one storytelling tradition are imposed upon another storytelling tradition; that is when the storyteller from the dominant culture says that you must tell stories the way I tell them, or when one storytelling tradition is seen as the mere subgenre of another. (249)

Thus, in incorporating African oral techniques, like repetition and storytelling, that Jones celebrates in her texts, Jones' stories are grounded in African cultural storytelling and not imposed colonialist criteria. Told in novel form, *Eva's Man* and *Corregidora* utilizes repetition and storytelling to develop the stories being told. In her seminal text *Liberating Voices: Oral Tradition in African American Literature*, Jones examines the significant role the oral tradition plays in African American literature; thus, it is no surprise that her texts rely heavily on orality and are examples of orature.

As Jones explores the various relationships—of men to women, women to men, and women to women—the duality of pleasure and pain, love and hatred, and the quest for self, she reveals the extremely detrimental effects that enforced gender roles, sexual abuse, and heteronormativity have on society and people in general. Her characters are unable to love themselves or those who look like them, and both the heterosexual and lesbian relationships are problematic. Jones has been accused of giving only token treatment to the lesbian character because she is "afraid to touch lesbianism with a heavy pen" (Shockley 89). While she does sketch lesbianism with an artful delicacy that is a marked contrast to the dark strokes with which she delineates the heterosexual relationship, and "The Women" is a strong portrayal of the effect of her mother's promiscuous lesbianism on a growing daughter, Jones does provide an in-depth exploration of lesbianism. She raises valuable questions concerning the lesbian's existence, her self-perception, and the perception of her by others. Even though Jones depicts lesbian themes, her works are niether affirmations of lesbianism nor condemnations of lesbianism. In an interview with Claudia Tate, Jones says, "Lesbianism exists, and that's the way I include it in my work. I'll have characters respond to positively or negatively, or sometimes the characters may simply acknowledge it as a reality" (Tate 98). In another interview with Charles H. Rowell, Jones further articulates, "of course some critics want a greater directness of political statement. I don't like direct political statements. . . My own preoccupation is with personality and in some of the work 'psychological obsessions and oppressions'" (Rowell 42). Lesbians are human beings in her presentation and not just political statements one way or the other.

The concept of lesbianism is treated differently in each of Jones' works. In *Corregidora*, Ursa, the female protagonist, rejects the lesbian embrace. However, the lesbian Elvira, in *Eva's Man*, is victorious in her seduction of the protagonist, Eva Canada. In Jones' short story "The Women," it is unclear whether the protagonist ultimately rejects or embraces lesbianism.

With the stories' focus on women, their voices, and their stories, a feminist theoretical perspective is certainly appropriate as well as the psychoanalytical approach because the stories portray and explore the psyche of their female protagonists and the psychological impact of living in a world that does not hear, see, or respect them. However, they each lack the cultural specificities necessary for an in-depth analysis grounded in an understanding of the culture and history. Therefore, the most appropriate theoretical approach is the womanist approach. These three texts can be effectively read from a womanist perspective; many of the womanist principles are applied to Jones' novels: there are strong women characters, nurturing women, and in some stories, intense friendships between the women, women who love other women "sexually and/or nonsexually," and "sometimes loves individual men, sexually and/or nonsexually" (Walker xi–xii). Quite frequently, the relationship with the foremothers affects the women's sexual orientation and bonding.

Having internalized the hetero/sexist oppression that regards them as whores, bitches, and/or the Other, Jones' women protagonists are unable to love themselves or others. However, this internalization is hardly unique to Jones' characters. Historically, Black women have been viewed as licentious and hypersexual. South African Sara Baartman, the Hottentot Venus, with her large buttocks on traveling display (her embalmed body continued on display at the London Museum until 1974) became the metaphor for Black women's hypersexuality in contrast with the white woman's chaste beauty. Jones' female characters suffer voicelessness, and like Sara Bartmaan, are unable to counter the prevailing narratives.

"The Women" is Jones' short-story account of a practicing lesbian and her observant daughter, neither of whom has become reconciled to lesbianism—in part, surely, because of the influence of heterosexist stereotypes and in part, perhaps, because the mother has never found in her experiences true female bonding. Jones called it "an initiation story—into womanhood—and something that complicates that, ideas of womanhood and what it means" (Rowell 51). Told from the viewpoint of the daughter, "The Women" is an account of the child Winnie's sexual development and learning from age 3 to 14 against a background of her divorced mother's series of lesbian encounters, each of which ends in bitterness. Winnie recounts only two memories of her parents' marriage. The first memory, "climb[ing] in the bed and sleep[ing] between the two of them in the early morning" (Jones 25)—seems idyllic when compared to the lesbian bedroom, which is closed to Winnie. The closed bedroom door suggests that what goes on behind it is wrong and perhaps unnatural since Winnie was welcomed into the heterosexual bed. The second compares the departure of their mother's first post-divorce lover to her father's leaving: "It was just like when my mama and daddy have the fight, and then my daddy didn't come back" (26). Perhaps from her husband, certainly from the heterosexist society, Gertrude Flynn gets her image of herself and her kind: she labels each ex-lover a "bitch's whore" (26), (31)

At three, Winnie learns of her mother's lesbianism and at five she learns the specifics from her ten-year-old cousin, Freddy. The first lover Mrs. Flynn take after her divorce is the mustachioed Ms. Maybell Logan, a "woman who wants to be a man" (26). Freddy shows and tells Winnie what is and "ain't gon' happen in there [in Gertrude and Maybell's bed]," because Miss Logan and Gertrude "ain't got no cock to crow" (27). He tells Winnie what her mother and Miss Logan do in the closed bedroom: "they feeling pussy . . . . They feeling titties" (29). And he predicts to Winnie, "when you grow up, you gonna be jus' like your mama" (27).

As Freddy initiates Winnie sexually, he demonstrates the callousness and "pervasiveness of sexual abuse that is even part of the consciousness of the very young" (Wade-Gayles 178):

> He raise my dress up and take my panties down and then he was Doing something to me but I didn't know what . . . I wont to get away . . . and then he did it. And then he put his hands down there and wipe it on my dress, but I just sit there. (Jones 28)

Winnie does not have the vocabulary to name the "it" that Freddy does. She does, however, know she does not like it and wants to escape. Freddy's dismissal of Winnie's humanity and his callousness is evidenced in his command that she "cover up your ass 'fore you get a cold pussy" (28), despite his having been the one to uncover it. Freddy's ideas about women and sex are from the street and the male double-standard. At 10, he has already been conditioned to oppress and degrade women, and speak to them in a condescending manner. When Winnie arrives in first grade, Freddy has spread the word on the playground that she is "fast" (35). Because this reputation precedes her, Winnie does not have the opportunity to introduce and define herself. At the age of six, Winnie has already been labeled and Othered. Freddy has done both. While Jones' narrative does not provide details of Winnie's ruined reputation, the reader can easily imagine the consequences of a little girl labeled "fast."

Being raised in a home where the father is absent, where the mother regards her women as bitches, whores, hussies, and pussies, and where the lovers establish no bond with the child, Winnie herself begins to see women as "whores" for her mother. When she begins school, the already-labeled "difficult child" tells her female teacher that her mother sleeps with Miss Fletcher, a shy old maid high school teacher, and she offers or threatens: "My mama sleep with you too" (33). But already at the age of six, having been "raked" by Freddy, she knows that any forced sexual encounter is a violation. Still unable to name the "it" and knowing only the dirty, violating side of "it," Winnie sees "it" as bad. As she says in a playground conversation, "Anybody do it to you bad" (36). Therefore, Freddy is bad.

Having had an unpleasant sexual encounter with the male in near-infancy, the prepubescent Winnie and her girlfriend Retta, on an overnight visit, experiment with sex. And they discover that it feels good:

"What you doing?"
"Trying to feel pussy Let me feel it."
"Feel good, don't it?"
"Yeah." (40)

With some inherent understanding of children's developmental stages, they justify their experiment because "they are little girls." Knowing that "when you get titties, you ain't supposed to let a girl do it" for that would "mean you queer," and they "ain't goin be queer" (41). These two young girls have also been conditioned by society and their mothers to judge lesbianism as "queer" and intolerable, a lesson perhaps first learned from Winnie's mother's closed bedroom door. Despite the good feeling their sexual act stimulated, the girls seem to already know that pleasure is forbidden and must reject an embrace that feels good.

Retta's mother directly voices the heterosexist disapproval to Gertrude Flynn when she leaves Retta for the overnight stay to attend a Baptist

Convention. That both Retta's mother and Freddy's attend a Baptist Convention is surely Jones' comment on the heterosexism of patriarchal religion. Describing her dissatisfaction with her work at the narcotics farm where men and women are segregated, she says, "It's this other stuff got me lookin' for someplace to go. You know, women hugging on each other. Guess when you're in a sit'ation where you ain't got nothing else . . . . But it just ain't right. I don't think it's right" (39). Imprisoned in heterosexist silence, with silence giving consent, Gertrude Flynn voices no defense of her sexuality and her life. Ironically, Gertrude Flynn is working in a largely female tobacco line, from which she takes a string of lovers. That she considers herself a "bitch" and her women as "whores" indicates the absence of genuine affection between lovers. Their relationships are all momentary physical passion, perhaps prevented from being anything more or deeper because of the influence of their community's standards on their self-image. Gertrude's inability to bond the lovers she takes subconsciously passes on to Winnie.

When Retta moves away, Winnie makes no effort to make new friends even though several girls try to be friendly. At the onset of her menses, Winnie sees her mother kissing at the back door a "big woman" who had hidden her car from public view at the back of the house, Winnie renews her vows, despite Freddy's prediction, not to be a "bitch's whore."

In high school, Winnie shows no interest in boys, not even Garland Morton, who is persistent in his determination that they "be keepin' company" (45). Winnie does not want him around, but she does not know why. He makes a shrewd assessment of Winnie: "You cold, ain't you?" (44). Winnie's coldness of one who is trying to possess herself, who remembers from her preschool encounter that "anybody do[ing] it to you be bad." When Garland surprises Winnie in her home at a time when her mother is out to visit a lover, he reveals the sexual situation in his own home: his father disparages his mother's artistic expression. Refusing to do any "female" chores, Garland avoids doing so by manipulating his mother with cunning. He does the same with Winnie. When Garland places his hand on her knees, she lets it remain, "thinking Mama gone to visit Miss Alice" (51). When Garland's hand touches her crotch, she responds physically: "My legs felt warm all inside. Then he put his hand on my crotch feeling for me, and then he was kissing me and feeling me through my panties. And then he said, 'Let's get out of the front room' " (52). By having sex with Garland, Winnie hopes to strangle any possibility of being like her mother. In a symbolic gesture, she takes Garland into her mother's bedroom. Jones thus ends her story, leaving her readers to ponder Winnie's sexual future.

Ann Allen Shockley says that Jones "should have said more" (89) with "The Women." Shockley would no doubt have had Gertrude find fulfillment with less "nebulous characters (89), and Winnie develop her sexual orientation without difficulty. Instead, in a nonlinear manner, Jones has shown the significance of the relationship between parent and child and the influence of sexist and heterosexist attitudes in the developmental process. Jones leaves us to wonder whether Winnie will ever accept the lesbian embrace or whether she will establish her heterosexuality, and whether in any case, she will develop a sense of self-worth and social relationships of mutuality. Or will she become a "bitch's whore" or a stud's fast woman?

Eva's Man tells the story of Eva Medina Canada, a woman whose life is tormented by male oppression, sexual abuse, and emotional silence, who is a prisoner of negative images and stereotypes of women and men. Consequentially, Eva Canada becomes a murderess who is either unable or unwilling to articulate her thoughts or her abuse. In an interview, Jones revealed that she deliberately wrote *Eva's Man* as an unrelentingly grim, non-linear, first-person narrative, interior monologue that moves back and forth in time: "I wanted to get a sense of different times and different personalities coexisting in memory" raising such questions as "how much of Eva's story is true and how much is deliberately not true: that is, how much of a game is she playing with her listeners/psychiatrists/others?" (Tate 143).

Despite the complexity of *Eva's Man*, much of the critic's analysis of the novel is grounded in their ideological disagreements with Jones' treatment of the male characters and the lesbian embrace. Jones recognizes the problem of writing about anything that concerning sexuality: "it appears as if you're supporting the sexual stereotypes about blacks" (Rowell 46). The problem, Jones further notes, "of appearing to support stereotypes further complicates the issue, as it complicates the issue of early novels having the black man—at least the early *published* novels and I keep insisting on this because that's what has been *seen* and assessments made on the basis of—at least from the viewpoint of the women storytellers, as the antagonists" (46). Unable to see Eva's actions as a reaction to her treatment at the hands of men, Melvin Dixon, for example, blames Eva: "Rather than acknowledging the part she played in abusing men . . . Eva persists in acting out with Davis the roles of women predators, the images of Eve, Medusa, and Queen Bee, which are really created by men out of their own castration anxiety and fears about their repressed femininity" (Dixon 247). Dixon is not alone in his assessment of the novel. He is accompanied by Jerry Ward who notes that Jones' novels and short stories "invite readers to explore the interiors of caged personalities, men and women driven to extremes," but also seem to be "indices of contemporary disorder as norm rather than deviation" (249). Ward sees Eva as a "victim of her own passivity, her tendency to accept the Playboy fantasy of what a woman is. Her life history contains a series of sordid, dehumanizing sexual encounters" (254). Succinctly summarizing Eva's life experiences, in a paragraph, Ward aptly notes that "Eva does not acquire a whole sense of personhood in her formative years" (255) as a result of childhood sexual abuse, lack of female friendship, an imprisoning marriage that does not permit a house phone, protective violence, and patriarchal stereotypes. While both Ward and Dixon offer insightful analyses, their analyses are short-sighted because they are "ideologically limited in their response to sexuality and gender" (Basu 196). In their analysis, both Ward and Dixon fail to see Eva as the woman Jones painted her to be. Like Eva is trapped in her experiences with men, Ward and Dixon, too, are trapped in their inability to see Eva as a victim of a misogynistic, patriarchal, and sexist society.

While Eva may indeed be a passive participant in her victimization as both Dixon and Ward note, Jones invites us to see and understand Eva in her totality, not just in her "culminating act, murder, and genital mutilation, in the light of everything else it offers—among other things, the multiple instances of the abuse of women" (197). In writing about topics that reflect poorly on the African American community and her refusal to engage in respectability politics, Jones faces the dilemma experienced by similar African American writers: "Should a black writer ignore such characters, refuse to enter 'such territory; because of the 'negative image' and because such characters can be misused politically by others, or should one try to reclaim such complex, contradictory characters?" (Davison 395).

Like Alice Walker's *The Color Purple*, much of the earlier criticism of *Corregidora* and *Eva's Man* was due to the belief the novels aired the Black community's proverbial dirty laundry. Jones answers in the affirmative to the latter question, stating, "I am interested in human relationships, but I do not make moral judgments or political judgments of my characters" (Jones *Black Women Writers* 233). Thankfully, Jones did not settle to write the idealist novel that portrayed Blacks at our best. Instead, because she is interested

> principally in the psychology of characters—and the word(s) in which they order their stories—their myths, dreams, nightmares, secret worlds, ambiguities, contradictions, ambivalences, memories, imaginations, their "puzzles." "For this reason, I cannot claim 'political compulsions' nor moral compulsions" if by either of these one means certain kinds of restrictions on "imaginative territory" or if one means maintaining a "literary decorum." (233)

Jones wrote *Eva's Man* and *Corregidora*, ground-breaking novels that explore the challenges of being a Black woman in a racist, sexist, patriarchal world and depicted the ugly realities of that existence. They tell the Black woman's story and her plight. These novels are like the blues in that they care about our pain, our wounds, bumps and bruises, scrapes with the law and hard times, and our broken hearts and broken spirits; however, they are also about our survival and our triumphs.

Unlike either Dixon or Ward, Margaret Davison reads *Eva's Man* in an entirely different way. She sees the novel as Jones' brilliant manipulation of biblical names and roles to undermine patriarchal stereotypes: "As the daughter of an adulterous mother Marie (Mary), Eva (Eve) assumes the role of moral arbiter who evades repeated attempts at violation . . . Eva definitively upsets the traditional framework wherein the temptress Eve is condemned as responsible for man's fall from God's grace" (406). More significantly, Davison sees Eva, who envisions "big, rusty nails sticking out of [her] palms" (Jones 95) as a Christ Figure: "This image is clearly consistent with the overarching portrait of Eva as a black woman crucified by her society" (Davison 406). Eva's story reads like a blues song, with repetitive choruses of sexual, physical, and verbal abuse. Margaret Davison describes Eva as a "figurative blues singer" (397), and *Eva's Man* qualifies as an extended blues experience. The story is replete with "repetitions and reversals and themes of love and violence. . ." (Davison 397) Eva's "narrative blues performance is meticulously rendered and constructed" (Davison 397). To every man she meets, Eva is a whore, a woman to be sexually exploited; she is consistently described as "a little evil devil bitch" (Jones *Eva's* 35). Eva hears her father tell her mother repeatedly: "Act like a whore, I'm gonna fuck you like a whore" (37). And her cousin Alfonso, like clockwork, beats his wife, Jean, in front of the same hotel, and she takes the abuse, "like they were working some kind of blues ritual" (Jones 131). Eva sees relationships as sadistic-masochistic. Eva is unable or unwilling to voice her blues to free herself from her painful past experiences, so she remains locked in passivity and incommunicado, refusing to explain herself or defend her actions to the court, the prison psychiatrist, the reporters, or her cellmate, Elvira: "I don't like to talk about myself" (73). Her "seemingly passive compliance is a way of resisting the double bind, what Cixous has called the 'phallocentric representationalism' " (144). While Eva withholds her story from those around her, telling it to whom she chooses and when it is Eva's voice we hear as we read her story. She controls her narrative, telling her listening readers what she does not tell the ones involved in her story: "This is the only way she has of resisting the dominant discourses that imprison her inside certain labels" (144). By controlling "what she will and will not tell is a way of maintaining her autonomy" (Tate 146–147). Eva refuses to be Ralph Ellison's Trueblood, who tells his story of incest and rape to an eager, voyeuristic White audience: "Even now people come in here and ask me how it happened. They want me to tell it over and over again. I don't mean just the psychiatrists, but people from newspapers and things. They read about it or hear about it someplace and just want to keep it living" (4–5). Her prison psychiatrist's name—David Smoot—echoes Eva's first molester—Freddy Smoot—and murdered lover—Davis Carter. With that name, we know that he will view Eva through the same lens as all of the other men and will thus be unable to help her: "They say they helping me. I'm forty-three years old, and I ain't seen none of their help yet" (5).

Eva's narrative, full of "imagined memories . . . [and] real ones" (10), is the interior soliloquy of a woman who is trying, without meaningful help of the prison psychologist, to understand her life. Eva piles memory on memory, weaves memory and fantasy together, free associates, blurs, condenses, and combines her experiences. Her meditation is structured on the framework of her recollections of a sordid five-day "affair," which culminates in her poising and emasculating her "lover" Davis Carter; within this structure, Eva brings the sex memories of her 43 years: "Davis squeezed my ankles. I squeezed a boy's dick. It was like squeezing a soft milkweed. The musician made me put my hands down between his legs" (49). She punctuates her interior monologue with accounts of the efforts of her cellmate, Elvira, to communicate with and seduce her as well the prison psychiatrist's efforts to unlock her voice. Despite the novel's title that suggests this is Eva's story, it really is a story about Eva's men who all coalesce into one man: "It is a story about men. About their obsessive sexuality and exploitative relationships" (Lionnet 145). It is their narrative of Eva that informs her narrative of herself. A passive player in her own life, it is to men's actions that Eva responds. Eva's own story, the story of Eva Medina Canada, we are not told. What we know of Eva is "what the men in her life (Freddy, Mr. Logan, John Canada, Tyrone, Davis, Alfonso, Moses Tripp, James Hunn, and finally David Smoot) have done to the women she knows." The narrative shows how they have made Eva herself into a "little evil devil bitch," a "sweet [castrating] bitch" (145). That Jones does not tell us Eva's own story but tells us Eva's story through the lens of sexist, misogynistic, and patriarchal men is evidence of the overwhelming authority of patriarchy to define, name, and other. Despite having a name that evokes the "first" mother, movement, and freedom, Eva Medina Canada is paralyzed by the various unwanted sexual encounters, stereotyped assumptions, the imprisoning silence that immobilizes her tongue, and the lack of woman friendship.

However, within that imprisoning silence, Eva seeks to name herself and create her own identity, resisting the labeling efforts of others to define her. She assumes the identity of "Eve, Queen Bee and Medusa, iconic women who have power and control, symbolic personages that have been very detrimental to men" (Tate 146). Reminiscent of Wright's Bigger Thomas, Eva's two voluntary actions, ones of violence and resistance, land her in prison, and the constant question of why. Lacking the voice and model to be proactive, Eva reacts to patriarchy and does so violently. Ironically, Eva refuses to speak while on trial where her words could free her, perhaps because she has been misunderstood and mislabeled her entire life by others. She chooses instead to speak in prison when she chooses to and thereby exudes control over her narrative, deciding when and to whom to speak: "All during the trial I wouldn't talk to anybody. But then, after I came in here [prison], I started talking. I tell them so much I don't even get it straight any more. I tell them things that don't even have to do with what I did, but they say they want to hear that too" (5). That we cannot determine if Eva's told story, told like a blues song, is true suggests Eva's deliberate resistance to a lifetime of pigeon-hole labeling. Like the gypsy woman Medina, who named her, Eva moves freely from state to state. Perhaps in a nod to her editor Toni Morrison, Gayl Jones' Eva resembles Sula, the person Eva could have been but was not. They are both educated and well-traveled: "Nashville, Detroit, New Orleans, New York, Philadelphia, Macon, and San Diego" (Morrison 120—Sula, like a man, is vocal and claims ownership of herself, freely owns her "own dirt" and proudly claims whatever is burning in her as hers. Like Sula, Eva is a traveler, noting "I've been everywhere. I could go anywhere" (Morrison 169). While Ajax calls Sula and Nel "pig meat", (Morrison 50), Moses Tripp, who wants to take Eva on trips, calls her "sweetmeat" (Jones 68). In her explanation of why she slept with Jude, her best friend's husband, Sula: "Well, there was this space in front of me, behind me, in my head. Some space. And Jude filled it up. That's all. He just filled up the space" (Morrison 144). Eva expresses the same sentiment to explain why she went with Davis: "Loneliness. I filled in the spaces. I filled in the spaces and feelings. Why did you kill him? I filled in the feelings" (Jones 169). Like Sula who wanted to know the essence of Ajax—"*If I take a chamois and rub real hard on the bone, right on the ledge of your cheek bone, some of the black will disappear. It will flake away into the chamois and underneath will be a folded leaf. I can see it shining through the black*" (Morrison 130, empasis mine)—Eva, after poisoning Davis, takes his essence into her mouth and bites it off and makes love to it, an act she describes as biting into a plum: "I opened his trousers and played with his penis. My mouth, my teeth, my tongue went inside his trousers. I raised blood, slime from cabbage, blood sausage. Blood an apple. . . I got back on the bed and squeezed his dick in my teeth. I bit down hard. My teeth in an apple. A swollen plum in my mouth" (Jones 128). Collapsing Freddy Smoot's penis with Davis', Eva says it felt like a "red swollen plum in my mouth. A milkweed full of blood" (128).

In the first meditation of the novel, Eva defines the fundamental difference between herself and her cellmate Elvira: "They let her go out more than they do me because they say she's got more control" (3). Elvira is a communicator; she reads newspapers and reports to Eva. She tries to share an article about Eva's crime, but Eva refuses to look. Still, in her soliloquy, Eva tries to understand her life and experiences.

Like Winnie in "The Women," Eva is initiated in sexuality when she is five-years-old. The experience is vulgar and nasty. She loses her virginity to a "dirty popsicle stick" in the hands of Freddy Smoot, who is so young, he's unable to have an erection. His penis feels like "soft milkweeds" (8), yet he has already been conditioned by society to abuse girls. The encounter leaves blood on the toilet paper. When he sees Eva again, he calls for a gang rape: "There's Eva, we can get some" (19). Jones plays on the words "dirty" and "popsicle stick." Dirty "symbolizes the baseness of sexual encounters in the community, and the popsicle stick, something found in a filthy gutter, stand throughout the novel for man's erection" (Wade-Gayles 178).

Eva finds no safety from or with men, even those who should protect her. Eva is molested by Tyrone, her mother's lover. He places her hand on his hardening penis. Even her cousin Alfonso assumes she has "had the meat" because she's "way too old not to had the meat" (58); most girls of her age have had the "meat *and* the gravy" (58). While taking her around to coarse cafes, with her mother's approval, to introduce her around, he, too, tries to molest her: "He had pulled me over where he was and starting kissing on the side of my neck.... He had hold of my hand ... it wasn't inside his pants. It felt like a wrist. It was throbbing like a wrist. I said Naw, and broke away from him and for the door" (71), and he constantly tells her "I just want to suck your tiddies" (94). Using the knife Freddy Smoot gifted her, 17-year-old stabs Moses Tripp, a man who "claimed he wasn't trying to do nothing but buy [her] a beer, but that wasn't all he was trying to buy" (98). He tells her he wants to "buy some pussy. Spread my legs so I'll be fucked in the ass again. Go fuck yourself, I told him. I don't want to fuck myself, I want to fuck you. I was seventeen when he tried to. Damn bitch" (153). Unwilling to accept Eva's rejection, he follows Eva outside: " 'Least feel on it for me. That ain't fair. Five dollars for a feel, that ain't ... Let me.' He reached down between my legs, then he screamed and pulled his hand back. He called me a 'bitch' " (98). From every man she encounters, she learns that all women, including herself, are "whores" and "bitches." Conditioned, too, by society to see all women as whores, Eva's husband treats her such upon seeing her in the company of a male classmate, echoing her father's treatment of her mother: "You think you a whore, I'll treat like a whore. You think you are a whore, I'll treat you like a whore ... he pulled my dress up and got between my legs. Think I can't do nothing. Fuck you like a damn whore. I'll fuck you like a whore" (163). Eva expected her father to respond violently to Tyrone who had violated his home; however, Tyrone escapes punishment because Eva's father and society regard women as "*naturally* sexually promiscuous" Davison 397).

Like Eva, all of the female characters are abused. Elvira was "handled" by a man when she was four years old: "He told me to get up in the truck and he'd give me some money. An old man with hair in his ears and skullcap on. He slid his hand up between my thighs and told me how nice and soft I was. He didn't have any teeth.... They got him for 'handling me'" (154). At the age of five, Miss Billie is molested by Mr. Logan: "I got another kind of stick you can see. . . . He got up real close and took his thing out. I swear it was right up in my face. He told me I could touch that one too. . . . He had it in his own hand, and he was rubbing on it till all this white stuff—I didn't know what it was then—came out" (12). Hating him from that day forward, she says Mr. Logan "ain't nothing but a shit. He ain't nothing but a ole shit" (11). And she admonishes Eva, "Don't let that old man mess you, now, cause he ain't nothing but a shit" (12). Perhaps seeing himself in young Freddy Smoot, Logan does nothing to protect Eva from Freddy who wants to "zamine" her again. Ignoring her request that he make Freddy leave her alone, Mr. Logan just "looked at me, grinning and walked on by" (14). Miss Billie's daughter, too, was molested: "He showed me what a man could do for himself. I mean, it couldn't do it . . . Naw he didn't beat it, he did something else" (90), that something else she never defined. By those in charge, Eva is molested: "The man in his office lays me on top of his desk. He pulls my dress up, takes his pants down" (135).

Eva has no role model for communication and understanding. Even in marriage, there is no communication between men and women on any level other than that of user and used. Her mother openly has an affair with Tyrone, a musician 10 years her junior, who eventually tries to rape 12-year-old Eva. Although her mother tells her father that the adultery "didn't happen because she didn't love him" (Jones 50), she fails to explain why it happened. There are no words to the blues soundtrack for the sadomasochistic dance between Alfonso and his wife Jean, who returns to him after each brutal beating. Thus, Eva is ill-equipped to voice her pain or her pleasure. On trial for stabbing Moses Tripp, the "ole feeler," Eva wouldn't talk, wouldn't say anything to defend herself" (70), a silence she acknowledges to Elvira: " 'I didn't tell anybody,' I said. 'I just let the man tell his side'" (98). Like Eva, young Freddy Smoot has no love language to express his "crush" on Eva. Instead, he lets a "dirty popsicle" do his talking. However, when he informs Eva of his family's impending move, he asks her if she will miss him, admitting that "I'm gon miss you," as he kissed her on the cheek and gifted her a "little pearl-handled pocketknife" (21) while repeating, "I'm gon miss you" as he ran back upstairs" (21). Though Eva liked for her lover Davis to penetrate her from behind, she never tells him: "I like to get up against my ass and come in that way. I never told him what I like, so he didn't do it a lot" (160).

Because Eva does not voice her disapproval or her pain, it is easy to read her as a passive participant in her victimization. A lifetime of constant abuse from all the men in and around her may well have rendered her mute, unable to articulate her innermost self and vocally resist their abuse. However, Eva's active refusal to speak when asked is an act of resistance. Her unwillingness to express or explain herself allows her to remain unengaged in the assumed stereotyped judgments about her that "categories of male constructions which position the female subject in a particular, and negative, relation to the male subject. The female is the passive victim of an excessive, and therefore irrational agent" (Basu 201). While Eva may be silent, she is not silenced: "in fact, hegemonic institutions invite and encourage her loquacity. Her participation would only provide 'data' which would allow her subject position to be gathered or recuperated into the different forms of institutional discourse" (199–200). Because of her life experiences, including when she was a young girl, Eva is both physically and psychologically imprisoned. Her psychological imprisonment, caused by her inability to distinguish men during her early and later encounters, leads to her physical imprisonment in a psychological institution.

Throughout her entire life, Eva gets no respect, no understanding, and no real caresses from a man. Instead, she sometimes gets unwanted sex and consistently constant negative assumptions about her character. Even though Eva searches for something with which to challenge men's assumptions that she's a "whore" and a "bitch," she cannot escape that image. Tyrone, Alfonso, and a stranger who offers Eva a ride all describe her as "a evil ole bitch. Your name ain't Eva it's evil" (10). Her husband, although good to her, thinks "I was that kind of woman. I could see it in his eyes. Like that other man. In the car. He opened the car door. He thought I was that kind of woman" (Jones 170). She's also called a "whore" by the landlady and the prison psychiatrist asks, "Is this the savage woman?" (141). From life she soon learns that ". . . always. They would . . . Always. No matter what I . . . . Just because the places I went, the way I talked or how I wore my hair" (171). In her interview for *Black Women Writers at Work*, Jones points out that Eva is disturbed by the fact that men repeatedly assume she's a whore or bitch: she eventually defines herself with the Queen Bee and Medusa image which men have created "out of their own castration anxiety and fears about their repressed femininity" (Dixon 247). Just as the men are unable to distinguish Eva from other women, Eva is unable to differentiate the men. Davis becomes a mixture of all the men who have abused her—Alphonso, Old Man Logan "the ole shit," Freddy Smoot, James Hunn, Tyrone, and Moses Tripp. Even prison psychiatrist David Smoot violates Eva. By insisting that Eva has to "open up sometime, woman, to somebody" (Jones 77), Smoot's actions are "tantamount to a form of sexual violation that Eva has experienced all her life and that the psychiatrist ironically reenacts" (Basu 200). Despite his declared effort, uttered in a soft voice like cotton candy, to help her, Smoot cannot penetrate Eva's fortress of silence because he sees her through his lens of patriarchy, unable to uncover and see the patriarchal abuse of Eva. His surprise that Eva has no physical scars indicates his inability to see beyond the surface. He derisively labels Eva's actions as a "crime of passion" (200) further reiterating the inaccurate summation of the lawyer: "*I submit the insanity of Eva Medina Canada, a woman who loved a man who did not return that love*" (Jones 150, emphasis author's). Eva eventually comes to regard all men as "shits" who always "mess with women" and think only about "where they going to get their next piece" (154). While Tyrone escaped punishment from Eva's father, Tyrone is one of the many men who sexually molested her and other women. Tyrone and his "phallocentered fraternity symbolically meet their retribution in Davis' murder" (Davison 397).

Davis' fatal mistake is when he picks Eva up and takes her to his cheap hotel room is he, too, assumes Eva is "that kind of woman" and treats her as such. He projects negative stereotypes of Eve and Medusa onto Eva; he "effectively renames her '*Eve Medusa Canada*,' thus inviting violent transgression" (Davison 404). He makes love to her during her menstrual cycle. He feeds her cabbage, and sausage with mustard that looks like "Baby's doodoo" and fills Eva with gas. He doesn't allow her to leave the room or comb her hair, letting instead it grow wild and look like snakes: "He wouldn't even let me comb my hair or nothing" (169). So ensconced is he in his own male stereotype that Davis is convinced of his sexual prowess and believes he's doing Eva a favor. He fails to see that Eva is not a whore, even though he knows that she "ain't been getting it" (17). Though Davis promised to wait the three days until she stopped menstruating, he has sex with her while she's asleep and menstruating, penetrating her from behind. Moreover, he hurts Eva: "After I came he kept touching my clit and it hurt. 'Please don't' " (156). Then he parted her hair with a comb, scratching her "scalp till it bled" (156). Calling Eva Eve, Medusa, a male lion, Davis connects Eva to women who "have been fatal to men" (Lionnet 143) thus foreshadowing his impending demise.

In retaliation for her devalued female being, Eva takes the essence of Davis' manhood into her mouth, bites it off, and wraps it in a silk handkerchief, a "brutal attack on phallocentrism" (Davison 396). She then retrieves her taken comb and the promised key. Davis' castration is "constitutes a literary blues statement, a testament to survival articulated by a woman who exists in the psychological, sexual, and spiritual margins of patriarchal society" (qtd. in Davison 397). This event is subtly foreshadowed by Davis' observation that Eva eats her food as if she's making love to it (130). Eva kills and mutilates Davis because "he came to represent all the men [she]'d known in [her] life" (81). Her act of violence is an explosion of the rage that has been festering from a lifetime of degradation. It is also a sex act in which she dominated this man who had told her, "Swallow me. Swallow me up. I know what kind of woman you are" (175). This is not a crime against an ". . .individual against society . . . it is present as a symptom of society's crime against the female individual. Struggle for the control of their own bodies determines the ultimate act of resistance and survival" (Lionnet 135). Significantly, as Davison points out, "Eva's act of castrating Davis and subsequently fantasizing that she is eating *fruit*—a 'red swollen plum,' 'blood from an apple' (Jones 128)—functions as an ingenious subversion, for it conflates crucial elements from both Eve and Medusa narratives. . . Eva reduces the phallus—the figurative fruit of her society's tree of knowledge—to food, and consumes it" (404).

Eva has never helped herself. Perhaps she has never had the role model to teach her how. Her mother has had a close woman friend, Miss Billie, who gives Eva a wooden "ancestor bracelet" that symbolically connects Eva to a female community, but she loses it when she is eight years old, which suggests her disconnection from that community. In a moment of clarity, Eva recognizes that her high school graduation visit to Miss Billie in North Carolina was really for her mother than for herself: "She'd have somebody she could talk things out with, because I knew she didn't feel she could talk thing out with me" (82).

But Miss Billie and Eva's mother also accept the male-imposed gender roles as patterns for their lives. Although they frown upon early sexual indulgence, believing that once a girl opens her legs, she cannot keep them closed, they admonish girls who don't eventually have a man. They validate self in terms of sexual encounters with men: "Whereas early promiscuity is frowned upon, validation of self in sexual encounters with a man is expected. In the cultural ethos of the community, a woman without a man is either insane or lesbian" (Wade-Gayles 179). Mrs. Canada encourages her daughter to experience and explore her womanhood. Miss Billie earlier spent an enormous amount of time trying to keep her daughter Charlotte's legs closed, but now that she is 27, unmarried and uninterested in men, Miss Billie spends an equal amount of time trying to get her to open them again. Miss Billie and Eva's mother also accept the male myth about women. It is from Miss Billie that Eva first learns of the Queen Bee, who "kills" every man who comes in contact with her, "who sucks men hollow" (73), an image so fascinating to her that she eventually accepts that role for herself and acts it out. Though Miss Billie and Mama comfort one another, they offer no redemptive pattern for Eva.

Miss Billie's daughter Charlotte, however, appears to have become a lesbian and to have become comfortable with her sexual orientation although her mother is not. On the North Carolina trip, she takes Eva for walks in the woods, explains the nature of a hurtful relationship she had once had with a boy, and tentatively offers Eva the lesbian embrace, telling Eva she "didn't want a man" (Jones 89). Eva is not ready for Charlotte's invitation; consequently, she does not acknowledge it. But after a life of male oppression and sexual brutality, Eva is ready to be seduced by Elvira.

And so, Eva is driven by a series of horrible events to a prison cell for the criminally insane and into the arms of Elvira, her lesbian cellmate. Perhaps in recognition of her as her self-titled name Queen Bee, Elvira calls Eva "honey" and offers her physical fulfillment (161). Unlike the men, in none of her propositions does she suggest using Eva: "I'll do it for you if you want me to, Eva . . . . You won't help yourself, that's why can't nobody else help you, cause you won't help yourself" (156).

Although Eva initially rejects Elvira, she realizes that she cannot continue to do so: "Last night she got in bed with me, Davis . . . I knocked her out, but I don't know how long I'm going to keep knocking her out" (176). After five years of prison, Eva is still so influenced by heterosexism that she reacts violently to Elvira and addresses her fears of weakness to Davis. At last, she accepts Elvira's tender lovemaking: "Tell me when it feels sweet, Eva. Tell me when I feels sweet, honey." I leaned back, squeezing her face between my legs, and I told her, "Now!" (177). The inevitability of their coming together is evidenced in their names since Elvira's name contains Eva's—"ElVirA" (Lionnet 145–46). Francoise Lionnet argues that "if Elvira can absorb and contain Eva, this icon of all the negative representations of women, then perhaps she can also re-engender her as a new female subject" (146). With their simultaneous names, we see in Elvira what Eva needs but never found in freedom—a female community. Ironically, imprisonment provides Eva the key to her liberation, "since it allows her to discover a female community in the transitional space of the psychiatric ward" (146). In accepting Elvira's lesbian embrace, Eva moves from her previous anti-lesbian embrace informed only by sexual desire to a full embrace. She realizes that what she wants is "nothing [he] can give" (176). In so doing, Eva "displaces her focus to a space outside of the politics of (male) aggression and power, offering passing resistance to the cultural scenarios that frame her as a *femme fatale*. Thus, the 'Now' (Jones 177) she utters as she surrenders to Elvira brings her into a present that suggests an alternative to her passive submission to, and acceptance of, the other's will to pleasure" (Lionnet 145).

In memory of a talk with the prison psychiatrist, Eva has equated opening up in oral communication with opening up sexually and "[keeps] her knees squeezed tight together" (Jones 76-77) as she refuses to talk to the male doctor. Wade-Gayles says that Elvira reopens Eva's closed legs by providing her with "an alternative to sexual victimization, that in embracing Elvira, Eva can move from "can't to can in sexual fulfillment" (183). If this is true, then perhaps Elvira can provide Eva with understanding and communication and can relieve her loneliness. In memory passage previously, however, Eva condenses the psychiatrist with Elvira and an obscene phone caller from her mother's past:

"How did it feel, Eva?" the psychiatrist asked.
"How did it feel?" Elvira asked.
"How do it feel, Mizz Canada?" The man asked my mama. (77)

If the verbal echoes in the closing passage of the novel are intentional, then perhaps both Wade-Gayles and Lionnet are wrong, and Eva had found only temporary physical pleasure but no real womanist bonding. In telling the stories of Winnie and Eva, Jones details the sexual and psychological abuse women from girlhood into adulthood experience from men in a patriarchal society that devalues, subdues, silences them. Their stories of repeated abuse suffered are indeed without joy, somber testament of suffered lives.

WORKS CITED

Basu, Biman. "Public and Private Discourse and the Black Female Subject: Gayl Jones' *Eva's Man*." *Callaloo*, vol. 19, no. 1, Winter 1996, pp. 93–208. *JSTOR*.

Claybough, Casey. "Afrocentric Recolonizations: Gayl Jones's 1990s Fiction." *Contemporary Literature*, vol. 46, no. 2, Summer 2005, pp. 43–274. *JSTOR*.

Davison, Carol Margaret. "Love'em and Lynch'em': The Castration Motif in Gayl Jones's *Eva's Man*." *African American Review*, vol. 29, no. 3, Autumn 1995, pp. 393–410. *JSTOR*.

Dixon, Melvin. "Singing a Deep Song: Language as Evidence in the Novels of Gayl Jones." *Black Women Writers (1950-1980): A Critical Evaluation*, edited by Mari Evans, New York: Doubleday, 1984, pp. 236–248.

Jones, Gayl. Ábout My Work." *Black Women Writers (1950-1980): A Critical Evaluation*, edited by Mari Evans. New York: Doubleday, 1984, pp. 233–235.

———. *Eva's Man*. Boston: Beacon Press, 1976.

———. Interview. By Charles Rowell. *Callaloo*, no. 16, October 1982, pp. 32–53.

———. Interview. By Claudia Tate. *Black American Literature Forum*, vol. 13, no. 4, Winter 1979, pp. 142–148.

———. "The Women." *The White Rat*. New York: Random Press, 1977.

Lionnet, Francoise. Geographies of Pain: Captive Bodies and Violent Acts in the Fictions of Myriam Warner-Vieyra, Gayl Jones, and Bessie Head. *Callaloo*, vol. 16, no. 1, Winter 1993, pp. 132–152.

Morrison, Toni. *Sula*. New York: Knopf, 1973.

Shange, Ntozake. *For Colored Girls who have Considered Suicide When The Rainbow Is Enuf: A Choreopoem*. New York: Scribner, 1975.

Tate, Claudia. *Black Women Writers at Work*. New York: Continuum, 1985.

Wade-Gayles, Gloria. *No Crystal Stair: Visions of Race and Sex in Black Women's Fiction*. Cleveland: Pilgrim Press, 1984.

Chapter 5

Grange's Grapple and Brownfield's Battle

Redefining Manhood in Alice Walker's Third Life of Grange Copeland

Lana N. Lockhart

As a lifelong proponent of the rights of women, author Alice Walker's writing and advocacy have been consistently shaped by the belief that women should exist, love, work, and play in a world that supports, affirms, and enables their humanity. Walker suggests that a "Womanist" or a "black feminist or feminist of color" (xi), in addition to being committed to making sure that her entire community survives and flourishes, must be concerned specifically with the plight of women. However, Walker also recognizes that the trials of women are often interconnected with the temperaments of men, which is evident throughout her writing. By using her writing as a form of activism, Walker has become a leader among African American women authors on how to navigate the complexities of the Black community and particularly on how to advance gender relations. She is often quoted from a February 2016 *Reader's Digest* piece in which she said, "Activism is the rent I pay for living on the planet" (164). Although Walker is often hailed for her literary exposition of the lives of women, I suggest that in the novel, *Third Life of Grange Copeland*, she strategically redefines the traditional performance of masculinity through her portrayal of the male characters. Published in 1970, Walker uses *Third Life of Grange Copeland* to critique the realities of masculinity in contemporary society by illustrating that (1) patriarchy should not include violence against women as a means of compliance; (2) oppressing Black women by perpetuating the patriarchal hegemony of White males will not garner their acceptance by White society; and (3) Black men must atone for their sins against Black women. As seen in *Third Life of Grange Copeland*, Walker is one of many Black Feminists authors who sought to get their male counterparts to become "comrades" against the patriarchal position that dominated their society by calling for a new idea of manhood.

> Due to the content of Walker's publications, particularly *Third Life of Grange Copeland*, she is probably one of the most acclaimed and controversial Black women authors of the late twentieth century. *Third Life* is the story of two men, a father named Grange and a son named Brownfield, who struggle to find their manhood in a racist society and within their family.

Critics of *Third Life* argue that Walker presents a haunting perspective of African American family life and demonizes Black men; however, I believe she is doing something greater. By depicting these two characters as she does, I suggest that Walker explores the following questions: How are Grange and Brownfield emasculated? How is their manhood affected by the pressures of white society and impacted by their interactions with women, especially Black women in the text? In the novel, Grange leaves his family behind in search of a new life up North, but he soon discovers that life is just as challenging up north for Black men as it is in the South. He returns to the South only to see the disarray into which, his son Brownfield and his family have fallen. In their quest to discover their manhood, each of them perpetuates a life of violence and abuse toward Black women, which are probably the most pivotal points of contention within the novel. For many, Walker's depiction of these two male characters was airing the community's "dirty laundry." However, I suggest that her goal was not negativity but an effort to use the power of the pen to speak out for Black women's rights and experiences, and use her writing as a form of activism through which, "the life we save is our own" (Walker 14). Furthermore, as Patricia Hill Collins states, "African American writers whose work seems to challenge dimensions of essential Blackness depicted as 'Truth' often encounter censure. . . . criticisms of Alice Walker's novels . . . often challenged Walker's accuracy in portraying the Black experience . . . holding her work to this standard allowed for its dismissal" (Collins 104). Walker's work was predominantly challenged by African American male leaders who despised her depictions of African American men. For instance, Addison Gayle's critique of *Third Life* hinged on Walker's alleged "inability to create complex male characters" (Dubey 108). However, being limited to depicting characters in the ways that the Black male leaders "approved," or that did not reflect her true experience went against Walker's principle of using her writing as a form of activism. Walker counters, "The writer . . . must be free to explore . . . . This means, very often, finding oneself considered 'unacceptable' by masses of people who think that the writer's obligation is not to explore or to challenge, but to second the masses motion's, whatever they are" (Walker 74). Hence, I suggest that Walker's portrayal of men in her novel, *Third Life* exhibits great complexity because of what she is saying about Black masculinity. Furthermore, Walker, among other women authors, rightfully claimed their freedom to create African American images that would influence social justice and change within their community and not be limited by the traditional gender constructs designed to protect a semblance of Black unity.

In *Third Life of Grange Copeland*, Walker is unapologetically presenting the problematics in the relationships of Black men and women, as she sees it, and presenting new concepts of masculinity through the characters, Grange and Brownfield. In *Third Life Grange Copeland*, Walker uses her experiences in her hometown to help shape the novel. Both Grange and Brownfield are sharecroppers like Walker's parents. In the afterward of *Third Life*, Walker remembers that her inspiration for the novel came from a visit to a funeral home that was next door to where she would babysit when she was younger. Her sister worked as a beautician at the funeral home and while visiting her, Walker saw the body of a woman who had been abused and murdered by her husband. In the novel, Mem, Brownfield's wife, faces a similar fate. Walker's father was a violent man too, and she sympathized with the dead woman because she knew that had a few circumstances been different, the dead woman could have easily been any of the women in her family. Walker writes that the violence that the men use on their families is a form of self-hatred through which,

> we have become more like our oppressors than many of us can bear to admit .... The white man's oppression of me will never excuse my oppression of you .... This is the understanding that is encoded in the lives of the 'soul survivors' of the novel, Grange Copeland and his granddaughter, Ruth. It is an understanding about the possibility of resistance to domination that all people share. (Walker 345)

By examining the concept of oppression within the novel, Walker is demonstrating that the oppression of Black women is because of patriarchal structures and warped views of masculinity within the novel. I argue that just as Walker is paying her rent to humanity by using her writing as a form of activism, she is also illustrating how Grange and Brownfield are paying their internal price to be seen as men in their society. The psychological emasculation of Black males in the United States dates back to enslavement and is rooted in Black men's need to feel affirmed as complete citizens and viable leaders, just as their white male counterparts had been affirmed for their entire lives. This affinity toward ideal manhood, which traditionally has meant white, middle-class, married, heterosexual and fully employed, is what author Judith Kegan Gardiner refers to as "hegemonic masculinity" in *Masculinity Studies and Feminist Theory: New Directions*. Gardiner states:

> All men are harmed by "hegemonic masculinity" . . . because it narrowed their options, forced them into confining roles, dampened their emotions, inhibited their relationships with other men, precluded intimacy with women and children, imposed sexual and gender conformity, distorted their self-perceptions, limited their social consciousness, and doomed them to continual and humiliating fear of failure to live up to the masculinity mark. . . . . Men are just beginning to realize that the traditional definition of masculinity leaves them unfulfilled and dissatisfied. (6)

Attempting to fulfill hegemonic masculinity is at the core of Grange and Brownfield Copeland's problems. Grange and Brownfield are mentally emasculated by their economic status and are held captive by the pressures and standards of white society.

Walker sets *Third Life* during the 1920s to the 1960s, a period in which Black economic mobility was greatly stifled. Like many Black families of this period, Grange and Brownfield are the targets of the sharecropping system, which Walker describes as one of the worst forms of racism because it left Blacks with nothing but a miserly lifestyle and insurmountable debt (Bates 8). Furthermore, Brownfield realizes after watching the loading of the truck for several weeks that "it was the man who drove the truck who caused his father to don a mask that was more impenetrable than his usual silence . . . the man was entirely different from his own father . . . Brownfield . . . filled with terror of this man who could, by his presence alone, turn his father into something that might as well have been a pebble or post or piece of dirt" (*Walker* 9). In this passage, I suggest that Walker is illustrating the idea that Black men must have the ability to present themselves in multiple ways and play according to the expectations of their audience for their survival, especially when interacting with someone who has superior power is called impression management (Majors 61). Being able to "manage" is a part of the "Cool Pose" concept that Majors and Billson developed, which analyzes how Black men interact with those around them. These authors argue that "the black male is socialized to view every white man as a potential enemy, every symbol of the dominant system as a potential threat. As a result, he is reluctant to expose his innermost feelings. Playing it cool becomes the mask of choice. Cool pose is a well-developed and creative art; it also exacts a stiff price in repressed feelings and suppressed energy" (Majors 27). Thus, in *Third Life*, Grange being compared to being low as dirt further demonstrates his position in society and why he acts the way that he does. His son Brownfield understands that the man whom his father fears is both white and successful—two things his father was not, and that he had enough control over their lives to turn his violent and boisterous father into a den of silence. The social order was clear. They farmed the land that white men owned, and they lived in a society in which they had to beg white men for rights.

Hence, Black men understood that because whites controlled their rights and their wages, they were slaves without the physical chains. However, if they wanted to survive in these conditions, they had to put on a mask of contentment.

Underneath this symbolic mask, many Black men coveted the patriarchal privileges that they had come to view as white hegemonic masculinity. To them, white hegemonic masculinity or ideal manhood encompassed social power, economic freedom, and societal respect. Unfortunately, Grange struggles mentally and emotionally because he has neither. When Brownfield is younger, he experiences his first sense of the concept of emasculation when he realizes that his father does not possess the socioeconomic supremacy included in ideal manhood. When his cousins came to visit him, they tell Brownfield "that his father worked for a cracker and that the cracker owned him. They told him that their own daddy, his Uncle Silas had gone to Philadelphia to be his own boss. . . . They bewildered, excited and hurt him . . . . He felt . . . as if he were waiting for something to happen that would take a very long time to come" (Walker 4). At this point in the story, Brownfield does not fully know how to articulate how he is feeling about his cousins' mean comments, but he senses that in the future, his pride and worth as a man will probably be controlled by this same set of societal rules and the dominant culture's power. In "Theorizing Progressive Black Masculinities," author Athena Mutua describes this power as a force that is socially structured but individually embodied but does not belong to all men equally. It is perpetuated in a society based on the hierarchy of races and the domination of men over others as one of the "central understandings and practices of masculinity" (17). Thus, Grange and Brownfield knew all too well that in terms of power and economic freedom, they had none. Thus, their "manhood" is continuously being questioned by themselves and challenged by others.

To further illustrate the effects of economics and white standards, Walker effectively highlights the extent of Black men's psychological emasculation by demonstrating how these notions of ideal masculinity caused some Black men to alienate themselves from their only intangible riches—their families—to pursue the tangible riches of money and status. For instance, knowing that he cannot hide his powerlessness because his son is observing him and knowing that his family does not think very highly of him only makes Grange's feelings of emasculation worse. His lowly state is likely the reason why he thinks of his family as a burden instead of a blessing. When examining their economic status, Walker writes,

> From the corner of his eye, Brownfield noticed that his father was also surveying the house . . . . While his son watched, Grange lifted his shoulders and let

> them fall. Brownfield knew this movement well; it was the fatal shrug. It meant his father saw nothing about the house that he could change and would therefore give up.... When Brownfield's mother had wanted him to go to school, Grange .... Knowing nothing of schools but knowing he was broke, he had shrugged; the shrug being the end of that particular dream. It was the same way when Margaret needed a dress and there was no way that Grange could afford to buy it. He merely shrugged." (Walker 14)

These are examples of Grange feeling trapped by his economic circumstances. He is powerless in his efforts to support his family or to give them a decent place to stay. Scholar Nancy E. Dowd notes that historically Black men's most fundamental way of proving their masculinity was by being an economic provider, and it was precisely in that respect that Black men were denied the means to be men in traditional terms (Mutua 264). Not only did the Eurocentric notion of success and inability to provide lead to internal conflicts, but it also led to problems with how they viewed and treated their families as well.

For many years Grange had dreamed of escaping to the north, but he was trapped by his economic circumstances and believed his family was an additional burden that kept him in his emasculated state. For instance, when Grange leaves, "Brownfield was crying silently and wanted his father to touch the tears. . . . He saw his father's hand draw back, without touching him. He saw him leave the room. He heard him leave the house. And he knew, even before he realized that his father would never be back, that he hated him" (21). Grange is determined to be free and to him, that means leaving behind any hindrances to that freedom. Grange's situation shares traits with author Ronda C. Henry Anthony's analysis of *The Narrative of William W. Brown, A Fugitive Slave* in her text *Searching for the New Black Man*. As we have seen throughout this study, when faced with disheartening economic conditions and racists standards, Black men sometimes viewed Black women and children as forces that held them back from attaining their freedom from slavery. As a result of this notion, Anthony points out that "attaining their manhood then becomes a game of deceiving whites as well as deceiving Black women and families" (40). In both Brown and Grange's situations, they both must choose whether their "manhood," which they envisioned as a reliable degree of financial stability and liberation from the confines of their white male oppressors, could happen while being honorable and staying with their families in the south, or, in contrast, whether it could ever come about as a result of them escaping to the North. Although Grange was not a literal slave, like Brown, his status in life made him a slave to his circumstances. For Grange, to stay would make him feel like the "overworked deacons, with rough pious hands that beat their women to death when they couldn't feed them" (154). Thus, in both cases, I suggest that the men choose liberty over family responsibility because they each believe that if they escape to the North, they will then have the opportunities to pursue "ideal manhood." As Collins argues, not being able to feed your family or advance in life is a violation of the "social class dimensions to hegemonic masculinity" because "real" men are not "financially dependent on others, but instead support others" (191). With Brownfield and Grange, the emasculating forces that come with economic status and white ideals of masculinity are so devastating that they, like some Black men, chose to seek their freedom from this emasculation even at the cost of hurting others in their lives. In each case, the men demonstrate that they would rather have the benefits of hegemonic masculinity than the combined burdens and benefits that come with a family.

Although Grange's journey is filled with many negative experiences because of economics and pressures of the dominant culture, I believe that Walker is illustrating in *Third Life* that Grange, like many African American men, has failed to define masculinity for himself, and thus, the attempt to fulfill Eurocentric masculinity leaves him with nothing to call his own. In the essay, "Bearing Witness and Paying Mind," Griffin argues that "black males are often seeking Eurocentric notions of success attributed to manhood that are characterized by wealth, notoriety, power, competition, and individualism opposed to embodying an Afrocentric worldview that positions relationships, reciprocity, interconnectedness, and collectivism as vital to being and becoming a successful black man" (171). We can see that Walker illustrates the latter in Grange's life. Although the battle to attain his manhood based on white standards is initially the catalyst through which Grange tries to experience his three lives, I assert that the "masculinity" through which he finds the greatest fulfillment is attained when he redefines manhood for himself. In his first life, he is a hopeless sharecropper with the burden of a family. In his second life, he goes north in an attempt to pursue "ideal manhood" through economic freedom. However, he discovers that the North is just as prejudiced as the South, and he is forced to hustle and steal just to survive. In his third life, he changes many of his negative ways and gains a sense of manhood by owning his own farm land as well as returning to his family. Thus, he also gets a glimpse of the idea that true freedom and manhood come from being one's own boss, making one's own decision about a livelihood, and interconnectivity with family.

By allowing Grange to commence his emancipation when he returns home Walker shows that it was not just Grange's hard work that afforded him a sense of emancipation: it is Josie's money, Ruth's love, Mem's death, and the memory of his dead wife that ultimately shape his perspective on his own masculinity. Walker writes, "With his money and hers he bought a farm. A farm far from town, off the main road, deep behind pines and oaks. He raised his own bread, fermented his own wine, cured his own meat. At last, he was free. But his freedom had cost him" (156). By using this as an aspect of Grange's liberation, I believe that Walker is illustrating several lessons. First, I suggest that Walker is giving a positive nod to the concept of ownership in the Black community by allowing Grange and Josie to own their land. Also, I believe that by allowing Grange to attain his manhood with the help of Josie's money, it is an illustration that Black men's greatest success comes when they work as comrades for community advancement with Black women instead of in competition. I suggest that she is acknowledging that Black men's concept of masculinity can include some aspects of traditional masculinity but that their greatest triumphs will come when they embrace a more relational approach to defining themselves. Grange finds his first sense of manhood when he returns to his family and embraces the members of his local community. He also finds success when he takes on the role of nurturer to his granddaughter, Ruth, which is a rejection of ideal masculine traits. However, Grange ultimately feels like a man when he accepts a more progressive, non-restrained masculinity that possesses some traits of hegemonic masculinity such as providing for his family and achieving a degree of economic advancement. Therefore, beliefs in unity and ownership within respective Black communities, and the concepts of Womanism in terms of being focused on relational worth and positive relationships with Black women, now combine to shape Grange's personal definition of manhood.

Walker uses Grange's new mindset to illustrate that a progressive view of manhood garners the most fulfillment when faced with the pressures that come from outside of the African American community. Walker also uses *Third Life* to address the intra-racial issues of the community as well. I suggest that while Walker is acknowledging that Black men have been the victims of a racist society, she is also presenting lessons about how they have victimized Black women in their effort to combat these pressures. Though Grange finds a sense of peace by changing his idea of masculinity toward the end of his life, it does not negate the negative interactions with Black women that he creates throughout his life and in his son Brownfield's life. Thus, Walker is using the male characters in her novel to illustrate that their emancipation from emasculation will also come when stop oppressing Black women and cease using violence as a means of compliance, because ultimately, doing so will not garner any greater acceptance of Black men in white society.

Additionally, Walker demonstrates that Black men's emancipation will not come at the cost of hurting Black women. Often Walker's characters were reflective of the significant problem of male dominance and female subordination within the community. Author Kimberly J. Chandler in the dissertation, "How to Become a 'Black Man,' " argues that Black men take advantage of the African American community's familiarity with the victimization that comes from racism use that to perpetuate the trope of the "oppressed black male." Chandler explains,

> This perception creates a perpetually subordinate position for Black females while guaranteeing a dominant position for Black males . . . the forces that support the privileging of black males assist in creating the perception that *that* privilege is extended because of the oppression they receive from greater society . . . . To not privilege Black males is to mirror the behavior of their oppressors. . . . They can use their oppressed position within society to substantiate their place of privilege within the black community . . . all the while, they benefit from having the privilege of remaining oblivious to the sexism impacting Black females. (82–83)

Thus, in *Third Life*, Walker acknowledges that Black men were victims of racist oppression, but she does not ignore that they could also be perpetuators of gender oppression.

Thus, Walker addresses the idea that when Black men feel emasculated, their frustrations often became apparent through their misogynistic and disdainful actions in relationships with Black women. Like many Black men, Grange's violent nature was often in response to the grim way he feels about his own life and prospects for happiness. Before his transition, not only do Grange's circumstances kill his dreams but they kill the dreams of his family as well. Although Brownfield later attains the same lowly status in his own life and adopts the same traits of dominance with his wife and family, he initially observes his mother's blind submission to his father with disdain. Walker notes, "Brownfield frowned. His mother agreed with his father whenever possible. And though he was only ten Brownfield wondered about this. He thought his mother was like a dog in some ways. She didn't have anything to say that did not in some way show her submission to his father" (*Third Life* 5). Although Brownfield recognizes that there is something inherently wrong in the dominate-subordinate relationship that exists between his parents, he later adopts the same behavior toward his own family. Just as his father Grange requires the childlike submission of Brownfield's mother, Margaret, Brownfield requires the same behavior from his wife, Mem. This requirement of submission is heavily connected to the previous two factors of emasculation, economics and white standards, because Black men know that they cannot control the white world outside of their home so they seek to control the world within their home. Grange had found that "wherever he went whites were in control; they ruled New York as they did Georgia; Harlem as they did Poontang Street" (140).

Brownfield feels similarly, telling his wife "you know how hard it is to be a black man down here . . . . You knows I never wanted to be nothing but a man! . . . the white folks just don't let nobody feel like doing right" (Walker 95). In each case, both Grange and Brownfield just want to be seen as real men, but in every way that they attempt to do so, they are held back by the emasculating factors that Black men face.

Yet it is important to recognize that Grange and Brownfield's emasculation is not caused nor perpetuated by the women in their lives. It is caused by racist forces, which cause them to take it out on the women whom they believe to be the only factors they can fathom controlling. Essentially, if the male did not have the resources to maintain his position as symbolic head of his family, he may seek to maintain a semblance of position through other means, which included the use of superior physical force because "the language of violence is one way to write a more dominative masculine script" (Majors and Billson 33). Author bell hooks notes that many underclass Black men are violent but will never act violently outside of the home but are abusive and violent in their private lives (hooks 56). Furthermore, hooks states that "Black male violence against black females is the most acceptable form of acting out. Since the racist sexist white world sees black women as angry bitches who must be kept in check, it turns away from relational violence in black life" (hooks 57). Hence, hooks suggest what Walker had already expressed through the characters, Grange and Brownfield.

Walker had essentially captured both the theoretical perspectives of the women victims and the male perpetrators in *Third Life*. Walker's depictions of Black life that included violence toward Black women from Black men was sometimes received negatively because her writing appeared at a time during the Black Power movement in the 1960s and 1970s, during which the artist was supposed to be representative of the Black voice and the artist was supposed to use his or her work to display the unity of the African American community. Although her writing depicted African American life, it did not do so in a way that reflected a positive image of Black families and her portrayal of Black men as domineering and violent was considered to be a factor that was against Black Power instead of for it.

In *Black Women Novelists and the Nationalist Aesthetic*, Walker argues that the men depicted in her novel *Third Life of Grange Copeland* were, in fact, real portrayals of men in the African American community. She notes that for many years, the Black men of the community have been taught that in patriarchal society that manhood is synonymous with controlling and dominating over others. Inherit in this teaching is the male attitude that assumes they have authority and should use violence and other means of control in order to maintain it. This type of patriarchal teaching is why Walker asserts that the depictions of domestic violence in her novels are realistic. Furthermore, in response to the Black Nationalism, Walker agreed that Black artists should portray and affirm a strong Black community, but she contended, "How can a family, a community, a race, a nation, a world, be healthy and strong, if one half dominates the other?" (107). I assert that unfortunately the concepts of masculinity that most men learn require that they suppress their emotions and perform in ways that are socially harmful to other members of the community, especially women. I further suggest that the assumption that the man has the right to dominate is often the main vehicle that leads to violence. In bell hooks' essay, "Understanding Patriarchy," she writes, "Clearly we cannot dismantle a system as long as we engage in collective denial about its impact on our lives. Patriarchy requires male dominance by any means necessary, hence it supports, promotes, and condones sexist violence" (2). Walker displays how the male characters in *Third Life* were maintaining this patriarchal culture by way of violence, but as I suggested earlier, she also demonstrates how the perpetuation of patriarchal violence stemmed from Black male subjugation to economic woes and racist oppression caused by White society.

As established through Grange and Brownfield's stories, as well as Walker's other male characters, Walker is clearly recognizing, though certainly not justifying, the Black man's own oppression. Though espousing her Womanist values by highlighting the sexual, economic, and physical oppression of Black women, Walker is also creating spaces for the reader to sympathize with Black men by demonstrating how they, too, suffer at the hands of white men. Nevertheless, through her characters, Walker demonstrates that masculinity pursuits, economic stress, and familial control are inextricably linked to intimate partner violence. It is not only the state of being economically disadvantaged that increases the risk of intimate partner violence but also the internalized implications of what such disadvantage implies about one's male identity (Peralta and Turtle 255).

Walker illustrates the disturbing images of violence that occur sometimes between Black men and women to gain domination, as when Grange threatens to kill his wife, Margaret; and Brownfield would later do the same to his wife Mem and their daughters. Walker writes, "Late Saturday night Grange would come home lurking drunk, threatening to kill his wife and Brownfield, stumbling shooting off his shot gun" (12). Later, she writes about Brownfield who beat "his once lovely wife now, regularly, because it made him feel, briefly good. Every Saturday night he beat her, trying to pin the blame of his failure on her by imprinting it on her face" (55). By telling these stories, Walker uses her work to expose the Black woman's oppression and bring communal and political awareness to this sensitive matter. She writes that liberation would require, "survival and wholeness of [the] entire people, male and female" (Walker xi). I believe that Walker knew that the philosophy of focusing on the Black man's liberation to liberating the entire community was not a proficient strategy because to do so would be forgetting about the other, very intricate parts of the Black community.

The next lesson of liberation from emasculation that Walker explores is that oppressing Black women does not garner the Black man's acceptance by white society. Often Black men who were seeking to advance themselves in society felt that if they conducted themselves the way white men did and treated others the way white men treated them, then they would gain the same status. This mindset came after Black men, who had attained freedom from enslavement wanted to assert themselves as the patriarchal powers that they had seen white men be in their lives prior to that time. Thus, by acting like white men did toward Black women, Black men believed that doing so would give them the power. However, the sad truth is that not only did it not give them the acceptance they desired in white society, but it also harmed their key supporters and comrades against injustice—Black women. In *We Real Cool*, hooks writes:

> Initially, when Brownfield imagines himself being married, he imagines himself as the benevolent patriarch. He simply wants to provide for and protect his family just as he has seen the white men of his society do with their families. Even as a young man Brownfield would daydream about what his life would be like when he got older. He imagined living in a beautiful mansion, having a chauffeur, a beloved wife, and two children. However, his dream was interrupted daily by the violent outburst of his father and the vile behavior of his mother. Although Brownfield hated his mother for interrupting his dreams, he blamed his father for making her the evil woman that she had become. Although, he initially blames his parents as the immediate interrupters of his dreams, he later realizes that their actions are a result of their own oppression.

Nevertheless, his determination to attain his manhood in white society causes him to treat his wife in the same negative way that his father does to Brownfield's mother. Initially when Brownfield meets Mem, she is educated, a beautiful "cherry-brown colored," shy, school teacher who reminds him of his mother. Their love for each other at the commencement of their marriage is strong, kind, and full of sincere dreams. Brownfield tells Mem, "We ain't always going to be stuck down here, honey. Don't you worry," and with a trusting heart she sat next to him, "holding her veil in her warm brown hands, and looking and smiling at him with gay believing eyes, full of love" (Walker 49). However, as reality set in and he was still working on the farm years later, with insurmountable debt and a growing family, Brownfield's hope faded slowly with his dreams. His dreams of a great life are doused by the need for survival.

Survival is one aspect of African American life that has made the concept of gender politics so controversial since slavery. Often African American families were unable to fulfill ideal roles of masculinity and femininity because survival needs within Black families mandated that both the mother and father work outside of the home. Brownfield realizes this at an early age. Walker writes, "His mother left him each morning with a hasty hug . . . . She worked all day pulling baits for ready money. Her legs were always clean when she left home and always coated with mud and slime from baits when she came back" (6). Just the basic necessities of food, shelter, and clothing automatically put Black men in a position of not realizing ideal manhood. Unlike the white men for whom they worked, the wives of Black men did not have the choice to tend solely to their own homes. Often their days included working very hard at the homes of their white employers with very little left of themselves to give to their own families. Brownfield realizes this reality is in stark contrast to the dreams he had for his own masculinity as a child. As a result, Brownfield takes on the same disdain for his family that his father, Grange, had for him and his mother. Brownfield realizes that his life is becoming a replica of his father's and he has lost hope for a better life. He realizes that under the hand of white oppression, he would never own his own land, never be able to give his wife all of the beautiful gifts that white men gave their wives and that his children would not have the same opportunities as white children. His solution to try to garner the same respect within his family that the white man feels is to control all aspects of his family's life. Walker writes,

> His crushed pride, his battered ego, made him drag Mem away from school—teaching. Her knowledge reflected badly on a husband who could barely read and write. It was his great ignorance that sent her into white homes as a domestic, his need to bring her down to his level . . . . He did not begrudge her the greater heart, but he could not forgive her the greater knowledge. It put her closer, in power to *them,* than he could ever be. (55)

In this passage, Brownfield turns against Mem because her education reminds him of everyone in his life, especially whites, who were superior to him. He feels lowly and degraded. Although Mem did not degrade him, he knew that everyone thought that she was "too good" for him and that began to weigh on him. As a Black man, he does not see her advancement as an asset, he sees it as an attack on his manhood. As with the previous chapter on *A Raisin in the Sun*, Brownfield, like Walter, did not see that if they worked together, as a united unit, they could get farther. All he saw was that he did not feel like a real man in or outside of his home.

Brownfield is so determined to have control over some aspect of his life that he does not realize that their greatest advancement as a family comes when they work in collaboration to follow Mem's lead after she temporarily decides to stand up to him for the good of their home. Under Brownfield's leadership, their family lived in a shack with rat holes on the land of the white man for whom they worked. Even though Brownfield hates their conditions and is insulted by the fact that Captain Davis has made a swap "as if he and his family were a string of workhorses" with another white landowner, Brownfield is still insistent that they will continue to live in these horrendous conditions simply because he said so" (79). Like the men of white society, Brownfield wants to have control over his life, but he fails to see that mistreating his family does not make him any more powerful. Although Mem is initially submissive, she eventually stands up to Brownfield. When Brownfield wakes up one morning, he arises to see her holding a shotgun aimed between his thighs. Mem says,

> I already told you . . . you ain't dragging me and these children through no more pigpens. . . . I want Daphne to be a young lady where there is other decent folks around, not out here in the sticks of some white man's property like in slavery times. I want Ornette to have a decent school. And little baby Ruth . . . I don't even want her to know there's such a thing as outdoor toilets . . . I ain't going to Mr. J.L.'s place . . . I have just about let you play man long enough to find out you ain't one. (Walker 84, 91)

Mem initially recognizes Brownfield's oppression in society and tries to make him feel like a man by following his leadership. However, when she notices that his pursuit of ideal hegemonic masculinity is destroying the family, she changes from the subordinate role to being more assertive. Her transition puts her in a kind of double role common to many working-class women that Patricia Hill Collins calls the "bitch" and the "mule." The "B***h" is pushy, loud, aggressive and rude, while the "mule" is passively stubborn and in need of supervision and prodding (124). These terms refer to stereotypical images of working-class women. Although Mem starts out as an intelligent woman of middle-class status, Brownfield turns her into a "mule" in his effort to feel like a man. However, when she is scorned by him, she turns into a more assertive character to get where she wants to be. Mem's transition is symbolic in multiple ways. Similar to the women during the time of the Black Power movement, often Black men thought that it was fine to not focus on the issues of women and were content to let Black women continue to be the *mules of the world*, to illustrate the hardships that Black women encounter. However, just as soon as they began to assert their rights and be more aggressive, then their image was viewed more antagonistically. The use of this negative image embodies how Black women are viewed when they get out of their allowable places.

    This transition also represents the concept that in order to gain success within the Black community the dreams of Black women and Black men must merge. As demonstrated with Mem and Brownfield, when they work antagonistically, the only result that ensues is doom. Sadly, Brownfield decides that the only way to prove that he is just as much of a man as his white counterparts to murder his own wife, the one person he could dominate. Brownfield's actions are unfortunately representative of the findings of Majors and Billson's study in that, violence often occurs in Black male-female relationships, "when a female criticizes her partner for his inability to support the family. . . . He takes this as further insult to an already jeopardized sense of manhood and self-esteem and may become violent to save face. Many black men feel that, even though they may not be able to control how society treats them, at the very least they should be able to control, 'their women' " (17). Black men were often using dominance and violence as an expression of their patriarchal power, which mirrored what they had seen in white society. When they noticed that they would not receive severe consequences for displaying violent behaviors toward their families, these behaviors became the normal expressions of manhood within the African American community. Expressing dominance through violence to affirm his manhood is exactly what leads to Brownfield's actions. Although he is sent to prison,

Brownfield knows that Mem's death, in the eyes of the dominant culture, is simply the death of a Black woman, nothing more and nothing less. He is not even remorseful because his only motive for killing her was to see if "he had any control over himself" in the oppressive white society in which he lives (165). Although he receives a temporary masculine feeling of affirmation from Mem's death, ultimately, Brownfield demonstrates the hopelessness that Black men of that period felt when attempting to control their own lives and have an impact on their families. As hooks says, "Black males socialized in patriarchal culture . . . make manhood synonymous with domination and the control of others, with the use of violence . . . . When . . . black males who acted violently, raping, killing, looting, it appeared that black males had finally arrived, their manhood was affirmed" (*hooks* 54). Brownfield's initial fulfillment is short-lived when he realizes that what he truly desires from the dominant society he will not receive. Eventually, he comes to grips with the idea that no matter where he goes or what he does—controlling his family or killing his wife—he is still not respected as a man in white society.

Furthermore, Walker clearly demonstrates that Black men's value cannot come from measuring themselves against ideal hegemonic masculinity because not only does it lead to their demise, but it also hurts the Black family. Even if Black men redefine their own masculinity and have a new sense of self, it is still important not to oppress Black women because doing so does not change their status outside of the community, especially with concerning their position in the dominant culture. Patricia Hill Collins supports this notion when she states, "The use of physical force, aggression, and violence as tools of subordination creates problems within the African American community in three areas. Specifically, . . . violence against women, . . . male aggression and violence that is damaging to everyone . . . the source lies in ideas about Black masculinity that in turn is situated within a larger context of hegemonic masculinity" (210). For centuries, Black men have been portrayed as angry and violent, which only reinforces the long-held stereotypes that cultivate fear as a marker of Black masculinity. Although some may contend that African American women authors such as Walker, and the others mentioned in this study, are only perpetuating this image of Black men, I argue that their depictions are meant to produce a completely different outcome. When white society depicts the Black men as angry and violent, they do so to justify their oppression. However, when Black women authors like Walker depict Black men as angry and violent, they do so as an expression of a negative reality that exists in the African American community but also as one that has the potential to positively change if African American men are willing to do so. Thus, if Black men continue to use ideal masculinity as the sole standard by which they measure themselves, they will continue to destroy their own community.

Finally, I suggest Walker is displaying that despite the reasons for what lead to a negative relationship with Black women or the outside forces that created it, Black men must atone for their sins against Black women. The definition of atone that I am using implies that Black men must make amends by doing what is right to make up for what they did wrong. Walker's male characters illustrate that Black men's atonement shall come by changing their outlook on ideal masculinity; changing their behavior and attitude toward Black women; and changing themselves toward a more progressive ideology of Black manhood. Change is seen most fully in Grange's character who takes on the role of nurturer, teacher, and care-giver to his granddaughter, Ruth, after the death of her mother, at the hands of his son. Grange treats Ruth with the honor and respect that he had never given to another woman in his entire life. He says to Ruth, "You're special to me because you're a part of me; a part of me I didn't used to want" (196). This is an indication of Grange's change because he acknowledges that initially there was a portion of his life that he was not willing to be responsible for and care for—his family. He was so concerned with fulfilling his original ideals of manhood that he did not realize until later that even if his economic status and the oppression of white society did not allow them to take care of them as he desired, he could still be a man through his loyalty and care for them. When he finally recognizes his new concept of manhood, Grange finds his true fulfillment as a man when he returns home and determines to make amends with the one person in his family who is still intact—Ruth. Walker writes, "The older Grange got the more serene and flatly sure of his mission he became. His one duty in the world was to prepare Ruth for some great and herculean task" (198). Being a better man became Grange's personal charge. Grange also repeatedly tells Ruth of the Hebrews children's exodus because he wants her to escape the conditions that have emasculated him for so many years. He saved up more than $900 for Ruth so that she would be able to get an education and not have to become the victim of a man's mistreatment just to survive. Although Grange knew that he could not correct what had happened to Ruth's mother, he was determined to make sure that Ruth experienced a different outcome. One day as he is confronting his unchanged son and trying to protect Ruth, Grange captures the complexities of Black masculinity when he says,

> I don't love but one somebody, black or white . . . An' what I'm talking about ain't love but being a man! . . . the crackers could make me run away from my wife, but where was the man in me that let me sneak off, never telling her I forgave her, never telling her how wrong I was myself . . . . And the white folks could have forced me to believe f--king a hundred strumpets was a sign of my manhood . . . but where was the man in me that let me take Josie here for such a cheap and low-down ride, when I didn't never care whether she lived or died . . . the white folks could have forced him to live in shacks; they might have even forced him to beat his wife and children like they was dogs, so he could keep on feeling something less than shit. But where was the man in him that let Brownfield kill his wife? . . . And if a cracker did cause him to kill his wife, Brownfield should have turned the gun on himself, for he wasn't no man. He let the cracker hold the gun because he was too weak to distinguish the cracker's will from his! The same was true of me. We both of us jumped our responsibility, and without facing up to at least some of his wrong a man loses his muscle. . . . If I had my life to live over . . . your ma and me would maybe have starved to death in some cracker's gutter, but she would have died with me holding her hand! For that much I could have done—and I believe she would have seen the man in me. (8)

Grange's monologue on manhood is by far the most powerful scene in the novel that captures what Walker is illustrating about Black masculinity and the lessons that would become the forerunner for masculinity studies. Grange recognizes that the violence and evil that he and his son enacted upon their families was unnecessary and cruel. Grange also realizes that he was wrong for degrading and turning his back on his wife because her liberation coupled with them working together is a part of both of their liberation. And finally, he realizes, just as he demonstrates with his granddaughter Ruth that he must atone for the evil acts that he has done to Black women in his past by endeavoring to change and do better in the future. I suggest that this is Walker's lesson to all Black men. Black men cannot go back and undo the mistreatment of Black women and children they have perpetuated in the past, but, yes, they can make every effort to make sure that one of the traits of Black manhood becomes a renewed attitude and dedication to making life better for those that have been previously damaged.

Readers can both sympathize with Grange and Brownfield as well as hold them accountable for their actions. In *Third Life of Grange Copeland*, Walker does display a love-hate relationship with Grange and Brownfield. I believe that this is why she presents the dichotomous ending for these two characters whose stories present them as if they are almost the same man. I suggest that Walker illustrates their contrasts as a part of Black men's liberation. Walker is demonstrating that advancement requires change. Brownfield does not change and as a result he lives and dies miserably, still trying to attain his manhood. However, Grange does change, and he gains fulfillment as a man in his third life because he has economic freedom by owning his own farm and land, he lives in isolation so that he does not have to be subjected to the standards of white society, and he finds a sense of purpose in his relationship with Ruth. He, in turn, dies a more honorable death than Brownfield because Grange dies protecting his newly found manhood.

Writing what she knew of the world and using her writing as a form of activism is exactly what Alice Walker did despite the many critics that she faced for her content. Walker knew that if African Americans were going to fight the oppression in mainstream society, then they must first acknowledge and oppose the oppression within the community. Fighting the oppression of Black women, at the hands of Black men is exactly what Walker does in her novels, especially in *The Third Life of Grange Copeland*. It is through these male characters that Walker presents the readers with solutions for male emancipation and female liberation.

WORKS CITED

Bates, Gerri. *Alice Walker: A Critical Companion.* Westport: Greenwood, 2005.

Chandler, Kimberly. "How to Become a 'Black Man': Exploring African American Masculinities and the Performance of Gender." Jackson and Hopson, 2014, 55–88.

Collins, Patricia Hill. *From Black Power to Hip Hop: Racism, Nationalism, and Feminism.* Philadelphia: Temple University Press, 2006.

Dubey, Madhu. *Black Women Novelists and the Nationalist Aesthetic.* Bloomington: Indiana University Press, 1994.

Gardiner, Judith Kegan. *Masculinity Studies & Feminist Theory: New Directions.* New York: Columbia University Press, 2002.

Griffin, Rachel. "Bearing Witness and Paying Mind: (Re) Defining the Meanings of Black Male Success." In *Masculinity in the Black Imagination: Politics of*

Communicating Race and Manhood, edited by Ronald Jackson and Mark Hopson, 167–186. New York: Peter Lang, 2011.

Henry, Anthony Ronda C. *Searching for the New Black Man: Black Masculinity and Women's Bodies*. Jackson: University of Mississippi Press, 2013.

hooks, bell. "Understanding Patriarchy." *The Will to Change: Men, Masculinity, and Love*. New York: Atria, 2004, 17–35.

———. *We Real Cool: Black Men and Masculinity*. New York: Routledge, 2004.

Majors, Richard, and Janet Mancini Billson. *Cool Pose: The Dilemmas of Black Manhood in America*. New York: Lexington, 1992.

Majors, Richard, and Janet Mancini Billson. *Cool Pose the Dilemmas of Black Manhood in America*. New York: Simon & Schuster, 1993.

Mutua, Athena D. *Progressive Black Masculinities*. New York: Routledge, 2006.

Walker, Alice. *In Search of Our Mothers' Gardens: Womanist Prose*. San Diego: Harcourt Brace Jovanovich, 1983.

———. *The Third Life of Grange Copeland*. New York: Harcourt, Brace, Jovanovich, 1970.

Chapter 6

Reconnections to Gendered Black Identities in Alice Walker's *The World Will Follow Joy*

Linda Mustafa

Alice Walker is best known for the book that won her the Pulitzer prize, *The Color Purple*,[1] and her formulation of womanist ideology. *In Search of Our Mothers' Gardens: Womanist Prose*,[2] Walker looked back into African American history and describes a womanist/womanism as: "A black feminist or feminist of colour. From the Black folk expression of mothers to children, 'you acting womanish,' i.e., like a woman. Usually referring to outrageous, audacious, courageous or willful behaviour . . . . Womanist is to feminist as purple is to lavender." With Walker's ideologist of a different kind of feminism, she opens the door for further ideological thought such as James Hal Cones, Jacquelyn Grant and Delores Williams' theological womanism.[3]

However, Walker is less known for writing poetry. Some of her collection of poems include *Once* (1968),[4] *Revolutionary Petunias and Other Poems* (1973),[5] *Good Night Willy Lee, I'll See You in the Morning* (1984),[6] and *Horses Make a Landscape Look More Beautiful* (1984),[7] *The World Will Follow Joy* (2013),[8] and others. While some see her poems as deeply rooted in oral tradition of African heritage, others explain her poems as conversational poems that do not conform to the form, style, and language of a poem. Yet, her poems are highly turgid with emotions and words that provoke intense empathy. According to Urquiaga and Cruz, Walker mostly writes her poems with the womanist ideology as the backdrop of telling her audience about the African heritage, which African Americans inherited. They assert that she is expressive when it comes to racist ideologies and believes that all skin colors are beautiful.[9]

It is surprising to note that despite Walker's popularity, very few of her poems have been critically analyzed. This is also reiterated by Urquiaga and Cruz when they contend that "...however in terms of it has been difficult for us [Cruz & Urquiaga] to find information."[10] This chapter seeks to add more knowledge to understanding and teaching of Walker's poetry; especially some of the poems contained in her book entitled *The World Will Follow Joy*. From the title of the book, it is likely that Walker seeks to add joy to her readers' experiences. To attain peace, happiness, and total contentment seems likely to be the message that Walker tries to pass on to her subjects; hence, this work analyzes the psychological implications of Black women reconnecting to their heritage/lineage to discover themselves, their identities, and their peace in a world that is riddled with discrimination of all sorts.

THEORETICAL FRAMEWORK

Stephen Frosh[11] in his introduction asserts:

> In psychoanalysis, it is the subjectivity of the individual which is the centre of concern, a subjectivity given not just by what can be easily expressed as a consciously available "1," but also by obscure and contradictory segments of a hidden self.[12]

An individual can develop a good psyche by long years of imbibing the environmental and social constructs of his or her community. According to Frosh, social factors contribute immensely to the build-up of the consciousness of a child who grows up into an adult. It is therefore paramount, according to Frosh, that

> the self can be thought of as a psychological structure that contains within it the various processes of mental life; it is implicit in this idea that there is something organised, stable and central about the self, that selfhood comprises a core element of each individual's personality and subjective existence.[13]

But Miller[14] asserts that "creating a self is like creating a work of art: it may not be worked on as consciously, although sometimes it is, but just as art to some degree involves taking the bits and pieces of the world and fitting them together to say something, so does the self."[15] The self, then, is an affirmation of what is humanly worthy and creative. Hence, this creative sense can evolve into an illusion used to deny an unbearable reality, which may invariably cause identity crisis. Erik Erickson equally agrees to identity formation being motivated by fragmentation. According to him, "Identity formation usually emanates from deep troubling thoughts and questions such as 'Who am I? What do I believe in? What will I live for?'"[16]

In describing the identity of African Americans, Du Bois insists that an African American identity is formed in the response of the "other gaze," which to him what he called "double consciousness."[17] Similarly, Fanon (1967)[18] asserts that Black identity is fashioned out of the oppressive sociopolitical structure of colonial culture as indicated in his statement here presented:

> The effective disalienation of the black man entails an immediate recognition of social and economic realities. If there is an inferiority complex, it is the outcome of a double process:—primarily, economic;—subsequently, the internalization—or, better, the epidermalization—of this inferiority.[19]

Hence, by making explicit the cultural construction of racial subjectivity, Fanon de-essentializes both race and psychoanalytic models of subject formation; psychoanalysis becomes a tool with which to evaluate relations of power and cultural hegemony.[20] Bergner[21] expresses that in Fanon's *Black Skin, White Masks*, women are subjects almost entirely in terms of their sexual relationships with men hence their feminine self is undermined.

Myles in her book entitled *Female Subjectivity in African American Women's Narratives of Enslavement* insists that "the figurative and literal rape of black women's identities, through the racialized, sexualized, and politicized stereotypes, is a result of the continual devaluation of black women and hegemonic oppressive practices."[22] The devaluation of Black women unfortunately comes from the past when white men tried to remove the "woman" from Black womanhood in order to make her a slave and an object or what is called commodification. However, the commodification of Black women did not stop after the abolition of slavery, instead it continued affecting their identities and ideologies.[23] Nikki Giovanni explains these connections among self, change, and self-empowerment: "We got to live in the real world. If we don't' like the world we're living in, change it. And if we can't change it, we change ourself. We can do something."[24] When Black women persist in defining themselves, the "act of insisting on black female self-definition [will] validate black women's power as human subjects" and authority as transformed African American women.[25]

Myles went on to insist on the fact that to recognize that visibility and voice constitutes the essence of selfhood, African American women, figuratively and literally, have searched for new "spaces" to articulate their existence away from female oppression and exploitation[26] because, Black women are reminded every day about their position, sex, race, and status in hegemonic society they are more engage in trying to assert their identities: hence, they go through extra efforts to reconnect their identity with a selfhood that is not demeaning. Lorde (1984) concurs with this and states thus:

"The oppressors maintain their position and evade responsibility for their own actions. There is a constant drain of energy which might be better used in redefining ourselves and devising realistic scenarios for altering the present and constructing the future."[27]

In conclusion, Patricia Williams (1991)[28] contends that hegemonic societies are actually a factor to African Americans distancing themselves from each other because of the fact that they are continually oppressed by the "other" [i.e., the other race, white]. Women are especially more predisposed to remaining in oppressive space or places and thus are unable to recognize their conditions in order to effect change. It is therefore necessary to state that isolating one's self from locating a definite identity is not utopian and can damage the consciousness of an oppressed woman; however, Black women can find strength when they identify with like women and share their trauma.[29] This chapter agrees with women moving from their constrained space to assert their identities in a hegemonic space such that they transformed from being subsumed in male identities to finding their identities without being subject to race, sex, gender, class, or status. It is therefore not out of place to express that in order for African American women to find their place and identities, they must rediscover their [self] locations outside patriarchal or Eurocentric locations as Chancy states in the following lines:

> [Safe space] functions as the language with which to repair the psychic damage of geographic and cultural alienation, provides the base by which to establish self-definition, the net by which to catch and gather Black women as they struggle to recuperate or recognize their ancestral, African heritage in their day-to-day life, and the bridge over which to cross, after having accomplished all of the above, on the long walk home. (22)[30]

From Chancy's opinion, African American women can locate and reconnect lost identities if they consciously move from points of oppressive intimidations to definite spaces that expressively define their psychological states as stable and new subjects.

RACE, GENDER, AND SEX AND THE RIGHTS OF WOMEN AS ANTECEDENTS OF LOCATING BLACK FEMALE IDENTITIES IN *THE WORLD WILL FOLLOW JOY*

In her foreword of *The World Will Follow Joy*, Alice Walker envisioned a world where "violence in all its hideous forms will cease very soon to appeal to even the most insulated of human beings."[31] She went on to shockingly reveal how women (mothers) and children are at the receiving end of bloody wars, whereby innocent lives are horribly terminated with the use of "saws, jackhammers, drills and bombs."[32] Barbara Christian notes that virtually all of Walker's works reverberates Walker's intention to present the Black woman as a creator and her attempt to be whole (i.e., have a definite identity/personality) in her society.[33] With this view as a backdrop, this chapter agrees with the Walker's vision of Black woman's quest to fashion out a definite self that is far from stereotypical conceptions of sex, race, status, and gender positions of the Black woman.

The poem "Democratic Womanism" comes from Walker's postulation of Womanism in her book *In Search of Our Mothers' Gardens: Womanist Prose* in which she discusses the woman of color, societal issues that affect a woman of color in a society, other rights that a woman should have as well as calling to attention, feminist values that exclude men and children. Walker in this poem reignites a new way of reconnecting feminine exploration of the woman such that she is not isolated from communal activities as well as ensuring that she develops a confident self. This is observed in the following lines:

Democratic Womanism.
I want to vote and work for a way of life
that honors the feminine;
a way that acknowledges
the theft of the wisdom
female and dark Mother leadership
might have provided our spaceship
all along.[34]

As Myles[35] envisioned that women are in a constant fight to locate their "space" away from oppressive ideologies, Walker in this poem also sees a new way of voting in "dark Mother leadership" and wisdom that can make a way for a new life for all women. Walker goes on to state that in locating identities unique to women of color, women must ensure that they: "want something else"; / "a different system entirely/one not seen on this earth" / "for thousands of years"/. These lines narrate the poet's deep feelings of wanting to see women establishing psyches that positively affects the world in such ways that the evils of the world will be reduced or entirely be eliminated. Walker's vision to see women rise above oppression and playing positive parts in their communities may have been the reason why she believes that a change should be the goal of every woman from "a talking head kind of gal" /happy to be mixing it up with the baddest boys/ to the situation "Where women rise/ to take their place/ en masse/ at the helm/ of earth's frail failing ship."[36]

The rather long poem eulogizes women who have alleviated the earth from one form of political, environmental, social and educational decadence. Such women include "Vandana Shiva, Aung San Suu Kyi, Wangari Maathai, Harriet Tubman, Yoko Ono, Frida Kahlo, Angela Davis, Celia Sanchez & Barbara Lee:"/ With new ones always rising.[37] But she also notes that the man is still ever present in the lives of their women and so cannot be disconnected from their activities to "mother the earth" as can be deciphered in these lines:

Democratic Womanism.
Notice how this word has "man" right in the
middle of it?
That's one reason I like it. He is there, front and
centre. But he is surrounded.[38]

The man is "surrounded" by all kinds of women who could teach him the good ways of life. From his mother, sisters, grandmothers, aunts, wife, nieces, and female cousins, a man can be cultured in such a way that his life is filled with a sense of responsibility to his family and the earth as well. An upbringing of responsibility to his community ensures that the men in the midst of women will instead sustain a nurturing ambience that allows for a healthy interaction of all humans, animals, and plant, hence his direct involvement with constituting a harmonious earthly living for all living things.

In the poem entitled "Turning Madness into Flowers #1," there is the feeling of loneliness, loss, and uncertainty and a curious inquest to locate the addressee of the poem. Walker uses iconic metaphors such as oil and ocean floor, to bring to the fore how people's identities can be distorted as a result of trauma. The trauma of a divided self is initiated by hurtful relationships with loved ones. She depicts metaphors of oil and ocean floor as relational words that express extreme trauma in an individual's lifetime especially when a person is embroiled in broken relationships such that the psychological state of the sufferer could lead to an unstable mind:

If my sorrow were deeper
I'd be, along with you, under
the ocean's floor;
but today I" learn that the oil
that pools beneath the ocean floor
is essence
residue
remains
of all our
relations. . .[39]

The persona is in a state of uncertainty and she is overwhelmed by her loss. Deep in sorrow, she endures a battle to locate her true self having lost her identity as a result of embittered love relationship.

However, in order to reconnect to her identity, the persona must connect to her ancestral past to be whole again. But this can only be done through a psychological connection because her loved ones are mostly the dead as can be read here:

our ancestors who have died and turned to oil
without our witness
eons ago.
We've always belonged to them.[40]

Walker addresses the struggle and resistance of Black Americans to overcome the oppressive ideals of white stereotypical thoughts. Like Fanon proposes, self-images are built on the observations of unstable racial identity, which mostly depends on masquerade, projection, and representation.[41] Walker's "Turning Madness into Flowers" illustrates the painful resistance Blacks endured while defining themselves. Their "unstable racial identity" activates a projection of self-image unto white standard of beauty, living and other parameters that denotes power: hence, a typical Black man/woman who has identity crises may be so engrossed in a psychological warfare to locate himself or herself, because he or she is juxtaposed between choosing white ideals over his or her Black heritage and identity. This kind of condition can be deciphered from these lines here stated:

We've always belonged to them.
speaking for you, hanging, weeping, over the
water's edge
as well as for myself.
it is our grief
heavy, relentless,
trudging
us, however resistant,[42]

The poem is devoid of rhyme, rhythm, and other apt poetic devices, but Walker's use of repetitions, single- or double-word lines brings out the significance of Black personae's urgent need to realign their psyches with a self that does not elicit a feeling of double consciousness. The poems ending with the words "to the decaying and rotten"/ "bottom of things"/ "our grief bringing" / " us home" heightens vividly the ruptured identities of Black Americans following slavery, segregation, and racism.

Another poem that touches the sensitivity of disjointed and misplaced gendered identities is "Democratic Motherism," which can be read as a sequel to "Democratic Womanism." In this poem, Walker speaks with a tensed and intimidating tone instructing the world on the need of mothering an earth, which is more engrossed in fighting wars at the expense of helpless and weak mothers and children:

In conversing about what
it will take to reclaim our planet we agreed
that what earth needs more than anything
is mothering. earth, Mother earth, needs
mothers, regardless of gender—though we all
recognize who most mothers have been, and
are.[43]

From the aforementioned lines, Walker is in a conversation with someone who also agrees with the earth needing mothers. The poem is also written without elements of rhyme, rhythm, and other literary devices but the tone talks about a persona who wants to tell the world of the importance of mothering. It is thus no surprise that Walker explains mothering in the poem, eliciting readers to have an idea of what mothering is as she defines in the following: "Mothering is an instinct, yes but it is also a practice."[44]

However, in the following lines, readers can deduce that mothering is not just for women. Men can also be mothers if they could channel all their resources toward taking care of the world: "It can be learned."/ "For women it has been an eons-long experience: the art and necessity of taking care of all, of everything, of mothering."[45] Hence, Walker summit that in a world of violence, chaos, enmity, anger, hatred, and other vices, the dire need of the world is not a government that sanctions killings and disruptions but one that ensures "Democratic Motherism."[46] According to Maria Stewart,[47] women should use their special roles as mothers to forge powerful mechanisms of political action. This is the same stance Walter depicts in the poem. She calls for mothers to take a stand to effect a change that would put an end to the suffering of children and women, here illustrated:

In any case, we will continue to endure,
and detest, the systems currently in place, in
which the condition of countless starving,
tortured, enslaved and murdered children
is seen as acceptable, unless we forthrightly
begin to envision, and work for, something
better: some way for humans to exist and

thrive, without suffering the despair of every
second of every day knowing our present
predicament's greatest cause is humanity's
fear of sharing equally with others, and its
rapidly growing, partly because of this fear,
self-hatred.[48]

The imagery of starving children, killings and enslavement, enables a feeling of fear, shock surprise, and anger that may influence a reader's sympathy (especially women) to call for women emancipation as envisioned by Walker. However, Walker tapers down the harsh call by suffusing her poem with a reminder that humans are supposed to live in equality and dissuade sufferings of every kind. To Walker, humanity's existence so far stems from past knowledge or revolutions that were done by "ancestors" who have walked and worked the earth such that their observations of the earth's horrors elicits "a new world political party."[49] It is thus not enough for mothers to fold their arms and watch as evil is being perpetrated; they should also "defend yourself [themselves]" and "unite all segments of the globe."[50]

In describing the functions of democratic mothers, Walker turns to the environment as a plausible partner in ensuring a peaceful and fruit bearing earth that is good enough for mothers and children to thrive. These lines below bring to the fore how the earth fights back to keep her sanity despite all kinds of natural and man-made catastrophes:

the earth fights back in the effort to reclaim
her freedom and integrity from the tyranny
imposed on her by humanity. Where dams
have burst, where forest fires have raged,
where hillsides have crumbled. Where rivers
have run wild. I am saying, as I believe, that
we must begin again to have conversation
with our planet.[51]

The earth, according to Walker, suffers just like a mother suffers. She is ravaged by both man and natural disasters; the earth is left to face her problems solely in isolation, because all the big politicians and government personnel don't care about her nor do they care about the woman/mother/girl child. This neglect has caused the earth to be disconnected from her position as the only place that can take care of human life so also is the Mother. The mother, too, is disconnected from herself, her dreams/desires, and herself in her children. There is, therefore, only one way to go back to a mother earth that responds to human touch and that is to have a conversation with the planet.[52]

Walker's activism in environmentalist discourse takes her further to enforcing a much deeper love for the environment. Just like a mother's love for her baby, Walker's love for the earth is an engaging relationship, whereby her intense love to free the earth from human destructions is transferred unto the love poems she writes to celebrate mother earth. According to Walker's Democratic Motherism, the earth is living and should be properly nurtured or else it dies silently and lonely death: "We were looking/ into a landscape that, though beautiful/ in the kodak-moment sense, was lifeless/ and uninspiring."[53] But when the earth is taken care of, more appreciated and valued, the earth's potentials can be easily harness such that the leaves of a tree may grow greener and radiantly, flowers may blossom more producing more scent for both humans and animal appreciation and even hold the earths surfaces more firmly through the planting of more trees:

As she sang in Hawaiian (a language
outlawed by U.S. colonial rule for decades; her
aunt had created a Hawaiian dictionary in an
effort to preserve the language) it seemed to
me the trees and other vegetation responded
by standing taller, fluffing themselves up. The
flowers among them appeared to fling their
scent. I became vividly aware of everything's
aliveness.[54]

From the preceding lines, the earth seems to bounce back after a passionate love shown to her by humans. It is therefore apt to say that the earth just like mothers and children need to be pampered with a definite and continuous love. Walker ends her poem by referring to the importance of every earthly being appreciating the earth: *"This token of gratitude, awareness, affection,"/ "might be our party's first step* (emphasis mine)."[55] This is a direct metaphor that implores everyone to appreciate mothers and their effort toward sustaining a peaceful earth for everyone. Walker's use of italics in writing the last two lines of her poems indicates her enthusiasm toward a reconnection to the earth with mothers' who are willing to channel their love toward bringing about a stop to wars, violence, killings, and poverty that plagues many countries.

Walker sees her patriotism to her nation, Black community and the African Diaspora, culture and love of women of all colors being replicated in the songs of Miriam Makeba, the South African who sang freedom songs that drew the world's attention to the struggles of her people during Apartheid Era. The poem "Don't be like those who ask for everything," explicitly narrates Walker's identification and reconnection to a sister who endured great lengths of standing just so she can tell the world about the traumas that bedevils her people. The following lines describe Walker's acknowledgment of Miriam's pain while singing in a crowded room:

Be like those who can see that my feet ache
from across a crowded room
that a foot rub
if i'm agreeable
never mind the staring
is the best way to smile
& say hello
to me.[56]

The pains it took for Miriam Makeba to resist White supremacy leadership ensured a connection between the two even though they were from different continents; different backgrounds and different cultures. The short poem berates those who are indifferent to the traumas Black women go through in order for them to heard/recognized. According to Hopkins (1988),[57] Black women can find strength when they identify with women who experience and share similar trauma in the course of their lives. As an activist; she sees the sacrifice of Makeba, which in this case is singing freedom songs at the cost of her life, as a challenge to other women who seek the luxury of life at the expense of their freedom. Walker therefore sternly admonishes the frivolities women indulge in by stating thus:

Don't be like those who ask for everything:
praise, a blurb, a free ride in my rented
limousine. They ask for everything but never
offer
anything in return.[58]

This bond of Black women who are raised in different cultural background displays "otherness," a situation whereby a person relates better with another because of shared similar problematic experiences.

In America, Walker battles the harsh laws of racism, segregation, and discrimination against Black women. Though they took different steps in their fight against discrimination against Blacks, Makeba and Walker are connected and become one in the songs and poems they sing and write against humiliation of the Black race hence the bond they have established through the songs they sing and the poems they write, gives both personalities the same identity; they find their true selves from the trauma they sing and write about.

The poem "Before I Leave the Stage" illustrates an identity crisis that finally gets to be resolved after the persona finally overcome fragmentation of self. The beginning of the poem indicates a persona anxious about what will be her fate by the time she leaves the stage; hence, she consults her subconscious self and she finds that she had to sing her pains away in order for her to achieve a confident state of mind as is indicated in these lines:

Before I leave the stage
I will sing the only song
I was meant truly to sing.
it is the song
of I AM.
yes: I am Me
&
you.
We Are.[59]

Like Frosh has declared, the self, then, is an affirmation of what is humanly worthy and creative. Hence, this creative sense can evolve into an illusion used to deny an unbearable reality, which may invariably cause identity crisis. Walker uses her traumatic experience and history to stabilize a lost self. She asserts that "I am me" to show that she has finally come to terms with who she is despite being "here nor there."[60] Also in this poem, Walker decides to love every Black man despite their sufferings and identity crisis indicating that she is proud of the Black man who is undaunting in trying to attain a true self/true identity in a world that classify the Black man as a second class citizen. So when Walker says; "I love Us with every drop"/ "of our blood"/ "-undaunted flags of being—/ "neither her nor there"[61] she reiterates a deep understanding of what it takes for an African American person to trace his identity back to his African roots. Even though he may be fragmented, Walker believes that an average African American person continues to resist an identity bestowed to him through the traumas of slavery, racism, and discrimination. Hence, an average African American becomes a true being by deciding to reconnect to his or her true self no matter the chaotic circumstances he or she may be living.

CONCLUSION

The analyses of the poems contained in walker's work brings to the fore Walker's zeal to believe in a world that discourages all forms of discrimination relating to skin color, sex, gender, age, or status. Walker's poems analyzed in this chapter narrate the different struggles the personae go through in order to overcome fragmented identities. For some like Miriam Makeba, standing for hours to sing of the struggles of her people over apartheid; segregation of Africans in their own father's land; discrimination against Black men and women; and the killing of innocent Africans was a sacrifice she had to make in order to bring the world's attention to the oppressive ideals instituted against the Black man by the white supremacist government of South Africa. As an activist herself, Walker has been in the forefront of advocating the rights of women to take up important positions in governments so as to help stop the violence against women and children; this is reflected in her poem "Democratic womanism." The plundering of the earth is only equal to the rape of a woman, which takes readers' imagination to the constant defilement of the earth as a result of environmental pollution and climate change, which are the direct manifestations of human disrespect of nature or mother earth.

Even though her themes are diverse, her poems are riddled with motifs of identity. Whether it is in relation to the environment, stereotypical, or oppressive ideologies, Walker's concern is to bring man, his philosophies, and the earth to a harmonious living. Therefore, with a careful psychoanalytic study of African American women's reconnection to their identity, most of the problems the earth is enshrouded in today would be history. Thus, this paper contends that the message Walker is determined to pass along is that every individual no matter who they are, where they may be or what linage/heritage they emanate from, must see to reconnecting back to the earth, their linage or culture and positively impact ideologies that will see to making the earth a better place for all humans to live in and as such dissuade the fragmentation of self.

NOTES

1. Alice, Walker, *The Color Purple* (Orlando: Harcourt.1982).
2. Alice, Walker. *In Search of My Mothers' Garden* (Orlando: Harcourt. 1983), p. 232.
3. Urquiaga, H. Yeni & Cruz, Garriga Y. "Blackwomen through Alice Walker's poetry (Characterisation of the valuating subjects of her poems)." *ELUA, 29* (2015): 174.
4. Alice, Walker. *Once* (1968).
5. Alice, Walker. *Revolutionary Petunians and other Poems* (1973).
6. Alice, Walker. *Goodnight Willi Lee, I'll See You in the Morning* (1984).
7. Alice, Walker. *Horses Make a Landscape Look More Beautiful* (1984).
8. Alice, Walker. *The World Will Follow Joy* (2013).
9. Urquiaga & Cruz: 183.
10. Urquiaga & Cruz: 172.

11. Frosh, Stephen. *Identity Crisis: Modernity, Psychoanalysis and the Self* (New York: Palgrave Macmillan, 1991).
12. Frosh: 2.
13. Frosh: 3
14. Miller, D. *Material Culture and Mass Consumption* (Oxford: Basil Blackwell, 1987).
15. Frosh: 13.
16. Gregg, S. Gray. *Culture and Identity in Muslim Society* (New York: Oxford University Press, 2007).
17. Bergner, Gwen. *Taboo Subjects: Race, Sex and Psychoanalysis* (Minneapolis: University of Minnesota Press, 2005), p. xiii.
18. Fanon, Frantz. *Black Skin, White Masks* (New York: Grove Press, 1967).
19. Fanon: 10–11.
20. Bergner: 4.
21. Bergner: 3.
22. Myles, Lynette D. *Female Subjectivity in African American Women's Narratives of Enslavement* (New York: Palgrave Macmillan, 2009), p. 24.
23. Myles: 25
24. Collins, Patricia Hill. *Black Feminist Thought: Knowledge, Consciousness, and The Politics of Empowerment* (New York: Routledge, 2000), p. 117.
25. Collins: 114.
26. Myles: 24.
27. Lorde, Audre. *Sister Outsider: Essays and Speeches by Audre Lorde* (Freedom, CA: Crossing Press, 1984), p. 115.
28. Williams, Patricia J. *The Alchemy of Race and Rights: Diary of a Law Professor* (New York: Harvard University Press, 1991).
29. Hopkins, Pauline E. *Contending Forces: An Illustrative Romance of Negro Life North and South.* 1900 (New York: Oxford University Press, 1988), p. 117.
30. Chancy, Myriam J. A. *Searching for Safe Spaces: Afro-Caribbean Women Writers in Exile* (Philadelphia: Temple University Press, 1997), 22.
31. Walker, Alice. *The World Will Follow Joy* (New York: The New Press, 2013), p. xiii.
32. Walker: xiii.
33. Christian, Barbara. "The Black Woman Artist as Wayward," in *Black Women Writers*, edited by Evans, Mari (New York: Anchor Press), p. 457.
34. Walker: 173.
35. Myles: 24.
36. Walker: 174.
37. Walker: 176.
38. Walker: 173.
39. Walker: 19.
40. Walker: 19.
41. Bhabha, Homi. "Remembering Fanon: Self, Psyche, and Colonial Condition," in *Remaking History*, edited by Barbara Krugel. & Phil Mariani (Seattle: Bay Press, 1989), p. 135.

42. Walker: 19.
43. Walker: 180.
44. Walker: 180.
45. Walker: 180.
46. Walker: 180.
47. Collins, Patricia Hill. *Black Feminist Thought: Knowledge, Consciousness, and The Politics of Empowerment* (New York: Routledge, 2000), p. 2.
48. Walker: 180–181.
49. Walker: 181.
50. Walker: 181–182.
51. Walker: 182.
52. Walker: 182.
53. Walker: 182.
54. Walker: 183.
55. Walker: 183.
56. Walker: 16.
57. Hopkins: 117.
58. Walker: 16.
59. Walker: 22.
60. Walker: 22.
61. Walker: 22.

BIBLIOGRAPHY

Bergner, Gwen. *Taboo subjects: Race, sex and psychoanalysis.* Minneapolis: University of Minnesota Press, 2005. http://www.upress.umn.edu.

Bhabha, Homi. "Remembering Fanon: Self, psyche, and colonial condition," *Remaking History*, edited by Barbara, Krugel. and Phil, Mariani. Seattle: Bay Press, 1989.

Chancy, Myriam J. A. *Searching for Safe Spaces: Afro-Caribbean Women Writers in Exile.* Philadelphia: Temple University Press, 1997.

Collins, Patricia Hill. *Black Feminist Thought: Knowledge, Consciousness, and the Politics of Empowerment.* New York: Routledge, 2000.

Fanon, Frantz. *Black Skin, White Masks.* New York: Grove Press, 1967.

Frosh, Stephen. *Identity Crisis: Modernity, Psychoanalysis and the Self.* New York: Palgrave Macmillan, 1991.

Gregg, S. Gray. *Culture and Identity in Muslim Society.* New York: Oxford University Press, 2007.

Hopkins, Pauline E. *Contending Forces: An Illustrative Romance of Negro Life North and South.* 1900. New York: Oxford University Press, 1988.

Lorde, Audre. *Sister Outsider: Essays and Speeches by Audre Lorde.* Freedom, CA: Crossing Press, 1984.

Miller, D. *Material Culture and Mass Consumption.* Oxford: Basil Blackwell, 1987.

Myles, Lynette D. *Female Subjectivity in African American Women's Narratives of Enslavement*. New York: Palgrave Macmillan, 2009.

Urquiaga, H. Yeni & Cruz, Garriga Y. "Blackwomen Through Alice Walker's Poetry (Characterisation of the Valuating Subjects of Her Poems)." *ELUA*, *29*, 2015, 171–190.

Walker, Alice. *The World Will Follow Joy*. New York: The New Press, 2013.

———. *In Search of Our Mothers' Gardens: Womanist Prose*. San Diego: Harcourt Brace Jovanovich, 1974.

Williams, Patricia J. *The Alchemy of Race and Rights: Diary of a Law Professor*. New York: Harvard University Press, 1991.

Chapter 7

Womanist Freedom Dreams
"Stay on the Battlefield" by Sonia Sanchez and Sweet Honey in the Rock

Michael C. Montesano

The evolution of Black feminism and womanism in the United States in the 1970s and 1980s grew out of Black women's continued efforts to critique and subvert the conditions of their oppression. Since Black women in the United States face multiple discriminations based on race, class, gender, and/or sexual prejudice, Black women in the 1970s and 1980s expressed their doubts about single-issue movements like white feminism and masculinist versions of Black Power. This chapter begins by examining the theories of oppression and liberation that Black women articulate as part of the discourses of Black feminism and womanism. Then, with a reading of "Stay on the Battlefield" by Sonia Sanchez and Sweet Honey in the Rock, this study connects Black feminist and womanist principles to artistic iterations of the emancipatory imaginary. Written and performed in the mid-1990s, "Stay on the Battlefield" exemplifies the resolute spirit of the womanist ethos. And with this act of creative resistance, the performers enact what Black Studies historian Robin D. G. Kelley calls freedom-dreaming.

In the freedom dream that "Stay on the Battlefield" brings into being, the artists invite every person committed to justice and truth to join them in their fight. However, despite the poem's radical inclusivity, this creative collaboration has been received in academia with many of the same exclusions that Black women were decrying in the 1970s and 1980s. The multiple exclusions that Black feminists criticized decades ago have migrated into U.S. scholarship through the relative disregard of Black women artists like Sanchez and Sweet Honey. The academic silence surrounding works like "Stay on the Battlefield" speaks to a larger trend of disciplinary fragmentation that ends up slighting some Black women's voices. This chapter pushes back on these exclusions first by interrogating their underlying issues in contemporary academia, and next by showcasing the insights on liberation that Black women so routinely deliver. Adopting Black women's emancipatory visions as a model of aspiration, this chapter argues for a recentering of Black women's voices in the U.S. university.

BLACK FEMINISM AND WOMANISM

The 1970 publication of *The Black Woman*, edited by the U.S. author and activist Toni Cade Bambara, marks a turning point in the development of Black feminist and womanist consciousness in the United States. With contributions from 27 authors and activist groups, the anthology includes poems, stories, and critical essays that scrutinize the interlocking systems of subjugation that Black women have faced in the United States. *The Black Woman* interrogates how Black women face multiple oppressions such as race, class, gender, and/or sexual discrimination, and the authors envision the conditions necessary to eliminating these inequalities. Bambara sets the tone for the anthology in her preface when she begins:

> We are involved in a struggle for liberation: liberation from the exploitive and dehumanizing system of racism, from the manipulative control of a corporate society; liberation from the constrictive norms of 'mainstream' culture, from the synthetic myths that encourage us to fashion ourselves rashly from without (reaction) rather than from within (creation).[1] (1)

With these opening words, Bambara creates a framework for critically interrogating systemic racism, corporate control, hegemonic norms, and an unthinking culture of frivolity.

Moreover, in addition to the sweeping critiques that Bambara articulates so concisely, she asserts her vision for liberation from these oppressive cultural and political impulses. Despite the discriminations that Black women face in a country like the United States, Bambara insists on "the value of a vision of a society substantially better than the existing one."[2] In the chapters that make up *The Black Woman*, contributing authors reiterate the double impulse that Bambara establishes at the start: (1) to expose the systemic violence of U.S. injustice, and (2) to envision and work toward a liberated future. Like Bambara does in the preface, Black feminist activist Frances Beale also invokes the emancipatory imaginary when she states that "the new world we are attempting to create must destroy oppression of any type."[3] In her chapter, "Double Jeopardy: To Be Black and Female," Beale scrutinizes the injustices of U.S. capitalism, which force Black women to work as domestic help in white homes where they are underpaid and vulnerable to assault. She condemns white men who unconscionably rape and exploit Black women, and she criticizes white women who fight against gender oppression without considering the race and class discrimination that benefits them and oppresses Black women. Beale also rebukes Black men who assert "their 'manhood' by telling Black women to step back into a domestic, submissive role."[4] She argues that "it is fallacious reasoning that in order for the Black man to be strong, the Black woman has to be weak," and she insists that the strength of one liberation movement does not need to weaken another.[5]

In contrast to what Beale calls the "counter-revolutionary position"[6] of Black men who are male chauvinists, she envisions a cooperative revolution in which all generations and genders take part in the liberation of Black people "and other oppressed peoples around the world."[7] Beale condemns society's injustices at the same time that she envisions a world in which all oppressed peoples can get free, and in this regard her contribution reflects the spirit of *The Black Woman* as a cohesive work. Following the publication of *The Black Woman* in 1970, Black women such as Angela Y. Davis, Audre Lorde, bell hooks, and the Combahee River Collective (CRC) continued to scrutinize the conditions of their oppression while simultaneously pursuing concrete action toward liberating themselves and others. With the intellectual contributions of these Black women, Black feminists envisioned a world that more explicitly included lesbians, all women of color, and working-class women.

Additionally, by the late 1970s, Alice Walker had developed the term "womanism" to better explicate the subversive subjectivity that Black women carve out in a white man's world. Walker first used the term "womanist" in her 1979 essay, "Coming Apart," and in 1983, she put forth a four-part definition in her book of essays, *In Search of Our Mothers' Gardens:*

> Womanist 1. From *womanish*. (Opp. of "girlish," i.e., frivolous, irresponsible, not serious.) A black feminist or feminist of color. From the black folk expression of mothers to female children, "You acting womanish," i.e., like a woman. Usually referring to outrageous, audacious, courageous or *willful* behavior. Wanting to know more and in greater depth than is considered "good" for one .... Responsible. In charge. *Serious.*[8]

In this first definition (1), Walker characterizes womanism by the boldness with which Black women and girls learn to assert themselves in a society that discourages their willful action. She follows this first definition with three more meanings that explore; (2) women's sexual and nonsexual love for other women, their culture, their emotional flexibility, their strength, as well as their commitment "to survival and wholeness of entire people, male *and* female,"⁹ (3) love for life-affirming behaviors and beliefs like music, dance, the moon, the Spirit, love, food, roundness, struggle, the Folk, and herself, "*Regardless*,"¹⁰ and (4) "Womanist is to feminist as purple is to lavender."¹¹ The breadth and depth of Walker's definitions elucidate womanist ways of being in the world. Womanism makes more visible Black women's experiences and struggles in the diaspora, and it celebrates the distinct perspectives and accumulated wisdom that is rooted in those experiences. Another hallmark of Walker's womanism is a commitment to acting toward collective liberation. Womanism highlights its love for struggle and its commitment to the well-being of entire people, and Walker sees the headwater of this impulse in the courage and willfulness demonstrated by young girls acting "womanish."¹²

The visions of liberation articulated by Black feminists and womanists give breath to what Black Studies historian Robin D. G. Kelley calls freedom-dreaming. In his 2002 book, *Freedom Dreams: The Black Radical Imagination*, Kelley describes freedom-dreaming as the courageous act of imagining and working toward a life beyond the limitations of one's immediate troubles. Kelley explains that his mother taught him this practice as a young boy growing up in their tenement apartment in Harlem/Washington Heights. As Kelley describes the practice, freedom-dreaming is a strategy of the disempowered to visualize and achieve their liberation. He describes how in spite of "the cops, drug dealers, social workers, the rusty tapwater, roaches and rodents, the urine-scented hallways, and the piles of garbage," his mother taught her children "that the Marvelous was free—in the patterns of a stray bird feather, in a Hudson River sunset, in the view from our fire escape, in the stories she told us, in the way she sang Gershwin's 'Summertime.' "¹³ Kelley's fond memory of his mother shows her teaching her children to appreciate life's simple wonders, and in doing so, she also demonstrates how to dream past the confines of their run-down apartment. With this model of willful resilience, Kelley's mother is one of the many Black women proving how some of society's most oppressed can render the most revelatory views a "new world" free of all oppressions.¹⁴

BLACK/WOMAN/POET

Born in 1934 in Birmingham, Alabama, Sonia Sanchez is a widely acclaimed award-winning poet, activist, and professor. At the age of nine, Sanchez moved with her father and stepmother to Harlem, and in New York, she graduated from Hunter College and did postgraduate work at New York University.¹⁵ She started her career as an educator in 1965 when she began teaching at Downtown Community School.¹⁶ Sanchez garnered fame in

1969 with her debut book of poems, *Home Coming*, and as a poet and activist, Sanchez became one of the most prominent voices in the Black Arts Movement (BAM). Sanchez's writing career embodies many of the fraught alliances and split allegiances that Black feminist discourse explores, and her substantial literary output coincides with the developing field of Black feminist and womanist thought. "Stay on the Battlefield," first recorded in 1995, comes long after the publication of *The Black Woman* and the high point of the BAM. Despite this temporal distance, the emancipatory vision that the poem elucidates is the same kind of freedom-dreaming that BAM, Black feminists, and womanists pursue.

Sweet Honey in the Rock is an all-woman a cappella ensemble whose compositions draw on blues, gospel, jazz, and African choral traditions. Founded in 1973 by Bernice Johnson Reagon, the group has been making music for more than 45 years. Based in Washington, DC, Sweet Honey has throughout the years engaged with different aspects of contemporary politics and African and African American culture.[17] In their collaboration with Sanchez in "Stay on the Battlefield," the artists bring into being what can only be described as a womanist freedom dream. Against the intersecting assaults that Black women face in a hetero-patriarchal white supremacist society, the artists boldly envision a future in which all oppressed peoples can get free. "Stay on the Battlefield" was first released as an audio performance on Sweet Honey in the Rock's album, *Sacred Ground*. Sanchez later printed the text as a poem titled "For Sweet Honey in the Rock" in her 1999 collection, *Shake Loose My Skin: New and Selected Poems*. In the audio performance of the poem, Sweet Honey in the Rock performs the chorus sections while Sanchez recites the verses.

In my reading of the poem, I will attend to aspects of the audio performance and to the poem as it appears on the page. I perceive eight distinct movements in the work's composition, and to be clear about the points I refer to in this chapter, I have noted in brackets on the right side of the page the points that I think mark the different movements. The poem begins and ends with the spiritual affirmation, "I'm gonna stay on the battlefield til I die," and when Sweet Honey in the Rock perform these parts, they do so in the style of the African American spiritual.[18] The spiritual is one of the earliest expressive practices of African American culture, and over the course of the poem's eight movements, Sanchez and Sweet Honey pay homage to the expressive patterns of spirituals, or sorrow songs. In *Call & Response: The Riverside Anthology of the African American Literary Tradition*, the editors explain that in the convention of the African American spiritual, "feelings of despair are often counteracted by a deepened sense of hope or affirmation. These sorrow songs are powerful calls for deliverance from collective oppression and exile and for redemption from individual hardship."[19] In "Stay on the Battlefield," the steady harmonies of the chorus' vocal style, the song's call and response format, and its lyrical theme and structure all work within and add to the African American spiritual tradition.

"Stay on the Battlefield" imagines a time when life-affirming values and actions are not just defended but celebrated and revered. Following the first movement performed by the chorus, the solo speaker makes a courageous entrance in the second movement (emphasis original to the poem):

Stay on the Battlefield

I'm gonna stay on the battlefield [i.]
I'm gonna stay on the battlefield
I'm gonna stay on the battlefield til I die
i had come into the city carrying life in my eyes
amid rumors of death,
calling out to everyone who would listen
it is time to move us all into another century[20]

The poem's speaker embraces the same affirmational values that Alice Walker cultivates with her concept of womanism. Even "amid rumors of death,"[21] the speaker adheres to the spirit of her values: "carrying life in my eyes."[22] The speaker grounds her perspective in what she knows to be right, and she spreads her message "to everyone who would listen."[23] As the speaker delivers these early declarations, it is always clear that her individual voice presupposes a community that shares her principles. If Sweet Honey in the Rock adopted the voice of the community in the performance of the poem, the speaker's solo voice is a testimony of one individual's journey on the battlefield.

The song's speaker-chorus format constantly reaffirms the individual's relationship to the wider community, and in the second movement, the speaker underscores this connection when she uses singular and plural first-person voices: "*i* had come,"[24] "spaces between us,"[25] "time to move *us all* (emphasis mine)."[26] Written at the end of the twentieth century, the speaker appeals to the community with her dream of moving "us all into another century."[27] With this speech act, the poem literally gestures to the forward progression of time, but the specificities of "time"[28] in this "*century*"[29] seem less important than what goes on there: "time for freedom and racial and sexual justice/ time for women and children and men time for hands unbound."[30] In avowing her commitment to comprehensive justice and freedom, the speaker shows readers the tremendous benefits of living out these beliefs: "i had come into the city wearing peaceful breasts/ and the spaces between us smiled."[31] Here, the speaker draws on the redemptive and regenerative possibilities of the ethics she endorses. In a social body fraught with a traumatic history and a tumultuous present, the idea of spaces smiling between members of the community is extraordinary. The poet transforms the society she imagines so that in spite of a world rife with cruelty and deception, she visualizes an active politics of grace. This image of collective joy appeals to anyone interested in equity and peace, and with this remarkable moment already in the second movement, the artists offer a glimpse of the worlds we stand to gain by valuing justice, truth, and unqualified freedom.

WOMANISM AND REVOLUTIONARY POETRY

The poetic vision of "Stay on the Battlefield" shares many affinities with Alice Walker's concept of womanism. Like womanism, Sanchez and Sweet Honey are "committed to survival and wholeness of entire people, male *and* female."[32] The poem also shares with womanism a love for the Spirit, struggle, the Folk, and so many other features essential to human life. During the development of Black feminist and womanist discourses in the 1970s and 1980s, Sanchez's poetic career was flourishing. However, her closest associations in that period were with the BAM. Sanchez was a prominent BAM artist, which as a movement has been described as the spiritual sister of the Black Power Movement. Among the many sociopolitical transformations brought about by the Black Power and BAM, the institutionalization of Black Studies in higher education was a direct consequence of these movements.

Sanchez was a founding figure in Black Studies as an educator and artist, and throughout her decades-long writing career, she has received awards from some of the most distinguished literary institutions in the United States. Despite Sanchez's numerous literary achievements, academics in the United States have generally not produced the scholarly studies of her work that her writing warrants. The relative paucity of publications on Sanchez's poetry in my view exposes the intellectual fissures in today's academic institutions. In the 1970s and 1980s, Black feminists diagnosed the exclusions they felt within Second Wave feminism, which they saw as overtly upper-middle class and white, and Black Power, which they felt was dominated by men's interests. Years later, the divisions between these camps account in some way for the scholarly oversight of Black women poets like Sanchez.

Two ideals that pervade Sanchez's poetry are (1) a healthy, proud, and politically conscious Black nation, and (2) a strong, liberated Black female consciousness. As a consequence of these two impulses, most studies of her work perceive two distinct poetic personas: Sanchez the poet-revolutionary and Sanchez the Black woman. For instance, in their headnote to Sanchez's poetry included in *Call & Response: The Riverside Anthology of the African American Literary Tradition* (1998), the editors summarize Sanchez's work by outlining the two personas that emerge in her verses. Editors Liggins Hill et al. describe "the dominant tone" of the first persona as an expression of "raw anger at white America for stripping blacks of their humanity and dignity."[33] They observe how Sanchez's first persona expresses her rage at the institutions and individuals upholding systemic racism in America (the United States).

Liggins Hill et al. argue that the righteous fury of Sanchez's first persona is complemented by her second poetic voice. For them, this second voice is more suited to reflecting on the meaning of womanhood in a patriarchal society. According to the editors, this second persona turns "more to metaphor than statement and more to the intimacy of female identity"[34] Liggins Hill et al. argue that these two personas complement rather than diminish one another since both facets of Sanchez's poetry continue to thrive in her work. But whereas the editors of *Call & Response* view a mutually affirming relationship between these two creative drives, U.S. scholar and poet Elizabeth A. Frost interprets a direct antagonism between them. In her book chapter on Sanchez's work, Frost asserts that Sanchez's verses contain ". . .a tension between two often-conflicting causes—those of black unity and of a specifically black *feminist* consciousness (original quote emphasized)."[35]

Frost includes a study of Sanchez's poetry in her book on feminist consciousness in twentieth-century verse, *The Feminist Avant-garde in American Poetry* (2003). In that work, Frost construes Sanchez's fight for a Black nation as naturally at odds with her life as a Black woman. She claims that Sanchez is "a black writer for whom feminist concerns were often suppressed in the interests of racial unity."[36] With this interpretive framing, Frost seems to believe that feminism and Black nationhood cannot coexist. Whenever Sanchez asserts a feminist consciousness within her poetry, Frost perceives this as a disavowal of Black nationalism. Frost's conceptual dichotomy fails to recognize the complexity both of Sanchez's poetry and Black feminism more broadly. It is true that many Black feminists were more thorough than Sanchez in their criticisms of the male chauvinism they saw in Black nationalist politics, but this does not discount the fact that Sanchez fought in her poems to make a place for Black women in the Black nationalist project. Like Toni Cade and Fran Beale do in their essays in *The Black Woman* (1970), Sanchez asserts her feminist consciousness within the liberated terrain of Black nationhood. The poet confronted gender conflict often in her early verses, but like Cade and Beale, Sanchez did so as a way of envisioning the Black nation as a place where Black women, men, and children could live and thrive together.

At the intersections of race and gender in contemporary U.S. poetry and politics, sexuality is a critical point of division. As Frost highlights in her book chapter on Sanchez, the heteronormativity and blatant homophobia in some of Sanchez's early verses have alienated many readers. In poems such as "to a jealous cat" and "To All Brothers: From All Sisters," Sanchez hurls the word "f----t" at Black and white men with the apparent intent of insulting their manhood. In these poems, respectively from *Home Coming* (1969) and *Homegirls & Handgrenades* (1984), Sanchez seems to view the implication of homosexuality as the ultimate insult against a man.

The hateful language that Sanchez once used in her verses gives substance to Frost's claim that the Sanchez is accepting of masculinist heteronormativity. When Sanchez envisions the Black nation in these poems, Frost notes how heterosexual love is the nexus of Black unity, and she speculates that Sanchez's exclusion of Black queerness, combined with the openly homophobic language in her work, has turned away many scholars of women's and gender studies. In Frost's estimation, "Sanchez has most often been seen not as a proponent of black women's consciousness but as an activist for black liberation more generally . . . . It is because Sanchez has most frequently chosen to emphasize racial unity, in keeping with Black Power and black nationalist concepts of the 1960s, that she is less frequently represented, or anthologized, as a feminist writer."[37] In this view, Sanchez's promotion of Black unity, which Frost perceives to be at the expense of her "black women's consciousness," is the reason that Sanchez has been overlooked by scholars of feminism.[38] Frost sees a "gap between feminism and black revolutionary politics," and she includes poets "Jayne Cortez, Carolyn Rodgers, and Nikki Giovanni" in a list of Black women poets who have been excluded from feminist anthologies.[39]

With her observations, Frost both diagnoses and repeats the uncritical presumption that supporting Black unity necessarily excludes one from feminist allegiance. Without excusing the homophobic attitudes in some of Sanchez's early work, it is necessary to underscore the dramatic shift that took place in her later career. From the 1980s to the 1990s, Sanchez's poetic language shifted from aggressively heteronormative to radically inclusive. Her poetry since the 1990s has consciously engendered inclusive values by denouncing chauvinisms and welcoming everyone regardless of race, religion, or sexuality. And as my reading of "Stay on the Battlefield" emphasizes, the freedom dreams that Sanchez envisions are spaces where everyone—male *and* female, straight *and* queer—can live and thrive. When Frost repeats the notion that Black unity is necessarily at odds with feminism, she normalizes the exclusion of Black women artists in contemporary academia.

In the 1990s, when Sanchez began adopting her poetics of inclusion, she continued to support Black unity; her verses explicitly embraced her queer brothers and sisters, but scholars of feminism mostly continued to ignore her work. Heterosexism may be the stated reason why feminists exclude Black women poets like Sanchez, but the poet's "raw anger at white America" may also explain why scholars of women's and gender studies—disciplines that continue to be overrepresented by white women, men, and gender nonbinary folks—choose to distance themselves from some Black women authors.[40] In other words, many white scholars editing feminist anthologies may exclude Black women poets like Sanchez because her verses stridently criticize the white supremacist institutions in which those editors may be complicit. To my knowledge, Frost is the only scholar of women's and gender studies to write on Sanchez, but scholars in these fields are not the only academics contributing to the exclusion of some Black women artists.

Among the articles and chapters on Sanchez's poetry by literary scholars in Black studies, Houston A. Baker, Jr. (1990), David Williams (1985), and Haki Madhubuti (1985) are some of the few authors to do in-depth readings of her poetry, and these studies focus on Sanchez's early work. The relative academic silence surrounding Sanchez's poetry, especially her later poetry (1990s to the present), suggests that the exclusions in white feminism and Black Power have developed into intellectual lacunae across academic disciplines today. In the 1960s and 1970s, activist organizing in the Women's Movement and the Black Power Movement transformed the political fabric of the United States, and these movements gave rise to innovative departments and programs such as Black studies and women's and gender studies. These academic disciplines are not equivalent to the movements that inspired them, but there is a strong correlation between these fields of scholarly inquiry and the activist imperatives that gave rise to their founding.

Over the years, women's and gender studies has been criticized for excluding working-class women, women of color, and women around the globe who are victimized by U.S. empire. Meanwhile, Black studies has been critiqued for being overdetermined by "Black heterosexual male leadership."[41] Both Black studies and women's and gender studies have taken steps to make their departments more inviting to all, but in the context of this study, it is evident that disciplinary tendencies have led to insufficient scholarly study of Black women poets like Sonia Sanchez. It is extremely unfortunate that a founding figure of Black studies who is also a renowned poet has not received more attention from scholars in this field. However, before proceeding, it is essential to note that it is actually inaccurate to describe poets like Sanchez as marginalized or silenced. The marginalization considered here of some Black women poets relates specifically to academia; poets like Sanchez have never been marginal to the community they write for—the African diaspora.

FREEDOM DREAMS AND BATTLEFIELDS

This inquiry aims to participate in a recentering of the tremendous wisdom that Black women artists bring to their work. Writing on Sanchez's poetry in 1990, Houston A. Baker, Jr. finds an important aspect of this poetic development in what he calls Sanchez's "Black woman poems."[42] Like Liggins Hill et al. (1998) and Frost (2003), Baker observes two personalities in Sanchez's verses. Yet, whereas others divide Sanchez's poetry into political and personal spheres of expression, Baker perceives more profound tensions at play. For him, "The sound that virtually everyone took as Ms. Sanchez's authentically revolutionary voice was, in effect, merely the ephemeral stuff of political rallies."[43] If many perceive Sanchez's politicized verses as her insurgent persona, Baker sees this personality as the louder but less politically conscious of her identities. He argues that Sanchez's "Black woman poems, by contrast, seem to me the truly *revolutionary* sound of resilient black survival motion—womanly blues filling nighttime air and converting 'noise'—transforming the noisy public moment into a traditional repetition and reworking of salvific wisdom."[44]

What Baker esteems most in Sanchez's work is that she "loves struggle. *Loves* the Folk. Loves herself. *Regardless.*"[45] He reveres the salvific wisdom of Sanchez's Black woman poems, for in those works he finds a spirit bold and lucid enough to cast off the psychic yoke of white supremacy. In Sanchez's (1985) own words, she seeks above all to be a truth-teller, and in her view "the most fundamental truth to be told in any art form, as far as Blacks are concerned, is that America is killing us."[46] Baker admires the resilient Black survival motion of Sanchez's poems because in the face of white supremacy's mass violence, she underscores how Black Americans "continue to live and love and struggle and win."[47] Against genocidal forces, Sanchez's womanist vision is triumphant in its resilience, and "Stay on the Battlefield" is an exemplar of this kind of Black woman freedom-dreaming.

In *Freedom Dreams: The Black Radical Imagination* (2002), Robin D.G. Kelley argues that radical ideas do not propel social movements, rather the most radical visions of a new society grow out of concrete struggles for transformative change.[48] With "Stay on the Battlefield," Sanchez and Sweet Honey declare their commitment to realize change, and the freedom dream that they offer is clearly rooted in an intimate knowledge of struggle. The third movement, for example, details the persecution that Black people face living in a white supremacist nation. After alternating between first-person voices in the first two movements, it is only in the third movement that a third-person "they" appears.[49] With the enunciation of the "I"[50] of the chorus, the "i"[51] of the speaker, and the speaker's call to move "us all into another century,"[52] the first two movements emphasize inclusion and fellowship. But in the third movement, it is the violent conduct of this *"they"* that excludes them from in-group membership (emphasis my own in the following lines):

And they followed us in their cars with their computers . . .
and they bumped us off the road turned over our cars,
and they bombed our buildings killed our babies,. . .[53]

"Stay on the Battlefield" is dense with what Sanchez calls the most fundamental truth for Black people in the United States: "America is killing us"[54] With a penchant for expressionism, the artists recognize the terror that threatens their lives, and the poem gets more specific about a context that up to this point has only been implicit. White supremacy in this poem is mostly a backdrop against which the performers choose to dream of a better world. Sanchez rarely attaches place- or time-specific details to the poem, but in the third movement, the persecutions the speaker lists allude to U.S. history of racial violence. When the speaker recalls how "they bumped us off the road turned over our cars," the poem gestures to the persecution of freedom riders and registration efforts for Black voters in the Civil Rights Movement. The speaker also refers to murder and bombing as a tactic of terror to intimidate Black Americans. The poet's word choices in these lines collapse the distance between the speaker of the poem and those who had their cars turned over and their babies killed. By expressing the trauma of racial terror in these terms, the speaker shares her sense of intimacy with the dangers and vulnerabilities of life in a white supremacist society.

In spite of the attacks described earlier, the speaker recounts the courageous response of the *"we"* group she represents in the fourth movement: *"but we kept on organizing we kept on teaching believing . . . but we held out our eyes delirious with grace* (emphasis mine).[55] As the speaker narrates the sequence, she and the chorus answer the threats on their lives with a stronger standard of moral conduct.

When the speaker contextualizes in the third movement the violent forces that threaten her life and freedom, readers can better apprehend the scope of this freedom dream. The poem's emancipatory imaginary builds in the fourth movement, and this epistemological shift embodies the audacious subjectivity that Alice Walker calls "womanism." The fourth movement is the speaker's answer to the despair that "they" wish to impose, and a collective spirit reaffirms her call in the fifth movement.[56] When the chorus responds to the speaker by affirming, "I'm gonna treat everybody right til I die,"[57] the path of the song's emotional journey follows the pattern of African American spirituals. In the way that "feelings of despair are often counteracted by a deepened sense of hope or affirmation,"[58] "Stay on the Battlefield" adds on the tradition of the African American spiritual. The hatred and violence that "they" personify may always be a physical and spiritual menace in this land, but the performers negotiate these dangers while holding to a higher plane of moral vision.[59]

With more flourishes of expressionism, the speaker appeals in the sixth movement to those who have not yet joined her on the battlefield. She calls to those "sitting still in domestic bacteria"[60] and those "standing still in double-breasted mornings."[61] The associations of immobility and stagnation ("sitting still" and "standing still") penetrate the gendered spaces of the "domestic" sphere and the "double-breasted mornings." The "bacteria" festering in these spaces makes clear the harm caused by complacency and inaction, and the speaker shifts from this expressionistic language to a straightforward call to "fight" or "stay on the battlefield" for our children and our community.[62]

The speaker continues inviting people to the battlefield in the seventh movement, and the poem's inclusivity counters the exclusions and oppressions that threaten her. This freedom dream envisions a world of collective liberation that reaches every space imaginable (the rain forests, the hood, the barrio, the schools, the abortion clinics, the prisons) and welcomes any person (brown, yellow, black, gay, white, lesbian). The only qualification for joining her and the chorus is a commitment to justice and truth.

At this point, the speaker welcomes audiences to the battlefield in a way that transitions to a sort of spiritual ascension. The chorus introduces the notion of the battlefield in the opening movement, and they repeatedly affirm their lifelong commitment to the struggle. Still, when readers learn that the battlefield the artists have been describing is called life, the late inclusion of this detail changes the perception of one's involvement in the struggle. On the battlefield called life, everyone is already implicated in the conflict, and so the artists' invitation for audiences join them does not require journeying to any far-off land, but it may demand personal and moral transformations. The poem conceptualizes every person as already involved in society's ongoing battle, and the artists encourage everyone to join them in their fight for "freedom and racial and sexual justice."[63]

"Stay on the Battlefield" assumes the momentous scale of expression that the African American spiritual established centuries ago. Sanchez and Sweet Honey in the Rock conjure the spirit of their ancestors by sounding out the dangers to which Black Americans continue to be exposed, and also by summoning the resilience, dignity, and visionary insight that Africans have so frequently employed in the diaspora. Considering the wellspring of wisdom that Black women like Sanchez and Sweet Honey offer in this work, the task remains to bring this news into classrooms as well as into rain forests, hoods, barrios, schools, abortion clinics, and prisons. Recentering Black women's voices in pedagogical practice is urgently needed at all levels of education today. In the U.S. university alone, this pedagogical project would help counteract the academic marginalization of women like Sanchez and Sweet Honey, and it would educate students and faculty on the liberating wisdom of Black women in the United States. In a nation doggedly committed to historical amnesia and willful ignorance about society's oppressive institutions, the womanist freedom dream of "Stay on the Battlefield" is fertile with redemptive possibility. In the poem's entreaty to audiences to join the artists on the battlefield, Sanchez and Sweet Honey invite us all to be greater than the systemic violence in which we are enmeshed. The poem demonstrates that there may always be a "they" group threatening the disempowered, but the artists insist that we can reclaim our lives by joining the fight for the collective future.[64]

NOTES

1. Toni Cade Bambara, "Preface," in *The Black Woman*, ed. Toni Cade Bambara (New York: Washington Square Press, 2005), 1.
2. Bambara, "Preface," 9.
3. Frances Beale, "Double Jeopardy: To Be Black and Female," in *The Black Woman*, ed. Toni Cade Bambara (New York: Washington Square Press, 2005), 121.
4. Ibid., 113.
5. Ibid.
6. Ibid.
7. Beale, "Double Jeopardy," 121.
8. Alice Walker, *In Search of Our Mothers' Gardens* (San Diego: Harcourt Brace Jovanovich, 1983), xi.
9. Ibid.
10. Walker, *In Search of Our Mothers' Gardens*, xii.
11. Ibid.
12. Ibid., xi.
13. Robin D.G. Kelley, *Freedom Dreams: The Black Radical Imagination* (Boston: Beacon Press, 2002), 1–2.
14. Beale, "Double Jeopardy," 121.
15. Patricia Liggins Hill, Bernard W. Bell, Trudier Harris, William J. Harris, R. Baxter Miller, Sondra A. O'Neale, and Horace A. Porter, "Sonia Sanchez," in *Call & Response: The Riverside Anthology to the African American Literary Tradition* (Boston: Houghton Mifflin, 1998), 1489.
16. Mari Evans, "Sonia Sanchez," in *Black Women Writers*, ed. Mari Evans (London: Pluto Press, 1985), 449.
17. Roger Catlin, "Sweet Honey in the Rock Has Been Making Music, and Taking a Stand, for 43 Years," *The Washington Post*, May 13, 2016, accessed July 21, 2019, https://www.washingtonpost.com/.
18. Ibid., line 3.
19. Liggins Hill, et al., "Spirituals," in *Call & Response*, ed. Liggins Hill et al. (Boston: Houghton Mifflin, 1998), 14.

20. Sonia Sanchez, "For Sweet Honey in the Rock," lines 7–10.
21. Ibid., 8.
22. Ibid., 7.
23. Ibid., 9.
24. Sonia Sanchez, "For Sweet Honey in the Rock," line 7.
25. Ibid., 14.
26. Ibid., 10.
27. Ibid.
28. Ibid.
29. Ibid.
30. Ibid., 11–12.
31. Ibid., 13–14.
32. Walker, *In Search of Our Mothers' Gardens,* xi.
33. Liggins Hill, et al., "Sonia Sanchez," in *Call & Response,* 1490.
34. Ibid.
35. Elizabeth A. Frost, *The Feminist Avant-garde in American Poetry* (Iowa City: University of Iowa, 2003), 65.
36. Frost, *The Feminist Avant-garde in American Poetry, 66.*
37. Frost, *The Feminist Avant-Garde,* 69.
38. Ibid.
39. Ibid.
40. Liggins Hill et al., *Call & Response,* 1490.
41. Patrick E. Johnson and Mae G. Henderson, "Introduction: Queering Black Studies/'Quaring' Queer Studies," in *Black Queer Studies,* eds. Patrick E. Johnson and Mae G. Henderson (Durham: Duke University Press, 2005), 3.
42. Houston A. Baker, Jr., "Our Lady: Sonia Sanchez and the Writing of a Black Renaissance," in *Reading Black, Reading Feminist: A Critical Anthology,* ed. Henry Louis Gates, Jr. (New York: Meridian, 1990), 335.
43. Ibid.
44. Ibid., 335–336.
45. Walker, *In Search of Our Mothers' Gardens,* xi.
46. Sonia Sanchez, "Ruminations/Reflections," in *Black Women Writers,* ed. Mari Evans (London: Pluto Press, 1985), 416.
47. Ibid.
48. Robin D.G. Kelley, *Freedom Dreams,* 9.
49. Sanchez, "For Sweet Honey in the Rock," line 17.
50. Ibid., 1.
51. Ibid., 7.
52. Sanchez, "For Sweet Honey in the Rock," line 10.
53. Ibid., 17–22.
54. Sanchez, "Ruminations/Reflections," 416.
55. Sanchez, "For Sweet Honey in the Rock," lines 23–27.
56. Ibid., 17.
57. Sanchez, "For Sweet Honey in the Rock," 30.
58. Liggins Hill et al., "Spirituals," in *Call & Response,* 14.

59. Sanchez, "For Sweet Honey in the Rock," 17.
60. Sanchez, "For Sweet Honey in the Rock," line 34.
61. Ibid., 35.
62. Ibid, 35.
63. Ibid., 11.
64. Sanchez, "For Sweet Honey in the Rock," line 17.

BIBLIOGRAPHY

Baker, Jr., Houston A. "Our Lady: Sonia Sanchez and the Writing of a Black Renaissance." In *Reading Black, Reading Feminist: A Critical Anthology,* edited by Henry Louis Gates, Jr., 318–347. New York: Meridian, 1990.

Bambara, Toni Cade. "Preface." In *The Black Woman,* edited by Toni Cade Bambara, 1–7. New York: Washington Square Press, 2005.

Beale, Frances. "Double Jeopardy: To Be Black and Female." In *The Black Woman,* edited by Toni Cade Bambara, 109–122. New York: Washington Square Press, 2005.

Catlin, Roger. "Sweet Honey in the Rock Has Been Making Music, and Taking a Stand, for 43 Years." *The Washington Post,* 13 May 2016, accessed 21 July 2019, https://www.washingtonpost.com/entertainment/sweet-honey-in-the-rock-has-been-making-music-and-taking-a-stand-for-43-years/2016/05/12/597a3eea-13cb-11e6-93ae-50921721165d_story.html.

Evans, Mari. "Sonia Sanchez." In *Black Women Writers,* edited by Mari Evans, 449–450. London: Pluto Press, 1985.

Frost, Elizabeth A. *The Feminist Avant-garde in American Poetry.* Iowa City: University of Iowa, 2003.

Johnson, E. Patrick and Mae G. Henderson. "Introduction: Queering Black Studies/'Quaring' Queer Studies.'" In *Black Queer Studies,* edited by E. Patrick Johnson and Mae G. Henderson, 1–17. Durham: Duke University of Press, 2005.

Kelley, Robin D.G. *Freedom Dreams: The Black Radical Imagination.* Boston: Beacon Press. 2002.

Liggins Hill, Patricia. Bernard W. Bell, Trudier Harris, William J. Harris, R. Baxter Miller, Sondra A. O'Neale, and Horace A. Porter. "Spirituals." In *Call & Response: The Riverside Anthology to the African American Literary Tradition,* edited by Liggins Hill, et al., 14–17. Boston: Houghton Mifflin, 1998.

———. "Sonia Sanchez." In *Call & Response: The Riverside Anthology to the African American Literary Tradition,* edited by Liggins Hill, et al., 1489–1497. Boston: Houghton Mifflin, 1998.

Sanchez, Sonia. "Ruminations/Reflections." In *Black Women Writers,* edited by Mari Evans, 415–418. London: Pluto Press, 1985.

———. *Shake Loose my Skin: New and Selected Poems.* Boston: Beacon Press, 1999.

Sweet Honey in the Rock. *Sacred Ground.* Rockville, MD: Omega Studios, 1995.

Walker, Alice. *In Search of Our Mothers' Gardens.* San Diego, New York, London: Harcourt Brace Jovanovich, 1983.

Chapter 8

Mothers Incognito in Toni Morrison's *Paradise*

Linda Mustafa

INTRODUCTION

In *Women in Chains: The Legacy of Slavery in Black Women's Fiction* (2000), Venetria Patton examines the position of slave women in America and the importance of this in the literature of Black women. Patton[1] begins her book by posing a theory on the degendering of slave women, which is an important part of what justified the continuing of slavery. Slaves to a large extent were considered chattels and not human beings and so the slaveholders recognized only their sex, but not their gender, they saw their sexual difference only in biological terms, not in social terms. Thus, female slaves were recognized as "breeders"[2] even though they had to do the same hard physical labor as male slaves. Enslaved African American women were therefore perceived to be "superbly strong" and this tradition or conceptualization of a mythologized/stereotypical view of Black mothers being "superbly strong" continues to plague African American women.

Barbara Christian argues that such idealized images have served as "content for some other major dilemma or problem the society cannot solve."[3] Such myths propose that Black mothers are matriarchal figures, overtly strong and protective, equally selfless, all-embracing, demanding nothing or little, and self-debasing, self-sacrificing creatures whose identities are subsumed by their nurturing services. Essentially, this conception invariably provoked an aura of Black maternity entrenched in the system of slavery and the inevitable separation of fathers (Black slaves or white owners) from their children. Thus, in the absence or unavailability of fathers, mothers became the only link that identified the Black slaves' parental heritage.

The ideology of defining African American matriarchy as being rooted in the slavery system and subsequently becoming a cultural fixture in Black communities has produced peculiar properties. One of such postulations as Judith Wilt puts it "is the myth of the black earth mother, indestructible under the heaviest load."[4] Equally, the ideology of Black motherhood is said to position Black mothers in restrictive roles and has contributed to the denial of individual growth and autonomy. This view is especially profound in bell hook's discourse about Black motherhood in which she expresses the fact that some women may see motherhood as a problematic situation that suppresses their identity and creativity, while others see motherhood as providing a means of asserting their rights.[5]

However, Christian contends that "the primacy of motherhood for women is a value that societies, whatever their differences, share"[6] no matter the varied conceptions of motherhood. Patricia Hill Collins concurs with Christian's position and also writes that "every culture has a worldview that it uses to order and evaluates its own experiences [of motherhood]."[7] Collins further posits that despite a worldwide appreciation of mothering, the experiences of Black women according to Collins resulted in their being marginalized, which is stated here:

> Black women's self-definitions enabled them to refashion African-influenced conceptions of self and community. These self-definitions of Black womanhood were designed to resist the negative controlling images of Black womanhood advanced by Whites as well as the discriminatory social practices that these controlling images supported. In all, Black women's participation in crafting a constantly changing African-American culture fostered distinctively Black and women-centred worldviews.[8] (10)

From the words of Collins, slavery, racism, classism, and gender segregation escalated racist and sexist ideologies against African American women.

Christian also points readers' direction toward the slave era explaining that slave women were valued mostly for their capacity to breed and their ability to nurture children.[9] This situation may have influenced Collins to acknowledge "the dominant ideology of the slave era fostered the creation of four interrelated socially constructed controlling images of Black womanhood, each reflecting the dominant group's interest in maintaining Black women's subordination."[10] The four controlling images that Collins examines are mammy, the matriarch, the welfare mother, and the Jezebel. By way of controlling images, Collins explains:

> Certain assumed qualities are attached to Black women and [then] used to justify [that] oppression. . . . From the mammies, jezebels and breeder women of slavery. . . to the smiling Aunt Jemimas on pancake mix boxes, ubiquitous Black prostitutes, and ever-present welfare mothers of contemporary popular culture,

the nexus of negative stereotypical images applied to African American women has been fundamental to Black women's oppression.[11](7)

Along the same line, hooks writes:

> The locus of women's oppression. Had black women voiced their views on motherhood, it would not have been named a serious obstacle to our freedom as women. Racism, availability of jobs, lack of skills of or education . . . would have been at the top of the list-but not motherhood.[12]

hooks, therefore, sums up her observations by attesting that the feminist theory of motherhood is racially codified and that there is an existence of a distinctly African American tradition of motherhood. These unique features of African American motherhood are that mothers and motherhood are valued by and central to African American culture and the other feature is that mothers and mothering can affect the physical and psychological well-being and empowerment of the African American people. With these two features clearly defining the mode of motherhood in African societies, the focus of most mothers in practice and thought is to preserve, protect, and empower their children for them to be able to resist racist harmful practices.

Since motherhood is a central theme and the figure of "mother" is a powerful and recurrent symbol in African American literature and culture (particularly as a signifier of the origins, tradition, family cohesion, strength, and survival), this chapter is framed upon motherhood discourse, with an in-depth analysis of the conceptualization of the mother, relationship with her children and the men in her life, as well as her psyche in a stereotypical African American society that seems to ignore mothers as valuable societal entities.

VARIANT DISCOURSES ON PSYCHOANALYTICAL CONCEPTION OF MOTHERHOOD

In her book *Of Woman Born: Motherhood as Experience and Institution* (1986), Adrienne Rich explained that the world's conception of a mother is one without identity. She further enthuses that maternal love must be selfless such that she tunes her life to conform to her children's life (22).[13] This stereotypical view of mothers as selfless and sacrificial may be the reason why Ruddick is cited in *Textual Mothers, Maternal Texts: Motherhood in Contemporary Women's Literature* (2010) as saying "maternal voices have been drowned by professional theory, ideologies of motherhood, sexist arrogance, and childhood fantasy. Voices that have been distorted and censored can only be developing voices" (Podnieks and O'Reilly 367).[14]

The notion of motherhood has undoubtedly elicited so much concern that from the 1990s to date there have been exponential studies of the phenomenon of mothers and their mothering abilities. This has invariably caused prejudiced categorization of mothers in the world's majorly patriarchal societies; so much that Marni Jackson noted that "Motherhood is an unexplored frontier of thought and emotion that we have tried to tame with rules, myth, and knowledge. But the geography remained unmapped" (9).[15] Jean O' Barr, Deborah Pope, and Mary Wyer, the editors of *Ties that Bind: Essays on Mothering and Patriarchy*, reiterated Jackson's statement by affirming that

> the geography of mothering is a complex, shifting terrain. On the one hand, there are routes assiduously travelled and surveyed, well-marked by popular sentiment and signposted by professional opinion, on the other, there are territories that remained obscured in turns and thickets, unarticulated in their reaches and vistas.[16] (i)

The continued exploration of motherhood as a phenomenal psychological entity in literary narratives reveals how motherhood is indeed a focal point of study in both local and world literatures. Studies such as Marianne Hirsch's *The Mother/Daughter Plot: Narrative, Psychoanalysis, Feminism* (1989); Chase-Lansdale, Brooks-Gunn, and Zamsky (1994); Jackson, 1991; Jarrett, 1994; Jayakody, Chatters, and Taylor, 1993 and others understudied the problems of motherhood in African American communities, generational mothering and female-headed Black families. Others like O'Reilly (2004) traces Morrison's view of "black mothers engage[ing] in maternal practice that has as its explicit goal the empowerment of [female] children" to develop a distinct female identity that is independent of the racial dominant culture (1).[17] Christian looks at motherhood in Buchi Emecheta's *Joys of Motherhood* (1979) and Alice Walker's *Meridian* (1976), and she argues that both texts present women-centered visions of motherhood that resist the prevailing empowerment theory. While she does acknowledge freedom for Black women was the need to keep their children by their side, Christian explains that the essence of this "freedom" emerges from the sacrifice of their own lives, literally and figuratively (109).[18]

However, one of the most researched topics of interest in women's psychology is female identity development and the relationship between mothers and daughters.

In *The Reproduction of Mothering* (1978),[19] Nancy Chodorow provides a psychological analysis of the female identity derived from the Freudian Oedipus model, although she aligns her analysis with object-relations psychology, which is based on the assumption that every individual's psychological life is created in and through personal relationships with others. Chodorow, however, claims that the female identity is dependent on the connection and closeness to the mother and the bonding between mother and daughter (100) (Marleen du Pree, 1–2).[20]

Chodorow's object relations invariably tries to explain the basis of women's identification with their inner self. Schreurs summarizes Chodorow's object relation theory in which Chodorow identifies the difference between boys and girls and the tendency of girls to identify with their mothers as a result of recognizing the m[other] in themselves here presented:

> Chodorow claims that mothering is reproduced by women and passed on to the next generation of women. The first human bond of both girls and boys is usually that with their mother. Because gender is an important aspect of individuals in our culture, difference becomes especially salient for boys and men. In contrast, sameness is important in the lives of girls and women. In order to achieve a male identity, boys have to separate from their mother and identify with their father, who is usually absent for much of the time. This leads to rigid ego boundaries in boys, and to a negatively-formulated identity, i.e. male equates with "not-female."[21] (1)

To Schreurs, object relations theory explains "many of the constancies in women lives" (4).[22] Yet the same theory cannot explain the changes and shifts a woman might undergo as she grows up and most probably eventually depart from the chains of mothering.

Susan Maushart, however, proposes that to experience "good motherhood" means a mother should be ready to be in a situation she termed "unmask motherhood." To be masked in motherhood, Maushart explains, "is to deny and repress what we experience, to misrepresent it, even to ourselves" (1–2).[23] More specifically, the mask of motherhood confers an idealized and hence unattainable image of motherhood that causes women to feel guilt and anxiety about their own (often messy and muddled) experiences of mothering. Therefore, the mask of motherhood, as Maushart elaborates, "keeps women from speaking clearly what they know and from hearing truths too threatening to face" (7).[24] The unmasking of motherhood thus necessitates what may be termed "an archaeology of maternity": an excavation of the truths of motherhood disguised and distorted beneath the mask (O'Reily 12).[25]

Finally, Daly and Reddy coined the term "daughter-centricity" to describe the fact that "we learn less about what it is like to mother than about what it is like to be mothered, even when the author has had both experiences" (2).[26] Adrienne Rich, therefore, concludes in her work *Of Woman Born* (1976) by affirming that "the words which are being spoken now, are being written down, the taboos are being broken, the masks of motherhood are cracking through" (239).²⁷ Whether such rebellions are conveyed by way of a sociological study of mothers or in a popular motherhood memoir, feminist writers and scholars alike endeavor to unmask motherhood by documenting the lived reality of mothering. In so doing, they counter the daughter-centricity described by Daly and Reddy earlier to create and compose what O'Reilly— has identified elsewhere as a matrifocal narrative.²⁸

THE "DIRTY GODDESSES" IN MORRISON'S *PARADISE*

Ruth de Kanteur without mincing words proposed that "the mother represents the dirty goddess, both source of and threat to their [children's] existence" (32).²⁹ In Morrison's *Paradise*, we find this to be both true and terrifying. The town of Ruby was named after the sister of one of the founding patriarchs of Ruby town. Ruby, who became the matriarch of the town in her death, was posthumously honored to compensate the grieving "friend and brother-in-law of [New Haven] who didn't make it back" (17).³⁰ The story is told of how in their quest to locate a place to build their town, the sister of the Morgan family, Ruby fell ill and died as a result of being refused medical care by white racists and the half-Black, half-white people they accosted for help. Angry and bitter at their rejection and the resultant death of their sister, these men vowed to keep their blue-black color untainted. In her death, therefore, Ruby becomes both the source of a new Black independent community and a threat to the peaceful existence of her descendants who could not bear the infiltration of their community by adulterated blood, what they called "detritus: throwaway people that sometimes blow back into the room after being swept out of the door" (4).³¹

Wanting to be independent, away from all the people that rejected them the help and assistance that they needed in their dire need, influenced the men of Ruby town to nurture their women to conform to their perceived "good women/mothers." With being rejected by "rich Choctaw and poor whites" (13),³² the people of Ruby decide to make their town as pure as they could with only black blood and so they made sure that "none of their women had ever worked in white man's kitchen or nurse a white child" (99).³³ This statement lucidly introduces readers to the stereotypical Mammy myth, of Black women being good mothers to white children while they abandon their biological children. The men of Ruby abhor the thought of having their women serve white men to erase any possibility of having fairer or light-skinned children will remind them of the unholy relationship between their Black "good" women and white "devilish" white men (who more than likely sexually assaulted Black women who worked for their wives and did not face punishment).

In order to forget the horrible experiences of slavery, the founding fathers of Ruby town, therefore, decided that children from raped women will further escalate their misery because both the raped mothers and their children are looked at as "breeders" (i.e., women/daughters only fit for breeding white children), hence they epitomized intra-racial discrimination against whites and fair-skinned Blacks as a way to permanently push away the trauma of slavery. Moreover, the sharp focus on racism by the men of Ruby and their insistence that Ruby's women avoidance of domestic work further draws readers attention to the derogatory categorization of Black women/mothers as matriarchs, the mammies, the Jezebels, the welfare mothers, and the modern-day aunt Jemimas as defined by Collins.[34]

Silva in her book entitled *Good Enough Mothering?* opines: "As individuals, women appear trapped between misery and joy, between full-time motherhood and the rejection of motherhood" (10).[35] This statement can be viewed as an embodiment of the different categories of women/mothers in Morrison's *Paradise*. Despite being demeaned by this categorization, the women in *Paradise* are "trapped" and in "misery," and their entrapment goes unnoticed. Their joy of mothering is only short-lived, and motherhood is burdensome. This situation is clearly illustrated in the Chapter titled "Mavis," so named after the distressed woman called Mavis. Here, we find a woman/mother who is demonized for having forgotten her twins in a locked-up Cadillac where they died of suffocation. Even though Mavis according to the journalist is "distraught and grieving" (21),[36] she is seen only as a Jezebel; a woman who does not love her children and is unfit to be a mother. Her "Jezebellian" love for herself supersedes her rapt attention to her children, thus she forgets leaving her babies in the back of the car as a sign of being distant a distant/unfit mother to her babies.

In sacrificing herself and time to care for her husband, Mavis loses her children, her peace, and her sanity. She is miserable, guilty and in the state of being a "masked mother," however, no one is ready to unmask the truth that is embedded in her and her trauma goes unnoticed:

> If she could, she would have slept out there, in the back seat, snuggled in the place where the twins had been, the only ones who enjoyed her company and weren't a trial. She couldn't, of course. Frank told her she better not touch, let alone drive, the Cadillac as long as she lived.[37] (25)

Mavis, in her grief, is abandoned even by her husband who should have shared the responsibility of the death of their children knowing fully well that she had to get what he would eat and at the same time, keep the children away from him to give him his space. She is further traumatized as she is considered self-centered mother not good enough to follow the rules of the mythological strong Black mother/woman. With her grown children, husband, and neighbors all against her, Mavis becomes incognito, hence she leaves home a broken mother.

Similarly, the other girls who took refuge in the convent are also maliciously seen as Jezebels all because they refuse to be submissive to men and do not conform to the rules of Ruby town. The narrator seemingly very casually relates the Ruby community's distaste for the seemingly free lifestyle of some distraught women (away from men), noting with much cynic criticism of the "sexually" hyped kind of dressing by the women at the convent. They [the community] demean not only the personality of the women of the convent, but they also categorize these women via the constricting conceptions that they had sworn not to condone.

These women are looked upon as horrible wild women who cannot be anything else but Jezebel's descendants: "They piled out of the car looking like go-go girls: pink shorts, skimpy tops, see-through skirts; painted eyes, no lipstick; obviously no underwear, no stockings. Jezebel's storehouse raided to decorate arms, earlobes, necks, ankles and even nostrils" (156–157).[38] The convent girls are avoided and even scorned. It even got to a stage where they are treated as ostracized and abominable humans: "The few local girls already there clumped together and withdrew. . ." (157).[39] Such is the hatred of assumed "dirty goddesses" and "unfit mothers"—a situation that led to the ghastly killing of the convent women.

In *Paradise*, Connie fits the features of both the mammy and a welfare mother. Stolorow and Atwood argue that subjectivity is always an aspect of intersubjectivity. That is to say, we are who we are because of our relationship (193).[40] Connie or Consolata naturally took after the white woman (Mary Magna) who took care of her at the convent. From her long years of relationship with Mary Magna, Consolata can identify "broken girls, frightened girls, weak and lying [women]" (222).[41] She becomes a mother to all the women who seek refuge in a place where Mavis Albright is observed to be a "swept world. Unjudgmental. Tidy. Ample" [a paradise for broken women] (48).[42] Kidnapped by the nun, Consolata is saved from a life on the streets and poverty and this association facilitates the training and rehabilitation of a poor child who transforms into a hard-working woman as can be read in the following: "learned to manage any and everything that did not require paper: she perfected the barbecue sauce that drove cattle-country people wild; quarreled with the chickens; gave hateful geese a wide berth; and tended the garden" (242).[43]

In time, Consolata grows to be an embodiment of diligence, steadfastness, and a reservoir of unreserved loyalty to her "Mother"; however, she is one who carries the misery of a disappointed love from one of the Morgan's sons, who rejects her for being white. The death of Mary Magna finally shatters her connection with the world, hence, consolidating her leaving a life incognito. Consolata's subjectivity to Mary Magna predisposes her to a life without attaining an identity. Thus, in her efforts to be the ideal mother just like Mary Magna taught her to be, Consolata lost her identification, her defining voice, and her zeal to live.

However, Edwards views women such as Consolata, Mary Magna, and the Morgan women as "community mothers," whom Nathani Wane explains to be women who "take care of the community" (112).[44] While Mary Magna, Sister Roberta, and later Consolata taught the girls and women of the convent the love of humanity as decreed by the Catholic Church, the women of Ruby taught their girls how not to wear make-up and perfumes; they accepted, conformed and passed on the unwritten law of "Disallowing" (meaning the refusal to marry other blacks such as fairer or light-skinned blacks), which resulted to what the character named Patricia called "8-Rock . . . Blue-Black people" (193).[45]

The concept of a communal mother is well understood by Consolata even though she is white. Consolata's acculturation amazes Mavis who, being Black, is familiar with communal mothering, Mavis is surprised at seeing the golden-skinned woman with moss green eyes (279) formally calling an old frail white woman, mother (whom she supposed is Connie's biological mother).[46] Consolata, however, does not see anything wrong with mothering unrelated persons as she clearly explains thus: "She [Mother Mary Magna] is my mother, your mother too" (48),[47] a statement a welfare mother would easily make.

The entrenchment of communal mothering such that generational continuity is firmly instituted, over clouds the people of Ruby such that the accepted mothering practice is that which promotes the negative continual of the racist trend of Disallowing, which is the patriarchal mandate for Ruby town dwellers. For instance, Menus is forced to "return the pretty sandy-haired girl from Virginia" (195);[48] forced to give up the house he bought for the girl and ended up trapped and in misery for the rest of his life. Menus suffers psychologically and becomes inebriated every weekend; yet, the community ignores his misery because of their selfish need to continue the discriminatory practice of disallowing fairer-skinned Blacks into their society as a means of preserving their identity and remembering how the founding fathers of Ruby town are similarly rejected by prejudiced, colored men.

O'Reilley argues:

> The African American tradition of motherhood centres upon the recognition that mothering, in its concern with the physical and psychological wellbeing of children and its focus upon the empowerment of children, has cultural and political import, value, and prominence, and that motherhood, as a consequence, is a site of power for black women.[49] (4)

The Morgan women and the women of the other eight founding families of Ruby town see themselves as a set of culturally forward-looking women whose right and political power is to uphold the virtues of "good mothering." They (mothers) make sure their children marry into the 8-rock families. They also made sure that their children also partake in "takeovers," frowning strongly at coupling outside marriage which could get a couple ostracized (196).[50]

Gloria Thomas Pillow writes in *Motherhood in Shades of Black* (2010) that the "most compelling aspect of the mother/child relationship is, in fact, its absence" (114).[51] A significant aspect of mothering in *Paradise* is the actual absence of mothering. Although the stereotypical labeling of "good mothers" and "not too good mothers" is a major contrast, still, the supposed good mothers are guilty of not loving their children enough. Patricia who is one of the accepted Ruby women/mother remembering her fight with her daughter, Billie Delia, realizes only years later that she has not been a good mother to her daughter and she traces this to her identity being fragmented as a result of not being wholly accepted by the 8-Rock people of Ruby town as presented thus:

> Trying to understand how she could have picked up that pressing iron, Pat realized that ever since Billie Delia was an infant, she thought of her as a liability some-how. Vulnerable to the possibility of not being quite as much of a lady as Patricia Cato would like. Was it that business of pulling down her panties in the street? Billie Delia was only three then. Pat knew that had her daughter been an 8-rock, they would not have held it against her . . . . But the question for her now in the silence of this here night was whether she had defended Billie Delia or sacrificed her.[52] (203)

Furthermore, Pillow opines: "A great deal of displaced mothering goes on by women who either cannot or will not nurture their own children" (114).[53] *Paradise* depicts such mothers who are displaced due to slavery, racism, economic inequality, and patriarchal oppression. Grace or Gigi seems to be a woman stereotypically categorized as a sexual icon, unfit for a good marital life. Right from the description of Gigi by K.D., she is looked down on based on her dressing, which in Ruby town is abominable: "she was—across the street from them in pants so tight, heels so high, earrings so large . . . (53) . . . . Supposed her navel had not peeked over her waist of her jeans or her breasts had just hushed" (54).[54] Gigi is inappropriately looked down on as a result of a displaced racist ideology by the people of Ruby town. The picture of a seemingly uncontrolled woman fits Ruby's ideology of Black women being the sexual pleasures of white men and in their efforts to stop the proliferation of this kind of ideology in their home town, they decide to rid the town of anything that reminds them of the promiscuity of their former white enslavers. Gigi's perceived underdressing and the flaunting of her feminine self, therefore, calls to remembrance the urge to desire a woman lustfully just like the white men sexually desire and rape Black women. The children born as a result of this abomination are rejected for being "adulterated." To the town of Ruby, a woman of such feminine attributes is an embodiment of independent ideals that the severely patriarchal town of Ruby does not want to exist.

Gigi and Arnette can be said to be displaced mothers because they both exhibit the carefree and unattached attitude of a stereotypical "Jezebel" and are erroneously believed to be hyper-sexualized—Arnette, not wanting to keep her pregnancy, and Gigi not wanting to be tied down by marriage and children. In fact, women such as the "pretty redbone girl Menus had brought home" are considered "loose women who could keep you from knowing who, what and where your children are" (278).[55] Pillow adds: "even when the biological mother is present, she is not—not for long, not in a truly nurturing or protective way" (114). For this reason, Pillows continues, "[there is] a sense of pervasive motherlessness underlies" in *Paradise* (114).[56] The mother of Seneca's boyfriend has the characteristics of "motherlessness." She sees her son Eddie as evil having run over a child and abandoning her. She was hurt by her son's irresponsibility toward her, especially as his only reason to send Seneca to her is to get her savings and also hurt that her husband had died leaving her lonely. So in her hurt, she refuses to be a mother to both Seneca and her son, Eddie (more like a Jezebel), and her loss of self and trauma of being abandoned goes unrecognized, which Seneca describes in the following:

> Alone, without witness, Mrs. Turtle had let go her reason, her personality, and shrieked for all world like the feathered, finned and hoofed whose flesh she never ate-the way a gull, a cow whale, a mother wolf might if her young had been snatched away. Her hands had been in her hair; her mouth wide open in a drenched face.[57] (134)

Lone is the perfect Mammy. She helped all the women in Ruby to birth their children and taught them how to continue mothering their children: "She taught them how to comb their breasts to set the milk flowing; what to do with the afterbirth; what direction the knife under the mattress should point" (271).[58] According to Susie Orbach and Luise Eichenbaum (2005), feminine power comes from the denial of personal needs to meet the needs of those around her (70).[59] Lone's nature of being a mammy to all the women in Haven and later Ruby empowers her so much that she influences the women of Ruby for 75 years but by the time she had turned 86, the women of Ruby rejects her midwife service and her sacrifice to be a mother to all mothers in the town of Ruby.

Halldis Leira and Madelien Krips declare that "[people] we must make a psychological choice, and in fact we are continually making a choice, as to what to internalize and what to reject of the various values, norms and ideals which are embedded in our culture" (80).[60] The people of Ruby chose to give up "Television, Policemen, Picture shows, filthy music . . . . Wickedness in the streets, theft in the night, murder in the morning. Liquor for lunch and dope at dinner" (274).[61] Yet they never stopped being like the racist whites whom they tried so hard to copy, neither did they stop the oppressive ideals of absolute patriarchy. And so the resolution was for the people of Ruby, whose culture is deeply entrenched in racism to stop the "ruination" (275).[62] So in their derogatory categorization of the convent women, as women who "don't need men and God"(276).[63] Without seeing that these women all bare a scathe psyche, the men of Ruby decide to kill the "free women" and preserve their culture of "Disallowing," "Takeovers," "ostracising," "unadulteration," and the upholding of emasculating patriarchal ideals.

Patricia Collins writes that "[the subordinating categorization of Black womanhood influences] the nexus of negative stereotypical images applied to African-American women has been fundamental to Black women's oppression" (Cited in O'Reilly 7).[64] At the burial of Consolata, Misner expresses his disappointment at Ruby's stereotypical categorization of the convent women: "Do you think this was a short pitiful life bereft of worth because it did not parallel your own?" (307).[65] In depicting the evils that come with racism and stereotyping, Morrison further brings to the fore the misconception of living a life away from the humiliating white man's principles/laws. After gaining their freedom, most Blacks had to live their lives as a replication of their former slave-masters. They know no other way of living and what has been passed down from generation to generation cannot be erased; hence, the people of Ruby imbibed the totalitarian patriarchal ideology of their former enslaver as which becomes the burden of Ruby town:

> They think they have out-foxed the whiteman when in fact they imitate him. They think they are protecting their wives and children, when in fact they are maiming them. And when the maimed children look for help, they look elsewhere for the cause. Born out of hatred, one that began when one kind of black man scorned another kind and that kind took the hatred to another level, their selfishness had trashed two hundred years of suffering and triumph in a moment of such pomposity and error and callousness it froze the mind . . . . Ruby, it seemed to him, was an unnecessary failure.[66] (306)

The dominant view of the negative categorization of the five convent women instituted the proliferation of controlling images of Black womanhood/

motherhood such that the four interrelated images of Black womanhood, which was conceived during the period of slavery, never ceased in the minds of the men of Ruby; hence, the men of Ruby instituted the emasculating control of their former enslavers in their Black only town of Ruby. The character, Bellie Delia who rejects the stereotypical labeling and excessive control of women, acknowledges Ruby's appalling flaws while she tries not to get fragmented in her zeal to be different as can be noted in the following: "A town that had tried to ruin her grandfather, succeeded in swallowing her mother and almost broken her own self. A backward noplace ruled by men whose power to control was out of control" (308).[67]

Finally, Audre Lorde argues, "It is axiomatic that if we do not define ourselves for ourselves, we will be defined by others—for their use and to our detriment" (as Cited in Collins 21).[68] Women such as Soane, Dovey, Sweetie Fleetwood, Arnette, and all the other women who are under the control of "men and God" could not define themselves just as Lorde argues. These women are defined by their men and mothers who forced them to continue the racist principles of Disallowing and "takeovers" to sustain their blue-black "pure" color, which disintegrates the degenerate town farther from the freedom to locate identities that are not racist inclined. For instance, Arnette had to marry K.D., not because her love for him is reciprocated but that she is mandated to marry within her historical heritage to procreate and save the Morgan's bloodline from dying out, hence sustaining the blue-black blood of Ruby's first family (215).[69] Patricia's mother is not wholly accepted in Ruby town because of her light skin. She is treated like an outcast as well as her children (They hate us because she looked like a cracker and was bound to have cracker-looking children like me [196]), even though they are fathered by one of the blue-black descendants of the founding fathers.

The ironic twist to *Paradise* is the women/mothers who choose to define themselves on their own terms. These women become detrimental to the society of Ruby for deciding to live away from men, recuperating from the traumas they suffer as a result of constitutionalized patriarchal dictates. These mothers are the broken women of the convent who take refuge at a place where patriarchal ideologies are nonexistent and because of their seemingly rebellious lifestyle, they are erroneously conceived as "slut, fangs and tails" (276).[70] Their bold act to discover themselves, away from instituted white adopted patriarchal norms, is conceived as an affront to Black patriarchy. Even though they can define themselves and love each other's company and refuse security and the patriarchal norms as instituted in Ruby town, they end up being the strong ones and people more responsible for their psychological make-up than those who myopically conform to the emasculating patriarchal hegemonies of Ruby town.

CONCLUSION

bell hooks declares, "Despite the brutal reality of racial apartheid, of domination, one's homeplace was one site where one could freely confront the issue of humanization, where one could resist" (42).[71] This indeed is what Patricia Best in Morrison's *Paradise* envisioned for Ruby. In her desire to be fully accepted by the people of Ruby, Patricia Best had to marry into the blue-black bloodline despite her being scorned for having lighter-skin. Becoming a mother, she juxtaposes her love for her daughter and her desire to pass on the racist patriarchal institutions of her hometown, which drove Bellie Delia away from her. Realizing later that her desperate actions against her daughter are actually to cover up for the trauma of being a "cracker coloured" mother (an insignificant woman/mother), Patricia regretted how she has also adopted the racist ideals of Ruby town and also being one of the "mammies" who is supposed to thoroughly teach her child the laws of Ruby town. Other women such as Soan and Dovey, Arnette's mother, Lone, and other conformists loved their children too much as a form of ensuring that their children do not get fragmented by the absolute racist patriarchal system. They pass on the unwritten laws of Ruby through a culturally knit practice of retelling the stories of the founding fathers and their oven oath.

However, in their effort to protect their children against developing an inferiority complex, these women are placated and they become irrelevant. They are used for the pleasure of the men in Ruby to their detriment, and in the process, they lose their identities. For instance, Arnette (despite being pregnant by K.D.) is forced to abort her pregnancy and suffers years of rejection by K.D. To K.D., she becomes irrelevant and irritating. She eventually gets married to him just to be a "breeder" woman. Arnette's identity is now tied to the Morgan family because she is expected to bear children to carry on the bloodline of one of the nine founding fathers of Ruby town. The women, who choose to define themselves unconnected to the men of Ruby town, endure much more marginalization and subjectivity. The convent women do not only suffer discrimination, but they are humiliated for their independence and tagged "dirty," "adulterated," "sluts," "godless," "evil," and "pests" only fit to be exterminated. The aggrieved men overlook the fact that these women all suffer and endured pains of unreciprocated love from both their children and spouses/lovers; being used to their detriment, and not having their own identities. In essence, *Paradise* depicts the enforcement of women or mothers to a life of sacrifice for their men and children. This erroneous myth of Black motherhood being a sacrificial norm thus becomes a destructive tool to the generational continuity of Ruby town.

NOTES

1. Patton, Venetria K. *Women in Chains: The Legacy of Slavery in Black Women's Fiction* (New York: State University of New York, 2000).
2. Patton: 1.
3. Christian, Barbara. *Black Women Novelists: The Development of a Tradition, 1892-1976* (Greenwood Press, 1980): 2.
4. Wilt, Judith. *Abortion, Choice, and Contemporary Fiction* (Chicago: University of Chicago Press, 1990):135.
5. Hooks, Bell. *Feminist Theory: From Margin to Center* (Boston, MA: South End Press, 1984): 176.
6. Christian, Barbara (1994). "An angle of seeing: Motherhood in Buchi Emecheta's Joys of Motherhood and Alice Walker's Meridian." In Nakano Glenn Evelyn, Chang Grace & Rennie Forcey Linda (Eds.). *Mothering, Ideology, Experience, and Agency* (New York: Routledge, 1994): 95.
7. Collins, Patricia Hill. *Black Feminist Thought: Knowledge, Consciousness, and the Politics of Empowerment* (New York: Routledge, 2000):10.
8. Collins: 10.
9. Christian: 97.
10. Christian: 71.
11. hooks: 7.
12. hooks: 133.
13. Rich, Adrienne. *Of Woman Born: Motherhood as Experience and Institution* (New York: W. W. Norton & Co., 1986).
14. Podnieks, Elizabeth and Andrea. O'Reilly (Eds.). Textual Mothers /Maternal Texts: *Motherhood in Contemporary Women's Literatures* (Ontario, Canada: Wilfrid Laurier University Press, 2010).
15. Jackson, Marni. *The Mother Zone: Love, Sex, and Laundry in the Modern Family* (New York: H. Holt, 1992).
16. O'Barr, Jean, Pope Deborah, and Wyer Mary. *Ties That Bind: Essays on Mothering and Patriarchy* (Chicago: University of Chicago Press, 1990).
17. O'Reilly, Andrea. *Toni Morrison & Motherhood: A Politics of the Heart* (Albany: State University of New York Press, 2004).
18. Christian: 109.
19. Chodorow, Nancy. *The Reproduction of Mothering: Psychoanalysis and the Sociology of Gender* (Berkeley: University of California Press, 1978).
20. Du Pree, Marleen. "The Mother/Daughter Relationship in Toni Morrison's *Sula* and Amy Tan's *The Joy Luck Club*." (Unpublished Thesis. July 2006).
21. Karlein, Schreurs. "Daughtering: The Development of Female Subjectivity." In Janneke van Mens-Verhulst, Schreurs Karlein, and Woertman Liesbeth (Eds.). *Daughtering and Mothering: Female Subjectivity Reanalysed* (New York: Routledge, 2005).
22. Schreurs: 4.
23. Maushart, Susan. *The Mask of Motherhood: How Becoming a Mother Changes Our Lives and Why We Never Talk about It* (New York: Penguin Books, 1999).

24. Maushart: 7.
25. O'Reily: 12.
26. Daly, Brenda O., and Maureen T. Reddy (Eds.). *Narrating Mothers: Theorizing Maternal Subjectivities* (Knoxville: University of Tennessee Press, 1991).
27. Rich: 239.
28. O'Reily, Andrea., and Silvia, Caporale-Bizzini (Eds.). "Introduction." *From the Personal to the Political: Toward a New Theory of Maternal Narrative* (Selinsgrove, PA: Susquehanna University Press, 2009).
29. De Kanteur, Ruth. "Becoming a Situated Mother." In Janneke van Mens-Verhulst, Schreurs Karlein, and Woertman Liesbeth (Eds.). *Daughtering and Mothering: Female Subjectivity Reanalysed* (New York: Routledge): 32.
30. Morrison, Toni. *Paradise* (New York: Alfred Knopf, 1998): 17.
31. Morrison: 4.
32. Morrison: 13.
33. Morrison: 99.
34. Collins: 5.
35. Silva, Elizabeth Bortalaia. *Good Enough Mothering* (New York: Routledge, 1996): 10.
36. Morrison: 21.
37. Morrison: 25.
38. Morrison: 156–157.
39. Morrison: 157.
40. Stolorow, R.D., and G.E.'Atwood. "The Mind & the Body." *Psychoanalytic Dialogues, 1* (1991).
41. Morrison: 222.
42. Morrison: 48.
43. Morrison: 242.
44. Morrison: 112.
45. Morrison: 193.
46. Morrison: 279.
47. Morrison: 48.
48. Morrison: 195.
49. O'Reilley, Andrea (Eds.). *Mother Matters: Mothering as Discourse & Practice* (Toronto: Association for Research on Mothering, 2004): 4.
50. Morrison: 196.
51. Pillow Thomas, G. *Motherhood in Shades of Black: The Maternal Psyche in the Novels of African American Women* (Jefferson, NC: McFarland & Company, 2010): 114.
52. Morrison: 203.
53. Pillow: 114.
54. Morrison: 53–54.
55. Morrison: 278.
56. Pillow: 114.
57. Morrison: 134.
58. Morrison: 271.

59. Orbach, Susie, and Luise, Eichenbaum. "Feminine Subjectivity, Counterference and the mother-daughter Relationship." In Janneke van Mens-Verhulst, Schreurs Karlein, and Woertman Liesbeth (Eds.). *Daughtering and Mothering: Female Subjectivity Reanalysed* (New York: Routledge, 2005): 70.
60. Leira, Halldis and Madelien Krips. "Revealing Cultural Myths on Motherhood." In Janneke van Mens-Verhulst, Schreurs Karlein, and Woertman Liesbeth (Eds.). *Daughtering and Mothering: Female Subjectivity Reanalysed* (New York: Routledge, 2005): 80.
61. Morrison: 274.
62. Morrison: 275.
63. Morrison: 276.
64. O'Reilley, Andrea. *Toni Morrison & Motherhood: A Politics of the Heart* (Albany: State University of New York Press, 2004): 7.
65. Morrison: 306.
66. Morrison: 306.
67. Morrison: 308.
68. Collins, Patricia. *Black Feminist Thought: Knowledge, Consciousness, and the Politics of Empowerment* (New York: Routledge, 1991): 21.
69. Morrison: 215.
70. Morrison: 276.
71. hooks, bell. "Homeplace: A Site of Resistance." *Yearning: Race, Gender, and Cultural Politics* (Boston: South End, 1990): 41–49.

BIBLIOGRAPHY

Boone, Alegrea M. "Searching for the Black Woman's identity in Alice Walker's fiction." (East Carolina University. An Unpublished Thesis, 2017).
Christian, Barbara. "An angle of seeing: Motherhood in Buchi Emecheta's Joys of Motherhood and Alice Walker's Meridian". In Nakano Glenn Evelyn, Chang Grace and Rennie Forcey Linda (Eds.). *Mothering, Ideology, Experience, and Agency.* New York: Routledge, 1994.
Christian, Barbara. *Black Women Novelists: The Development of a Tradition, 1892-1976.* Greenwood Press, 1980.
Chodorow, Nancy. *The Reproduction of Mothering: Psychoanalysis and the Sociology of Gender.* Berkeley: University of California Press, 1978.
Collins, Patricia Hill. *Black Feminist Thought: Knowledge, Consciousness, and the Politics of Empowerment.* New York: Routledge, 2000 [1991].
Daly, Brenda O., and Maureen T. Reddy (Eds.). *Narrating Mothers: Theorizing Maternal Subjectivities.* Knoxville: University of Tennessee Press, 1991.
De Kanteur, Ruth. "Becoming a Situated Mother." In Janneke van Mens-Verhulst, Schreurs Karlein, and Woertman Liesbeth (Eds.). *Daughtering and Mothering: Female Subjectivity Reanalysed.* New York: Routledge, 2005.
Du Pree, Marleen. "The Mother/Daughter Relationship in Toni Morrison's *Sula* and Amy Tan's *The Joy Luck Club.*" Unpublished Thesis. July, 2006.

Edwards, Arlene. "Community Mothering: The Relationship between Mothering and the Community Work of Black Women." *Journal of the Association for Research on Mothering* 2, no. 2 (Fall/Winter 2000): 66–84.

Hirsch, Marianne. *The Mother/Daughter Plot: Narrative, Psychoanalysis, Feminism*. Bloomington: Indiana University Press, 1989.

Hooks, Bell. *Feminist Theory: From Margin to Centre*. Boston, MA: South End Press, 1984.

———. "Homeplace: A Site of Resistance." *Yearning: Race, Gender, and Cultural Politics*. Boston: South End, 1990: 41–49.

Jackson, A.P. "Black, Single, Working Mothers in Poverty: Preferences for Employment, Well-being, and Perceptions of Preschool-age Children." Paper presented at the meeting of the Council on Social Work Education, New Orleans, 1991.

Jackson, Marni. *The Mother Zone: Love, Sex, and Laundry in the Modern Family*. New York: H. Holt, 1992.

Jarrett, R. L. "Living Poor: Family Life Among Single Parent, African-American Women." *Social Problems* 41, no. 1 (1994): 30–48.

Jayakody, R., L. Chatters, and R.J. Taylor. "Family Support to Single and Married African American Mothers: The Provision of Financial, Emotional, and Child Care Assistance." *Journal of Marriage and the Family*, 55 (1993): 261–276.

Karlein, Schreurs. "Daughtering: The Development of Female Subjectivity." In Janneke van Mens-Verhulst, Schreurs Karlein, and Woertman Liesbeth (Eds.). *Daughtering and Mothering: Female Subjectivity Reanalysed*. New York: Routledge, 2005.

Maushart, Susan. *The Mask of Motherhood: How Becoming a Mother Changes Our Lives and Why We Never Talk about It*. New York: Penguin Books, 1999.

Morrison, Toni. *Paradise*. New York: Alfred Knopf, 1998.

O'Barr, Jean, Pope Deborah, and Wyer Mary. *Ties That Bind: Essays on Mothering and Patriarchy*. Chicago: University of Chicago Press, 1990.

Orbach, Susie, and Eichenbaum Luise. "Feminine Subjectivity, Counterference and the mother-daughter Relationship." In Janneke van Mens-Verhulst, Schreurs Karlein, and Woertman Liesbeth (Eds.). *Daughtering and Mothering: Female Subjectivity Reanalysed*. New York: Routledge, 2005.

O'Reilly, Andrea. *Motherhood at the 21st Century: Experience, Identity, Policy, Agency*. New York: Columbia University Press, 2010a.

O'Reilly, Andrea and Caporale-Bizzini Silvia. (Eds.). *From Motherhood to Mothering: The Legacy of Adrienne Rich's of Woman Born*. Albany: State University of New York Press, 2004.———. (Eds.). "Introduction." *From the Personal to the Political: Toward a New Theory of Maternal Narrative*. Selinsgrove, PA: Susquehanna University Press, 2009.

———. (Eds.). *Mother Matters: Mothering as Discourse & Practice*. Toronto: Association for Research on Mothering, 2004.

———. *Toni Morrison & Motherhood: A Politics of the Heart*. Albany: State University of New York Press, 2004.

Patton, Venetria K. *Women in Chains: The Legacy of Slavery in Black Women's Fiction*. New York: State University of New York, 2000.

Pillow Thomas, G. *Motherhood in Shades of Black: The Maternal Psyche in the Novels of African American Women.* Jefferson, NC: McFarland & Company, 2010.

Podnieks, Elizabeth and Andrea. O'Reilly. (Eds.). Textual Mothers /Maternal Texts: *Motherhood in Contemporary Women's Literatures.* Ontario, Canada: Wilfrid Laurier University Press, 2010.

Rich, Adrienne. *Of Woman Born: Motherhood as Experience and Institution.* New York: W. W. Norton & Co., 1986.

Ruddick, Sara. *Maternal Thinking: Toward a Politics of Peace.* 1989. Boston: Beacon Press, 2002.

Stolorow, R.D., and G.E. Atwood. "The Mind & the Body." *Psychoanalytic Dialogues,* 1 (1991): 181–195.

Walkerdine, V. 'Growing up the hard way'. In V. Walkerdine, and H. Lucey (Eds.). *Democracy in the Kitchen.* London: Virago Press, 1989.

Wane, Njoki Nathani. "Reflections on the Mutuality of Mothering: Women, Children, and Othermothering." *Journal of the Association for Research on Mothering* 2, no. 2 (Fall/Winter 2000): 105–116.

Wilt, Judith. *Abortion, Choice, and Contemporary Fiction.* Chicago: University of Chicago Press, 1990.

Chapter 9

Love in a Time of Pretentiousness

The Social and Personal Consequences of Romance in Chimamanda Ngozi Adichie's Americanah

Anna E. Schmidt

In an interview with *The Guardian* in 2014, Nigerian author Chimamanda Ngozi Adichie described her novel *Americanah* as "just a love story." This description contrasted with the ways most reviewers characterized the novel at the time, downplaying its commentary on love and romance. One reviewer, in the June 10, 2013, edition of the *Washington Post*, described the novel as "social satire masquerading as romantic comedy" (Raboteau para 3). Another reviewer wrote in the *New York Times* that "though the book threatens to morph into a simple story of [the protagonists'] reunion, it stretches into a scalding assessment of Nigeria" (Peed para 6). Another reviewer in *The Guardian* called the novel "ostensibly a love story . . . but it is also a brilliant dissection of modern attitudes toward race" (Day para 2). Words like "masquerading" and "ostensibly" illustrate these reviewers' inability to consider that love may actually be the novel's primary theme. And understandably so. Western readers expect that postcolonial literature will always be politically driven. As Ama Ata Aidoo's introduction to the anthology *African Love Stories* explains, love stories in contemporary African novels are *"never* revealed as such" but are instead "completely subsumed under 'the more important social and political issues' which the modern African writer (thinks she/he) has to deal with" (xi, emphasis in original).

Moreover, Western literary critics generally assume that love stories with happy endings are out of touch with reality. In the late 1990s, writer Vivian Gornick persuasively wrote that romantic love could no longer function as a literary symbol of personal growth and success because contemporary relationships prove that love is tenuous. Consequently, many readers and critics prefer novels with a clear pedagogical, if not political, purpose. For example, when I ask my students what brought them to an African American or U.S. ethnic literature course, they consistently tell me they want to learn more about the cultures they will be reading. Although I also value the cultural and political meanings of texts, I wonder if something is missing when we focus exclusively on what a novel teaches us about a group or a time period instead of what it reveals to us about the interior life, including the consequences of loving another. Shifting our focus to the interior life does not, of course, mean rejecting the political meanings of texts. As Adichie points out, some critics have assumed love stories by women are *solely* about love and private emotions (what I would call the interior life), whereas they are more willing to see political meanings in love stories written by men. Adichie explained it like this:

> All literature is about love. When men do it, it's a political comment on human relations. When women do it, it's just a love story. So, although I wanted to do much more than a love story, a part of me wants to push back against the idea that love stories are not important. I wanted to use a love story to talk about other things. But really in the end, it's just a love story. (Interview)

I agree with Adichie—the novel is a love story. But the romance at the heart of the novel is not only about the relationship between Ifemulu and Obinze: it is also a story of cultural belonging.

This chapter explores how love is portrayed in *Americanah* by looking at the romance of Ifemulu (also called Ifem) and Obinze, which scaffolds the narrative, as well as the relationships they ultimately abandon with other characters. In addition, it extends the notion of love to the protagonists' engagement with Nigerian and American societies. My analysis draws on Chela Sandoval's concept of "decolonial love" as a means of imagining new forms of relationality across differences, a theory that suggests social transformation is possible when alliances are not based only on identity or a shared experience of suffering. Sandoval writes that literature and art are essential in presenting these new ways of thinking and of relating to others. In *Americanah*, the protagonists seek love *sans* politics, believing it is the most lasting form of love. Identity politics or empathy for those who are different from us cannot revolutionize society, the novel implies, because these stances rarely go beyond surface appearances. On the other hand, romantic love can transform people when it leads them to live without pretentiousness. In Ifemulu's words, it "twists you and wrings out and makes you breathe through the nostrils of your beloved" (366–7). This transformation begins within the self and extends to the relationship and the broader community as Ifem and Obinze discover their individual identities and seek honesty in their interpersonal relationships.

To be sure, this is an idealistic claim. In the course of their journeys—separate and together—the characters learn that this love without politics and without pretense may be impossible because society (Nigerian, American, and British society) is structured in such a way that no relationships can truly avoid being touched by their broader sociopolitical contexts.

In the six years since the book's publication, literary scholars have analyzed the novel's criticism of Nigerian and American society and its representation of Black female agency and double consciousness. As well, Jennifer Leetsch recently discussed the love story between Ifem and Obinze, concluding that in the novel, "love stands for fluidity and fractiousness—sometimes ugly, painful and twisted, but always disturbing boundaries" and thus "it functions as a site of resistance and resilience for oppressive ideologies" (12). These boundaries and ideologies are most obvious in terms of race and class hierarchies and social mores regarding romance and marriage in Nigeria, the United States, and the United Kingdom, which cause Ifem and Obinze to feel alienated from their social circles until they reunite at the end of the novel. The other characters with whom Ifem and Obinze form long-term romantic relationships only increase this feeling of discontent. Mary Jane Androne argues that Ifem's relationships with Curt and Blaine (an independently wealthy white man and an African American professor at Yale, respectively) fail because they cannot "bridge misunderstandings emerging not only from race and race consciousness but also differences between African Americans and Non-American Blacks" (237). I would add that Obinze's marriage to Kosi fails because neither partner acknowledges what the other has had to do to—and to give up—maintain the appearance of what wealthy Nigerians in the novel would call a good life. Scholars have not closely examined Obinze and Kosi's relationship, but it is key to understanding how the novel represents love and is therefore worth considering in conjunction with Ifem's relationships.

Ifem and Obinze fall in love through a shared imaginative encounter with American culture, a place they believe would offer them the freedom to grow as individuals in ways they could not at home. They criticize middle-class Nigerian society for its emphasis on the appearance of material success and its expectation of conformity. Their desire for a love independent from social expectations is evident the first time they meet. At a social gathering for secondary school students, Obinze's friend introduces him first to Ifem's friend Ginika because "it was the natural order of things, that the gods should match Obinze and Ginika" on account of them both being good looking by Nigerian standards (67). But Obinze is immediately attracted to Ifem because of her sharp wit and intelligence, her refusal to be anyone other than herself, whereas he believes Ginika is too willing to please others. Throughout the first stage of their romance, Ifem falls in love with America because Obinze introduces her to American books and television shows. The narrator says that his "longing [for America] took on a minor mystical quality and America became where he was destined to be. He saw himself walking the streets of Harlem, discussing the merits of Mark Twain with his American friends, gazing at Mount Rushmore" (288). Seeing America through his eyes, Ifem begins to dream of living "in a house from *The Cosby Show*" and going to school where "students [hold] notebooks miraculously free of wear and crease" (122).

Attaining this American dream seems within reach when the professors at their Nigerian university repeatedly go on strike, and the two must find another place to study. Ifemulu transfers to a New England university and ultimately prospers in her new country. She is initially disappointed by the real Brooklyn where "the street . . . was poorly lit, bordered not by leafy trees but by closely parked cars, nothing like the pretty street on *The Cosby Show*," but she is nevertheless eager to "discover America" (130). By contrast, Obinze's dream is never fulfilled. Ifem cuts off contact with him shortly after moving (for reasons that will be explained further), and Obinze tries to get to America via England. He moves to London on a temporary work visa and attempts to enter a green card marriage but is deported before the ceremony. Upon returning to Nigeria, he goes into business as a real estate developer, becomes wealthier than he ever imagined, and marries a woman who caters to his every need without argument. Though he is outwardly successful, Obinze is dissatisfied with his work and his marriage because they feel inauthentic to him. During their 13-year separation, Ifem completes university studies and creates a popular blog on race in the United States that leads to a Princeton fellowship and many speaking engagements. Yet she grows dissatisfied with America and with her relationships there because she does not feel she can be true to herself.

Ifem "tries on" and discards two versions of America represented by Curt and Blaine. She meets Curt when her friend Ginika (who had been living in the United States for a few years by then) connects her with a family in need of a nanny. Ifem considers being Curt's girlfriend "a role she slipped into as into a favorite, flattering dress" (241–2). She loves that he desires her. He is the first white American man who looks at her as a woman rather than as "the help" because she is a Black woman working as a nanny in his cousin's home. She loves that he can unexpectedly whisk her away to Paris for the weekend. Adichie uses optimistic, sunshiny metaphors to describe their relationship: "With Curt, she became, in her mind . . . a woman running in the rain with the taste of sun-warmed strawberries in her mouth" (241). To describe Curt, she writes, "He believed in good omens and positive thoughts and happy endings to films, a trouble-free belief, because he had not considered them deeply before choosing to believe; he just simply believed" (243).

Curt's beliefs are not entirely trouble-free, however, and he invites Ifem to complicate his understanding about some things. He listens to her explain the difficulty of finding, for instance, magazines that discuss makeup and hair-care tips for women of color. And he stands up for Ifem when a salon refuses to wax her eyebrows saying they "don't do curly," assuming the texture of her eyebrows would match her hair. He also finds Ifem a well-paying office job she would not have been able to get without his connections. But his effervescence and his belief that their racial differences were unimportant ultimately blind Curt to Ifem's experiences and desires. He does not see that his friends look down on Ifem because of her dark skin or that his mother views Ifem as another exotic object her son brought home from his many travels. He does not recognize the possessiveness of his love when he tells her he does not want to be her "sweetheart" but "the fucking of love your life" (278). Eventually, Ifem tires of being the teacher who shows him how race matters in American society. When she cheats on him—an act that ends their three-year relationship—Curt berates her for giving herself to another man. He does not understand when Ifem says she "took" from the man what she wanted (357). When Ifem reflects on why she cheated, she realizes that she longed "to hold emotions in her hand that she never could" when she was with Curt (355). On the surface, Curt gave her everything she wanted and more. In some respects, he made it possible for Ifem to succeed in the United States, and he helped her to recognize her values. But their love story could not last because his love was ultimately shallow, and it restricted Ifem's freedom.

Shortly after the two breakups, Ifem begins writing a blog called *Raceteenth or Various Observations about American Blacks (Those Formerly Known as Negroes) by a Non-American Black*. The blog describes her observations on how American perceptions of race structure friendships, romantic relationships, politics, humor, language, ideas about beauty, and so forth. It becomes so popular that she is invited to universities and businesses to talk about diversity and cultural awareness, and it earns her a prestigious research fellowship. More importantly, it becomes a virtual community in which she can freely voice her opinions and observations about American culture and connect with Black women and other people of color who have had similar experiences. Interpersonal love, community, and self-acceptance are entwined in her blog posts. Ifemulu's first post argues that romantic love is "the simplest solution to the problem of race in America." She continues:

> Not friendship. Not the kind of safe, shallow love where the objective is that both people remain comfortable. But real deep romantic love, the kind that twists you and wrings you out and makes you breathe through the nostrils of your beloved. And because that real deep romantic love is so rare, and because

American society is set up to make it even rarer between American Black and American White, the problem of race in America will never be solved. (366–7)

Given the failed relationship with Curt—amusingly called "The Hot White Ex" in the blog—Ifem is understandably pessimistic about Americans' ability to love in this manner. Her description is more aptly applied to her intimacy with Obinze with whom she says "My eyes were open but I did not see the ceiling" (24). Ifem's understanding of love—life-changing, transformative love—expands an individual's awareness and transcends barriers people create to prevent others from seeing or potentially harming their interior lives. The problem with American culture—as represented by Curt—is that it is preoccupied with a "shiny falseness of surfaces" that prevents people from connecting deeply with one another (231).

Of course, such love is impossible if the person does not feel safe enough to be vulnerable with another, as is the case when Ifem allows a man to sexually touch her for money that she desperately needs in her first months in the United States. This is the truest representation of "colonial love" in the novel. The man is a white, upper-class tennis coach who hires Ifemulu, a young Black woman who desperately needs financial help because he needs "help to relax" in a most exploitative way (177). As literary scholar Carolyn Ureña writes, colonial love is "based in an imperialist, dualist logic" that "dangerously fetishizes the beloved object and participates in the oppression and subjugation of difference" (87). Ifem feels she has no choice, and the coach takes advantage of that. After the violation, Ifem—now feeling alone and ashamed—breaks off all contact with Obinze and tells no one about it until she meets him again in Lagos. She sinks into a depression, "swallowed, lost in a viscous haze, shrouded in a soup of nothingness." Moreover, "She cared about nothing. She wanted to care, but she no longer knew how; it had slipped from her memory, the ability to care" (192). In the space of the novel, this depressive state does not long persist. She soon is hired as a nanny, meets Curt, and comes to love herself and those around her once again. The internal effects linger, nevertheless, such that when she finally tells Obinze the truth, her eyes fill with tears while Obinze holds her hand and sits in silence with her. From Ifem's perspective, "She was inside this silence and she was safe" (543). This space is shared, allowing them to be safe and honest with one another.

Furthermore, this space of silence Ifem shares with Obinze, in the end, is absent of analysis or politics—characteristics that often overshadow her other romance in America. Blaine is African American, a professor of comparative politics at Yale, a reader of only academic, high-brow sorts of books, and a consumer of organic food. "He knew about everything," the narrator explains, and Ifem changes her eating and exercise habits to match his. She thinks of Blaine as a "salutary tonic" because "with him, she could only inhabit a higher level of goodness" (384). Moreover, she begins to revise her blog posts upon his suggestions, but she becomes resentful when the posts start to sound too academic. She would rather observe the way things are than explain *why* they are that way. For instance, in a post titled "Why Are the Dankest, Drabbest Parts of American Cities Full of American Blacks?" Blaine tells her to explain how government policy and redistricting caused those conditions. When Ifem takes down the post because it does not sound like her perspective anymore, Blaine calls her "lazy" (387). In contrast with Curt, Blaine reasons through his beliefs and positions so deeply that Ifem sometimes finds it surprising that she had not already arrived at the same conclusions. The narrator explains, "She felt a step removed from the things he believed, and the things he knew, and she was eager to play catch-up, fascinated by his sense of rightness" (387).

Ifem romanticizes Blaine as the perfect man the moment she meets him on a train. She imagines them "hand in hand, going to the mall in Stamford, she teasing him, reminding him of this conversation on the day they met, and raising her face to kiss him" (221). When they meet again a few years later, they quickly pick up where they left off. Ifem cooks for him despite her dislike of cooking and imagines them "with ginger on their lips, yellow curry licked off her body, bay leaves crushed beneath them" (383). The reality is different, though. Blaine is much more practical, which fact she learns by his "slipping on of the condom with such slow and clinical concentration" (383). Blaine's sense of what is right and proper is precisely what dissolves their relationship when Ifem chooses not to attend a demonstration Blaine organizes to protest the unfair treatment of a Black employee at Yale. Blaine's consternation with her causes Ifem to hear, "in his tone, a subtle accusation, not merely about her laziness, her zeal and conviction, but also about her Africanness; she was not sufficiently furious because she was African, not African American" (428). Ifem feels this disconnect with Blaine's close friends as well:

> They were youngish and well-dressed and righteous, their sentences filled with "sort of," and "the ways in which" ... were they serious, these people who were so enraged about imported vegetables that ripened in trucks? They wanted to stop child labor in Africa. They would not buy clothes made by underpaid workers in Asia. They looked at the world with an impractical, luminous earnestness that moved her, but never convinced her. Surrounded by them, Blaine hummed with references unfamiliar to her, and he would seem far away, as though he belonged to them, and when he finally looked at her, his eyes warm and loving, she felt something like relief. (388)

Despite her occasional feeling of being an outsider, Ifem feels secure in this relationship, and she even tells her family and friends in Nigeria about Blaine.

After their fight regarding the missed demonstration, their relationship is mended during Barack Obama's 2008 presidential campaign. The two are bolstered by the hope and optimism of the campaign and the fact that Obama was one thing they could agree upon.

Nevertheless, Ifem ultimately decides to leave Blaine and return to Nigeria, and she cannot give him a satisfactory reason because "there was no cause; it was simply that layer after layer of discontent had settled in her, and formed a mass that now propelled her" (8). From her perspective, their relationship had been "like being content in a house but always sitting by the window and looking out" (9). Ifem knows that she cannot be what Blaine wants her to be. Like Curt, Blaine wants Ifem to be entirely devoted to him and to what matters to him. In distinct ways based on their individual racial and class identities, both men echo an imperialist attitude of American society that requires immigrants to swear allegiance to a narrow vision of Americanness. Katherine Hallemeier writes that men's absolutism in matters of love is shaped by their racial identities and experiences. Curt's whiteness, she says, enables his optimism and makes it difficult for him to understand why Ifem would not absolutely return his love. In regards to Blaine, she writes, "[his] experience of growing up black in America has left him unprepared to function in a relationship in which his goodness, which is to say his advocacy for racial justice, does not result in the absolute solidarity he desires and expects" (240). For Hallemeier, Ifem's romantic relationships are allegories for understanding how race structures American relationships.

I would add that they can be read as two versions of Americanness that are offered to immigrants—an optimistic and upwardly mobile one that accepts differences while glossing over real injustices, and a critical one that acknowledges injustice and works to change it, believing that at its core, American society is structured to make such transformation possible. Ifem is not at home in either version because they do not allow her to form her own opinions or to respond to social injustices in her own ways. This fact is most evident when she realizes the organizations that invite her to speak on diversity and cultural awareness have no intention of changing their practices, but only want her to make them feel better about themselves and the progress society has made. By the end of her time in the United States, Ifem is the "right kind" of immigrant. She's well-educated, is not dependent on government assistance, and maintains socially acceptable markers of her heritage (she wears her hair in braids and speaks clear and proper English). She uses her blog to create a sense of community among other women of color, and when she criticizes American society, she does so without inciting revolution. It is not surprising, then, that she returns to Nigeria; she was tired of playing a role predetermined by Curt or Blaine or any other social circle she entered.

Lest we think that such predetermined social roles only exist in the United States, however, *Americanah* illustrates parallel issues in Nigeria. Obinze's marriage to Kosi and his relationship with the upper echelon of Lagos society suffers from many of the same problems as Ifem's relationships. When Obinze is deported from England, his connections at home lead to him reluctantly accepting a job in "evaluation consulting," which a friend describes this way: "You undervalue the properties and make sure it looks as if you are following due process. You acquire the property, sell off half to pay your purchase price, and you are in business!" (32). His wealth and properties grow until people start treating him differently, which makes him feel like an interloper in his own life, as if it "had become this layer of pretension after pretension" (533).

He marries Kosi, "a touchstone of realness," because she is "so extraordinarily beautiful and yet so ordinary, predictable and domestic and dedicated" and might then make him believe this new life is really his (565–6). To put it another way, Kosi becomes a version of Nigeria that Obinze tries on, feeling flattered at first but soon realizing the relationship is not a good fit. The narrator uses a rather sardonic simile to describe Kosi's presence in the marriage. She only looked "more beautiful, fresher, with fuller hips and breasts, like a well-watered houseplant" (566). Obinze grows frustrated with her shallowness, her inability to recognize the problems in Nigerian society, and her allegiance to social mores. When their daughter is born, Kosi's first response is "Darling, we'll have a boy next time," to which Obinze feels "a gentle contempt towards her, for wanting a boy because they were supposed to want a boy" when he did not at all care about their child's sex (565). Moreover, Kosi always presents herself as appeasing and agreeable to others. At a professional gathering in which Kosi speaks with the wives of other wealthy men, Obinze criticizes her inwardly because "she was always taking two sides at once, to please everyone; she always chose peace over truth, was always eager to conform" (36). Indeed, Kosi's characterization is of a piece with that of the other Nigerian women in the novel who seem to only be concerned with their appearance and with attracting wealthy men. Upon Ifem's return to Lagos, she notes that many women there "define their lives by men they can never truly have, crippled by their culture of dependence, with desperation in their eyes and designer handbags on their wrists" (521). This culture of conformity in Lagos frustrates Ifem and Obinze. Like Ifem with Curt and Blaine, Obinze feels as though being Kosi's husband is a role he performs alongside her, one that does not allow him to be true to himself. By contrast, when he reunites with Ifem, he is relieved that she is still honest about who she is even if she disagrees with him. Obinze's marriage fails because it is socially meaningful, but not personally so.

Obinze and Ifemulu seek love and belonging independent from social expectations, and they seem to find it in one another. Because their love story departs from social expectations, *Americanah* supports Chela Sandoval's concept of decolonial love. In *Methodologies of the Oppressed*, she describes decolonial love as a method of relationality that can lead to social change by ensuring others' freedom and allowing for change in both parties over time. According to Sandoval, romantic love can help us imagine this revolutionary love, which requires a willingness to be changed by love and to allow change in another. It allows for complexity insofar as it is not dependent on any single identity or allegiance. It goes beyond such surface appearances. Audre Lorde's definition of the erotic is useful in explaining this idea. In "Uses of the Erotic," she distinguishes between the erotic and the pornographic. The latter "represents the suppression of true feeling" by "[emphasizing] sensation without feeling" (54). The erotic, by contrast, carries a depth of feeling. It is a "sharing of joy, whether physical, emotional, psychic, or intellectual" that "forms a bridge between the sharers which can be the basis for understanding much of what is not shared between them," and thus it "lessens the threat of their difference" (56). Turning back to the novel, we can see that this joy, or eroticism, is missing in the relationships Ifem and Obinze have with other people. Ifem romanticizes her relationships with Curt and Blaine, and they, in turn, maintain unrealistic expectations of how she should act in the relationships. Consequently, the initial bliss of those relationships disappears. The novel does not go into as much depth with Kosi and Obinze's relationship, but it appears their marriage is only a surface sort of love that does not bring joy to either party.

For Lorde and Sandoval, there is a revolutionary love that can lead to more equitable social relationships. Sandoval cautions, however, the western narrative of falling in love is not an adequate model of this idea because it requires reciprocation and exclusivity. That is, if I love someone but see no hope of my love being returned, I will stop loving them, and the two of us will go our separate ways. This is indeed what happens to Ifem after her relationships with Curt and Blaine end, and her phone conversations with them later are polite and stilted. They do not go on loving her because she does not fit their image of love or the form it should take. Ifem is likewise guilty of expecting an exclusive love. When she returns to Lagos and rekindles her romance with Obinze, she refuses to be "the other woman" in Obinze's life. She demands all of him or none of him. As I understand Sandoval, such insistence would not be in keeping with the idea of decolonial love, which is perhaps why Sandoval says romantic love is but an entry point into the concept.

Even though the lovers reunite at the end, the love story in *Americanah* suggests that decolonial love is impossible between two people because no relationship can escape politics and the social structures in which we all participate. Even Blaine, who is the most highly educated and arguably the most thoughtful character in the novel, cannot love another person in a way that allows her to be free, nor will he let himself be changed by the relationship. There are limits to his love. Ifem and Obinze are the only ones in the novel able to love freely. Jennifer Leetsch interprets the love story as one that troubles the boundaries that divide people, saying that Ifem's "Come in" to Obinze at the end of the novel resists the terminal ending of traditional love stories (7). Be that as it may, it is worth noting that this interaction occurs after they have fought about the nature of their relationship when Obinze says "You are the woman I love . . . . But I feel this sense of responsibility about what I need to do." Ifem wonders what "responsibility" means: "Did it mean that he wanted to continue seeing her but had to stay married? Did it mean that he could no longer continue seeing her?" When he remains silent to her questions, she tells him to leave (558). After some time, Obinze decides to divorce Kosi but live nearby so he can see his daughter every day. Only after he makes this decision does he pursue the relationship with Ifem again. Their romance is exclusive. Yes, their love opens a space for both characters to feel whole within themselves, but that space is exclusive to the two of them. They feel distanced from everyone else in the novel and from the various cultures through which they move; it is primarily within the space of their relationship that they find a sense of true belonging.

That being said, during the months that Obinze is working out his feelings about his marriage, Ifem discovers another kind of love. It is a love for Nigeria—and herself as Nigerian—that she had not previously experienced. Ifem's observations of Lagos upon returning home are at first mocking and poignant, but they lead to self-reflection. She meets with a group of other "Americanahs" (the name given to someone who leaves Nigeria for America and then returns) where the group laughs about the things they miss in America. One person mentions a new restaurant saying, "they have the kinds of things we can eat," meaning fresh vegetables and not much meat. At this comment, "An unease crept up on Ifemulu. She was comfortable here, and she wished she were not. She wished, too, that she was not so interested in this new restaurant, did not perk up, imagining fresh green salads and steamed still-firm vegetables" (503). When she begins writing a new blog titled "The Small Redemptions of Lagos," she comments on this discussion, noting: "Nigeria is not a nation of people with food allergies, not a nation of picky eaters for whom food is about distinctions and separations. It is a nation of people who eat beef and chicken and cow skin and intestines and dried fish in a single bowl of soup, and it is called assorted, and so get over yourselves and realize that the way of life here is just that, assorted" (520).

As she had done in her American blog, Ifem pokes fun at stereotypes and the assumptions people have of how those unlike themselves should behave.

The humor in both blogs is essential to the narrative, and it is a kind of humor only possible from someone that loves enough to pay close attention. The romantic love narrative is not the sole form of love that brings Ifem joy and fulfillment. Her blogs create a virtual community among people who may not have made such connections elsewhere. In a post titled "A Michelle Obama Shout-Out Plus Hair as Race Metaphor," Ifem mentions the uproar that would occur if Michelle Obama "got tired of all the heat and decided to go natural and appeared on TV with lots of woolly hair, or tight spirally curls." She concludes that "she would totally rock but poor Obama would certainly lose the independent vote" (368). She updates this post with a note that a reader asked for her hair-care routine, which she provides and then asks other readers to post their own. Her Lagos blog likewise creates a forum for readers to voice concerns they may not have had space to discuss in the past. Within a week of her post about Nigerian foodways, 1,000 people visit her blog, some of whom thank her for finally speaking up about this issue. Adichie continued *The Small Redemptions of Lagos* for some months in 2014 after the novel was published. In wide-ranging posts that cover similar topics as her U.S. blog, Ifem (and sometimes her friends) comments on social issues such as the Ebola crisis, commercial development in Lagos, and stereotypical representations of Africa in popular culture; she mentions organizations and leaders she and Obinze admire; and she provides tips about hair and skincare products for her readers and updates them about her relationship with Obinze. Although Ifem feels distanced from people throughout the novel, her blogs—like her relationship with Obinze—enable her to be true to herself and to meaningfully connect with others. The narrator remarks that by writing her blog in Lagos "she had, finally, spun herself fully into being" (586).

Through humorous critique and romantic comedy, *Americanah* insists that a meaningful life is oriented around joy, not suffering. Lorde speaks to this idea when she describes an "erotic knowledge" that "empowers us" and "becomes a lens through which we scrutinize all aspects of our existence, forcing us to evaluate those aspects honestly in terms of their relative meaning within our lives." Erotic knowledge entails recognizing one's "capacity for joy" and choosing to pursue paths in life that create joy within the self and for others (57). An emphasis on joy contrasts with the representations of violence and exploitation that are common in postcolonial texts. Consider, for example, Junot Díaz's *The Brief Wondrous Life of Oscar Wao*. In an interview, Díaz said that decolonial love in that novel centers on the question of: "Is it possible to love one's broken-by-the-coloniality-of-power self in another broken-by-the-coloniality-of-power person?" He described it as a search for love that could "liberate [the Dominican-American characters in the novel] from that horrible legacy of violence." Yomaira Figueroa's analysis of the novel contends that representations of decolonial love invite readers to imagine and create a future in which love for self and community transforms society and breaks down the structures that divide people and treat some as less than human. Díaz's novel describes a different geography and cultural context, of course, and recent allegations of sexual harassment against Díaz may rightly make readers suspicious of any claims he makes for decolonial love. His definition is worth considering, nonetheless, because it points to a common presentation of postcolonial literature that begins in a state of brokenness and suffering. In *Oscar Wao*, generations of women characters are raped and assaulted by men who often have experienced their own forms of violence, racism, and poverty. Scenes of rape are ubiquitous in postcolonial and American ethnic works of literature not only because rape is a real and common experience, but also because it is a powerful symbol of the effects of colonialism on women and their communities.

Americanah resists such a narrative. As Leetsch and others have pointed out, the novel departs from works like Chinua Achebe's *Things Fall Apart* that focus on the traumas African nations experienced during colonization and the lasting political and social effects of them (4). Adichie spoke to the common problem of people outside Africa associating the continent's people with suffering in her TED Talk "The Danger of a Single Story." She notes that when she left Nigeria to attend an American college, her roommate was shocked that she could speak English and cook on a stove and that she listened to Mariah Carey. In her roommate's "single story," Adichie says, "there was no possibility of Africans being similar to her in any way, no possibility of feelings more complex than pity, no possibility of a connection as human equals." She does not blame her roommate for her preconceptions but notes that stereotypes are common when people encounter only one story about a people. In *Americanah*, Adichie acknowledges the political climate of Lagos and the racism in the United Kingdom and the United States, and her characters do suffer from these realities. But the narrative does not begin in a place of trauma, nor does suffering define any character's experience. Love is equally a part of human experience, and the novel presents love in multifaceted ways. Ifem's love directs her to live free of pretentiousness and the opinions others think she should have, and through her blog, she helps others do the same.

Although the novel is on the surface a fairly traditional love story, it illustrates the internal work necessary for personal and social transformation. In no particular order, this work entails identifying stereotypical narratives that structure one's thoughts and behaviors (as Curt does), taking action through a process of self-acceptance and working on behalf of a community (as Blaine does), and allowing for the possibility of being changed through the encounter with others and with the self (as Obinze does). Ifemulu goes through all these stages, illustrating a key element of decolonial love. Sandoval explains that "the only predictable final outcome" of this revolutionary way of thinking "is transformation itself," as the individual changes social reality and is herself changed by the process (156).

Ifemulu's transformation involves complicating the link between the personal and the political, a link that distinguishes Nigeria, "where boundaries were blurred" and "work blended into life" (483). She desires a romantic love separate from politics, but with Obinze, she is forced to consider that this ideal may be impossible. For this reason, she insists on clarity about their relationship when she returns to Nigeria. Perhaps she can only do so after she has left the country and then returned after she has witnessed in two different cultures and how social structures delimit interpersonal relationships. By the end of the novel, Ifem does not feel compelled to be political or to love in circumscribed ways based on her identity or social status. Her love for Obinze and Lagos are not diminished by her criticisms, and those relationships are transformed through her process of seeking an honest relationship that accepts the uniqueness of both without demanding that they change. For Ifem, there is a difference between accepting and understanding someone. She calls Obinze "the only person with whom she had never felt the need to explain herself" (7). Love does not necessarily require knowing or understanding another person because the only one we can truly understand is ourselves (and even that is not certain). Likewise, Ifem's love for Lagos grows only when she begins to accept it without comparing it to the United States, or analyzing the problems in Lagos by that comparison, as do the other Americanahs she meets.

Although *Americanah*'s vision of decolonial love involves an exclusive romantic relationship, it also extends that relationship to encompass a virtual community and a nation. The criticisms of American, British, and Nigerian societies present in the novel are effects of this love. By beginning in a place of love, rather than trauma and continued suffering, Adichie invites readers and scholars to complicate their conceptions of postcolonial literature and the realities it represents. Such reconsiderations may not transform society, but they may help us view society (our own and others) in ways that recognize a wider range of human experiences, including love.

WORKS CITED

Adichie, Chimamanda Ngozi. *Americanah*. Anchor/Random House, 2013.

———. "The Danger of a Single Story." TED, 10 March 2014, www.ted.com/talks/chimamanda_adichie_the_danger_of_a_single_story.

———. Interview by Emma Brockes. *The Guardian*, 21 Mar. 2014, https://www.theguardian.com/books/2014/mar/21/chimamanda-ngozi-adichie-interview.

———. *The Small Redemptions of Lagos*, Aug. – Nov. 2014, americanahblog.wordpress.com/. Accessed 11 Aug. 2019.

Aidoo, Ama Ata. "Introduction." *African Love Stories: an anthology*, edited by Aidoo, Ayebia Clarke, 2006, pp. vii–xiv.

Androne, Mary Jane. "Adichie's *Americanah*: A Migrant Bildungsroman." *A Companion to Chimamanda Ngozi Adichie*, edited by Ernest N. Emenyonu, James Currey/Boydell & Brewer, 2017, pp. 229–43.

Day, Elizabeth. Review of *Americanah*. *The Guardian*, 15 Apr 2013, https://www.theguardian.com/books/2013/apr/15/americanah-chimamanda-ngozi-adichie-review.

Díaz, Junot. *The Brief Wondrous Life of Oscar Wao*. Riverhead/Penguin, 2007.

Figueroa, Yomaira C. "Reparation as Transformation: Radical Literary (Re)imaginings of Futurities Through Decolonial Love." *Decolonization: Indigeneity, Education & Society*, vol. 4, no. 1, 2015, pp. 41–58.

Gornick, Vivian. *The End of the Novel of Love*. Beacon, 1997.

Hallemeir, Katherine. "'To Be from the Country of People Who Gave': National Allegory and the United States of Adichie's *Americanah*." *Studies in the Novel*, vol. 47, no. 2, Summer 2015, pp. 231–45. *Project Muse*, doi: 10.1353/sdn.2015.0029.

Leetsch, Jennifer. "Love, Limb-Loosener: Encounters in Chimamanda Ngozi Adichie's *Americanah*." *Journal of Popular Romance Studies*, vol. 6, April 2017, pp. 1–14.

Lorde, Audre. "Uses of the Erotic: the Erotic as Power." 1984. *Sister Outsider: Essays & Speeches*, Crossing Press/Random House, 2007, pp. 53–9.

Moya, Paula M.L. "The Search for Decolonial Love, Part II: An Interview with Junot Díaz." *Boston Review*, 27 June 2012, bostonreview.net/archives/BR37.4/junot_díaz_paula_moya_2_oscar_wao_monstro_race.php. Accessed Nov. 2016.

Peed, Mike. "Realities of Race." *The New York Times*, 7 June 2013, https://www.nytimes.com/2013/06/09/books/review/americanah-by-chimamanda-ngozi-adichie.html

Raboteau, Emily. Review of *Americanah*. *The Washington Post*, 10 June 2013, https://www.washingtonpost.com/entertainment/books/book-review-americanah-by-chimamanda-ngozi-adichie/2013/06/10/a9e5a522-d1de-11e2-9f1a-1a7cdee20287_story.html?noredirect=on.

Sandoval, Chela. *Methodology of the Oppressed*. University of Minnesota Press, 2000.

Ureña, Carolyn. "Loving from Below: Of (De)colonial Love and Other Demons." *Hypatia*, vol. 32, no. 1, Winter 2017, pp. 86–102.

Chapter 10

Endless Love

The Evolution of Healers in Octavia Butler's Patternist *Series*

Ebony Gibson

In a 1988 interview, Octavia Butler explains, "In my novels, generally, everybody wins or loses something . . . because as I see it, that's pretty much how the world is."[1] In other words, no matter how good or evil—though Butler disliked those labels too[2]—and no matter how powerful, no character emerges unscathed from the complex and often violent worlds he or she inhabits. Healers are central to the *Patternist* world. They are Black women with the ability to heal the mental and physical wounds of others;[3] however, their abilities and understanding of the human body also make them dangerous enemies.

This chapter examines the evolution of healers in the *Patternist* novels. I analyze them in order of publication moving from Amber (*Patternmaster*), Rachel (*Mind of My Mind*), and their ancestor who is introduced as Emma (*Mind of My Mind*) before she is fully developed as Anyanwu (*Wild* Seed). This order of analysis is intentionally chosen to reinforce that as Butler writes prequels to *Patternmaster*, she reinscribes issues of race, gender, and African Worldview in the earlier novels. They are now generally read in the chronological sequence of the narrative. I will explore the relationship between the healers and how these women shape each other; in other words, when Butler writes about Rachel and then Anyanwu, she continues to add more depth to the issues of race, gender, and African Worldview than originally present in reading Amber in a standalone text.[4] Moreover, while Butler's exploration of gender and othering is present from her earliest novel, the evolution of the healer reflects her growing purposeful use of West African culture.

PATTERNIST SYNOPSIS

The *Patternist* series centers on the origins and rise to power of a community of telepaths and the violent struggles to maintain power. It consists of five novels: *Patternmaster* (1976), *Mind of My Mind* (1977), *Survivor* (1978), *Wild Seed* (1979), and *Clay's Ark* (1980).[5] The texts were not published in order of events. Butler had written and rewritten stories for several of these characters since adolescence. She explains in an interview with Charles Brown that these were novels she "could write quickly"; she comments, these were the "novels that were 'in my trunk.' "[6] In other words, she continues unpacking the lives of central characters. Butler explains, "I just kept taking them back in time, after wondering, 'How'd they get like that?' And that's how they got plugged in to wherever they are on that timeline."[7] Thus, the first novel published is *Patternmaster*—the last of the narrative events—and the larger narrative is fleshed out with prequels and origin stories.

The synopsis that follows is in the chronological order of narrative, since that is generally how the books are read; however, the later analysis of the characters will be in the order the books were published. The description below primarily focuses on the three novels containing the healers. More details are provided about *Wild Seed* because more of the argument is focused on Anyanwu and her connection to the other healers.

In *Wild Seed*, the immortal 4,000-year-old Doro cannot die. Whether he chooses to or not, his essence jumps to a new body. To conquer "loneliness and boredom,"[8] he begins the project of breeding together people in which he senses special psychic or telekinetic abilities. The opening of the novel is set in 1690 in West Africa. Doro is wandering and distraught over the destruction of one of his seed villages. He discovers Anyanwu, an Igbo woman whom he considers "wild seed"—someone with exceptional abilities that he discovers outside of the people who follow him. Anyanwu has lived nearly 300 years; she has exceptional strength, can become any animal whose flesh she ingests and analyzes, heal sickness within her own body, and use the fluids of her body to heal others.

Doro lures her from her home by promising her the possibility of children that will never die and an empty promise to leave her existing children alone.[9] She soon discovers how fully Doro owns his people; he presides violently over them by taking bodies to maintain order, for pleasure, and breeding. You obey him or he will soon be wearing your skin. Once they are in New England, he forces her to marry his son Isaac, something she considers an "abomination" because she is married to Doro. She does it only to spare her children and because she is not ready to die.

Anyanwu grows to love Isaac and builds a life with him for over 50 years. She finds some happiness despite the emotional and sexual violence Doro repeatedly inflicts as a form of control and humiliation. Both she and Isaac have slept with many others as part of the breeding program. Isaac has grown up with Doro's way of life as normal; therefore, Isaac does what is expected of him and happily returns home to his wife and children. For Anyanwu, it continues to be a humiliating experience. However, Doro grows tired of her resistance and is only waiting for Isaac to die before he kills her. Doro knows her healing abilities are all that keep his favorite son alive. The second section of the novel opens in 1741.[10] Doro returns to the New England village Wheatley where Anyanwu, Isaac, and their children reside. One of Anyanwu's daughters, Nweke, is entering transition; it is an emotional and physical painful event that many do not survive; if they do, the gift is usually extraordinary telepathic or telekinetic powers. Nweke's transition goes horribly wrong leading to her death and Isaac's. Sensing Doro's plan to kill her, Anyanwu escapes before the funerals.

Nearly a century later in 1840, Doro tracks Anyanwu down in Louisiana. She runs her plantation by taking the shape of an older white man as needed. Yet, the people on her land are not enslaved. However, Anyanwu, without serious efforts, has gathered her own group of people with special abilities. They thrive and have created a family. Instead of killing Anyanwu, Doro reaches an uneasy agreement where he sends her some of his people to look after. The relationship is tenuous, but they eventually find affection for each other again; Anyanwu suffers the death of loved ones indirectly and directly due to Doro's decisions. Anyanwu decides she is "tired" and ready to die. Doro begs for her not to leave him. She is the only thing in his life that is not "temporary." They reach an understanding; he will no longer simply kill his people who have served their purpose as breeding stock. Anyanwu heads west with her people due to the rumors of impending war; she changes her name to Emma.

In *Mind of My Mind*, approximately 150 years after the end of *Wild Seed*, Doro's millennia of experimenting creates his daughter Mary—a descendant of Anyanwu (who now calls herself Emma). Mary surpasses his expectations. Once through "transition" (a painful and often deadly process when telepathic or telekinetic powers are fully realized), she produces the Pattern—an unseen but powerful mental string connecting her to Doro's six most powerful and stable "actives." Actives are those who have survived the horrible transition to realize their full abilities. While "latents" are those who carry the genetic material of abilities but cannot use it. Mary believes her goal is to help latents. Because they have no control over their ability, they often suffer; it is an endless and uncontrollable noise of other people's thoughts that leads many latents to violence, depression, and often suicide. These offcasts are unimportant to Doro and due to thousands of years of breeding people all over the world, there are now thousands of latents who suffer. Rachel extends the

Pattern by helping latents through transition. Over the course of two years, Mary adds hundreds to the Pattern. Doro is threatened by this growth and tells Mary she must stop. However, not only does she choose not to stop, Mary is physically unable to stop. She must continue to add. In the inevitable confrontation, Mary can link with other Patternists and defeat Doro. Learning of Doro's death, Emma decides to die.

Clay's Ark is the origin story of Clayarks. A group of humans is infected by an alien virus carried back by an astronaut on an exploratory spaceship returning to Earth. The virus compels the infected to spread the disease to others and rewards the carrier with increased strength. Clayarks are the violent enemy and the most present danger to telepaths in *Patternmaster*—beyond the struggles for power with each other. *Survivor* follows a missionary colony that leaves earth to escape the Clayarks. The protagonist Alanna is kidnapped from the colony by Tekhon—one of two alien groups on the planet. She must learn to survive among them—and in some ways eventually finds a more satisfying life than she had among the missionaries.

Patternmaster is set in the distant future where the Pattern is now controlled by Rayal—a man who killed most of his siblings and married his sister, Jansee, as his lead wife to consolidate power. It is a feudal system organized by households. Hours after leaving school, the protagonist Teray's plan to become a housemaster is quickly shattered. Instead of being an apprentice and preparing to one day have his own house, he is sold to the housemaster Coransee; Teray soon learns that he and Coransee are both the sons of Rayal and Jansee. Coransee wants to eliminate Teray as competition to be the next Patternmaster. Teray's wife Iray is taken from him and also now belongs to his brother. Teray is given the household job of looking after mutes; they are non-telepathic humans who are mentally enslaved to carry out most of the domestic tasks of the household. He meets the healer Amber when a mute is severely beaten by another member of the house. She is an independent and belongs to no single household and uses her services as a healer. Teray eventually decides to try to escape Coransee, hoping he can make it to his dying father's household to train and perhaps have a chance of beating his much more experienced brother. He and Amber leave together and travel a deadly wilderness full of Clayarks and other housemasters loyal to Coransee. Amber teaches him the skills to kill Clayarks more quickly. Amber also stands by his side ready to die when attacked by a housemaster and her people. After surviving the attack, Teray asks her to be his head wife. She makes it clear she loves him, but she wants a house of her own. Coransee finds them soon after and takes the two as prisoners. Coransee plans to continue the journey to their father's house, kill Teray, and take the position of Patternmaster. A showdown between the brothers is inevitable and Teray is waiting for the right moment, hoping he can catch his brother off guard and gain some advantage. Amber admits to Teray, she has conceived their baby with Teray; that provides an even greater incentive for Teray. She also points out to Teray his advantage is that he has the natural gifts of a healer. When the fight does take place between the two brothers, Teray is victorious and kills his brother—in large part because he embraces the techniques of a healer to use in conjunction with the more common talents of a telepath.

AMBER

It is established at the opening of *Patternmaster* that power may only be maintained through violence. Rayal explains to his lead wife that their children will one day fight and kill each other for control of the Pattern, just as Rayal killed his brothers and married his strongest sister. This conversation foreshadows the main conflict of the novel—the battle for control of the Pattern between the brothers Teray and Coransee. Nevertheless, while the plot centers on Teray's path to gain the Pattern, he is only successful because of Amber.[11]

Amber's first appearance is healing the violence that a man has inflicted on a mute woman. Amber has little patience for Teray's ignorance of the situation. His responsibility in the household is caring for mutes; however, he has been so self-involved with his concerns that he has neglected the welfare of those in his care. Teray has not done much more than the minimum, feeling the job is beneath him. Amber functions in a world where most women are wives or concubines; these women must gain and maintain their power through men. However, she is independent and strong but weary of healing the violence that telepaths inflict on mutes simply for sport and amusement; she opens her mind to Teray, allowing him to see the extent of the depravity. Her actions pull Teray out of selfishness and remind him of responsibilities outside of him. She is the one that repeatedly mends the bodies of the powerless, and she also negotiates how to maintain her agency and ambitions among powerful enemies.

Amber can maintain her power because she is an excellent healer and an exceptionally knowledgeable killer; she understands the bodies of humans and animals and can heal or destroy their organs with a simple thought. Because of this training, she is an efficient killer of Clayarks and must push past Teray's arrogance and naiveté to teach him how to kill them more quickly for both of their survival. Moreover, Hampton argues, "It is through Amber's control over her own body and the bodies of other characters in the narrative that her value and identity become unbounded."[12] Therefore, it is her ability to manipulate the body in a society that has a telepathic ruling class that sets her apart. She has a highly valued skill that constantly reminds her to respect and protect her body but also survive in a society that rarely views a woman's body as more than a sexual object.

Amber's empowerment also comes from her relationship with another woman.[13] A great deal of her knowledge comes from her former lover Kai who is a woman, housemaster, and healer. Kai helps her through transition and gives her 15 years of memories and knowledge as a housemaster. This offers a different perspective from the male housemasters who refuse to apprentice anyone who has the potential to one day be stronger.[14] On the other hand, Amber stays at Coransee's house for two years because she "didn't want to be just a copy of Kai, running on memories."[15] She wants to add to her knowledge and find her path as a future housemaster. However, Coransee stops accepting her as an independent and only seeks to categorize her into one of the common (and oppressive) roles of women in his house when he learns from digging around in Amber's thoughts about her relationship with Kai. The thought of Amber having a strong sexual, emotional, and intellectual bond with another woman is threatening to him. This is when Amber decides to leave with Teray.

Amber leaves with Teray because it is her best chance at freedom. A few days later, after escaping a deadly standoff, Teray asks Amber to be his wife. She explains, " 'I want what I want. I could have given my life for you back there if we had to fight. But I could never give my life *to* you' " [italics in original]. When he continues trying to convince her, she offers, " 'How interested would you be in becoming a lead husband?' . . . 'I am after all going to need a lead husband.' "[16] With a few sentences, she calls attention to the lack of equality he expects her to accept in the role of spouse. It would not and could not be a true partnership. She wants a house of her own. Love does not change that. She does not subordinate her goals for a man.

While she chooses not to be a wife, Amber does choose to be a mother. She conceives a child and later tells Teray she has done it. As Hampton points out, "Amber's openness to impregnation is not completely clear in the narrative. What is important is that Amber made all of the decisions pertaining to her body alone. . . . By impregnating herself without the consent of Teray, she has taken the traditionally debilitating title of motherhood and transformed it as a symbol of liberation and power of the female body."[17] Thus, Amber has added a sense of empowerment and choice to a condition often largely associated with sacrifice and loss. Furthermore, it speaks to Amber's outlook on the world. Despite the hardships and suffering that surround her, she is purposely bringing life into the world. Moreover, in addition to other ambitions that she has, she chooses to be a mother; it is not something forced upon her by social pressure or that has happened by accident. This reinforces the surety and confidence already embodied in her character.

In Amber's world, race is not a primary determining factor of success; it generally ties to power, gender, and telepathic ability. Canavan also points out that in this novel "racial markers" are "completely incidental."[18] And in her 1980 article "Lost Races in Science Fiction," Butler stresses, "*Patternmaster* takes place at a time when psionic ability is all that counts. People have who have enough of the ability are on top whether they're male or female, black, white, or brown. People who have none are slaves. In this culture, a black like the novel's main woman character would, except for her coloring, be indistinguishable from characters of any other race."[19] Yet, Butler does take time to make sure the reader is aware of her color and her name even reinforces it. Teray describes Amber as "a lighter golden color beneath her clothing. Honey-colored. The cap of black hair was softer than it looked and the woman was harder than she felt."[20] In fact, the word "amber" itself may be used to describe something as honey-colored. The substance is so beautiful in appearance that it has been used for centuries as jewelry. It is also hard and may preserve whatever is trapped inside for millennia. Amber preserves the core values, survival instinct, and psionic abilities of her ancestors. Moreover, Amber gains more power as a symbol as Butler writes the prequels and enriches the legacy and power of Black women healers with Anyanwu and Rachel. In her society, Amber is not immediately judged by her race; but the reader is made aware of it—and even more so if they have read the novels chronologically leading up to her.

No blatant signs of an African Worldview are in the novel; however, when viewed through the lens of West African mysticism, the Pattern may be read as a symbol of community and valuing the group over the individual. In the Pattern, individuals are tethered to others and relationships and households are built based on how "close" individuals are to someone else in the Pattern.[21] For example, Joachim has a reputation for picking members of the household based on the closeness in the Pattern. In other words, strength and power come through linking with others. Simply put, individuals *are* stronger together than apart and even stronger if they are closer together in the Pattern. Teray and Amber embrace that link and the intimacy that comes with that connection. They are loyal to each other—and their personal goals and desires. They are more successful than those who are not.

RACHEL

Butler continues to develop these themes of how women use the power within and without as she later writes the stories of Amber's ancestors. For example, in *Mind of My Mind*, Mary creates her strategy for dealing with the disgruntled actives by reading their minds. However, the pivotal scene that demonstrates Mary's dominance and establishes her as the first Patternmaster is when she attacks the bodies of Jesse and Rachel—as opposed to their minds. Taking down Jesse is quick and easy. However, when Rachel—who is the most stable and strong healer Doro has—is taken down, the other actives accept Mary's role as their leader.

Rachel is the daughter of Emma's[22] most successful granddaughter.[23] She is rarely discussed in analyses of *Mind of My Mind*. Critics generally focus on Mary—or Emma as the first sketch of Anyanwu. However, Rachel serves as an important bridge between Amber and Anyanwu.

Rachel maintains the implication—that begins with Amber—that a healer has fierce and deadly abilities and should be viewed as a threat. Initially, Rachel is Mary's biggest threat. In the first few weeks of the actives in the Pattern being drawn to Mary, Rachel does not suffer well-being on a "leash."[24] Unlike Amber to whom the Pattern is a natural thing, Rachel is one of the two who resists the hardest; she is used to being in control and answering to no one (except Doro). Even Doro does not underestimate her ability. He warns Rachel that until Mary has fully recovered from transition, Mary "better not even catch so much as a cold, *healer*."[25]

Rachel never inflicts harm for entertainment as seen in *Patternmaster*; however, before the Pattern, she sucks energy from those she healed. That is not to say that the first Patternists do not inflict emotional violence and mental violations on mutes. It is Mary and Rachel as part of the original six actives in the Pattern who establish how mutes are to be treated. Mutes are resources and while protections are put in place, the powerful abuse the defenseless. Mutes may be programmed to be content and not aware that they are enslaved, but they are enslaved nonetheless.

Rachel displays sexual freedom and domination in her incestuous relationship with her cousin. She uses her distant cousin Eli to fulfill her most important needs, but once the Pattern is created, she pairs with an active that provides more balance. Eli serves essential roles as a business partner and lover. Because Eli is a latent, she has mental dominance. Before the Pattern, the only role that he does not seem to play is supplying the energy she feeds on, which she receives from those she heals. Her dominance over him seems natural to her and she seems impatient when he does not immediately comply. This also raises speculation as to whether she dominates him in the same way sexually. There are no hints of romantic affection and she quickly pairs with another active once the Pattern is created; there seems to be more affection and parity in her relationship with Jesse. Before the Pattern, two actives could not be near each other; it would have been two painful and uncomfortable. Perhaps Rachel finds comfort in someone she considers more of her psionic equal. While Amber and Teray are joined in their hate for Coransee and willingness to risk death for a better life, Rachel and Jesse bond over the initial hatred for Mary and the desire to return to their previous lives. They are also the only two that do more than talk of attacking Mary. Rachel is also ready to sacrifice her life when she believes Jesse is dead from his failed attack. Later, when Butler writes the origin story of Doro and Anyanwu, there is an even more complex version of a bond that is full of the tension and hate between two powerful and immortal, something only hinted at in *Mind of My Mind*.[26]

While Rachel initially fights the Pattern, she eventually embraces it and becomes a more selfless healer; thus, Rachel has a dramatic shift in her moral character. Moreover, like Amber, one of Rachel's most important relationships in catalyzing her growth as a healer comes from another woman. Rachel's biggest progression comes after she is defeated by Mary. Once she accepts that she is a permanently part of Pattern, like the other original actives, she finds fulfillment in her work helping to recover latents. It is painful and demanding work, yet Rachel seems much more at peace than she was posing as a faith healer, feeding off of a congregation. There are no more crowds of adoration, instead, there are mentally and physically broken latents who are slowly killing themselves.

Rachel's growth is reflected in her relationship of mentoring another healer. While Rachel does not have children or speak of motherhood, she is shown to develop into a mentor and mother figure for the healer she is training. Rachel patiently guides Miguela through a particularly bad scene of recovering latents from their home and encourages Miguela even in the mentee's moments of frustration. This is far different from when earlier in the novel Mary asks for help in learning healing skills and Rachel refuses because no one taught her. Moreover, this is very different from Amber whose overall demeanor and worldview are consistent. The biggest shift in character in *Patternmaster* takes place in the naïve Teray who must grow up quickly. Amber's love for Teray is important in making his quick shift possible—but even more influential is her frankness and mentoring in healing. Most importantly, she unapologetically holds on to her ambition to be a housemaster, which is rarely accomplished by women.

ANYANWU

Butler first introduced Anyanwu as Emma in *Mind of My Mind*. In this novel, we only hear of her abilities to heal and see them carried out by her descendants Rachel and Mary. In *Wild Seed*, after writing the stories of Amber, Rachel, and Mary, Butler writes the origins of Anyanwu and creates who Ruth Salvaggio refers to as "Butler's most fully developed and intriguing heroine."[27] Butler adds understanding and depth to the hard-won bond between Doro and Emma. She also adds a deeper understanding of the violence and sacrifice that gives birth to the Pattern and creates a bookend to the *Patternmaster*.

Butler establishes a setting of violence from the first paragraph of *Wild Seed*. It opens to devastation that is even beyond the control of immortal Doro. One of his seed's villages has been destroyed and pillaged by slavers. The setting is quickly used to establish death, greed, and destruction: "With their guns and their greed, [slavers] had undone in a few hours the work of a thousand years. Those villagers they had not herded away, they had slaughtered. Doro found human bones, hair, bits of desiccated flesh missed by scavengers. He stood over a very small skeleton—the bones of a child."[28] Thus, slavers took what they wanted and killed the rest; animals fed on the dead bodies. Humans and animals alike consume without mercy. But Doro is no more merciful. He leaves bodies in his wake. He enslaves too. And while Anyanwu can pretend for a short while that Doro is not as bad as the enslavers and enslavement she has known in her life, she begins to quickly learn that as soon as he found her and understood her abilities—it was inevitable that she would become a possession that would enrich his breeding program.

Like her descendants, Anyanwu negotiates how to use her power in a violent and oppressing world. While I am limiting my argument to the healers, and at this moment Anyanwu, Sarah Outterson argues that Butler makes a pedagogical argument about violence throughout her novels: "violence is inevitable. Despite the thin veneer of culture that we pretend exists, violating power is an independent force that we can't avoid. . . . Furthermore, survival requires violence. Butler demonstrates again and again how the harsh reality of confrontation with the ugliest forms of natural, determined behavior demonstrates the essential presence of violence in the human character."[29] And Doro is a clear embodiment of that "detached force." An immortal being—a force that wears bodies but does not have one of his own. He has moved through the world thousands of years without any true challenge to that power. Yet Anyanwu is the first. And over the first 50 years of their relationship, Doro uses the tactics of seduction, emotional and sexual violence, and physical threat to control their relationship. Yet, even among this violence, Anyanwu continues to heal herself, care for others, and find a loving husband and partner in Isaac.

Anyanwu approaches violence and ugliness with kindness and from the perspective of a healer. As J. Andrew Deman points out, "Anyanwu does not 'shift' herself into some masculine trope by taking power and finding a way to kill Doro, executing him with the same brand of violence that is his defining characteristic. Rather, Anyanwu finds a new way, the way of a healer."[30] In other words, her natural response is not to use brutality. It is to continue to help others even amid her pain and oppression. The most vivid representation of this is in her handling of Thomas. To humiliate her, Doro sends her to sleep with Thomas.[31] A man so haunted by the thoughts of others he has to live miles away from a town to avoid the proximity of other people. He is a lonely, bitter alcoholic who has let his body deteriorate to the point of emaciation and being covered in stinking open sores. Anyanwu does not even retaliate against his verbal abuse but approaches him with compassion and understanding that he is no less a prisoner of Doro. She can find emotional common ground and begin to heal Thomas both mentally and physically. Even in moments of oppression, she resists. Anyanwu makes meaning of her life and gives meaning to others by choosing to heal.

Anyanwu and Doro operate in a space of tension with the former resisting the latter. And while their dynamic changes over the course of centuries, Anyanwu generally acts as a *nonviolent* resister. In arguing for the role of violence in the way we live, Outterson presents a helpful framework for viewing the dynamic between Anyanwu and Doro when she cites a passage from Martin Luther King, Jr.'s "Letter from a Birmingham Jail":

> My citing the creation of tension as part of the work of the nonviolent resister may sound rather shocking. But I must confess that I am not afraid of the word "tension." I have earnestly opposed violent tension, but there is a type of constructive, nonviolent tension that is necessary for growth. Just as Socrates felt that it was necessary to create a tension in the mind so that individuals could rise from the bondage of myths and half-truths to the unfettered realm of creative analysis and objective appraisal, so must we see the need for nonviolent gadflies to create the kind of tension in society that will help men rise from the dark depths of prejudice and racism to the majestic heights of understanding and brotherhood.[32]

King offers this perspective to white clergymen not wanting to violate southern racial custom. Outterson uses this as a principle to reflect: "We must constantly renew our minds and perceptions of the traditions of the past. The answer is not a single, final pedagogical method, but a constant willingness to undergo compulsive, violent death and renewal of self."[33] In other words, Outterson alludes to the tension between custom and the need to thoughtfully (and often painfully) question tradition to give birth to a new identity. Therefore, while Doro holds fasts to the customs and expectations of wild seed he has created over thousands of years, Anyanwu resists him by quietly maintaining core principles from her 300 years of life, such as motherhood and healing—yet still adapting when necessary for survival.[34] Doro has a constant need for her to see him through the lens of all others that generally adore him—or at least fear and blindly obey. He is angry with himself that he even cares that she hates him.

This is not to say Anyanwu never uses physical violence; it is done when she needs to defend herself or those she loves. She chooses animal forms to carry out her most physically violent acts, such as turning to a leopard to kill Lale for projecting pictures of her having sex with him into her mind and planning to rape her. And she turns into the dangerous cat again to kill Joseph after he kills her favorite son Stephen and attempts to rape and later attempts to kill her 11-year-old daughter Helen. In these cases, she changes her body to a weapon—instead of picking one up. And she does not simply change her shape but becomes them.

She also changes form for connection and escape. When married to Isaac, who could fly, she would take the form of a brightly colored bird in case hunters ever spotted them, knowing she could heal if shot. This creates a bond between the two. When Isaac and Nweke die, she escapes Doro by flying away as an eagle and living for years as a dolphin. As a dolphin, she finds peace and later when Doro tracks her down and is indirectly the reason for the death of her son Stephen and the suicide of her daughter Margaret, she goes again to the sea to refresh and heal herself. The dolphin form is also how she finds lost treasure on the bottom of the sea that she uses to help run the plantation.

Yet, she also pragmatically uses race and gender as a disguise—or more accurately a tool when needed. To create a life and home in Louisiana for herself, slaves she has bought and freed, and white outcasts, Anyanwu creates the guise of a white plantation owner Edward Warrick. To Anyanwu, it is a practical disguise, one she predicts over a century earlier in a conversation with Thomas who does not understand why she does not choose to be white when she can be: " 'I'm content,' she said. 'If I have to be white someday to survive, I will be white. If I have to be a leopard to hunt and kill, I will be a leopard. If I have to travel quickly across land, I'll become a large bird. If I have to cross the sea, I'll become a fish.' She smiled a little. 'A dolphin, perhaps.' "[35] While there's no doubt Anyanwu understands the cultural and political capital of whiteness and maleness, she finds contentment and pride in who she is. She considers white skin only another tool for survival. However, she is also aware of the effect of wearing white skin and how after a time she can get used to the effects of the privilege. She meets Stephen's father because he calls to her in her native language when she passes him; he is in chains and has just survived the middle passage and she is shaped as Warrick. He asks, " Anyanwu! Does that white skin cover your eyes too?" She understands at that moment that she had become "oblivious" to seeing slaves around her. And explains, "I had been white for too long."[36] Therefore, she understands the dangers of this tool; it must be wielded with care like any other. Furthermore, this disrupts the usual trope of passing. She does not seem to suffer from the dilemma or duality of walking between two unaccepting cultures. Anyanwu can choose which skin to wear—and when she does, the skin and shape she reverts to and prefers are that of herself as a 19-year-old Igbo woman. That form is "home" for her body.

While in the shape of Warrick, Anyanwu marries and builds a family with a woman, reflecting a shift in her earlier views on sexuality. Anyanwu not only marries but has children with her wife, Denise. Denise is well aware of Anyanwu's gifts. However, Denise is also special in that she sees ghosts. Thus, no matter men or women, Anyanwu's lovers are witches. Moreover, it is not simply a marriage of convenience of a white wife and white children; they "pleased each other."[37] This is a clear shift from the earlier belief that such things were "abominations"[38] or the inability to get an erection when forced to have sex with Doro with him in a woman's body and Anyanwu shaped like a man.[39] However, it is also worth noting that Anyanwu's relationship with Denise—and Amber's relationship with Kai are presented as backstory with few details. The focus seems to be more on the emotional connection than the sexual. Moreover, unlike many of the sexual interactions between men and women in the novels, there is no subtext residue of force, oppression, or inequity.

Anyanwu is the only healer to have a shapeshifting ability; it points forward to concepts Butler will more fully realize in the Oankali aliens of the *Xenogenesis* series. In her interview with Marilynn Mehaffy and AnaLouise Keating, Butler admits she was "uncomfortable" about the abilities that she had given Anyanwu; she explains that by the time she gets to the *Xenogenesis* series, she "understood more of what [she] was trying to get at."[40] Thus, Butler continues to explore the power of reshaping the body and its implications. The Oankali change shape from generation to generation by careful genetic programming to suit the needs of caring for their spaceships and to adjust their appearance in hopes of making genetic trade partners more comfortable. And after taking cancer from humans, they also use it to increase their abilities to regenerate. On the other hand, Anyanwu can read the flesh of any animal she ingests to become another living entity. Yet her essence or spirit remains. She still holds on to the experiences and identity. The abilities of Anyanwu and Oankali raise questions about defining the essence of humanity. Butler interrogates it with Anyanwu by making her more than human. Anyanwu can see the beauty of other species through a human lens. Later, in *Xenogenesis*, it is explored by making the Oankali aliens at times more *humane* than human beings. And it also raises questions about the limits of perspective.

Anyanwu's ability of endless motherhood also points forward to the antihero Lilith in the *Xenogenesis* series—and back to Amber in *Patternmaster*. Anyanwu continues to give birth throughout *Wild Seed* and by the last section, she is giving birth at 450-years-old. Lilith can give birth at that age due to genetic modification by the Oankali. Anyanwu is born with her abilities. Also, when Butler writes *Wild Seed* as a prequel to *Patternmaster*, she gives this gift to control motherhood to Amber's ancestors and therefore continues to use the healers and the choice to become a mother as a symbol. They control every aspect of their baby's conception and genetics with their wombs. They can bring healthy children into the world; however, they must still suffer the same burdens of not being able to protect a child once it enters the world.

Anyanwu also maintains a connection to her Igbo culture and reflects a shift in Butler's writing to make purposeful and apparent connections to Igbo and Yoruba culture and *Wild Seed* becomes the earliest in publication to often be connected to African Worldview by critics.[41] Canavan points out that Butler studied African history and culture in college.[42] And Butler draws heavily on Igbo culture to create Anyanwu. She studied Igbo ethnography and dialects to create Anyanwu.[43] Butler created Anyanwu from an Igbo story: "Atagbusi was a shape-shifter who had spent her whole life helping her people, and when she died, a market gate was named after her and later became a symbol of protection. I thought to myself, This woman's description is perfect—who said she had to die? And I had Anyanwu give 'Atagbusi' as one of her names."[44] Thus, Butler chooses a woman who represents strength, community, and prosperity, and reimagines her with even greater power.

In *Wild Seed* and *Mind of Mind*, Anyanwu functions as a "living" ancestor—and after her death, she is framed as an ancestor for *Patternmaster*. The reader is more aware of Amber as Black and female because of the culture and images of Anyanwu in her native West Africa. And these signifiers are even more apparent once juxtaposed against the backdrops of seventeenth- and eighteenth-century upstate New York and nineteenth-century Louisiana;[45] she holds on to West African language and culture that she passes on to her children. And we as readers retain these memories as we meet Amber.

To encapsulate the healer, a scene from *Wild Seed* seems appropriate. Immediately after the death scene of Anyanwu's daughter Nweke and her husband Issac, Anyanwu knows she must leave. She cannot stay for the funeral and grieve the losses with family and friends. Nweke was the product of her few days with Thomas—one of her greatest challenges as a healer. She has lost her husband of 50 years. Nonetheless, she must escape because Doro intends to kill her now that Isaac has died. Anyanwu has already experienced a great deal of loss. And even greater pain awaits her in the final section of the novel. The pain never ends. Yet neither does the instinct to not just endure or survive. Instead, Anyanwu and her descendants resist, heal, protect, grow, and pursue their dreams. They find moments of joy and purpose in the violent worlds they inhabit.

NOTES

1. Larry McCaffery and Jim McMenamin, "An Interview with Octavia E. Butler," in *Conversations with Octavia Butler*, ed. Consuela Francis (University Press of Mississippi, 2010), 20.

2. Butler was clear in her interviews that she did not like simple labels of good and evil being tied to her characters. One such interview that is often cited is the NPR interview with Juan Williams.

3. The term "Black" is used as opposed to "African American" to identify race; the first term is often recognized and used interchangeably with the second; however, in this case, it is also being used to recognize the African Diasporic and interracial background of many of Butler's character.

4. As a new generation finds and reads Butler for the first time (and even most readers in the past decade), they will usually read the novels in chronological order of events. The *Patternist* novels were originally published between 1976 and 1984. However, they were republished (excluding *Survivor*) and repackaged in the order of narrative events as *Seed to Harvest* in 2007.

5. Butler wrote *Survivor* at 19. It was the first written but third published. *Survivor* connects through *Clay's Ark*; missionaries leave earth hoping to escape the mutated humans known as Clayarks. Butler planned to do a whole series of "Missionary" stories on different planets but that never came to fruition. See Canavan (31–35) for more details.

6. Charles Brown, "Octavia E. Butler: Persistence," in *Conversations with Octavia Butler*, ed. Consuela Francis (University Press of Mississippi, 2010), 181.

7. Brown, "Octavia E. Butler: Persistence," 181.

8. Octavia E. Butler, *Seed to Harvest: Wild Seed, Mind of My Mind, Clay's Ark, Patternmaster* (New York: Grand Central Publishing, 2007), 100. For clarity and specificity, all endnotes that follow will have the title of the novel as opposed to the compilation *Seed to Harvest*.

9. At the opening of *Wild Seed* (27), Anyanwu has already had 47 children and 10 husbands.

10. The novel alludes to the Christian allegory in naming its three sections after books from the Bible; for analysis of the names and meanings, see Hampton, *Changing,* 40–44 and Shinn, "Sigynifyin(g)," 79–80.

11. Gerry Canavan believes that Amber "often threatened to steal the book from its male 'chosen one' " (81).

12. Gregory Jerome Hampton, *Changing Bodies in the Fiction of Octavia Butler: Slaves, Aliens, and Vampires* (Lanham, MD: Lexington Books, 2010), 59.

13. Amber identifies as bisexual, and explains to Teray, " 'When I meet a woman who attracts me, I prefer women' . . . 'And when I meet a man who attracts me, I prefer men' " (*Patternmaster* 717).

14. Amber even seeks to empower Iray by stopping Teray from making decisions for Iray and making sure Iray can decide for herself if she wants to run away from Coransee (*Patternmaster* 691).

15. Butler, *Patternmaster*, 718.

16. Butler, *Patternmaster*, 716.
17. Hampton, *Changing*, 63–64.
18. Gerry Canavan, *Octavia E. Butler* (Urbana: University of Illinois, 2016), 51. Canavan goes on to argue that "this 'colorblind society' has reinscribed the privileges of whiteness into an even more monstrous and permanent form . . . slavery has become a universal condition that's not simply for the mutes but for all but the most privileged Patternmasters, with essentially no reason to hope that this system will ever be abolished or overthrown" (52).
19. Octavia E. Butler, "Lost Races of Science Fiction (1980)," in *Octavia E. Butler*, edited by Gerry Canavan Urbana: University of Illinois, 2016), 186.
20. Butler, *Patternmaster*, 692.
21. It is never clearly explained what it means to be "closer" in the Pattern. My educated guess is that it refers to genetic compatibility and often having similar telepathic gifts—even if not developed.
22. Emma is used when referring to events related to *Mind of Mind*. Anyanwu is used when referring to events in *Wild Seed* or the character in general.
23. Emma's granddaughter Catherine had the potential to outlive Emma. However, she also had psionic abilities but not a strong mental shielding to keep out the noise of others. Like Emma would do so eventually, when she could not take it anymore, Catherine lay down and died—at the age of 39; moreover, "Everyone of Doro's previous healers had made similar decisions" (*Mind of My Mind*, 346).
24. Butler, *Mind of My Mind*, 348.
25. Butler, *Mind of My Mind*, 348 (emphasis mine).
26. The relationship between Mary and her forced marriage to Karl also explores the tensions of power shifts between two powerful beings, especially when a woman gains more power.
27. Ruth Salvaggio, "Octavia Butler and the Black Science-Fiction Heroine," *Black American Literature Forum* 18, no. 2 (1984): 80.
28. Butler, *Wild Seed*, 5.
29. Sarah Outterson, "Diversity, Change, Violence: Octavia Butler's Pedagogical Philosophy," *Utopian Studies* 19, no. 3 (2008): 448.
30. J. Andrew Deman, "Taking Out the Trash: Octavia E. Butler's Wild Seed and the Feminist Voice in American SF," *Femspec* 6, no. 2 (2005): 13.
31. Butler, *Wild*, 144–161. The story of Thomas is one of the most significant examples of Anyanwu as a healer and her resistance to Doro's tactics to punish and humiliate her.
32. Martin Luther King, Jr., "Letter from a Birmingham Jail," University of Pennsylvania, accessed June 28, 2018, https://www.africa.upenn.edu/Articles_Gen/Letter_Birmingham.html.
33. Outterson, "Diversity," 453.
34. See Christopher Okonwo's *A Spirit of Dialogue: Incarnations of Ọgbañje, the Born-to-die, in African American Literature* for his observation of what Anyanwu has lost and tries to retain of her Igbo culture (72–79).
35. Butler, *Wild Seed*, 150.
36. Butler, *Wild Seed*, 191.

37. Butler, *Wild Seed*, 195.
38. Butler, *Wild Seed*, 94.
39. Butler, *Wild Seed*, 145.
40. Marilynn Mehaffy and AnaLouise Keating, " 'Radio Imagination': Octavia Butler on the Poetics of Narrative Embodiment," in *Conversations with Octavia Butler*, ed. Consuela Francis (Jackson: University Press of Mississippi, 2010), 111.
41. For analysis of Yoruba and Igbo culture in *Wild Seed*, see Shinn (74–75); Okonkwo; Piziks (50).
42. Canavan, *Octavia E. Butler*, 36.
43. McCaffery and McMenamin, "An Interview," 23.
44. McCaffery and McMenamin, "An Interview," 23.
45. For an extensive analysis of signifying in *Wild Seed* and Butler's work, see Shinn.

BIBLIOGRAPHY

"amber, n.1 and adj." OED Online. March 2018. Oxford University Press. Accessed May 29, 2018, https://www.oed.com/view/Entry/6112.

Brown, Charles. "Octavia E. Butler: Persistence." In *Conversations with Octavia Butler*, edited by Consuela Francis, 181–188. Jackson: University Press of Mississippi, 2010.

Butler, Octavia E. "Lost Races of Science Fiction (1980)." In *Octavia E. Butler*, edited by Gerry Canavan, 181–86. Urbana: University of Illinois, 2016.

Butler, Octavia E. *Seed to Harvest: Wild Seed, Mind of My Mind, Clay's Ark, Patternmaster*. New York: Grand Central Publishing, 2007.

Bynum, Edward Bruce. *The African Unconscious: Roots of Ancient Mysticism and Modern Psychology*. New York: Cosmio Books, 2012.

Canavan, Gerry. *Octavia E. Butler*. Urbana: University of Illinois, 2016.

Deman, J. Andrew. "Taking Out the Trash: Octavia E. Butler's Wild Seed and the Feminist Voice in American SF." *Femspec* 6, no. 2 (2005): 6–14.

Hampton, Gregory Jerome. *Changing Bodies in the Fiction of Octavia Butler: Slaves, Aliens, and Vampires*. Lanham, MD: Lexington Books, 2010.

Idowu, E. Bolaji. *African Traditional Religion: A Definition*. Maryknoll, NY: Orbis Books, 1973.

King, Martin Luther, Jr. "Letter from a Birmingham Jail." University of Pennsylvania. Accessed June 28, 2018. https://www.africa.upenn.edu/Articles_Gen/Letter_Birmingham.html.

McCaffery, Larry, and Jim McMenamin. "An Interview with Octavia E. Butler." In *Conversations with Octavia Butler*, edited by Consuela Francis, 10–26. Jackson: University Press of Mississippi, 2010.

Mehaffy, Marilynn, and AnaLouise Keating. "'Radio Imagination': Octavia Butler on the Poetics of Narrative Embodiment." In *Conversations with Octavia Butler*, edited by Consuela Francis, 98–122. Jackson: University Press of Mississippi, 2010.

Okonkwo, Christopher N. "Of Power, Protest, and Revolution: Wild Seed and Mind of My Mind." In *A Spirit of Dialogue: Incarnations of Ọgbañje, the Born-To-Die, in African American Literature*, edited by Christopher Okonkwo, 59–87. Knoxville: University of Tennessee Press, 2008.

Outterson, Sarah. "Diversity, Change, Violence: Octavia Butler's Pedagogical Philosophy." *Utopian Studies* 19, no. 3 (2008): 433–56.

Piziks, Steven. "An Interview with Octavia E. Butler." *Marion Zimmer Bradley's FANTASY Magazine*, no. 37 (1997): 46–51.

Salvaggio, Ruth. "Octavia Butler and the Black Science-Fiction Heroine." *Black American Literature Forum* 18, no. 2 (1984): 78–81.

Shinn, Thelma J. "Signifyin(g) Science Fiction." In *Women Shapeshifters: Transforming the Contemporary Novel*, edited by Thelma J. Shinn, 73–85. Westport, CT: Greenwood Press, 1996.

Williams, Juan. "Octavia Butler." In *Conversations with Octavia Butler*, edited by Consuela Francis, 161–80. Jackson: University Press of Mississippi, 2010.

Chapter 11

"I Would Restore What Could Be Restored"

Reclaiming Identity in Octavia Butler's Fledgling

Rashell Smith-Spears

In the folktale, "The People Could Fly" Africans brought to the New World once possessed wings. Through the harshness of the middle passage and the cruel treatment they endure during enslavement, they lose their wings and even the knowledge of how to use them. Not everyone has forgotten, however, and one day when the overseer and driver mistreat a young mother, the old man who remembers speaks a forgotten language and the woman remembers. She spreads her black wings that were actually still a part of her and she flies back home to Africa, escaping the cruelty of slavery. The old man also helps others, speaking the words and inspiring remembrance in them that also leads to their escape.

This story is significant in several ways. First, it recognizes the incorporation of the supernatural-as-natural in African American life. From miraculous provisions to tales of ancestral visitations, the supernatural plays a prominent role in African American culture, arguing for the possibility of the unseen having influence on daily activity and providing an explanation for the seemingly unexplainable. In this story, the wings are an ordinary part of the anatomy, like arms or legs or tonsils that, although unseen, do not simply fall off like a mystical anomaly. They are always there even if invisible or forgotten. Second, and most prevalent to this chapter is the notion of forgetting. Because of their oppression, the people neither remember their language, their power, nor who they are. Their identity, however, is still a part of them and only needs to be coaxed to the forefront of their remembrance. When they realize their power, through language nonetheless, they can become autonomous and in charge of their individual/collective destinies. At the end of the story, the audience is told that the enslaved who were left behind recount the tale to future generations and they tell it to their offspring. However, not everyone believes in the power and autonomy of the people. The slave owner in the story refuses to acknowledge the event as truth. He must instead create his own story explaining the disappearance of the people. Although we are not told what his invention is, we can assume, it will be a narrative that fits within his understanding of the world and Black people.

In addition to being a literary tool of empowerment, this story speaks to the necessary connections between memory and the search for identity. Certainly, the African American experience has been one of orphanage, disconnect, and amnesia as the enslaved and their descendants were violently assimilated into their inferior positions in American society. This process has caused Black people to lose not only their memories of their cultures of origin but also themselves. It then becomes necessary to move beyond this cultural amnesia to seek an understanding of the past to find the self.

Black women writers ask us to confront the past and interrogate this memory loss all of the time. They challenge us to answer such questions as: How does the collective pain of oppression shape our identities even when we do not consciously acknowledge them? Furthermore, as a race, how do we create a sense of wholeness that will allow for the forward progression of the community when there are gaps in our racial memory? Through realism, romance, detective fiction, and even the fantastic, they speak to these questions by portraying the necessity and possibility of confronting the past to discover one's identity. One writer, in particular, Octavia Butler, utilizes vampire literature to explore issues of memory as it relates to a discovery of self. Butler's discussion of the vampire and identity is especially significant because African Americans, reduced and redefined by colonizers and enslavers, are in constant search of their identity. Furthermore, her discussion is significant because as Cynthia Staples points out, "Vampires . . . link the past with the present," thus making them a unique and fitting trope to discuss the African American confrontation with the past.[1] In her novel *Fledgling*, Butler illustrates how a lack of knowledge of self can instill vulnerability in oppressed individuals, which may appear as a weakness. Butler shifts our understanding of weakness, vulnerability, and power, however. Instead of power over others, Butler claims a truer, more productive power comes from responding to the unknown past by defining one's self, the telling of one's own story, and accepting one's weaknesses and strengths, moving forward despite missing knowledge.

Butler's use of the vampire trope draws on a tradition of employing the vampire to create discourses on identity. Writers of mainstream literature express society's anxieties through the vampire as well as reveal the society's understanding of its identity. W. Scott Poole asserts in *Monsters in America* that past societies have created a feared figure, which represents those who are "othered" in society and bear the flaws of humanity. This hatred of the "Other" originates from a fear of the instability of the dominant class' own identity, a fear that they might "yield to the difference" that the Other embodies.[2] As their identities are encompassed in their bodies, Poole suggests that the vampire serves as a threat because it can "puncture, rend and ultimately destroy [that] body."[3] Certainly, it follows that if the vampire can destroy the body, it can destroy one's identity. To survive, a vampire must either destroy/kill a human or turn an individual into something else (a vampire).

Discourses on identity are also expressed through the vampire's disruptions of established binaries: life/death, good/evil, masculine/feminine, heterosexual/homosexual, and desirable/repulsive. The vampire embodies both sides of the binary making it difficult, if not impossible to satisfactorily categorize the individual. This difficulty both disturbs and fascinates society as it speaks to the possibilities for change in identity. During the nineteenth century, this inability to categorize served to disturb more than fascinate. Concerned with the rapid social, economic, and scientific changes that were occurring, many white Americans and Europeans experienced anxiety about their identity and place in the world. Consequently, they seized upon racial identity as a stabilizing marker. They sought homogeneity and purity, deeming those who were racially different as not only "Other," but an inferior "Other." According to Felipe Smith in *American Body Politics*, "The consensus of social scientists was that the impossibility of sharing national kinship with black Americans had to do with innate and ineradicable deficiencies in black bodies."[4] Black people could not be included in the national family, could not be regarded as a part of the national body politic, because they were different and deficient. Wander, Martin, and Nakayama explains that definitions of who was white and Black, particularly in America, were not always easy to establish, despite the attempts to draw legal lines around them.[5] To this end, issues of racial hybridity created problems for society because they suggested the possibility of unknowable blackness. Individuals with both Black and white heritage could be somatically white, but according to pseudoscientific ideas about the polluting effect of Black blood, would be Black. In this way, that which is alien could sneak into the homes of white people and be undetected and undetectable, changing who they are and understand themselves to be. The term, *mulatto*, for instance, was used to designate a person with a mixed racial heritage but was also telling in that it means "little mule." A person with both Black and white heritage was considered to be a deceptive and sterile thing without the ability to reproduce and consequently, a danger to a thriving white nation.

This transformational power of undetected Black blood did not only apply to the individual. Social scientists, writers, and politicians alike also shared the notion of the polluting effect of the Black race within the nation. Thomas Dixon, in his novel that would chronicle and valorize the inception of the Ku Klux Klan, writes, "One drop of Negro blood makes a negro. It kinks the hair, flattens the nose, thickens the lips, puts out the light of intellect, and lights the fires of brutish passions. The beginning of Negro equality as a vital fact is the beginning of the end of this nation's life."[6] He catalogs the sentiments of the day that argued the threat of Black regression. The belief existed that a Black presence in the nation would be detrimental to the nation therefore such invasion had to be guarded against.

These fears created the African American as a menace, monstrous even. One can easily see how Dracula, Nosferatu, and other vampire figures, then, come to stand in for the terror of uncertainty, difference, change, and attitudes of powerlessness regarding race and the Other. The vampire figure, especially as it was warded against and destroyed by white masculine Christianity, worked to reassure the mainstream of its identity and power. In "Black Girls Are from the Future," Susana M. Morris asserts the vampire—then and now—reifies whiteness and its supremacy. She writes,

> [They] often underscore some of the anxieties mainstream culture has with our current multicultural and "postracial" society by seeking to "reinstate" the supremacy of whiteness, often through such tropes as the triumph of a lily-white vampire slayer or through nostalgia for an all-powerful white man who is a vampire.[7]

Even in our contemporary, more inclusive culture, vampires like Edward Cullen from Stephenie Meyer's *Twilight* series, Lestat from Anne Rice's *The Vampire Chronicles*, and Angel from Joss Whedon's *Buffy* and *Angel* maintain for society the power of white masculinity even as the vampires question their place in the world and ultimately find it on top.

In her novel about a Black vampire/human hybrid, Octavia Butler contends with these notions of race, hybridity, and an unknowable heritage with an eye toward shifting our understanding of power. Through her text, we are made to understand how our own world considers these issues and perhaps a better approach. Morris claims that Butler "advocates transgressing repressive social norms and rejecting heteropatriarchy, while centering (or creating) a variety of experiences from across the Afrodiaspora."[8] Butler's characters illustrate paradigm shifts that offer possibilities for reshaping our concepts of community. And as Ali Brox states, that community "is not free of problems but rather one where problems are confronted and dealt with."[9] Much of Butler's literature gives us worlds that confront and deal with problems within the community that stems from identity and power. In each she proposes transformational notions of what it means to be an individual, to know the self, and to be in community with others. In her 1980 novel, *Wildseed*, the main characters Doro and Anyanwu are both powerful individuals who conceive of their abilities and the inherent responsibilities of possessing them in differing ways. Doro, the masculine figure, wields his power to command obedience from humans as well as enhanced humans and ultimately to kill them. Power for him means the ability to manipulate and destroy. Anyanwu, whose form is most often a woman, uses her power to heal. She can also alter her form to imitate any living creature down to the cellular level, connecting to them through a supernatural empathy. The difference between their power is life and death. And while some may read their connection as the yin and yang of existence, their attitudes toward their abilities differ as well. Doro kills without passion or connection until he meets Anyanwu who bribes, begs, and bargains with him to temper his lethality, to be discriminate in whom and how he kills. For her, to have power over others is not for controlling others, but for helping them.

Similarly, Dana, in Butler's *Kindred*, uses her power to help and to heal. Dana is not enhanced with supernatural abilities, but because she time travels to the past, her power is of a more cognitive nature. Each time she is pulled into the past, she must heal or act as a savior for her ancestor, Rufus. She uses her contemporary knowledge of basic medicine and antibiotics, literacy, and history to assist Rufus in navigating the life-threatening dilemmas he often creates for himself. Through Dana's use of her power, Butler complicates the notion of power as self-serving and manipulative because Dana, as a Black woman, must use her power for the benefit of a white man who is a slaveholder.

Dana must work to save the man whose inclination is to marginalize her while remaining ignorant of her true self. It is not until later in her relationship with Rufus that she discovers her true connection to him as one of his descendants. Through history-as-life, she has to experience a discovering of herself and heritage in a way that actual African Americans must do through books and artifacts. Nonetheless, Butler acknowledges that it must be done, but the initial ignorance does not indicate a lack of power even as it does leave Dana somewhat vulnerable. Both Dana and Anyanwu serve as precursors to Shori who must discover herself but does not abdicate power in doing so.

In *Fledgling*, Shori is an amnesiac. She awakens in a dark cave, naked, hungry, and hurt. Her injuries—she has been burned, scarred, and given trauma to the head—have caused her to have no idea where or even who she is. While her immediate physical needs of hunger and cessation from pain must be met initially, she quickly embarks on a journey to discover the answers about her identity. Through interactions with other humans and vampires as well as through research and empirical experiences, she comes to learn basic aspects of her being. She is 53 years old (although she appears to be ten); she is a hybrid, the result of an experimentation between a Black human woman and an Ina (a separate species that drinks blood like vampires, but is not supernatural); and she is the victim of a xenophobic attack that decimated her entire family and permanently erased her memory.

Marie-Luise Löffler and Floriant Bast claim that it is this experience of adversity and growth that positions Butler's novel as a vampiric *Bildungsroman*. As Shori progresses in her personal development, she reveals a "self-determination that is linked to central concerns of African American women's literature."[10] White supremacist mythologies about Black female hyper promiscuity and aggression along with well-intentioned characterizations of the enduring Black matriarch posited Black women as the object of others' narratives of identity. Even the tradition of the *bildungsroman* itself marginalized Black women as it historically centers the white male's story of growth. Furthermore, the male who is at odds with society's values and customs eventually accepts them. Black women are often at odds with society's values and ways because those values marginalize them. For self-actualization to occur, those values cannot be accepted by Black women. In their literature, Black women wrote against these narratives that marginalized them in order to reclaim their subjectivity.

In *Fledgling*, the marginalization of Shori is portrayed as xenophobic, and that manifests as speciesism in the novel but reads like real-life racism. As with racism, individuals attempt to define Shori according to their narrative constructions. These constructions work to reify homogeneity and power within the established hierarchies. Shori's difference aligns her with humans, whom the Ina see as inferior and thus she threatens their understanding of themselves. So, for those Ina who hate her, Shori must fit within the narratives they have created about humans (and Blacks even as they argue race does not matter to them). Because she is Ina and human, she does not easily fit within their understanding of society's classifications: she is too Ina to be human and too human to be Ina. Ironically, this difference makes her stronger than both groups. As Ina, she can move with greater speed than humans, she has more strength, she lives significantly longer, she is self-healing, she does not suffer from disease and she can command the loyalty and obedience of any human she bites. As a human, she can stay awake during the day unlike the Ina who become comatose, and due to her dark skin, she can remain in sunlight with minimal pain or damage. Additionally, her humanity allows her to empathize more readily with her human symbionts, individuals who are emotionally attached to her and physically dependent on the venom in her saliva. Scholar Melissa Strong says this connection to her symbionts permits her to collect them more easily, which enhances "her adaptability and make[s] her less vulnerable than other Ina."[11] Because of the traits that make her different, she can survive more easily.

Shori's abilities are proof that the experimental hybridity performed to create her is a positive aspect in the Ina community, but the bigots among them refuse to recognize her as more than a "murdering black mongrel bitch" as her attacker, Russell Silk calls her.[12] Another attacker, Katharine Dahlman, says of her, "No one can be certain of the truth of anything you say because you are neither Ina nor human. Your scents, your reactions, your facial expressions, your body language—none of it is right."[13] Part of the Ina's strength is being able to sense the truth in individuals. Shori, however, is unreadable to them and thus, she is deemed an illegitimate imposter who does not fit in any group, which according to Katharine, invalidates her words and her very existence. Strong explains this attitude, claiming that "Shori's hybrid status troubles the sacred Ina/human binary, rendering characters like Katharine not simply unwilling to recognize the advantages of genetic engineering but also eager to destroy Shori."[14] Katharine, like Russell and the Silk family, sees Shori as an inferior "other" who threatens their very identity. Russell charges, "What will she give us all? Fur? Tails?"[15] His charges are reminiscent of the claims Thomas Dixon makes in *The Leopard's Spots* (1903) about the regressive effect of the African American presence in America. The Silks and Katharine Dahlman use Shori's hybridity to define her as less than even human. They see her like an animal or even a nonentity. Brox offers Homi Bhabha's theory on the hybrid as an explanation for this marginalization. According to Bhabha, "The hybrid figure opens up a space of cultural uncertainty and instability . . . . this ambivalent space, or Third Space, disrupts the unity and homogeneity of cultural identity to create an in-between that can be read anew."[16] Identities formed within this space create an ambivalence that is subversive to the established authority. Strong agrees, explaining that for the Silks, Shori threatens their "honor and strength, which [they] believe 'flows from [their] uniqueness and [their] unity.' "[17] Her newness imperils their idea of themselves and therefore they must create an identity for her that will validate who they believe themselves to be. They must define her narrative against their own to maintain their own identity story.

The Silks and Katharine are malevolent in their definitions of Shori, but Butler illustrates that even the most well-intentioned, when in a position of power, will attempt to define those whom they deem less powerful. Shori's encounter with her first human symbiont after she leaves the cave illuminates this point. Although Wright, believing her to be an injured child, offers her assistance, he repeatedly attempts to take her to the hospital against her will. He assumes he knows what is best for her. Throughout their relationship, even after she is proven to be the older and stronger of the two, he continues to attempt to control aspects of her life such as her movement and her relationships.

Wright's attempts to control Shori and construct a narrative for her include the seminal act of naming her. In "Authority, Alienation and Social Death," Orlando Patterson examines the process of social and economic control of an individual begins with alienating that individual from his/her previous identity. It involves social and emotional isolation and renaming. While Wright is not consciously trying to gain authority over Shori—he assumes he already has it—he does operate within his role as a heterosexual white male to name and define her. Soon after their initial encounter, Shori inadvertently bites him and sucks his blood. Revealing her truth, she tells him, "I don't think I have anyone . . . . I don't remember. I need to find out who I am and what happened to me and . . . and everything."[18] She expresses her vulnerabilities, although she does not express a need for him to answer any of her questions. Yet, he tells her, "You're a vampire, you know."[19] Wright defines her with confidence and authority.

Wright's assessment of her as a vampire is reminiscent of the erroneous manner in which Black women have been defined and classified historically. In "Hearts of Darkness," Barbara Omolade explains that the first encounters between European settlers and African women were layered with European perspectives on sexuality. She writes "He perceived the African's sensual ways according to his own cultural definitions of sex, nudity, and blackness as base, foul, and bestial. He did not attempt to understand how Africans defined their own behavior. He made assumptions and invented knowledge about their behavior as he created conditions for this 'knowledge' to become reality."[20] Cultural insensitivity and arrogance had an impact on the European's perspective of the African woman, but these factors also worked to determine how she would be regarded for centuries thereafter.

Similarly, Wright uses his experiences and worldview to determine Shori is a vampire based only on his limited knowledge of her and vampires. Because she bites him and drinks his blood, he makes assumptions that are not necessarily proven. Shori is not a vampire. Vampires are supernatural creatures who exist in a liminal state between life and death. Traditionally, they are considered to be evil and must destroy human life to maintain their own. Shori and her people are a species of living beings whose bodily processes can be explained scientifically, not magically. Like humans, they must make choices whether to be moral or not, but their livelihood depends on the continued existence of humanity. The "vampires" of Butler's novel challenge us to rethink what we regard as monstrous or non-monstrous. She troubles our established understanding of what we think we know about monsters and vampires, much in the same way Black people are defined according to traditional racial parameters yet do not resemble any of those ideas.

Wright not only assumes and claims Shori to be a vampire, but he also assumes the right to label her as jailbait because she appears to be so young, and he claims the right to give her the name Renee. He names her "vampire," "jailbait," and "Renee" based on his understanding of the world. Each of his assessments is wrong, but his position as a White man confronted by a Black female "child" does not allow him to question his authority to make these valuations. Of course, Butler is disrupting the reader's perceptions of the powerful and powerless through Shori's experience with Wright. She appears to be the weaker of the two, the least empowered because she occupies marginalized positions—she is Black, she is female, she is a child, and she has a disability. However, her truth is that she is older than Wright, she is stronger than he is, and she has the power over his life or his death. So, we learn that not only is Wright incorrect in his construction of who Shori is, but she is the one with the power to define herself and him if she chooses.

Shori does assume the power to define herself by constantly telling her story. She relays to everyone she meets what has happened to her so that the truth of her life story is her own. According to JoAnne Banks-Wallace, storytelling is a means by which the spirit-self is nurtured.[21] As Shori tells her story, she is claiming herself, but also healing her spirit. She is connecting to who she is and to her community. Storytelling has a significant history in African culture and maintains a prominent role in African American culture. Embracing an oral tradition, African griots, or storytellers, were considered to be the keepers of the culture and the history. They told the tales that governed the people's mores and values, which maintained their sense of self as a people and a community. Citing Senegalese griot D'Jimo Kouyate, Banks-Wallace notes that "without stories in an oral tradition there is no history, no reference."[22]

Banks-Wallace goes on to explain the power of storytelling in the African American tradition.

> Storytelling in the African American oral tradition is first and foremost about healing and nurturing through communion with The Spirit and one another (L. Brown and L. Goss, personal communication, November 19, 2000). The collection and sharing of stories are considered sacred work. Major functions of folklore and storytelling include nurturing a harmonious African American community, sustaining a unique cultural identity, and undergirding the struggle for spiritual and material freedom (Cannon, 1995; Stewart, 1997). Gillespie (1998) argued that storytelling empowers people by unshrouding the lives of those who have come before them, thus enabling people to have a clearer picture of their situation and the options available to them. Gates (1989) asserted that using stories to ask and answer epistemological and ontological questions in our own voices has played a critical role in the survival of African Americans.[23]

Shori taps into a potent and consistent tradition as she uses the power of storytelling to establish her personal and historical truth even though she does not know the full story. She is healing, she is connecting, and she is empowering herself to define herself. Strong agrees, claiming "The storytelling strategy establishes her as an individual and temporarily thwarts the learned and ingrained compulsion to affix to her conventional markers of identity."[24] Telling her story teaches her who she is and it denies others the opportunity to determine her person. It serves as a means to allow her to claim agency and to set the parameters for who is going to be and who will be a part of those definitions. Banks-Wallace says "Some stories support the development of intimate relationships among tellers and listeners by serving as touchstones. Touchstones are things that remind people of a shared heritage and/or past. Certain stories bring forth a whole series of deep-seated memories about experiences that either cannot be or are not easily articulated."[25] When Shori tells her story to others, she allows them to fill in the gaps for her when they can (such as her father or her symbionts), which not only creates a connection between her as a storyteller and the others as listeners in a shared event, but it also creates a connection between the two parties in a shared history and heritage. Moreover, she uses their contributions to weigh their knowledge against her new experiences so that she can make her own assessments.

Butler illustrates the value in the tradition of storytelling, but she also acknowledges the need for Shori to understand the story that has been written for her. Using traditional mainstream resources such as books and the internet, Shori considers Wright's definition of her as a vampire, comparing it with the details of the story she knows. She reads of porphyria, a disease that makes people so vulnerable to light they lose body parts. She places this information in comparison to her story and assesses, "That was interesting, but it awakened no memories in me. After all, I had proved that if I were badly burned or wounded, I would heal."[26] She recounts for herself her tale of awaking in a dark cave burned and suffering a head injury, but after four days or so, being nearly healed. Her story reveals the conflict of who she is and others' assessment of her kind. However, the myths and the folklore, even the science, all fall short of categorizing or even describing her truly. She says of the books, "Whoever and whatever I was, no one seemed to be writing about my kind. Perhaps my kind did not want to be written about."[27]

Although Shori does not find answers to her past and identity in written books, she can use her own empirical experiences to fill in the gaps of her knowledge. Each time she relays what has happened to her whether to herself or others, she compares the details to the memories her body has. Her physical body acts as a repository of her life story and telling the story as she knows it allows her to access the stored data in her person. She cannot remember her life and culture before the attack, yet her body does remember and contains evidence of who she is. Questions from others and interactions with them trigger memories. In several instances, actions that she performs automatically, "feel right" or familiar because her body is familiar with the activity even if her mind cannot remember it. In her first sexual encounter with Wright, her body not only grows excited at the prospect of being with him, but the sensations are familiar, like she has been in the situation with someone before and it feels as if the activity is appropriate and necessary. When she is in the cave, in a primordial state, her body knows that it needs meat to survive and on instinct, she kills the "animal" that comes near her. Soon after, she kills a deer with skill and aplomb because her muscles remember. Finally, even after the attack, she finds that her body heals itself. Not only is this healing another example of her body remembering, but it also reveals to Shori that she possesses that power to heal. This healing is her body telling her about herself. It also speaks to her experience and what has happened to her. Loffler and Bast explain that scars are often used in Black women's literature as a trope for the violent suffering in the women's experiences.[28] The scars are not simply the leftover residue of an injury, but instead serve as physical reminders to the individual of what has transpired in their lives, and in Shori's case, what has been done to her. Furthermore, Loffler and Bast state, "This conflation of the categories of body and memory is an insistence on the necessarily embodied character of any narration of a violent past."[29] Shori's physical scars are a part of her story; they are bodily illustrations of her attack and the efforts expended to disrupt her way of life if not her very being. These scars speak to the violence that has been done to her body and even to her spirit, but ultimately, they heal. Her largest scar, her memory loss, however, remains to tell others of her pain and to remind the community that her identity and culture have been stolen from her. It also serves as an indictment on the members of the community who can see the grave wrong that has been committed against her but choose to remain complacent in addressing it.

Regardless of the commitment of the community-at-large, Shori assumes her agency in addressing the injustices she has endured. She confronts the unknown past and the mystery of her identity through the legal system. She utilizes the Ina's system of justice to bring charges against those who attacked her and her family in what the Ina call Council of Judgment. Here, before a jury of impartial Ina family representatives, she formally charges the Silks with a crime against her, understanding that she does not remember all the facts of the events nor does she remember all of the customs of the Ina. Despite her obvious deficits, Shori goes before the court to seek justice and in doing so, she claims the truth of herself as she yet again tells her story. Shori uses the Ina justice system to further establish her personhood, an act that recalls the process of dehumanizing Black people through the legal system in American history. In addition to disparate sentencing practices, blatant miscarriages of justice, as well as the law declaring Black people as 3/5 a man, the legal/court system has worked to relegate and maintain second-class personhood for African Americans. Butler is certainly aware of this history as she places Shori in the vulnerable position of bringing a case against a powerful and respected family although she is young, different, and an amnesiac. Her detractors use her amnesia, caused by her perpetrators, to argue against her Ina identity and to negate her belonging within the community. In this way, Butler is commenting on society's practice of using the consequences of racism and poverty (unemployment, crime, incarceration, etc.) against African Americans to negate their identity and their right to inclusion.

However, when relaying the story of perceived deficiencies within the African American race, the tale rarely includes the reason for the deficiencies because they would implicate the perpetrators and would not fit neatly within the parameters of their narrative. One of the arguments the Defense makes against Shori is that she cannot be trusted because she is impaired. Although her impairment results from the attack on her person and her family, many believe she is incapable of presenting an accurate account of the wrongs she has endured. One adjudicator says, "I don't believe Shori's memories and accusations should be trusted. I'm not convinced that Shori understands the situation as well as she believes she does. She believes what she says, that's clear. . . . I'm not willing to disrupt or destroy the Silk family on the word of someone as disabled as Shori Matthews clearly is."[30] In this judgment, there is no acknowledgment of the perpetrator's guilt or how Shori came to be disabled. There is only a statement that she is disabled and therefore, untrustworthy, especially against the reputation of an established family. The narrative of their respectability takes precedence over the truth of Shori's injury.

During the trial, she is allowed and expected to question her attackers, the Silks and their symbionts about the attacks and their motivations. In this way, although their answers are not always truthful, she learns more about who she is and what her status is in her community. As African Americans have learned, there is a great deal to be discovered about history not only through what is told but also what is omitted and what is reshaped. Toni Morrison makes this claim in *Playing in the Dark: Whiteness in the Literary Imagination* (1993) when she examines the seeming absence of the Black presence in American literature. She writes:

> It [canonical American literature] assumes that this presence [African Americans]—which shaped the body politic, the Constitution, and the entire history of the culture—has no significant place or consequence in the origin and development of that culture's literature. Moreover, such knowledge assumes that the characteristics of our national literature emanate from a particular "Americanness" that is separate from and unaccountable to this presence.[31]

As scholars have historically crafted the American narrative, they have omitted the Black presence, not simply marginalizing, but erasing Black people from the national discourse. This deliberate omission speaks to the values of the nation concerning how they see themselves even more so than how they see others. Morrison explains that American literature's "coded language and purposeful restrictions" allow it to "deal with the racial disingenuousness and moral frailty at its heart."[32] Ultimately, what Morrison helps us to understand is that this omission of the Black presence was "crucial to their sense of Americaness."[33] Similarly, as the Silks and Katharine try to erase Shori's presence, they inform readers and Shori of who they are and the power she has in their estimation to disrupt their sense of stability. This is certainly a lesson that Shori learns and makes us privy to as readers.

Shori also learns that one of the abilities of the Ina is to discern a person's truthfulness through their words, their scent, their facial expression, and their body language. As Shori tells her story repeatedly, she is watched for these clues. Her body becomes the story and the storyteller. The way she tells her story becomes just as important in this situation as what she says. Her body, including her scars, visible and invisible, relays information about not only Shori's identity and experiences that she can learn from but also the people with whom she interacts.

In the end, Shori's story, and thus her person, is validated when the judgment is found in her favor. Although one of her enemies, Katharine Dahlman, asserts that she is inconsequential, thus nothing, the judgment officially recognizes her as Ina and, in accepting her story, recognizes her on her terms. She is a hybrid; she is Black; she is an orphan; she is an amnesiac. These traits could be regarded as deficits, but that is not how Shori classifies them in her story. "[My mothers and sisters, my father and brothers, my memory] were all gone. The person I had been was gone. I couldn't bring anyone back, not even myself. I could only learn what I could about the Ina, about my families. I would restore what could be restored."[34] Shori acknowledges the loss in her life, but she accepts that the people, as well as the loss, are a part of her experience and she is determined to move forward with that knowledge. She accepts herself and many in Ina society accept her, too. One of her distant relatives, Joan Braithwaite, speculates that Shori would "make a damn good ally someday." Accepting herself, Shori responds, "She's right. I will."[35]

Shori's potential for the future goes beyond being a good ally. Her presence and acceptance in the community represent the possibility for change and growth. Strong explains, the "storytelling serves important legal and social functions that can pave the way for change."[36] Because Shori, as a hybrid, as a Black woman, as an orphan with no immediate family, as an amnesiac—all things foreign to the Ina—is officially accepted by the community as she is, change can occur within the society that will make them all the better for it. Her acceptance opens this thousands-year-old species to new ways of being and functioning within the world. Butler's texts often advocate for adaptability and change as a means for continued survival. Fledgling is no different. After all, it is Shori's difference that allows her to survive the attack on her families and it is her difference that causes her enemies to underestimate her, which ultimately gives her the advantage in her confrontations with them.

In this novel, Butler illustrates the power and potential of a confrontation with an unknown past. She challenges oppressed peoples who are marginalized to claim themselves and their stories even as they lack the full knowledge of their identity and culture. Shori acts as a literary representative of Black people who are relegated to the margins of society; she faces the unknown past, the unremembered past, by telling her story and refusing to allow others to take it from her. She faces the past by filling in the gaps with knowledge from within herself and knowledge from others. And she faces the past by forging an identity based on what she knows and accepting herself for who she is, imperfections and all. Like those slave ancestors who flew home in the folktale, Shori may not remember the past, but she knows that the power to soar is within her. She faces the future unafraid to take flight.

NOTES

1. (Staples 2006).
2. (Poole 2011, 14).
3. (Poole 2011, 14).
4. (Smith 1998, 6).
5. (Wander, Phillip C., Judith N. Martin, & Thomas K. Nakayama 2005, 31).
6. (Dixon 1902, 242).
7. (Morris 2012, 146).
8. (Morris 2012, 155).
9. (Brox 2008, 392).
10. (Loffler, Marie-Luise and Floriant Bast 2011, 7).
11. (Strong 2010, 30).
12. (Butler 2005, 300).
13. (Butler 2005, 272).
14. (Strong 2010, 31).
15. (Butler 2005, 300).
16. (Brox 2008, 391).
17. (Strong 2010, 33).
18. (Butler 2005, 12).
19. (Butler 2005, 12).

20. (Omolade 1995, 362).
21. (Banks-Wallace 2002, 411).
22. (Banks-Wallace 2002, 412).
23. (Banks-Wallace 2002, 412).
24. (Strong 2010, 28).
25. (Banks-Wallace 2002, 411).
26. (Butler 2005, 33).
27. (Butler 2005, 39).
28. (Loffler, Marie-Luise and Floriant Bast 2011, 8).
29. (Loffler, Marie-Luise and Floriant Bast 2011, 8).
30. (Butler 2005, 296).
31. (Morrison 1990, 5).
32. (Morrison 1990, 6).
33. (Morrison 1990, 6).
34. (Butler 2005, 310).
35. (Butler 2005, 310).
36. (Strong 2010, 28).

BIBLIOGRAPHY

Banks-Wallace, JoAnne. 2002. "Talk That Talk: Storytelling and Analysis Rooted in African American Oral Tradition." *Qualitative Health Research*, 12(3), 410–426.
Brox, Ali. 2008. "'Every Age Has the Vampire It Needs": Octavia Butler's Vampiric Vision in Fledgling." *Utopian Studies*, 19(3), 391–409.
Butler, Octavia. 2005. *Fledgling*. New York: Grand Central Publishing.
Dixon, Thomas. 1902. *The Leopard's Spots*. New York: Doubleday.
Loffler, Marie-Luise and Floriant Bast. 2011. "Bites from the Margins: Contemporary African American Women's Vampire Literature." *Kultur & Geschlecht*, 8, 1–19.
Morris, Susanna M. 2012. "Black Girls Are from the Future: Afrofuturist Feminism in Octavia E. Butler's Fledgling." *WSQ: Women's Studies Quarterly*, 40(3/4), 146–166.
Morrison, Toni. 1990. *Playing in the Dark: Whiteness and the Literary Imagination*. New York: Vintage Books.
Omolade, Barbara. 1995. "Hearts of Darkness." In *Words of Fire: An Anthology of African-American Feminist Thought*, edited by Beverly Guy-Sheftall, 362–378. New York: The New Press.
Patterson, Orlando. 2017. "Authority, Alienation and Social Death." In *Critical Readings on Global Slavery*, edited by Damian Alan Pargas and Felicia Roşu, 90–146. Boston: Brill Publishers.
Poole, W. Scott. 2011. *Monsters in America: Our Historical Obsession with the Hideous and the Haunting*. Waco: Baylor University Press.
Smith, Felipe. 1998. *American Body Politics: Race, Gender, and Black Literary Renaissance*. Athens: The University of Georgia Press.
Staples, Cynthia. 2006. "'Meanwhile, Back at the Crypt." *Black Issues* 42–43.

Strong, Melissa J. 2010. "The Limits of Newness: Hybridity in Octavia E. Butler's *Fledgling*." *Femspec*, 11(1), 27–43.

Wander, Phillip C., Judith N. Martin, and Thomas K. Nakayama. 2005. "The Roots of Racial Classification." In *White Privilege: Essential Readings on the Other Side of Racism*, edited by Paula S. Rothenberg, 29–34. New York: Worth Publishers.

Chapter 12

Audre Lorde's *Zami* as a Speculative Womanist Guide to Self-Actualization in Octavia Butler's *Dawn*

Roslyn Nicole Smith

Black women who embark upon a quest to become self-actualized also commit to the discovery of their intrinsic personhood, despite marginalizing societal narratives that undermine their humanity. For over 200 years, Black women authors in the United States have cautioned that erasing their perspectives from American narratives potentially obliterates the communities Black women have historically held together, and the roles Black women continue to play in spearheading and supporting sociopolitical movements. This erasure also dismisses art forms—such as literature—that reflect the related triumphs and struggles associated with the ways Black women engage their journeys toward self-actualization amid interlocking oppressions of race and gender.

Audre Lorde in her 1982 biomythography *Zami* illustrates an alternative model for self-actualization that is not stunted by racial and gendered oppression. Readers who engage Lorde as the protagonist in her biomythography bear witness as a combination of her innate desires and her lived experiences influence her self-actualization. Lorde indicates in the introduction to *Zami* that while she always possessed an intrinsic sense of the qualities that defined her personhood, she also understood early on that the resulting selfhood would run counter to societal constructs of womanhood. Lorde's perspective illustrates the significance of considering the *self* as an integral force in engaging oppression and exemplifies bell hooks' arguments regarding self-recovery as a liberatory act. hooks writes, "Before many of us can effectively sustain engagement in organized resistance struggle, in the Black liberation movement, we need to undergo a process of self-recovery" (hooks 7). Lorde's journey toward selfhood can also be viewed as revolutionary. "Revolution," writes Toni Cade Bambara, "begins with the self, in the self" (Bambara 133). Therefore, self-recovery and self-actualization both speak to the process of connecting or reconnecting, to one's inner-compass as a mechanism for navigating external environments. As revealed in many texts by Black women authors, once a Black woman decides to follow her internal compass toward self-actualization, her intrinsic desires define her approach to achieving full personhood despite external environments that invalidate their humanity. To this end, this study proposes Audre Lorde's text *Zami* as a speculative text that presents a womanist speculative archetype who models a version of self-actualization that is uninterrupted by racial and gendered oppression. Framing *Zami* in this manner also provides an opportunity to examine protagonists in woman-authored Black speculative fiction texts as womanist speculative archetypes who, like Lorde, self-actualize outside of the dominant narrative of what Lorde identifies as the mythical norm.

While Black women author fictional texts in a variety of genres, Black speculative fiction offers a unique opportunity for readers and writers to imagine a reality where Black women's evolutions are not hampered by racial and gendered constructs in literature and reality. Toni Morrison analyzes White authors' unwillingness to include Black characters as integral components of their fiction in her text, *Playing in the Dark: Whiteness in the Literary Imagination* (1993). Here she writes that the absence of Black people within the pages of American fiction paradoxically speaks to the importance of their presence (Morrison 5–6) in American culture. In a sense, this dismissal reads as willful regard. White authors' rejection tasks Black writers with the sole responsibility of writing literature that integrates or centers the Black perspective (Morrison 5–6). Morrison writes of this effort, "Living in a nation of people who *decided* that their worldview would combine agendas for individual freedom *and* mechanisms for devastating racial oppression presents a singular landscape as a writer" (Morrison xii). Morrison further notes that writing both "within and without" of this literary landscape presents an opportunity to consider the "resilience and gravity, the inadequacy and the force of the imaginative act" (Morrison xiii) of non-Black writers. As a genre that offers authors opportunities to reconstruct reality, Black speculative literature written by women offers a unique response to such dismissals while simultaneously participating in the tradition of Black women writers who radically imagine strategies for engaging oppression through writing. In addition to examining intersectional oppression through a fictional medium, the speculative genre enables these writers to design worlds where Black women are chosen to be the heroines and their efforts are recognized as integral to the viability of their world. As such, the protagonists model a reality that the dominant narrative of American literature often disregards. An even more contextualized meaning can be mined from discovering how Black women employ this type of agency in their counternarratives when we read these works from a womanist theoretical viewpoint.

Alice Walker introduced the term, "womanism," in her 1979 short story, "Coming Apart," and later defined the word in 1983 in her text, "Womanist." She developed the term *womanist* during the second wave of the feminist movement, a time that ranges from the 1960s to the 1980s. Walker's term provided an antidote to the dismissal of Black women's concerns during the second-wave feminist movement. While authors such as Chinkwenye Okonjo Ogunyemi (1985) and Clenora Hudson-Weems (1989) have produced important texts that expand Walker's definition, the *Color Purple* author's description of womanism offers a perspective of the term that aligns with an analysis about Black women's self-actualization as represented in woman-authored Black speculative fiction. Walker's definition of this term speaks to the importance of Black women loving and valuing themselves as well as their communities. The adoration Walker promotes in her definition of womanism extends to Black culture, Black histories, activism, sexuality, and mental health. Her metacognitive term describes not only how Black women struggle with oppression but also how they endure within the struggle.

One of these traditions expressed in Walker's definition is love. Walker writes that a womanist, "Loves music. Loves dance. Loves the moon. *Loves* the Spirit. Loves love and food and roundness. Loves struggle. *Loves* the Folk. Loves herself. *Regardless*" (Walker xii). Audre Lorde, a contemporary of Walker, echoed the importance of loving one's self even when the larger culture says, "You, you are not worthy of such love." Walker's perspective incorporates and moves beyond the feminist goal of equal rights. These authors' viewpoints include a conversation about healing from historical traumas such as slavery, Jim Crow laws, systemic racism, that specifically affect Black women. The abstract nature of parts of Walker's definition of womanism—"Loves the moon. *Loves* the Spirit"—invites the imaginative language and concepts that the Black speculative fiction genre offers to engage the process of healing. To this end, this study employs Lorde's biomythography *Zami* as a womanist, theoretical example of an other-worldly, mythic, approach to engaging racism and gender inequities beyond the dichotomy of resistance and assimilation toward a womanist ethos of value and worth.

A womanist reading of *Zami* frames Lorde's narrative as a liberatory text wherein she creates a counternarrative that enables her to unearth, construct, and nurture her personhood on her terms. The mythos element Lorde employs to communicate her real-world journey toward constructing her identity positions her narrative as an ideal womanist, Black speculative, theoretical template. Audre Lorde's eponymous revisionist myth *Zami* presents the author's coming of age experiences as inseparable from her sexual, sociopolitical, and personal liberation. In this manner, Lorde presents her life experiences as a heroic womanist, African diasporic quest toward an empowered and nonconforming identity, rather than as a tale from a survivor who struggles to navigate a Western, oppressive sociopolitical narrative of someone else's design. Her resulting text reconstructs conventional, hegemonic, racial, and gendered elements of the myth genre. Using *Zami* as a template, one can frame the mechanisms woman-authored Black speculative fiction use to center Black women as important actors in the American literary landscape. *Zami* then becomes a biomythography that provides a theoretical lens through which one can read Black speculative fiction written by women as *liberation biomythographies*. Lorde's revised African diasporic and Western hybrid mythos genre, with Black feminist underpinnings, results in a womanist speculative archetypal heroine within a *liberation biomythography* who presents *self-actualization* as a key component toward creating her liberation from gendered and racial oppression.

Lorde's womanist speculative archetype interrupts the mythos literary structure wherein the woman's role is a, "hidden agenda of gender norms, where 'adult' means learning to be dependent, submissive, or 'nonadult' " (Pratt 16). The author's resolution of the heroine's quest in *Zami* offers an integral illustration of this interruption. According to Carl Jung and Joseph Campbell, in the traditional—*read male*—quest narrative the signal that the hero has resolved the quest would be a sacred marriage (Ball 62). This, "sacred marriage," would take place between the hero and a "sacred divine female figure who represents his anima or his soul" (Ball 62). Lorde's text subverts this hallmark of the myth genre as this sacred union takes place in *Zami* between two women—Lorde and Kitty, the shortened moniker of Afrekete (Lorde 247–251). The name Afrekete comprises the numerous, varied characteristics and diasporic iterations of the African deity represented as Esu/Elegbara in many West African and related diasporic spiritual traditions (Provost 46–51). Of these deistic characteristics, Provost writes that the "verbal dexterity, indeterminacy, gender ambiguity, and ability to mediate seeming contradictions . . . offer Lorde both a model survivor/fighter and particular linguistic strategies which aid her struggle against oppressive beliefs and behaviors" (Provost 47). So, to unite with Kitty is to unite with more than Lorde's soul; it is to connect to multiple layers of herself that exist beyond time, location, and social constructions of identity.

As Lorde and Kitty join in a same-sex, loving and intimate manner, Lorde supplies the reader with imagery that connects the reader to these blossoming layers of selfhood with words that are bountiful and lush and reminiscent of the tone in her description of Carriacou, her parents' birthplace and also a place that resonates with Lorde as home. In describing Afrekete's effect on her Lorde writes, "There are certain verities which are always with us, which we come to depend upon. That the sun moves north in summer, that melted ice contracts, that the curved banana is sweeter. Afrekete taught me roots, new definitions of our women's bodies—definitions for which I had only been in training to learn before" (Lorde 249). Later she describes their love-making using similar language related to nature and growth. Here, Lorde's description of her visit to a market with Kitty transitions to a description of time they later spent together: "There were green plantains, which we half-peeled and then planted, fruit deep, in each other's bodies until the petals of skin lay like tendrils of broad green fire upon the curly darkness between our spread thighs" (Lorde 248). In comparison, when Lorde thinks of home, her parents' birth country Carriacou, and even her mother, she sometimes represents these views with similar nature imagery, albeit not as erotic. Of her mother, Lorde writes, "She breathed exuded hummed the fruit smell of Noel's Hill (an area in Carriacou) morning fresh and noon hot, and I spun visions of sapodilla and mango as a net over my Harlem tenement cot in the snoring darkness rank with nightmare sweat" (Lorde 176). And when she describes Carriacou, a place she had not seen yet as a child, did not yet exist on a map, and only knew from her parents' descriptions, Lorde writes, "But underneath it all, as I was growing up, home was still a sweet place . . . . It was our own, my truly private paradise of blugoe and breadfruit hanging from the trees, of nutmeg and lime and sapodilla, of tonka beans and red and yellow Paradise Plums" (Lorde 256). These similar images indicate that Lorde's intimate encounters with Afrekete offer her a path to a complete, synchronized self that comprises Lorde's Carriacou ancestry, her Blackness, her womanness, and her sexual orientation—toward ultimately home.

Lorde's revisions of Western mythos conventions illustrate Annis Pratt's perspective on archetypes as, "an original, of a series of variations" (Pratt 3). Pratt describes and analyzes the various representations of archetypes in women's fiction definition as archetypal patterns—the focus of the author's studies. Pratt writes that archetypal patterns "represent categories of particulars, that can be described in their interrelationships within a given text or body of literature" (Pratt 5). As such, these archetypal patterns are not rigid categories imposed on literary texts, but rather fluid categories that are inductive from within literature (Pratt 5). Pratt understands the need for this revised view of archetypes when she notes that "quest patterns described by Jung, Campbell, and Frye" compared to "plot structures of women's novels . . . create narratives manifesting an acute tension between what any normal human being might desire and what a woman must become" (Pratt 6). Pratt proposes that one of the reasons women's fiction differs so radically from that of men is that women's efforts for personal development are encumbered by societal conventions (Pratt 6, 168–169). As such, she argues that women's "desire for responsible selfhood, for the achievement of authenticity through individual choice, comes up against the assumption that a woman aspiring to selfhood is by definition selfish, deviating from norms of subservience to the dominant gender" (Pratt 6). Further, from a Jungian perspective, in literature, the feminine only serves "as exterior containers for male projections or subordinate elements of the male personality" (Pratt 8). Conversely, Pratt argues, "women authors treat the domestic enclosures that women accept as a condition of social survival" (Pratt 9). In her review of 300 years of women's fiction, Pratt finds that Western bildungsroman heroines who resisted these roles usually became societal outcasts whose fate ended in madness, maiming, or death (Pratt 9).

Throughout her text, Pratt identifies science fiction as a genre that enables women to create new images of heroines or heroes without concerns about social retaliation. Heroines in women's science fiction cognizantly pursue self-actualization, along with societal goals (Pratt 36), "to realize and exercise his (or her) inner powers" (Pratt 36) without perceived punishments such as death or illness. Pratt also notes that "when a woman sets out to manipulate language, to create new myths out of old, to write an essay or to paint a painting, she transgresses fundamental social taboos in that very act" (Pratt 11). For instance, Pratt writes, "Only in the fantasy cultures of science fiction does she retain freedom to control her own body and to fulfill an adult social function" (Pratt 168). This control often extends to the authors' approach to presenting their protagonist's sexuality.

Pratt indicates that within science fiction, authors such as Ursula K. Le Guin, Joanna Russ, and Anne McCaffrey create heroes who decide not to be female, "transcending the gender limitations characterizing more conventional novels" (Pratt 35). This notion is true for individuals as it relates not only to gender but also to race and sexuality. Extending Pratt's analysis to race and sexuality, then, calls for analyses of Black women writers' texts, which combat these representations of oppression from racial and gendered perspectives. As Lorde writes, "To examine Black women's literature effectively requires that we be seen as whole people in our actual complexities—as women, as human—rather than as one of those problematic but familiar stereotypes provided in this society in place of genuine images of Black women" (Lorde 287). Science fiction as written by women, therefore, enables the heroine to complete a fully realized bildungsroman where her choices to achieve a full personhood are not limited (Lorde 35) by prescribed gender roles of mother, wife, daughter, or crone.

Not only are definitions of biomythography and female archetypes integral to this analysis but also an understanding of the terms "speculative fiction," "Black speculative fiction," and "Afrofuturism." Robert Heinlein first used the term "speculative fiction" in his 1948 essay, "On Writing of Speculative Fiction" (Jackson and Moody-Freeman 2). Heinlein describes, "speculative science fiction" or the speculative story as one that considers how people engage new technology or science (Jackson and Moody-Freeman 2). He writes, "science and established fiefs are extrapolated to produce a new situation, a new framework for human action. As a result of this new situation, new human problems are created—and our store is about how human beings cope with those new problems" (Jackson and Moody-Freeman 2). Judith Merril, noted science fiction writer, offers an expanded definition in 1966 that considers—more closely—the creative and writerly mechanisms that encourage the instructive nature of speculative fiction. Merril writes that speculative fiction is a genre "whose objective is to explore, to discover, to *learn*, [sic] by means of projection, extrapolation, analogue, hypothesis-and-paper-experimentation, something about the nature of the universe, of man, or reality" (*Science Fiction Encyclopedia*). David Wyatt's 2007 text suggests that the speculative fiction genre offers liberation because it specifically challenges cultural hegemonies. Wyatt describes the genre as "a term which includes all literature that takes place in a universe slightly different from our own. In all of its forms, it gives authors to ask relevant questions about one's own society in a way that would prove provocative in mainstream forms" (qtd. in Jackson and Moody-Freeman 2). Wyatt goes on to name speculative fiction as a "literature of freedom" for the author and reader who are able to speculate outside of conventional ideas for societal change (Jackson and Moody-Freeman 2).

Of these definitions, Wyatt's consideration of speculative fiction is most relevant to this project. His view of speculative fiction as liberatory suggests limitless opportunities to reimagine one's place in, and significance to, local and global communities that combat intersectional oppression. However, when employing this genre to address intersectional oppression, it is important to connect extrapolation and exploration to a specific sociopolitical concern. The product of this necessary fusion of terms for Black writers of speculative fiction is *Black speculative fiction*. Sheree Thomas, the editor of the first comprehensive collection of the genre, titled *Dark Matter* (2000) describes Black speculative fiction as, "a diverse range of speculative fiction from the African diaspora" (Thomas xii). The synchronicity of *speculative* and *Black* also supports a view of Black women speculative writers as explorers presenting unique methods for engaging oppression that open dialogue, outside of their fictional texts, for sustainable, imaginative solutions to racial and gendered oppressions in the real world. This study considers the intersection of not only Womanism and Black Speculative fiction but also Afrofuturism as components of a liberation biomythography that illustrates modes of Black liberation through the mechanism of a womanist speculative archetype.

In her study focusing on the term "Afrofuturism," Lisa Yaszek writes, "In its broadest dimensions, Afrofuturism is an extension of the historical recovery projects that Black Atlantic intellectuals have engaged in for well over two hundred years" (Yazsek 4). Therefore, writers of African descent who employ speculative and Afrofuturistic tropes to engage gendered and racial oppression do so to seek alternative options for liberation or survival against the rippling effects of geographic, personal, and social displacement. Displacement, then, emphasizes the fluidity and dynamic nature of speculative literature written by Black women in the United States as an ongoing legacy of employing writing as a tool for engaging intersectional oppression. Viewing female-authored Black speculative texts in this manner offers an opportunity to name displacement as the condition that acts as a catalyst for redefining selfhood in the real world and symbolically in the person of a fictional Black female protagonist who helps to refashion humanity. The Afrofuturistic strategy employed in these Black speculative texts extends that tradition by "reorienting the intercultural vectors of Black Atlantic temporality towards the preoptic as much as the retrospective" (Eshun 289). Often these writings illustrate methods for expanding or recreating their notion of selfhood, as well as navigating and surviving an initially arbitrary alien community. Furthermore, the writers learn to create new or participate in existing communities to sustain this new selfhood. Additionally, they often choose to avoid or eschew those communities that are a detriment to their journey toward self-actualization. Species survival in the context of liberation biomythographies requires an ideological investment in the future of the African diaspora. Kodwo Eshun's definition of Afrofuturism presents a manifestation of this proposition: "Afrofuturism may be characterized as a program for recovering the histories of counter-futures created in a century hostile to Afro Diasporic projection and as a space within which the critical work of manufacturing tools capable of intervention within the current political dispensation may be undertaken" (Eshun 301).

Eshun describes this task of futuristic speculation for writers of African descent as a practice that is not compulsory, but rather essential (Eshun 289) and refers to Afrofuturism as a "field" that "does not seek to deny the tradition of counter-memory" (Eshun 289). Eshun's view stresses the importance of considering the harrowing reverberations of the past on the present, as well as how these time frames contribute to a vast, diasporic cultural database. This examination potentially reprograms members of the African diaspora's response to contemporary and future concerns in a manner that reflects radical imagination. Likewise, Lysa Rivera offers the perspective that "Afrofuturist writers and texts recognize that just as history is a contested discursive terrain, so too is the concept of futurity" (Rivera 159) and presents the future as a plain that must be cultivated and tended. Tending the future requires, in part, artistry that is a generational part of Black women's creativity as executed—in part—in Black women's writing. In this way, many Black women rewrite their female ancestors into existence even while continuing the work of projecting themselves, and future generations into the future. Creating liberation biomythographies is not just women's work, this is Black women's work.

Susanna Morris refers to the writings of Black women from the Afrofuturist genre as "Afrofuturist feminisms." In her text, "Black Girls Are from the Future: Afrofuturist Feminism in Octavia E. Butler's *Fledgling*," Morris argues that people of color who write vampire stories use these texts to interrupt the dominant trope of whiteness, power, fantasy present in most vampire texts (Morris 145–146). Morris offers an analysis of Butler's novel *Fledgling* as an example of how a Black woman writer accomplishes this task through a "black feminist Afrofuturist epistemology that transgressively revises the contemporary vampire genre" (Morris 145–146). Morris titles this epistemology, "Afrofuturist feminisms," a term, that highlights the theoretical characteristics that Afrofuturism and Black feminist theory share (Morris 153). This analysis extends Morris' perspective of the similar points of discourse between Afrofuturism and feminism. It presents an Afrofuturistic/womanist analysis of Black speculative fiction. In other words, this analysis broadly uses the Afrofuturist theoretical lens, but within that framework, employs a womanist focus. For this reason, the terms "liberation biomythography" and "speculative womanist archetype" aptly encapsulate the Black speculative genre as well as Afrofuturistic theories methods.

Lorde's template for a liberation biomythography requires a womanist speculative archetype who is on a quest for self-actualization, a quest that enables this person's journey to self to unfold without the social or biological confines of gender, and a community to support and nurture this journey. This chapter analyzes liberation mythology through the actions of the texts' womanist speculative archetype. More specifically, the analysis examines how Black women, and the communities they engage, can free themselves of racial and gendered oppression. To this end, the alien invasions provide a new myth within which to examine a womanist speculative archetype's journey and her reconsideration of gendered roles as an element of the journey to self-actualization.

A womanist lens provides the reader with the analytical language to frame these authors' counternarratives, as liberation biomythographies that reflect the authors' and/or protagonists' intrinsic identity. A womanist reading of these texts also opens the way to viewing these heroines' journeys as a synergistic relationship between recovering or discovering one's self and engaging one's outside environment. Black heroines must surmount hurdles that originate in a Western ethos that denies their consciousness and ability for self-reflection and self-actualization. Given this reality of such an obstacle, there is a need for alternative ways of understanding Black female interiority as represented in American literature. Pratt writes of these protagonists, that when one considers a young Black heroine's "attempts to achieve a full personal development (she is) hampered at every turn" (Pratt 32). Arguably, the Black heroine's diminished development in American literature reflects the degrees of unworthiness and inhumanity extant in American culture. As such, through the conventional lens of the American literary imagination, the Black female protagonist "faces a double alienation" in that she is encouraged to adhere to the standards of purity and decorum as represented by "white femininity" while understanding that according to a master narrative, she is inherently impure (Pratt 32). Dr. Kim Marie Vaz's analysis offers a useful perspective regarding how a womanist framework ameliorates the Black heroines' paradoxical condition. She writes that womanists "concoct something that makes sense for how we are living in complex gender, racial, and class social configurations" (Vaz 234). In other words, womanism does not offer a static approach or critical lens for understanding self-actualization. Instead, womanism reveals the shifting systems of healing that constitute a multiplicity of responses to a dynamic and often pernicious environment. More specifically, womanism emphasizes that an evolving self, based on an internal compass rather than a response to external influences, is one such scenario. To this end, the analysis that follows in this chapter examines how a womanist reading can offer a more expansive and nuanced analysis of Black women's speculative narratives. Using a womanist lens, this chapter explores the protagonist's experience as a journey toward self-actualization, highlighting a path to liberation through counternarratives that contest interlocking modes of oppression. Specifically, this analysis identifies the main characters' approaches to create or discover their intrinsic personhood as a counternarrative to racial and gender inequities through the use of a heroic *womanist speculative archetype*.

Audre Lorde exhibits this synergistic approach to self-actualization in *Zami*. Throughout this work, which she identifies as biomythography, Lorde presents herself as a Black woman whose quest toward self-actualization requires acts of racial and gendered liberation. Indeed, *Zami* represents Lorde's ongoing interrogation of racial and gendered systems of interlocking oppression. Five years before Lorde published her biomythography, she produced a printed rebuke, "The Master's Tools Will Never Dismantle the Master's House." In this text, Lorde cautions the organizers of the 1979 "Second Sex Conference" against upholding a narrative that marginalizes people who are not white, heteronormative, and members of the middle or higher class. Her speech was precipitated by the lack of diversity among the panels at a conference slated to presumably address *all* women's concerns. Lorde asks in this text, "What does it mean when the tools of a racist patriarchy are used to examine the fruits of that same patriarchy?" (Lorde 111). The answer to her query, writes Lorde, is that "only the most narrow perimeters of change are possible and allowable" (Lorde 111). In other words, one cannot purport commitment to the liberation of women while narrowly designating which women merit liberation. One year later, in her 1980 essay, "Age, Race, Class, and Sex: Women Redefining Difference," Lorde designated the "tool of a racist patriarchy" she discussed in her earlier text as part of a "mythical norm" (Lorde 116–117). Lorde further argued that those who exist within this mythical norm view others as different or deviant. An extension of this limited viewpoint, Lorde continued, is the belief that all members of any of these othered groups share a homogenized experience of oppression (Lorde 116). In this example, all women's oppression becomes subsumed under one purview—white and middle class. Lorde's overarching argument in these two essays, as well as in *Zami*, supports the indeterminable value of a womanist perspective, which connects Black women's worth to a praxis of empowerment as represented in the *womanist speculative archetype*.

When readers encounter Lorde as the womanist speculative archetype in her counternarrative *Zami*, they witness Lorde implementing her theories of rejecting both the master's tools and the mythical norm. The author enacts this effort by changing her name to a term that represents women in community and by curating an evolution-focused narrative. These two strategies signal Lorde's commitment to proposing a new paradigm of how Black women reclaim their personhood. Collectively, these two strategies exhibit three attributes of Walker's definition of womanist—*adaptability, universality*, and *boldness*. These characteristics undergird womanist-based, tangible approaches to disrupting interlocking oppression and are common traits authors infuse into their womanist speculative archetypes. A brief overview of how these characteristics serve to create and incubate Lorde's intrinsic sense of self *Zami* will support further analyses of how the protagonists of *Dawn* present similar womanist characteristics.

Lorde first signals the imperativeness of self-actualization by boldly renaming herself in the title of her biomythography: *Zami: A New Spelling of My Name*. Zami is a Carriacou term used to describe "women who work together as friends and lovers" (Lorde 255). This definition of Lorde's new name signals interdependence, a key component of Lorde's evolution. Second, the structure of Lorde's narrative illustrates her intentional approach to self-actualization. Rather than present a narrative shaped solely by time, Lorde presents a hero's narrative primarily framed in the order of self-discovery. While chronology certainly exists in this narrative, time does not drive the evolution of the text or the heroine's journey—Lorde's metamorphosis does. As a result, the reader engages a womanist speculative archetype's quest toward self-actualization, rather than a survivor's tale of navigating an oppressive sociopolitical climate.

Before Lorde can earnestly begin a quest of self-discovery, she has to recognize the connection between recovering her *self* and survival; the first step of this process is valuing her uniqueness. Therefore, although—as discussed in the "Introduction" of this chapter—Lorde naturally exercises her bent in *Zami* toward individuality at an early age, she does not consciously and actively view herself and her actions as different until adolescence. It is during this time that she begins to exhibit the three characteristics that center the womanist ethos: *adaptability*, *universalism*, and *boldness*. Once Lorde begins high school, she comes to understand that she is unique, "not because I was Black, but because I was me" (Lorde 82). It is important to note here that this revelation does not disregard her Blackness, but places equal importance on her intrinsic need to be herself as it includes her Blackness. Lorde's response to this revelation was to locate like-minded people—regardless of race—rather than to suppress her unconventionality. She eventually joins a group of young women who have named themselves "The Branded" (Lorde 81). The author characterizes The Branded as "a sisterhood of rebels" who were united by the differences that separated them from others (Lorde 81). Lorde also describes the group as "the Lunatic Fringe, proud of our outrageousness and our madness, our bizarre-colored inks and quill pens" (Lorde 81). Establishing solidarity with this network of young women allows Lorde to employ the womanist view of universalism. Her interdependent approach to community supersedes any concerns about their dissimilarities. Lorde's friendship with The Branded precipitates the boldness she will need for the next leg of her journey toward personhood. At 17, an adolescent Lorde finds that to continue her transformation, she needs to move into her own apartment. As she began to pursue her authentic personhood, her home environment became a battleground where her need for privacy and introspection were constantly under attack. Lorde writes of her family, "A request for privacy was treated like an outright act of insolence for which the punishment was swift and painful" (Lorde 83). The stress of this seemingly interminable battle on Lorde was telling. When she slept at night, she would often experience nightmares and wake up to her, "pillowcase red and stiffened by gushing nosebleeds during the night, or damp and saturated with the acrid smell of tears and the sweat of terror" (Lorde 83). Thus, Lorde learns at a young age that sometimes adapting to a condition means exercising the audacity to move outside of it. Walker includes this observation in her definition of a womanist is a woman who is: "Not a separatist, except periodically, for health" (Walker xi). Lorde says of her move that while she was nervous, she was also committed to, "an adolescent's wild and powerful commitment to battling in my own full eye, closer to my own strength" (Lorde 104). These early experiences of the dissonance between an emerging self and a restrictive domestic environment seem to shape Lorde's steadfast commitment to creating her own spaces for transformation, no matter the cost. As a result, any adversities Lorde faced after leaving her parents' home—whether it was poverty, an abortion, another move—Lorde adapted. She remained committed to creating a literal and figurative space where she was able to have solitude to write, to be depressed, to socialize with members of The Branded—in essence, and to self-actualize.

At one moment in the text, she goes to work, two nights after an abortion, to ensure her ability to pay her expenses for the month. A maid whom Lorde encounters sees Lorde's wan complexion and fatigued posture, evidence of her pain and blood loss, and says to Lorde, "Chile, why don't you go on back home to your mama, where you belong?" (Lorde 114). However, what the maid could not know was that Lorde was responding to an internal compass that would lead her true north, toward self-actualization. As sickly and despondent as Lorde may have appeared, any alternative—such as going back to her mother—would have been even more detrimental to her sense of self. In this regard, Lorde was exactly where she belonged. One year later, Lorde's continued boldness and mutability drove her to move from New York to Connecticut to work in a factory, and at 19, to fly to Mexico to live and study as an independent student. In each of these spaces, she engaged or created zamis that, similarly to The Branded, bonded because they understood that their personhood existed outside of the mythical norm. However, all of these experiences indicate the *adaptability, universalism,* and *boldness* that informed Lorde's early sense of the person she was becoming.

As with Lorde in *Zami*, Lilith in Octavia Butler's novel *Dawn* (1987) exemplifies this womanist framework as she adapts to radically new environments introduced by aliens. Like Lorde, Lilith learns the nature of—and navigational methods for—their new environments. A radical change to the outside environment indeed precipitates the protagonists' evolutions; however, the sense of displacement was always present based on preinvasion, interlocking social oppressions. Therefore, for the speculative womanist archetype, a radical change in the outside environment allows the protagonist to reemerge in an environment where the characteristics that would be devalued would be viewed as leadership potential. An integral part of the protagonists' evolution is their ability to nourish innate talents in and of themselves, because as Bambara writes, "The individual, the basic revolutionary unit" must debride the ego and heart of toxins that "assault . . . and threaten" them (Bambara 133). Otherwise, the poison will spread to subsequent "units," such as relationships, families, and communities (Bambara 133). Because these heroines nurture their inner revolution they are then able to create communities that nourish their proficiencies and interface with groups that value them as assets. Lorde, by necessity, leaves the familiarity of home to create her own new and uncharted environment, while Lilith regains consciousness in a new environment created by the alien Oankali.

"Alive" (Lorde 153). "Alive!" (Butler 9). For Audre Lorde, the word *alive* speaks to the moment her journey toward authentic personhood leads her away from an emotionally toxic relationship toward an international journey—at the age of 19—to Mexico. Butler's protagonist, Lilith, speaks this word as she awakens from a 250-year chemically induced sleep that followed an apocalyptic nuclear world war. While the circumstances connected to each iteration of "Alive" differ, the most obvious being the genres, one may extrapolate a similar meaning from each heroine's statement from a womanist standpoint—it is time to adapt. As Lilith's exclamation mark indicates, her utterance of the word is an emphatic confirmation of her renewed existence. She speaks herself into existence and ignites her journey toward self-actualization. Once Lilith realizes that she has indeed survived the nuclear war, she begins to reorient herself to her new environment. This practice of assessment and then reorientation is an important aspect of Black women's agency as writers and/or activists. Oftentimes, they describe injustices in a clear and unadulterated manner as a call to action or as a precursor to identifying a prescription for how to solve the problem. We see such an approach in Lorde's texts, and the reader witnesses it again in Lilith's approach to engaging in her new environment. Upon awakening, Lilith considers whether she had been drugged, she contemplates the dimensions of the room and she considers the practical question of whether there are clothes for her to wear, and so on (Butler 5–11). These early assessments provide Lilith the opportunity to evaluate her environment and the resources available to her. In this regard, central to Lilith's dawning awareness of her new surroundings is the understanding that what she perceives is the reality (Butler 5). She employs this perspective as she takes stock of her new conditions and later centers her training philosophy on this notion. Thus, Lilith's attempts to come to terms with her reality also signals that her self-actualization will also mean a complete transformation of her personhood and perception of herself within a new world. Understanding her reality underlines Lilith's commitment to realism continues to serve her well as she meets her Oankali handler, Jdahya. Her ability to leave the isolation room the Oankali placed her in rests solely on Lilith's ability to accept Jdahya's appearance, tolerate being near him, and agree to her assigned task. Adapting to this new species would be no small feat. Butler describes Jdahya's appearance as a "humanoid, but it had no nose—no bulge, no nostrils—just flat, gray skin" (Butler 12). Lilith also learns that what originally appeared to be hair growing out of his head, around his eyes, from his throat, were actually tentacles (Butler 12–14). Her eventual adjustment to the dissonance of this new environment and an alien race is taxing but not fearful. Lilith says of this new experience, she has had many fears to overcome already, "She was not afraid . . . . The unknown frightened her. The cage she was in frightened her. She preferred becoming accustomed to any number of ugly faces to remaining in her cage" (Butler 12). From this perspective, Lilith's decision to remain grounded in the environment she could engage with her five senses, rather than to pretend or imagine she was somewhere else, is an exercise in boldness and adaptability. Lilith's perspective reflects an aspect of womanism that Layli Phillips Maparyan, editor of *The Womanist Reader*, defines in part as "a social change perspective rooted in Black women and other women of color's everyday experiences and everyday methods of problem-solving" (Phillips Maparyan xx).

As Lilith becomes accustomed to her liaison Jdahya, he explains the job the aliens have assigned to her. He informs Lilith that her task is to "awaken a small group of humans, all English-speaking, and help them learn to deal with us. You'll teach them the survival skills we teach you" (Butler 35). When Butler presents Lilith as the human the Oankali choose to prepare the first group of humans to travel to earth, she ensures that the reader understands the significance of the alien's choice. The reader learns that after interacting with humans for over 200 years, Lilith was the only one the Oankali viewed as equipped to assist them in forming sustainable earth-bound family units with humans (Butler 31–32). A close reading of the text provides a view of Lilith as conflicted about accepting this role. A deeper reading of Lilith's job assignment offers an opportunity to evaluate her position as antithetical to the mythic norm as represented in American literature and especially science fiction. As a Black woman protagonist, Lilith is moved from the margins of the text to the center as the womanist speculative archetype. As the archetype the aliens' task to guide the renewal of the earth, the reimagined planet reflects a womanist, commonweal approach toward humanity.

Several characteristics mark Lilith as an ideal candidate to prepare humans to integrate with a select group of Oankali and return to earth. In addition to her training as an anthropologist, she had been a mother and a wife until her family perished in the nuclear war. These characteristics frame her as a nurturer. Additionally, she has a family history of cancer, which, for the Oankali, means she can regenerate cells easily. The Oankali find this aspect of Lilith's DNA almost mesmerizingly seductive because regenerative cells mean the Oankali, adept at biological engineering, gain access to new biological possibilities—such as regenerating limbs. Lastly, she is adaptable. Lilith has been willing to develop an openness to learn about her new, alien environment. Lilith's decision is bold, for she understands what this compliance means in terms of her future children: "Medusa children. Snakes for hair. Nests of nightcrawlers for eyes and ears" (Butler 43). Lilith also understands that her acquiescence will signal, for some of the humans that she has taken on the role of a "Judas goat" or Oankali sympathizer (Butler 66). Once Lilith decides to comply with the Oankali demands, they remake her. The Oankali enhance her biologically as a defense mechanism to be stronger than the humans she will awaken. They also adjust her chemical makeup to enable her to open the ship's doors with her saliva, which, until this point, could only be controlled by Oankali secretions. Lilith's name also changes. Unlike Lorde, Lilith does not choose her new name; the Oankali rename her. Lilith Iyapo becomes Dhokaaltediinj-dahyalilith eka Kahguyat aj Dinso (Butler 64). Her Oankali name informs other Oankali that Lilith is an adopted member of the Oankali species and is now part of a specific Oankali kinship group (Butler 64). Lilith's new name signals to humans as well that the Oankali have coopted her into their social and familial structure. It is important to note here that despite what many of the humans may think of Lilith, her decision to comply with the Oankali does not also indicate her apathy to restoring or preserving humanity. Quite the contrary, she also complies because as an anthropologist she cares for humanity and wants to have a hand in her species' survival.

Once she understands how she is unique among humans and orients herself to her new environment, she then, like Lorde, has to connect to like-minded people. This task is especially difficult for Lilith because, unlike Lorde and her group, The Branded, Lilith has no existing group of people she can connect with; she has to select the people to awaken from suspended animation. Once Lilith strategically chooses the humans she to awaken, there are two characteristics that the group have in common. Everyone, including Lilith, is eager to move from the Oankali ship back to earth. Second, as Lilith suspected, many of the humans view her as a traitor to her kind. This is arguably a position Black women are sometimes faced with, the eagerness for the principle they are advocating to be achieved, but the contempt—or in some cases erasure—they have to face to be effective. bell hooks addresses this concern when she writes:

> If you think about the brave books dealing with Black womanhood from the 1960s and 1970s, so many of them had to span pages and pages dealing with the "Are you Black first or are you a woman first?" question . . . (we) will not be able to address our lives and our mental and physical health adequately if we cannot address the interlocking systems. (bell hooks 157)

Throughout the *Xenogenesis* trilogy, Lilith continues to be vilified as a traitor to humankind among the group of humans called the resistors. These humans refuse to create interspecies families with the Oankali even though the Oankali have rendered them sterile and unable to produce children without capitulating to the Oankali family structure (Butler 268, 281).

Despite the criticism Lilith receives from the human resistors, she displays her love and concern for her humanity and that of the resistors. Viewed in a womanist context, Lilith displays the characteristic of a universalist. Patricia Hill Collins interpolates Walker's meaning of universalist as the belief that everyone can coexist equally, no matter their differences (Hill Collins 10). Therefore, she nurtures her humanity by taking moments for herself—an action that harkens back to Walker's view of a womanist as one who values the need for solitude. During these sojourns, she travels out beyond the Oankali camp to be alone and to plant edible crops for human resistors. Their unwillingness to literally, and figuratively, partner with the Oankali means most of the humans are unfamiliar with the altered, edible vegetation on the Oankali-restored earth. Lilith, more than anyone, understands how her decision to comply with the Oankali could be viewed as reckless, rather than bold. She often felt that way about the decision herself. But she did not view the decision as one made without love for humanity. Arguably, the ongoing conflict she displays throughout the trilogy about the family she is creating is proof of her love for humanity, her womanist sense of universalism. She even supports the idea of a human colony on Mars led by one of her construct children, even though the Oankali believe sending humans to Mars equates leaving them to humans' fatal flaw that dooms them to hierarchical behavior and thus potential annihilation of the human race (Butler 561, 474–475). Lilith's universalist approach to the Oankali, human and her hybrid children are necessary to serving her environment. Her universalist approach is also how her commitment to survive her new environment manifests.

For the womanist speculative archetypes in *Zami* and *Dawn* survival is the catalyst that propels them toward actualizing their innate desires. The impetus for this catalyst is new environments. In Lorde's case, she seeks out new environments that support her ability to survive the racial and gendered counternarrative she is creating regarding her personhood. In each new environment, Lorde connects with women who reify her innate sense of self as antithetical to racial and gendered social constructs. Lorde's journey toward self-actualization yields more than one reason to define herself. Decades later, Lorde would define herself not only as the eponymous *Zami* but also as an assemblage of names: Black, lesbian, mother, warrior, and poet. All of these names represent a collectively whole Lorde. For Lilith, aliens choose the protagonists' new environment. The new earth becomes a crucible wherein apocalyptic circumstances force her to reconsider who she becomes. The result is, as is for Lorde, multifaceted. Lilith becomes a doula that ushers in Oankali-human families; she also becomes a betrayer of humanity. In each case, self-actualization for these archetypes does not mean distilling the expression of their intrinsic desires into one label. Rather, the journey to self-actualization results in a unique, genuine expression of oneself in presentation and expression.

WORKS CITED

Anderson, Reynaldo and Charles E. Jones, ed. *Afrofuturism 2.0: The Rise of Astro-Blackness*. Lanham, MD: Lexington Books/An imprint of the Rowman & Littlefield Publishing Group, Inc., 2016. Kindle Edition.

Baccolini, Raffaella. "Gender and Genre in the Feminist Critical Dystopias of Katharine Burdekin, Margaret Atwood, and Octavia Butler." In *Future Females, the Next Generation: New Voices and Velocities in Feminist Science Criticism*, edited by Marleen S. Barr, 13–34. New York: Rowman & Littlefield, 2000.

Ball, Charlene. "Old Magic and New Fury: The Theophany of Afrekete in Audre Lorde's 'Tar Beach.'" *NWSA Journal* 13, no. 1 (Spring, 2001): 61–85.

Barr, Marleen S. ed., *Afro-future Females: Black Writers Chart Science Fiction's Newest New Wave Trajectory*. Columbus: The Ohio State University Press, 2008. Print.

Boyce Davies, Carole. *Caribbean Spaces: Escapes from Twilight Zones*. Champaign: University of Illinois Press, 2013. *Project MUSE*. Web. 27 Jun. 2015.

Burdekin, Margaret Atwood, and Octavia Butler." In *Future Females, The Next Generation: New Voices and Velocities in Feminist Science Fiction Criticism*. Ed. Marleen S. Barr. Oxford: Rowman & Littlefield Publishers, Inc. 2000.

Burton, Justin D. "From Barthes To Bart: The Simpsons Vs. Amadeus." *Journal Of Popular Culture* 46, no. 3 (2013): 481–500. *Literary Reference Center*. Web. 8 Apr. 2016.

Butler, Octavia. *Dawn*. New York: Aspect/Warner Books, 1997. (Originally published in 1987). Print.

———. *Kindred*. Boston: Beacon Press, 2003 (Originally published in 1979 by Doubleday). Print.

———. *Xenogenesis*. New York: Warner Books, 1987.

Canavan, Gerry. "Far Beyond the Star Pit." Isiah Lavender III, Ed. *Black and Brown Planets: The Politics of Race in Science Fiction*. Jackson, MS: University Press of Mississippi, 2014.

Eshun, Kodwo. "Further Considerations of Afrofuturism." *CR: The New Centennial Review* 3, no. 2 (Summer 2003): 287–302 (Article). doi: 10.1353/ncr.2003.0021.

Franklin, Bruce H. *Future Perfect: An American Science Fiction of the Nineteenth Century*. New York: Oxford University Press, 1966.

Hill Collins, Patricia. *Black Feminist Thought: Knowledge, Consciousness, and the Politics of Empowerment*. 2nd ed. New York: Routledge, 2009. Print.

Hooks, Bell. *Sisters of the Yam: Black Women and Self-Recovery*. New York: Routledge, 2014.

Jackson, Sandra, and Julie Moody-Freeman. "The Genre Of Science Fiction And The Black Imagination." *African Identities* 7, no. 2 (2009): 127–132. *Academic Search Complete*. Web. 8 Apr. 2016.

Jones, Esther. "Africana Women's Science Fiction and Narrative Medicine." Reynaldo Anderson and Charles E. Jones, eds. *Afrofuturism 2.0: The Rise of Astro-Blackness*. Lanham, MD: Lexington Books/An imprint of the Rowman & Littlefield Publishing Group, Inc., 2016.

Jue, Melody. "Intimate Objectivity: On Nnedi Okorafor's Oceanic Afrofuturism." *Women's Studies Quarterly* 45, no. 1/2 (Spring/Summer 2017): 171–188.

Kilgore, De Witt Douglas. "Beyond the History We Know: Nnedi Okorafor-Mbachu, Nisi Shawl, and Jarla Tangh Rethink Science Fiction Tradition." (119–129). Marleen S. Barr, Ed. *Afro-future Females: Black Writers Chart Science Fiction's Newest New Wave Trajectory*. Columbus: The Ohio State University Press, 2008. Print.

Le Guin, Ursula K. *The Language of the Night: Essays on Fantasy and Science Fiction*. Ed. Susan Wood. New York: G.P. Putnam's Sons, 1979. Print.

Lorde, Audre. "Age, Race, Class and Sex: Women Redefining Difference." *Words of Fire: An Anthology of African American Feminist Thought*. (284–291). New York: The New Press, 1995. Print.

———. "Learning from the '60s." *Sister Outsider: Essays and Speeches by Audre Lorde*. Berkley: Crossing Press, 2007. Print.

———. *Zami: A New Spelling of My Name*. Berkley: Crossing Press, 1982. Print.

Melzer, Patricia. *Alien Constructions: Science Fiction and Feminist Thought*. Austin: University of Texas Press, 2006. Print.

Morris, Susana M. "Black Girls Are from the Future: Afrofuturist Feminism in Octavia E. Butler's Fledgling." *Women's Studies Quarterly* 40, no. 3/4 (2012): 146–166. *Education Source*. Web. 4 Apr. 2016.

Okorafor, Nnedi. *Lagoon*. New York: Saga Press, Reprint edition, July 14, 2015. Kindle Edition.

Phillips, Layli. *The Womanist Reader: The First Quarter Century of Womanist Thought*. New York: Routledge, 2007. Print.

Pinto, Samantha. *Difficult Diasporas: The Transnational Feminist Aesthetic of the Black Atlantic*. New York: NYU Press, 2013. *eBook Collection (EBSCOhost)*. Web. 22 Dec. 2016.

Pratt, Annis (with Barbara White, Andrea Lowenstein, Mary Wyer). *Archetypal Patterns in Women's Fiction*. Bloomington, IN: Indiana University Press, 1981. Print.

Provost, Kara and Audre Lorde. "Becoming Afrekete: The Trickster in the Work of Audre Lorde." *MELUS* 20, no. 4 (Winter 1995): 45–59. Web.

Rivera, Lysa. "*Mestizaje* and Heterotopia in Ernest Hogan's, *High Aztec*." 146-162. *Black and Brown Planets: The Politics of Race in Science Fiction*. Ed. Isiah Lavender, III. University Press of Mississippi, 2014. Print.

Russell, Heather. *Legba's Crossing: Narratology in the African Atlantic*. Athens, GA: University of Georgia Press, 2009. Print.

Smith, Faith. Sex and the Citizen: Interrogating the Caribbean, University of Virginia Press, 2011. ProQuest Ebook Central. Web.

Stein, Arlene. Sex and Sensibility: Stories of a Lesbian Generation. Berkley: University of California Press, 1997. Print.

Tate, Claudia, ed. *Black Women Writers at Work*. New York: Continuum, 1983. Print.

Thomas, Sheree, ed. *Dark Matter: A Century of Speculative Fiction from the African Diaspora*. New York: Aspect/Warner Books, 2000. Print.

Vaz, Kim Marie. "Womanist Archetypal Psychology: A Model of Counseling for Black Women and Couples Based on Yoruba Mythology." 233–245. *The*

Womanist Reader: The First Quarter Century of Womanist Thought. Ed. Layli Phillips. New York: Routledge, 2007. Print.

Walker, Alice. "Saving the Life That is Your Own." *In Search of Our Mother's Gardens: Womanist Prose.* Orlando: Harcourt, Inc., 1983. Print.

———. "Womanist." *In Search of Our Mother's Gardens: Womanist Prose." In Search of Our Mother's Gardens: Womanist Prose.* Orlando, Harcourt, Inc., 1983. Print.

Yaszek, Lisa. "Afrofuturism, Science Fiction, and the History of the Future." *Socialism and Democracy* 20, no. 3 (2006): 41–60.

Chapter 13

Arc of Memory in Natasha Trethewey's Works[1]

Nagueyalti Warren

The doorway into the future is through the past. Memory, historical, personal, and nostalgic, infuses Natasha Trethewey's writing as a kind of spiritual subtext. Her works are singularly important because they interrogate the past, insist on our remembering what some would just as soon forget or have already forgotten, and what she also tried desperately but without success not to remember. Poetic memory is more than biographical facts and does not depend on the accuracy, linearity, causality, or facts of life (Gosmann 1). However, Trethewey's poetry contains both kinds of memories, historic and poetic.

Memory and the emotional fire of nostalgia enliven poetry but are elements often rejected as being too subjective or confessional. Lucille Clifton's poem, "Why Some People Be Mad at Me Sometimes," says that people want her to remember but to recall their memories instead of hers (*Blessing the Boats* 38). Trethewey digs deeply into the storehouse of her memories and in doing so remembers the fractured American past. She unearths what Robert Pinsky calls buried memory. One might ask why the past, and to that question, Trethewey joins a host of other Southern writers concerned with the past. Faulkner insists, "The past is never dead. It's not even past." O'Connor understands "Where you came from is gone," from which Trethewey quotes in the introduction to *Beyond Katrina*. Katherine Anne Porter believes, "The past is never where you think you left it"; Margaret and Alice Walker recover the Black past by writing historical novels, and Zora Neale Hurston declares, "The present was an egg laid by the past that had the future inside its shell!" At the beginning of this new century, Huston Baker (2001) declared, "Black critical memory is a memory which refuses to relinquish its racial roots. . . . The clarity bestowed by black critical memory is painful. It is a terrible lucidity casting dark light on a deeply troubling racial idea" (9–10). The reason historical and poetic memory matters is that it saves lives. Indeed, the life Trethewey saves will be her own and perhaps others as well.

Even though no peace and reconciliation commission exists for the citizens of America's South, as it does in South Africa where apartheid mirrored Jim Crow; and few efforts to remember, acknowledge, forgive injustice, and make peace with the past have occurred, Trethewey confronts this Southern history through the fabric of her own experience. One can only make peace with what he or she knows, a convincing reason to excavate the past. Other equally compelling reasons to retrieve the past are power in the story and freedom in the telling. History is semantically ambiguous. Historian Michel-Rolph Trouillot observes that story can be fiction or nonfiction with both based upon interpretation (5–6). (His)story, well documented by conquerors and ruling elite, is another story when narrated by ordinary people and produces contested memories.

History contained in artistic mediums sometimes is unnoticed; thus, Trethewey's fondness for the ekphrastic poem that engages other art forms. Clifton Johnson's photographs, a northerner documenting the South, as well as family pictures are subjects in *Domestic Work*. The photographs of (E. J.) Bellocq provide the inspiration as well as the historical evidence of the red-light district of Storyville, New Orleans, in *Bellocq's Ophelia*. Visual representation tells only part of the story, despite the adage, "a picture is worth a thousand words," especially when those words come from a poet intent on revealing the inner lives of those captured in the photographer's frame. In Trethewey's first two volumes of poetry, photographs, public and personal, provide the context for her writing.[2]

DOMESTIC WORK

In *Domestic Work*, "Three Photographs" situates the reader in 1901. In "Daybook," the first section of the poem, a white photographer has come south to capture the "Negro" who is "Always easy to pose" (6). Trethewey captures the racist stereotypes prevalent at the time when W. E. B. Du Bois declared the problem of the twentieth century to be the color line. The two black men in the photographer's frame are objects even though the persona in the poem claims "they make such good subjects./ Always easy to pose,/ their childlike curiosity" (6). Narrating from the photographer's viewpoint, the poet captures the historical objectification of those caught unwittingly in his shutter, like the two men gathering flowers for their sweethearts. The subtle irony of the first of the three photographs is more apparent in the second, "Cabbage Vendor." Narrating from the female vendor's perspective, the persona resists becoming an object and interrogates the idea of being caught on film as natural. She believes her photograph is "unnatural like hoodoo love," and she threatens to turn the table on the photographer "and make him see himself/ like he be seeing me—/ distant and small—forever" (7). The poem's form is equally feisty. The repetition of keywords, "Cabbages" and "cabbage," "hole" and "hold," and "natural," creates the cadence of Southern speech in the 28-line poem—and is an excellent example of Trethewey's use of free verse, which is not free of form. While the lines are unmetered, the line lengths, line breaks, enjambments, and use of alliteration—*what/want/ watch/when/when/kin/keep/keep*—provide the rhythm that meter provides in metrical verse.

Trethewey dedicates the second section of *Domestic Work*, entitled "Domestic Work," to her maternal grandmother, born in 1916; she is 21 years old in the first poem. "Domestic Work, 1937" opens in the heart of the Great Depression. This free-verse poem dances with rhythm and refrain: *"Let's make a change, girl"* follows the stanza in which the grandmother cleans someone else's house, and the line, *"Cleanliness is next to godliness . . ."* comes after the grandmother cleans her own house; the refrain, *"Nearer my God to thee,"* introduces the final stanza that ends with the grandmother's "wish for something better" (13). "Speculation, 1939" begins and ends with rhyming couplets. Between the couplets, a shift to four-line stanzas with alternating rhyme fits the change, the leap of faith, the New Deal the young woman makes by leaving the job as an elevator operator and following her dream to attend beauty school. The signs in "Speculation, 1939" contain familiar superstitions, like black-eyed peas for good luck; but "Signs, Oakvale, Mississippi, 1941" is a sonnet with both regular and perfect end rhymes, as well as some internal rhyme. While the form is classic, the content conjures the blues. The line, "On Highway 49, heading North" suggests the Cross Road Blues, the place where bluesman Robert Johnson is said to have sold his soul to the devil. Big Joe Williams (Howlin' Wolf) is famous for "Blues on Highway 49." U.S. Highway 49, constructed in 1926, was the first interstate highway in Mississippi. In a mere 14 lines, Trethewey evokes her grandmother's history, her marriage to her first husband with the gap in his teeth (a sign of a liar), blues legends, and the development of the state with "cotton and road signs—*stop* or *slow*" (16). "Tableau" reveals the coming apart of the marriage, like the hairline crack the woman sees in the bowl, a stress fracture poised to split the union in half. "At the Station," a poem anchored with an epigraph from bluesman Robert Johnson, chronicles the split.

The poems in the "Domestic Work" section are women-centered, as they must be, for not often do men engage in domestic tasks or suffer the boredom of pregnancy and lying in wait. "Expectant" traces the birth of Trethewey's mother and moves to her birth in the third section of the book. In the last poem in the second section, "Self-Employment, 1970," the grandmother is fifty-four, finally working only from her home, but always reinventing herself with the changing of her wigs. In the Charles Rowell interview, Trethewey reveals her intent to memorialize her grandmother's history, the many jobs that she held, and the grace with which she kept evolving.

Section three of *Domestic Work* begins in 1965, before the poet's birth in April 1966. Her parents are in Frankfort, Kentucky, their Black/white love illegal, and this fact leads their daughter to ponder the meaning of her personal history, so entwined with public law and custom. Mississippi records obscure the poet's history as her birth certificate indicates. The document lists her mother as "colored" and her father, "Canadian." Like American, Canadian is not a racial designation. To legitimize a link between Black and white in the public record was illegal, as well. Trethewey's personal history is not unique. In the South, especially, biracial and mixed-race children are not unusual. African Americans are hybrids, much as whites are a conglomeration of shared genes. DNA reveals the ridiculous construction of race. However, in a society in which racism still operates and in which people judge by external appearances, a person who appears Black has a different experience from one who appears white. Being Black and looking white produces a variety of experiences, such as the one described in the poem "Flounder" where the persona is not mule but fish to "flip-flop" from Black to white, to fight back and resist being caught in the dichotomy (*Domestic Work* 35).

Trethewey says that almost all of her poems begin with questions such as "What are those things that happened in the past that have everything to do with this moment and me in it?" (Cavalieri). The trauma of the Black Atlantic past and the segregation laws against miscegenation are dated historical facts. Conversely, poetic memory appears in "Cameo," where the persona remembers the dark mornings as she watched her mother dress and then attach a cameo to her neck. The poem itself becomes a cameo: a portrait of the mother framed in the poet's mind. The poem's emotional truth and visual imagery resonate with any daughter who has ever watched her mother dress.

The focus on memory in postmodern writings might be a delayed response to great trauma. The Maafa (African holocaust), and slavery's aftermath, account for the resurgence of memory in African American writing. Baker asserts that the South, in particular, was "flung into existence by that rupture of modernity that was the transatlantic trade" (187). Trethewey states that she wants to inscribe the erasure of Black history and poetic truth "into public memory" and "to create a public record of people who are often excluded" (Rowell 1025). Alice Walker has written, "Each writer writes the missing part of the other writer's story" (49), and until all the parts emerge, the truth will not be known. Trethewey echoes Walker when she says, "I think poems are in conversation with other poems" (Rowell 1026). *Domestic Work* depicts the life of ordinary people that history texts often exclude.

Domestic work symbolizes more than the denotative meaning of a person paid to perform menial tasks such as cleaning; it encompasses the work that we do to live. Trethewey claims that domestic work, finally, is "work that we do as human beings to live with or without people that we've lost, the work of memory" (Rowell 1026). The fourth and final section of the book circles back to the grandmother's picture gallery, to Aunt Sugar, and to the murdered mother. "Limen," meaning threshold or doorway, the book's closing poem, is an elegy for Trethewey's deceased mother. The poem's final words, "hearts flutter," make perceptible the poet's grief.

Bellocq's Ophelia

Trethewey's second collection, unlike *Domestic Work*, is a deliberate effort to step outside of herself. *Bellocq's Ophelia* is a persona poem that imagines the interior life of another. Trethewey extensively researched the facts surrounding the Storyville district in New Orleans and studied Bellocq's photographs. As a University of Massachusetts graduate student in a class focused on photography, Trethewey studied Roland Barthes' idea of "punctum," that which pierces the viewer, or as she explains, "the power of the image" (Rowell 1028). The reference to Barthes is appropriate because his diary reveals his sexual encounters with "boys" in Morocco, where he engaged the sexual exotic; Trethewey writes about the elaborate, sexually exotic arrangements in Storyville.

Trethewey ensures that Ophelia does not become a victim, even when the circumstances of her life would seem to make her one. Always would-be victims can become survivors. For Ophelia, her ability for self-reflection and her audacity to stare back at the sexualized gaze seeking to dehumanize her is salvation. In a time when women were seen and not heard, her options for earning a living were severely restricted, even had she been purely white and of a higher social class. By law, Ophelia must follow the condition of her mother—Black, uneducated, and poor—despite Ophelia appearing white and being the daughter of a white father. Confined to sharecropping in her Mississippi hometown and vulnerable to white male exploitation, she can only escape by passing for white and seeking an office job where she is unknown. Her move to New Orleans proves unsuccessful, and to avoid starving, she ends up working in the sex industry.

Ophelia encapsulates the gendered history of Black women in Africa and the Diaspora. The eroticization of blackness ranges from the sexualized gaze on Saartjie nee Sara Baartman, the Khoikhoi woman who was taken to France and displayed as the Hottentot Venus, to the literary characters like the unnamed African woman in Conrad's *Heart of Darkness*. Blackness, when not viewed as sinister, becomes an exotic, sexual fetish. Slaves and prostitutes to satisfy lascivious male desire replaced purely white women, who were viewed as virginal and passionless. If the women appeared white, as did the quadroons and octoroons, whiteness increased their desirability because as Annette Debo points out, they looked white, but men considered them sexually Black.

The creation of race as a tool for manipulating the masses was recognized early: "In the 1940s [Francis] Ashley-Montagu called race 'a mischievous and retardative term' and in 1942 published *Man's Most Dangerous Myth: The Fallacy of Race* that stated the only race was the human race" (Warren *W.E.B. Du Bois* 84). Notwithstanding the scientific evidence that biological race is an illusion, the social construction of the idea still fuels sexual fantasies. Trethewey takes a specific cameo, Ophelia, and opens the memory of sexual exploitation complicated by the racialized idea of blackness. Alecia P. Long writes: "The sexual status quo in antebellum New Orleans made all enslaved women vulnerable to their owner's sexual whims, while those sold as fancy girls were implicitly marketed as sexual slaves" (10). Various chapters in Long's history text coincide with the events Ophelia describes. Long's first history chapter is titled "It's Because You Are a Colored Woman: Sex, Race, and Concubinage after the Civil War." Trethewey frames her book with two epigraphs, one from Toni Morrison, who declares as a "Colored Woman" Ophelia, and by extension, Black women, "had nothing to fall back on; not maleness, not whiteness, not ladyhood, not anything" (178). As a result, they invent themselves. Trethewey grants this agency to her character.

The title poem, in the narrator's voice, sets the tone for the persona's voice that follows. Referring to Millais' painting of Ophelia dead in the pond, Trethewey's version of Ophelia says, "there for the taking [her body]. But in her face, a dare" (3). The penultimate stanza, also reflecting on the photograph, reads, "Her body limp as dead Ophelia's," but the final line changes everything—"her lips poised to open, to speak" (3). The poet passes the pen to Ophelia, who in the next poem writes a "Letter Home." The letter describes her efforts to pass as white and her failure to do so.

In Section II "Countess P—'s Advice for New Girls" is the advice given to all girls, even today, either by verbal instruction or more often through glossy advertisements and celluloid images that say, as the Countess says: "You must learn to be watched. Empty/ your thoughts . . . See yourself through his eyes—Wait to be/asked to speak" (11). The line breaks are revealing. The essence of the advice is: wait to be. The fourteen Storyville letters are written in free verse. In the first letter, Ophelia understands her value. Alecia Long in her book writes the chapter heading, "As Rare as White Blackbirds." Ophelia writes, "I am the *African Violet* for the promise/ of that wild continent hidden beneath/ my white skin" (13). Ophelia's next letter tells her friend and former teacher Constance that she has chosen to become a prostitute. She claims a sense of agency, insisting that now her labor is her own. Ophelia confronts only one instance of self-doubt. In the *"March 1911"* letter, she wonders if the work that she recognizes as "spectacle and fetish" (20) suits her. Trethewey interrogates the roles that women accept and endure by having Ophelia question whether women somehow are suited for or predisposed to accept subordinate positions. Here, too, is a subtle indictment that feminists have long leveled at mothers for upholding the strictures of patriarchy. Ophelia recalls that her mother taught her to "curtsy and be still" (20) so that she would please the white man—her father.

Bellocq's Ophelia and *Domestic Work* are both women-centered and concern the work that women do while exposing their limited choices. The choices available to Ophelia cause her to wish to forget. She "want[s] freedom from memory" (24), and the anesthesia "in the white space of forgetting" (24) is compelling. Unable to forget, she purchases a camera of her own, and Bellocq, who has been photographing her, instructs her in its use. The camera represents the third eye for Ophelia and provides a way for her to see, rather than to just be seen in someone else's gaze. Patriarchal society grants men the freedom to look, and in many cultures, a woman was/is brazen, if she looks back. Ophelia's instructions are to train herself "not to look back" (11). The camera empowers her, however. *"March 1912,"* a postcard written in renga form, announces Ophelia's westward trip into the sunset and suggests the freedom and adventure reserved for men. Trethewey has chosen the renga, a Japanese form of linked haiku because it encourages collaborative compositions. Trethewey dons at least two and possibly three masks in *Bellocq's Ophelia*: the poet's narrative voice, Ophelia's voice, and perhaps Bellocq's. At least he collaborates with Ophelia to take her photographs and teach her how to use the camera. The renga then is appropriate for the penultimate poem in the book's central division. Thematically the form requires pastoral language, discusses the seasons, and observes nature. Trethewey is within the tradition with winter shedding its "gray husk" and the anticipation of spring (33).

Section III contains 10 unrhymed sonnets and a vignette. The sonnets are Ophelia's diary entries and reveal more intimate details than her letters. "Father," in which Ophelia recalls being chastised for using *lay* and *lie* incorrectly, exposes the paradoxical parallels between the words and her occupation—she lies down to work, and she lies to project a faux image of what men want to see. Men lay the ground rules for her behavior. Irony dominates the final lines that expose her fear of meeting her father as a customer. Not only might he be chagrined for how she earns her living but disgusted at the freewheeling sexual exploits that produced siblings who would not recognize each other. The sonnet explains, as well, how from childhood Ophelia has learned the lesson of exchange. For the apples, candy, and other rewards from her father, she writes, "In exchange I must present fingernails/ and ears, open my mouth to show the teeth" (38). The exchange is mirrored in the sex trade. Fortunately, Ophelia steps "out of the frame, wide-eyed, into her life" (48). In addition to restoring historical facts, either unacknowledged or erased, Trethewey wants to understand her existence, and she longs for what is lost: her mother and grandmother and our ancestors.

Native Guard

History and the poetry of nostalgia are also overarching themes in *Native Guard*, her third collection of poetry, which won the Pulitzer Prize. Ange Mlinko's review says that the book is structured like an argument—a dialectic with the biographical as thesis, the historical as antithesis, and part three as a synthesis (59). Another way to think about the structure is memory (of her mother), history (of the Native Guard), and nostalgia, a desire for what is lost. Mlinko suggests *Native Guard* is "a formula" introduced by Robert Lowell that "begins with a psychological 'I,' piquing prurient curiosity, then elevates that 'I' beyond memoir by placing it in a larger context of recovering cultural memory" (60). She insists the formula is outmoded and never a good idea to begin with because "it reinforces the prejudice against 'mere' poetry (lyric, that trivial thing) by requiring that poetry keep memory alive or raise consciousness" (60). Her conclusion is curious given the lyrical quality of Trethewey's poetry.

The opening poem, "Theories of Time and Space," is a frame that introduces history, memory, and nostalgia. The couplets, white spaces, and long line lengths create a poem intended as a meditation. Trethewey's theory coincides with Alice Walker's (*The Same River Twice*), and Heraclitus' belief that one cannot enter the same river twice. Her poem declares: "Everywhere you go will be somewhere/ you've never been" (1). This poem as contemplation is more than a device to introduce the collection but also structures what follows and questions the essence of there and here. Is *there* past and *here* present? Can one get to the past from the present? Is memory the entryway? "Theories of Time and Space" calls memory a "tome" that one must carry. Another poem declares memory "flawed, changeful—that dulls the lash/ for the master, sharpens it for the slave" (25). Trethewey's epigraph from Charles Wright, "Memory is a cemetery," reinforces the contemplative mood of the collection.

The poet selects the lyrics from "Wayfaring Stranger," a traditional hymn, as a bridge from "Theories of Time and Space" to the poems for her murdered mother, gone now for 20 years. The daughter/poet/narrator is finally ready to meet the mother. The River Jordan, in the African American religious tradition, represents salvation, a baptismal crossing over from trouble to peace and freedom. The opening poem, "The Southern Crescent," begins the first major section of the book with an inherited memory passed to the daughter from the mother. In 1959, the mother rode the Crescent to meet her father in Los Angeles, but her father never appeared. In 1979, before AMTRAK took over the Southern Crescent, the mother and daughter share one last ride. Memory is an overlay in the poem—another train trip to meet the poet's father ends in a derailment with people killed and the mother's disappointment that another trip has gone wrong. The poem ends ambiguously with the mother's reflection in the window as night falls. The final stanza states that the mother is "sure" this time, but ends by saying, "my mother's face appears, clearer now/ as evening comes on, dark and certain" (6). Is it the mother or the approaching night that is dark and certain?

"Genus Narcissus," which directly follows "The Southern Crescent," admits the narcissism of childhood—childish vanity the poet calls it. In childhood's innocence, she knows nothing of how life's ironies play out—that the name of the flower she chooses for her mother connects to Narcissus in Greek myth, one so lovely he can only love himself, or that his love will be the death of him. The foreshadowing is clear only years later. The final revelation from the flowers called Narcissus is riveting: *"Be taken with yourself,* / they said to me; *Die early,* to my mother" (7). Hindsight as perfect vision is cliché, but memory, at least sometimes, is a way to see clearly.

"Graveyard Blues" is a poem that captures history, memory, and longing in a form that exerts magisterial control of the poet's emotions. The poetic form holds the weight of emotion in a hybrid structure that deviates from the standard blues in that the second line, rather than repeat the first, amplifies it. The rhyming aaa/bbb/ccc/ddd/ee carries the poem forward with rhythm and blues. While the poet mourns the loss of her mother, Giorgia De Cenzo correctly points to the mention of names in the closing couplet, "I wander now among names of the dead:" a subtle but certain allusion to other murdered and lynched bodies in this Mississippi graveyard. Ironically, the last line in the poem, "My mother's name, stone pillow for my head" (8), is a hard pillow because the mother's name represents a conundrum for the daughter. In Jake Adam York's interview, Trethewey reveals that her mother's grave has no headstone. She could not bring herself to put the last name of the murderer on the marker. Paralyzed by the murderer's name, she finally realizes that she can use her mother's maiden name, which she does in the dedication of *Native Guard.*

The sonnet "What is Evidence" is also highly structured to control the emotion that it contains. The end rhymes/slant rhymes play much like a song out of tune, which reveals the pain controlled within the fourteen lines—the bruises, broken bones, and her mother's quivering voice are evidence. The poet chooses form as a means of restraint. Freeform might have spilled over into maudlin verse. She uses Evidence to reveal the truth—in this case, the "site of memory" where truth resides is in the mother's body. What is evident here is not just race but gender. Audre Lorde's poem is a reminder, "This woman is Black/ so her blood is shed into silence" (Warren *Temba* 651). While controlling her rage, Trethewey captures the evidence so that what happened to her mother will not be lost in silence.

The outpouring of the daughter's emotions, contained by strict form, appears again in "Myth," a palindrome or mirror poem. The rhyme scheme repeats in the reflecting three stanzas. The repetition creates a haunting quality in the tercets. The opening line, "I was asleep while you were dying," pulls the reader into the narrator's dream, where the dead mother lives. The poem refers to the myth of Erebus or the darkness of the underworld personified. The poet tries in vain to bring her mother from the dream into the light of day, but upon awakening, she finds her mother has not followed. "Myth" also refers to Orpheus and Eurydice. Orpheus looks back and loses his wife, who was leaving the darkness of the underworld to follow him to the outer world. When he looks back, she disappears, like the image of the poet's mother. Myths often present contrary meanings, which add to their mystery. On one hand, examining history requires looking back, yet some myths warn against it. Orpheus loses his beloved, and Lot's wife in the biblical story turns into a pillar of salt for looking back. Nostalgia can facilitate a return to the past, however. Trethewey comments on her need to circle back, rather than use linear narrative, which she beautifully achieves in "Myth."

The final poem in Part I, "At Dusk," also is a circling back. Ostensibly, about a neighbor and her cat, the poem concerns the poet's ability to call someone out there—to "call someone home" (15). To call the mother back returns the reader to "Theories of Time and Space," and takes us from here to there, to find our loved ones if only in dreams, and in that magical darkness, the last stage of twilight. Thadious Davis observes, "Trethewey adheres to a postmodernist narrative of impossible reunion" (71). Indeed, Trethewey's reunion occurs only in remembering. In the next section, the poet moves from memory and longing to history.

The epigraph "Everybody knows about Mississippi" from Nina Simone's song "Mississippi Goddamn," introduces Part II. The song, signifying the state's history, also frames the first poem, "Pilgrimage." By choosing to title the poem "Pilgrimage," the poet creates the lofty tone of a spiritual journey juxtaposed against her irreverent epigraph. The pilgrimage is to Vicksburg. The poem contains the unforgettable ending lines: "the ghost of history lies down beside me, / rolls over, pins me beneath a heavy arm" (20). The arm is weighty with slavery, cotton, the 1874 Vicksburg massacre that killed Black citizens, and the murders during the civil rights era. The poet resurrects this history in the poem as it is preserved in "stone, white/ marble, on Confederate Avenue," or in museums. The Mississippi River is a "graveyard/ for skeletons" (19), the poem says, and "of sunken riverboats," and history also says it holds Black unclaimed bodies. The Mississippi River symbolizes a pilgrimage to the real heart of darkness, the poet's native source, and a metaphorical source for all of "us" who've "come 'cross the water" (Clifton, *All Us Come Cross the Water*). Trethewey, like the mighty river forging its path to the sea, creates her path in terms of style and subject matter. Her history challenges the Vicksburg Spring Pilgrimage that takes place annually and invites visitors to "relive an era when cotton was king" (Online Highways Home). Her "Pilgrimage" is a spiritual knowing expressed in the epigraph; however, she accepts the invitation to revisit the time when cotton ruled with her visit to Vicksburg.

The poem that follows "Pilgrimage," "Scenes from a Documentary History of Mississippi," set in 1907, begins with "*King Cotton.*" This villanelle with rhyming tercets creates a marching rhythm. The banner that announces, "Cotton, America's King," and the images including the plague of weevils, the president with his back to the Blacks—reveal the history that privileges the white cotton, land-owning kings and ignores the pickers as if the cotton has bagged itself. The poetic form that contains this history subverts Trethewey's narrative impulse that she admits is an issue when dealing with historical facts. The poet is guided by Rita Dove's advice, "If you can get the edges into the form, then that form becomes transformed—it hurts much more, it's much more disturbing if something horrific is described so eloquently that you see the beauty in the background even while the horror is happening before your eyes—the glistening of a raindrop on a bright green leaf as someone's throat is slit—well, your defenses are down, and emotion slips in" (Alexander). Trethewey captures the horror of history in the form that is repetitive because history tends to be. The poem "Flood" reflects the repetitive nature of history. The poet quotes from a photograph of flood victims, "*One group of black refugees*, the caption tells us" (22), and the rhetoric of 2005 is familiar; citizens of the United States called refugees in 1927 and again in 2005, demonstrate the circularity of history. In the "Native Guard" sequence, the title poems are a crown of sonnets, 10 unrhymed poems connected by the last line of one stanza and the opening line of the next. The Frederick Douglass epigraph addresses the Civil War. "*If this war is to be forgotten, I ask in the name of all things sacred what shall men remember?*" appropriately introduces the forgotten Native Guard. Douglass' address, "The Unknown Loyal Dead," given at Arlington National Cemetery on May 30, 1871, also is appropriate; for not only were the Native Guard forgotten, but they were also never known for many people.

The sonnets, dated November 1862 to 1865, are a record kept in a journal that one of the guards usurps from an abandoned mansion. As with Ophelia, Trethewey transfers the pen to the Native Guard, empowering him to write his own story. "Truth be told, I do not want to forget/ anything of my former life," introduces the change in voice. The line is an affirmation for memory, as De Cenzo points out, and the opening words, "Truth be told" (25), is an idiomatic expression in African American vernacular. People use the statement when what they say is likely to be challenged or denied, like the soldier's history that has been denied with deafening silence.

The guard who keeps a record in the secondhand journal writes over the original record; this action symbolizes that in many respects, African American history is a story told over the official versions. The Native Guard was not infantry, but a supply unit left to perform the duties no one else wanted. A colonel calls it *"nigger work,"* but the most surprising part of their duties is to guard the confederate prisoners captured by the Union soldiers and brought to Mississippi's Ship Island. The former masters and "would-be masters" (27) are not abused by the formerly enslaved men. The literate guard writes letters to their families. They fear the one who writes the letters, but he is sympathetic. He sees "X binds them to the page—a mute symbol/ like the cross on a grave" (27). The war makes slaves of all, and their master is death. Sonnet eight says, "Death makes equals of us all: a fair master" (29). Sonnet ten, dated 1865, reckons with the past and calls to account those responsible for the massacre at Fort Pillow, Tennessee, when under the white flag of surrender, African American Union troops were murdered.[3] Various sources differ regarding the number, but most report upward of 200. Some denied that the massacre ever happened. Truth be told, research demonstrates otherwise. The army changed the name of the Native Guard to Corps d'Afrique. As the naming of the 1927 and 2005 flood victims as refugees challenged their identity as U.S. citizens, the name change of the Guard effectively disowns the Black native sons of the South.

The final section of *Native Guard* focuses on the magnetism of Southern geography. Walt Whitman's epigraph emphasizes the dichotomy of good/ evil, love/hate in the South. For Trethewey, the dichotomy is Black/white. The poem "Pastoral" is reminiscent of Rita Dove's poem, "Upon Meeting Don L. Lee in a Dream." Dove uses free verse and Trethewey an unrhymed sonnet, but the poems match philosophically. Don L. Lee is to the 1960s Black Arts Movement what Robert Penn Warren is to the 1920s Fugitive Poets. Dove's poem is a dream in which the poets meet, and she tells Lee the past is gone and asks what is there now? Trethewey's poem also is a dream; but rather than confronting one poet, she finds herself in the company of all of the Fugitive Poets. They line up for a photograph, and the photographer says, "*Say 'race'* " (35). The poet/narrator is in blackface, and there is a question, but not posed by the poet. The men ask her if she doesn't hate the South. She does not answer. In Dove's poem, Lee does not answer; but his face, perhaps seen as a mask, begins to disintegrate. In Trethewey's dream-poem, she is a stereotyped image of a Black person, an exaggerated caricature. The camera freezes her fake image; and, even after she announces that her father is white, the question she must face is *"You don't hate it?"*[4] The poems juxtapose the younger poets, Dove and Trethewey, against the older poets, Lee and the Fugitives.

The most interesting form used in the *Native Guard* collection is the ghazal. In "Miscegenation" the form restrains a narrative that might have read like the hackneyed tragic mulatto tale, but the seven couplets, each ending with Mississippi and echoing the poem's title, turn the "tragedy" on its head. Trethewey uses Faulkner's Joe Christmas as a tragic mulatto or not since he does not know his identity, but there are plenty of figures in nineteenth and twentieth-century African American literature from which she could have chosen. William Wells Brown's *Clotel or the President's Daughter* and Nella Larsen's *Passing* or *Quicksand* offer examples. Trethewey selects Joe Christmas because he fits perfectly with her name. Her father named her Natasha, which means *"Christmas child,"* even though she was born near Easter. She is neither lynched like Joe nor crucified like Jesus. Self-knowledge ("I know more than Joe Christmas did") is what saves the poet from a tragic end.

"Southern History," a sonnet with a regular rhyme scheme, is an example of distorted history. In the poem, a teacher shows the film *Gone with the Wind* as a depiction *"of the old South"* (38). Although presented as *"a true account,"* the poet recognizes it is no more a documentary history of the old South than *The Birth of a Nation* is for the Reconstruction era. The poem's final stanza demonstrates how silence empowers a lie. The narrator blames herself for not speaking up and challenges those who keep silent when confronting a lie. In another autobiographical poem, "Incident," the interracial couple and their daughter are not silent, but the narrator claims, "Nothing really happened" (41). The poet employs litotes because the Klan burns a cross on their lawn. A pantoum with interlocking quatrains, the form of the poem is perfect for repetitive thoughts or actions. Every year the story is repeated. Each time the story is retold, they are thankful for what did not happen.

The final poems in this collection include the personal "Monument" written for the mother and the collective "Elegy for the Native Guard." "South," the closing poem, is both personal and collective. The monument for the mother is set in the cemetery, where there still is no grave marker; ants busily bring up the soil, and the daughter grieves for what she has not done. In the elegy, Trethewey quotes Allen Tate, one of the Fugitive Poets, and borrows from his "Ode to the Confederate Dead" for the epigraph. Only the fort on

Ship Island remains; the graves have washed open, with "fish dart among their bones" (44). "South" traces the poet's return to the state that made her a crime, but she claims her native land and vows to have her body buried in the place of her birth. The poem speaks for all who are prone to psychological exile from their native land.

Beyond Katrina

Robert Penn Warren's *Segregation: The Inner Conflict in the South* (1956) influences the form of Trethewey's *Beyond Katrina: A Meditation on the Gulf Coast* (2010). Warren's book is a mixed genre that blends memoir in conversational prose and interviews. In conversation with Joycelyn Heath, Trethewey states her preference for "creating literary hybrids." *Beyond Katrina* combines poetry and prose, history and memory in a way that elucidates the Southern, African American lived experience in the twenty-first century. Katrina is still alive in the collective memory and less likely to inhabit the realm of contested memory than what took place more than one hundred years ago. Nevertheless, there still are two groups with disparate narratives, one grounded in penury, and another enabled by redress of their grievances; one group of people viewed as native, and entitled to compensation, while the other group is viewed as refugees—interlopers. Trethewey bridges the disparate groups with herself, being both Black and white as well as experiencing both privilege and exclusion. Of the South, Warren wrote it "was a necessary part of my life. I was going back to look at the landscapes and streets I had known . . . to look at the faces, to hear the voices, to hear, in fact, the voices in my own blood" (*Segregation* 3). Trethewey returns for similar reasons. Her meditation ponders the geography and the sociology of the Mississippi Gulf Coast couched, both literally and symbolically, in the memory and history of storms.

In 1991, Trethewey wrote the words *"Natural Disaster"* (*Beyond Katrina* 1) in her journal. Not only are the storms along the Gulf Coast star-crossed, but because they spawn off the coast of sub-Saharan West Africa, they create fodder for the imagination. The path of the storms follows the course of the Middle Passage. Ancestral spirits seem to wreak havoc from the deep. Whether or not Trethewey meditated on the path the storms take, she does consider providence in a poem of that title included both here and in *Native Guard*. The poem centers on the 1969 storm Camille. Of particular importance is the line "boats washed ashore, a swamp / where graves had been" (*Beyond Katrina* 29), which could allude to the Atlantic from which the hurricane has come, a grave of the Middle Passage. The poet's memory is a trembling reflection that disappears; like the identity that forms in a society that refuses to reflect one's true image—a Duboisian concept—"a sense of always looking at one's self through the eyes of others" (Du Bois 3). For the poet, it is the eye of water.

In this meditation on Katrina, Trethewey recalls personal tragedies, like her brother's arrest and the death of her grandmother, and the formidable effort to tell her brother's story. These narratives speak for the unspoken accounts from the Mississippi Gulf Coast, for Katrina usually brings to mind New Orleans. Talking to storm survivors, Trethewey finds that recovery is slow; some people have lived in FEMA trailers for more than a year. Of course, those with money rebuild. State officials including Governor Haley Barbour insist that the state does not discriminate by race or income when giving aid to storm victims, but many poor residents cannot afford homeowners insurance and are ineligible for some aid programs.

After her initial journey home, following the storm to retrieve her grandmother, Trethewey postpones returning for too long; she carries the burden of guilt for not fulfilling her grandmother's wish to see Gulfport one more time. Bringing the grandmother home to the storm-ravaged church for burial is made more traumatic because, as Trethewey confesses in a National Public Radio interview ("Natasha"), the grandmother is not returned whole. She lost her leg to amputation just before dying, the result of a wound that would not heal. The chapter "Redux" ends the memoir and indicates how going back can help to move one forward. The history of storms, the memory of bygone days, and knowledge of what makes a place home characterize this meditation on the Mississippi Gulf Coast.

Thrall

Trethewey has a love—not quite love—relationship with her South. Angered by the injustice, saddened by the destruction caused by nature and humanity, *Thrall* questions love with a Robert Penn Warren epigraph: "What is love? / One name for it is knowledge." Trethewey's writing focuses on self-knowledge and the relationship of the self to the past. Dedicated to her father, the collection begins with an elegy, even though her father was alive. The poem laments the past in unrhymed couplets. The narrative voice is nostalgic for the "river . . . thick / with salmon" (3), and resigned to the outcome for all things living, her "back to where" she knows they are headed (5).

"Miracle of the Black Leg," inspired by the myth of twin physicians who transplant the leg of an Ethiopian onto a white recipient, in some ways may have been influenced by Trethewey's memory of her grandmother's leg amputation. The free-verse poem, written in four parts, condemns the sacrifice of one man to save another when that choice is predicated upon race/color. The poem declares that always the dark body is "hewn"; and one need only recall the Tuskegee syphilis study, the Henrietta Lacks research, and numerous other experiments performed on the Black body to understand the poet's conclusion. The story of the transplant continues to change, and the poet intends to unearth the truth. Part two of the poem suggests a sexualized reading with the Moor on the floor, his "hands crossed at the groin" (10). In the corner of the room, the curved form of a snake emerges from the "mouth of a boy like a tongue—slippery / and rooted in the body as knowledge" (10). Captured in wood—"in words / or wood or paint—" read "wood" as trees, and read "paint" as paintings or photographs of violence performed on the Black body. James Allen's *Without Sanctuary: Lynching Photography in America* and Trudier Harris' *Exorcising Blackness: Historical and Literary Lynching* provide evidence for a historical reading of "Miracle of the Black Leg." The mutilation of the Black body is part of what Trethewey calls "the body as knowledge" (10). The repetition of the myth is a trajectory of Black history.

Part three of "Miracle of the Black Leg" describes the suffering of both the white patient and the *"blackamoor"* (11). Always injustice is a two-edged sword that cuts both oppressor and the oppressed. Section four of the poem established the injustice of deeming some people worthy, and others expendable. The poet also emphasizes the degree to which people are bound in symbiotic relationships, how the Black is a modifier of the white, and how the story of the relationship is still being written.

Poems influenced by the *Casta* paintings of Juan Rodriguez Juárez begin with "Taxonomy," normally a classification of organisms, but in this case, the cataloging of races. The poem explains, *"this plus this equals this"* (16); a Black person mating with Spaniard produces a mulatto. In Mexico, classifying race was more elaborate than in the Southern United States. Black and Indian would produce a lobo. In the South, one drop of Black blood, as if there were such a thing, rendered a person Black. In "The Book of Castas," the poet names a "typology of taint," a "sullying spot" (24). The poems in this collection, unlike in Trethewey's other books, are mostly free verse, but carefully executed. The white spaces work perfectly with the question in the poem, *"What do you call / that space between / the dark geographies of sex?"* The answer is "Call it the *taint*—as in / T'aint one and t'aint the other—" (25).

"The Americans," describing a photograph by Robert Frank, returns to Southern states. Dr. Samuel Adolphus Cartwright on Dissecting the White Negro, 1851 reveals the obsession with race, color, and blood. Dr. Cartwright is the physician responsible for the curious term Drapetomania, a mental disease that caused African Americans to run away from slavery. The reference to Cartwright exposes scientific racism and the predilection for viewing Black behavior as pathological. In this persona poem, Dr. Cartwright is talking to students or other physicians as he performs the dissection, while he looks for what makes a Black person Black.

The poet's research and recovery of the past, hers and ours, illuminates what was, in a way that history texts cannot achieve with mere facts and dates. The final poem from *Thrall* testifies to the absolute need for poetic memory. Trethewey writes, "Always there is something more to know/what lingers at the edge of thought" (76). There is something more of history, something more to remember, and homesickness for what is lost. That which is spiritual is the subtext unseen but felt, enigmatic and present in Trethewey's poetry of mothers and grandmothers, women's work and their exploitation, the past and how it lives in the present moment.

Congregation and *Monument*

In 2014, Trethewey won the William Meredith Foundation award for poetry. The award-winning work, *Congregation*, is a "love letter to the Gulf Coast, a praise song, a dirge, invocation and benediction, a requiem for the Gulf Coast" (iii). Poems contained in this chapbook also appear in *Beyond Katrina*. Trethewey's last book of poetry, published in 2018, contains poems from her four previous collections. The first poem preceding the selected ones is an "Imperative for Carrying on in the Aftermath"—an aftermath not only of her mother's death but of the Civil War dead, the old South statues that repress freedom and a culture still wrestling with the concept that Black lives matter and Black women's lives matter.

MEMORIAL DRIVE: A DAUGHTER'S MEMOIR

Trethewey's latest work and her most poignant demonstrates why history for her is crucial. Her personal history has haunted the poet and writing her story and her mother's has provided some relief from emotional and psychic pain. Two quotations frame the book's opening: "The past beats inside me like a second heart" from *The Sea* by John Banville and "All journeys have secret destinations of which the traveler is unaware"—Martin Buber. The second heart in the first quotation is mirrored in the memoir's last sentence when Trethewey recalling road trips with her mother writes, "we'd drive like that: so close we seemed conjoined, and I could feel her heart beating against me as if I had not one, but two" (213). Trethewey's memoir chronicles the loss of her mother to domestic violence. As one might expect, the prose is poetic, and some parts of the narrative are ethereal. The page before the prologue is written in italic and relates a dream the daughter has of her dead mother. The mother's final questions. "*Do you know what it means to have a wound that never heals?'—a refrain.*" The refrain for the daughter is her wound that never heals. At 19, the traumatic loss of her mother to murder is an eternal wound. The question also embraces the grandmother whose unhealing wound ended in her leg being amputated.

In graduate school at the University of Massachusetts, Amherst, a creative writing professor asked Trethewey if she would ever move on from what the professor thought was an obsessive focus on what had happened to her mother (Hall). This rather crass question is evident that the professor had absolutely no knowledge of "a wound that never heals." The Prologue describes a photograph of her mother at the age of forty. Trethewey reads the image of her mother as a new beginning, thinking that her life was before her, thinking perhaps of unlimited possibilities. Her mother had come far, divorced her first husband, Natasha's father, moved from her hometown, Gulfport, earned a graduate degree, remarried, and extricated herself from that abusive relationship, or so she thought. She must have been hopeful. For years, however, Trethewey told herself that her mother was aware of her approaching demise. Going back to the crime scene enables her to see things differently. Shakespeare's, Sonnet 3 ends the Prologue and introduces Part 1 of the memoir. The lines Trethewey chooses from the sonnet are perfect: *"Thou art thy mother's glass, and she in thee/ Calls back the lovely April of her prime."* These words capture the irony of the mother's prime occurring early because her life is cut short and equally reveal the "lovely April," which is Trethewey, born April 26, 1966.

Aptly titled *Memorial Drive* not only does the name mark memories the poet must unpack and examine the street on which she and her mother lived. Memorial Drive is a long road going from downtown Atlanta east to Stone Mountain, Georgia. Recalling their lives together is painful. She must reconstruct what she has long suppressed. Memorial Drive is where her mother was murdered by her ex-husband. Trethewey was 19 when it happened, a just-becoming adult, and the event would shape the person and the artist she became.

In the shadow of Stone Mountain, a monument to the Confederacy, Trethewey makes clear how personal history, the tragic loss of her mother, and social history, Stone Mountain, Confederate monuments, and symbols of racism and oppression all intertwine on a street named for memory. The wound that will not heal is both personal and historical. Trethewey recalls that in 1966 when she was born, the state of Mississippi rendered her persona non-grata because interracial marriage between her mother and father was illegal. She felt wounded by her native state. The most significant wound, however, is the loss of her mother to violence and murder in a patriarchal system that creates monsters. Regarding the man who took her mother's life, Trethewey says she tries to see him as someone who was once a child, one damaged by his experience in Vietnam, and perhaps one unduly influenced by toxic masculinity.

Trethewey's body of works, with the memoir being the crowning jewel, is a living monument to her mother and grandmother and other women of similar experiences that historical erasure cannot obliviate. Her works are memorial statues and corrective to willed amnesia.

NOTES

1. Parts of this chapter appeared as "History, Memory, and Nostalgia in the Works of Natasha Trethewey," *The Southern Quarterly: A Journal of Arts & Letters in the South,* 50, no. 4 (Summer 2013), 75–98.
2. The name Ophelia, generally traced to Shakespeare's *Hamlet,* has a long past, deriving from the Greek word meaning help. The poet Jacopo Sannaazaro used it in the poem "Arcadia." Shakespeare probably borrowed from him. By choosing to name her persona Ophelia, Trethewey joins a host of other artists, including Richard Brautigan, *The Rape of Ophelia,* and Arthur Rimbaud (*Ophélie,* a poem based on the Waterhouse painting). The name situates the work within white canonical literature, but its meaning also speaks to the Black literary tradition. Help, helper, or helped applies to the context of a worker, and the bodacious literary character, Shug Avery who in *The Temple of My Familiar* declares: "Helped are those who know" (289). Trethewey's Ophelia knows how to avoid the angst of Shakespeare's Ophelia, and as Julia Roberts quips to her husband in the film, *Larry Crowne,* Ophelia is out of the pond.
3. John Cimprich. *Fort Pillow: A Civil War Massacre and Public Memory* (Baton Rouge: Louisiana State University Press, 2005).
4. Quentin Compson in Faulkner's *Absalom, Absalom!* says, "I don't hate it," meaning that he did not hate the South. Trethewey's question echoes Faulkner.

BIBLIOGRAPHY

Alexander, Elizabeth. "An Interview with Rita Dove." *Writer's Chronicle* (October/November 2005). AWPWriters.org. Web. 20 September 2019.
Baker, Houston. *I Don't Hate the South: Reflections on Faulkner, Family, and the South.* New York: Oxford University Press, 2007.
Cavalieri, Grace. Interview. www.gracecavalieri.com. Web. 19 September 2019.
Clifton, Lucille. *Blessing the Boats.* Rochester, NY: BOA Editions, 2000.
———. *All Us Come Cross the Water.* New York: Henry Holt, 1973.
Davis, Thadious. *Southscapes: Geographies of Race, Region, & Literature.* Chapel Hill, NC: University of North Carolina Press, 2011.
Debo, Annette. "Ophelia Speaks: Resurrecting Still Lives in Natasha Trethewey's *Bellocq's Ophelia.*" *African American Review* 42, no. 2 (Summer 2008): 201–214.
Douglass, Frederick. "The Unknown Loyal Dead." www.theatlantic.com/national/archive. Web. 12 September 2019.

Gosmann, Uta. *Poetic Memory: The Forgotten Self in Plath, Howe, Hinsey, and Glück*. Madison, WI: Farleigh Dickinson University Press, 2012.
Hall, Joan Wylie, ed. *Conversations with Natasha Trethewey*. Jackson, MI: University Press of Mississippi, 2013.
Heath, Joycelyn. "Interviews & Essays," (February 12, 2012). www.Smartishpace.com
Long, Alecia P. *The Great Southern Babylon*. Baton Rouge, LA: Louisiana State University Press, 2004.
Mlinko, Ange. Rev. of *Native Guard*. *Poetry* 1911 (Oct. 2007): 59–61.
Morrison, Toni. *Song of Solomon*. New York: First Vintage, 2004 [1977].
Pinsky, Robert. "Poetry and American Memory." *The Atlantic Monthly* 284, no. 4 (1999): 60–70,.
Rowell, Charles Henry. "Inscriptive Restorations: An Interview with Natasha Trethewey." *Callaloo* 27, no. 4 (Autumn 2004): 1022–1034.
Trethewey, Natasha. *Domestic Work*. Saint Paul, MN: Graywolf, 2000.
———. *Bellocq's Ophelia*. Saint Paul, MN: Graywolf, 2002.
———. *Native Guard*. Boston, MA: Houghton Mifflin, 2006.
———. *Thrall*. Boston, MA: Houghton Mifflin Harcourt, 2012.
———. *Congregation: Poems by Natasha Trethewey*. Takoma Park, MD: Dryad Press. 2014.
———. *Monument New and Selected*. New York: Mariner Books, 2018.
———. *Memorial Drive: A Daughter's Memoir*. New York: Harper Collins, 2020.
Trouillot, Michel-Rolph. *Silencing the Past: Power and the Production of History*. Boston, MA: Beacon, 1995.
Walker, Alice. *In Search of Our Mothers' Gardens*. New York: Harcourt Brace Jovanovich, 1983.
Warren, Nagueyalti, ed. *Temba Tupu! (Walking Naked): Africana Women's Poetic Self-Portrait*. Trenton, NJ: Africa World Press, 2008.
———. Interview with Trethewey, July 2016 for an entry in *Critical Survey of American Literature*. Ed. Steven G. Kellman. Amenia, NY: Greyhouse, 2016.
———. *Grandfather of Black Studies: W.E.B. Du Bois*. Trenton, NJ: Africa World Press, 2011
York, Jake Adam. "Jake Adam York Interviews Natasha Trethewey." *Southern Spaces*, 25 June 2010. Southernspaces.org. Web. 20 September 2019.

Chapter 14

Seen and Unseen

The Role of the Venus in N. K. Jemisin's **The Fifth Season**

Jasmine H. Wade

N. K. Jemisin's *The Fifth Season* begins with a provocative suggestion: "Let's start with the end of the world, why don't we? Get it over with and move on to more interesting things."[1] With this invitation, the narrator brings the reader into an apocalypse that spans the entire trilogy. Another way to view these lines is as an encouragement to view the world a new way, to think a bit differently. Through her complicated and sometimes unlikeable protagonist and the world she helps end, Jemisin challenges what Patricia Hill Collins calls a "controlling image," the stereotypical images that justify and reinforce Black women's oppression.[2] The Black Venus is the stereotypical image most relevant to Jemisin's trilogy.

Who is the Black Venus? First, Saartje Baartman (also known as Sarah Baartman) is often associated with the moniker Black Venus or Hottentot Venus. She was a South African woman who was enslaved by Europeans and put on public display for much of her life. She was mocked for her genitalia and the protuberance of her buttocks. The distorted view of these body parts then became the model for the Black female "other" under the white gaze. She was not truly laid to rest until 2002 when she was returned to South Africa and buried.[3]

Second, in "Venus in Two Acts," Saidiya Hartman talks about another Black Venus. "She is found everywhere in the Atlantic world. The barracoon, the hollow of the slave ship, the pest-house, the brothel, the cage, the surgeon's laboratory, the prison, the cane-field, the kitchen, the master's bedroom—turns out to be exactly the same place and in all of them she is called Venus."[4] This Black Venus is present but silent in the slavery archives.

She does not look a particular way, but rather she is defined by her demeaned position in society.

Third, the Sable Venus, an imaginary woman, appears in pro-slavery poetry and paintings. She is presented as a woman empowered by destructive sexuality. She is complicit in her captivity, if not dangerous for the white master.[5] The Sable Venus' counterpart is a goddess who has similar provocative sexuality.

What makes a Black Venus? The literature offers three foundational tenets in how the Black Venus is constructed: (1) "the invocation of Black beauty ultimately is employed to show the beauty and superiority of whiteness," (2) even though the Black woman is described as inferior, she is still considered desirable, and (3) the white man's attraction to her seems to threaten white supremacy, making her dangerous.[6]

By drawing on the image of Hartman's Black Venus and the mythology of the Sable Venus, I propose a fourth Black Venus: the Afrofuturist Venus.[7] This Black Venus still experiences the oppressions and distortions of the other Venuses, but she is given a voice and has agency. N. K. Jemisin's protagonist in *The Fifth Season* (and the subsequent books in the trilogy) is a Black Venus. This essay will draw clear connections between the Sable Venus and Jemisin's protagonist to illustrate how she is part of the lineage of Black Venuses. Through this, I argue that as the protagonist evolves, she moves from a Sable Venus figure to an Afrofuturist Venus figure. This shift in the portrayal of the Black Venus not only underscores the importance and potential of Afrofuturism, and more specifically Jemisin's work but also illustrates the power of morphing old archetypes.

BACKGROUND ON THE SABLE VENUS AND *THE FIFTH SEASON*

The original Sable Venus appears in "The Sable Venus: An Ode," Isaac Teale's famous poem from 1793. Teale, a clergyman and a tutor, wrote the tale of the "sable queen of love," a Black goddess with potent sexuality who lives among the Greek gods on Mount Helicon. "The black goddess's fanciful voyage from Angola to Jamaica in a chariot, bedecked with precious materials, drawn by flying fish, and accompanied by a host of sea creatures."[8] The Sable Venus travels from Africa to the Caribbean, inciting desire in everyone she encounters.

The speaker says:

The loveliest limbs her form compose,
Such as her sister Venus chose,

In Florence, where she's seen;
Both just alike, except the white,
No difference, no—none at night,
The beauteous dames between[9]

    The speaker expresses deep love for the Sable Venus and asserts her beauty, which is no different from the white Venus, especially at night. This poem is the main text through which I look at and understand the Sable Venus.

    Isaac Teale's Sable Venus is a Black "female subject held up to European standards of beauty, conveyed by the classical Roman goddesses, Venus."[10] She is a contradiction: alluring and repulsive, appealing and odious, seen and unseen. Even the name itself—Black Venus—is an oxymoron. The name suggests Blackness can be coupled with the power and privilege a European goddess would have. Applying a Black feminist framework to Teale's Sable Venus requires attending to the contradictions as well as questions of agency and self-identification.

    Teale's "The Sable Venus: An Ode" describes the Sable Venus' journey through the Middle Passage, from Angola to Jamaica. It presents the journey as fanciful and exciting, full of sea creatures and lustful gods. The Sable Venus is a woman with a terrible power who has captured the hearts of white men.[11] In this way, the poem frames the Middle Passage as a journey of love and desire rather than horror and social and physical death. In the ode, the Sable Venus represents early views of the over-sexualization of Black women, the beginning of their hypervisibility. Teale is hyperaware of the Black women around him—enough that he chose to write about their sensuality. He also, at the same time, does not see the Black woman—the real, human, flesh and blood women around him in Jamaica. Instead, he sees what he has imagined, what society has trained him to see.

    The image of the Sable Venus has persisted through the centuries, long after Teale's poem. The archetype of the sensually powerful yet undesirable Black woman is sometimes called a Jezebel and appears throughout popular culture. It appears in the continued over-sexualization of Black girls.[12] Connecting the Sable Venus to N. K. Jemisin's main character illustrates how Afrofuturism has the potential to shift old, negative archetypes into revolutionary figures.

    N. K. Jemisin's Afrofuturist Venus functions differently in the world of *The Fifth Season* than Teale's Sable Venus. In Jemisin's world, the Earth is prone to periods, known as Fifth Seasons, when natural disasters make the planet nearly uninhabitable. Jemisin's glossary describes a Season of Teeth when humans were so unprepared they had to turn to cannibalism to survive, and the Boiling Season, when acid rained for three years. The main premise of the trilogy is that the Earth enters its final season. As the narrator says,

This is what you must remember: the ending of one story is just the beginning of another. This has happened before, after all. People die. Old orders pass. New societies are born. When we say "the world has ended," it's usually a lie because the planet is just fine.

But this is the way the world ends.
This is the way the world ends.
This is the way the world ends.
For the last time."[13]

Essun, the protagonist, is an orogene, a kind of human who can sense and manipulate the energies and atoms of the Earth. Orogenes can cause and quell earthquakes; they can raise coral and pull rocks up from the flat ground. They are superhuman, and yet they are also vulnerable to attacks from people who look down on them or fear them. Orogenes who are considered "good" are trained at the Fulcrum, a site where orogenes are confined and programmed, to serve the state. They are dispatched to solve matters of the earth, like earthquakes.

"The orogenes of the Fulcrum serve the world . . . . You will have no user name from here forth, because your usefulness lies in what you are, not merely some familiar aptitude. From birth, an orogene child can stop a shake; even without training, you are an orogene. . . . With training, however, and with the guidance of other skilled orogenes at the Fulcrum, you can be useful not merely to a single comm, but all the Stillness."[14]

While the comparison is not one-to-one, the orogenes do represent Black people. Jemisin confirms this in interviews and on her blog.[15] The links between orogenes and Black people lie in their inability within society to fully access the benefits of humanity. They are a servant species, best meant to subjugate for the good of society, and also a species to fear because there is much about them that is outside the knowledge of the Sanzeds, the human species. Not to mention, orogenes are immensely powerful, and that power is threatening to others.

While *The Fifth Season* appears to have three protagonists, Damaya, Syenite, and Essun, it becomes clear that they are all the same person. Damaya is Essun as a child. Syenite is her name after she is trained by the Fulcrum and grows to be a young woman. She becomes Essun after she leaves Fulcrum-life. While this chapter touches on all three characters, the focus is on Damaya and Syenite (also called Syen) to demonstrate the connections between Teale's Sable Venus and Damaya/Syenite's life as an orogene.

DAMAYA'S MIDDLE PASSAGE

Teale's ode to the Sable Venus chronicles, in part, her Middle Passage, the voyage from Angola to Jamaica. Damaya has a similar journey, her personal Middle Passage, when she is taken to the Fulcrum, where she will be enslaved and trained to serve the state. When Damaya's family discover she is an orogene, they lock her in the barn and wait for a Fulcrum Guardian to come. Schaffa, Damaya's Guardian, is tasked to watch over her and protect the world from her. He convinces her to come with him by getting her to believe he cares for her. By the time she and Schaffa leave her small town on a horse, Damaya "does not want Schaffa angry with her. He's the only person who cares about her in all the world."[16] She expresses complicated feelings, desperately seeking someone to care for her as she has just been sold into slavery by the people who were supposed to be her family.

As they travel, Schaffa tells Damaya a story, an old myth. Misalem, an orogene, was on a quest to kill the emperor. He killed thousands of people on his way to the emperor's palace to demand the emperor's death. When he arrives in the capital of the empire, he finds that the entire city has been destroyed. Shemshana, the emperor's bodyguard, ordered that everyone burn the city down, destroy everything they could, and leave. This is because orogenes draw their energy from the world around them. When Misalem arrived, there was not enough energy for him to pull on to do any lasting damage. This distracted him long enough for Shemshana to kill him.

When Damaya hears this story, she first imagines herself as Shemshana, the clever woman who outsmarted the killer. Then, she realizes she is not Shemshana. She can never be Shemshana. She is Misalem, the madman. This is the indoctrination of her new life as an enslaved person. Schaffa ends the story by saying, "I am your Guardian now, and it is my duty to make certain you remain helpful, never harmful."[17] Through this story, he impresses upon her the imperial fact that: "You are lightening, dangerous unless captured in wires. You're fire—a warm light on a cold dark night to be sure, but also a conflagration that can destroy everything in its path."[18] Here, Schaffa emphasizes the kind of contradictions associated with the Sable Venus—beautiful and destructive, helpful and harmful. These contradictions justify Schaffa (and Teale's) desire to control the Black Venus.

In this section, Schaffa sounds similar to Teale. Teale describes the Sable Venus as beautiful and powerful. But unlike her European counterpart, she is dangerous, capable of great destruction. She has captured the hearts and minds of the white men around her. She is the one they adore, the one to whom they confess. Her power is so great, her throne is constant. Her power is presented not as benevolent, but destructive.

Damaya, like the Sable Venus, is also destructively powerful. While Teale categorizes the Sable Venus' power as sexual prowess, I am not casting Damaya's power in that light. Instead, I posit that these are two imaginary female figures who are considered dangerous and must be watched closely because of a biological fact. For the Sable Venus, it is the combination of her blackness with her womanness. For Damaya, it is orogeny. Moreover, the Sable Venus and Damaya are perceived as dangerous in part because of their powers but more because they are positioned as inferior in society and are still desirable. For Teale, lust for a woman who is considered subhuman threatens the status quo of white supremacy. For Jemisin, Damaya's existence and Schaffa's very real—though dysfunctional—love for her also threaten the status quo. Both societies (European and Sanzed) concluded that they needed to enslave the Black Venus. If Damaya's power, what makes her desirable and different, is controlled by the empire, then it is the empire's power, not Damaya's. This creates an illusion of a restored balance of power.

After Schaffa tells Damaya the story and she realizes he thinks of her as destructive, she resists. She fights against this external definition. When she asserts herself and declares that maybe she's not what he says she is, Schaffa breaks her hand. "All her awareness has focused on her hand, and his hand, and the horrid wet pop and jostle of things that have never moved before, the pain of which is sharp and immediate and so powerful that she screams."[19] Schaffa's justification is that he needs to know that when she is scared, hurting, or feeling any kind of intense emotion so that she can control herself and not do damage. She needs to prove herself to be one of the good ones. He breaks her hand in three places and then threatens to crush all the bones, to which Damaya reacts with a fierce "no."

Schaffa responds: "Orogenes have no right to say no. I am your Guardian. I will break every bone in your hand, every bone in your *body*, if I deem it necessary to make the world safe from you."[20] Here Schaffa emphasizes that despite Damaya's extraordinary power, despite the good she can do, she is not in control of her body. Schaffa, and by extension the state, is.

He lets her process that for a moment and then his next words to her are: "I love you."

Going through the scene of Schaffa breaking Damaya's hand, which will always ache after this, by the way, I am reminded that Teale's "The Sable Venus: An Ode" is supposed to be a love poem. Whether we believe the sincerity of the speaker or not, he is professing undying love, attraction, and desire for the Sable Venus. Yet, just as Schaffa's declaration of love, just after his threat en route to a life of enslavement is disturbing, so too is Teale's profession of love and awe of the woman's power as she travels from Angola to Jamaica for similar enslavement. In reading Teale's poem, the critical reader is forced to try to reconcile two images: the beautiful, powerful Sable Venus of the poem and all the Black Venuses who died unnamed, unburied along the Atlantic.[21] Damaya is doing similar work in this scene, trying to reconcile Schaffa's "I love you" with her broken hand. With all these parallels, Damaya is a Black Venus, whose hypervisibility means she is always at risk of danger or death and whose simultaneous invisibility means she loses the freedom to define herself.

BREEDING SYEN

The Black Venus archetype holds through the protagonist's other identity, Syenite, in how female orogenes, in particular, are prized. Damaya learns the initial lesson that her body is not her own through Schaffa on that Middle Passage. By the time Damaya becomes Syenite, the four-ringed (advanced) Fulcrum orogene, this message has been fully ingrained in her mind. So much so that when she approaches Alabaster, the ten-ringed Fulcrum orogene, intending to sleep with him, she treats it as one of her many Fulcrum chores. Because of Syenite's gender and orogeny skills, she is tasked to make a baby with Alabaster. "Even Feldspar never came right out and said *Your assignment is to produce a child within a year with this man.* That lack of acknowledgment is supposed to make it easier, somehow."[22] Pregnancy is her "assignment," and the lack of transparency does not make this easier. It only underscores her lack of agency. "She's the one who has to carry a child she doesn't want, which might kill her, and even if it doesn't will change her body forever, if not her life."[23] The consequences for failing to produce a child or failing at her orogene duties are dire. "If she lets herself get labeled difficult, they will kill her career and assign her permanently to the Fulcrum, leaving her nothing to do but lie on her back and turn men's grunting and farting into babies."[24] Even in this moment of forced reproductive labor, Syenite still tries to grasp at an agency that is not there by controlling the details of the situation. She approaches Alabaster, she undresses, she provides the lubricant, and she tells him to not move. While these small actions make it "well, not right. But better, somehow, that she's the one in control," in actuality, Syenite has no more control over her body than the Sable Venus did.[25]

Syenite's duty for the Fulcrum, for the empire, raises complications around the idea of desire. In Teale's "The Sable Venus an Ode," the Black Venus' power is primarily sexual. It is in her ability to draw men to her with a taboo desire.

Teale writes:

Do thou in gentle Phibba smile,
In artful Benneba beguile,

In wanton Mimba pout;
In sprightly Cuba's eyes look gay,
Or grave in sober Quasheba,
I still shall find the out.

In these lines, Teale comes closest to talking about actual Black women. He sees the Black Venus in the smile of one enslaved woman, in the pout of another, in the bright eyes of yet another. The illusion Teale created through the mythology of the Sable Venus becomes more transparent in this stanza, and his illicit desires for real enslaved women come forward. In thinking about Syenite as a Sable Venus and her duty to breed as fundamental to that, I come to think about desire a little differently.

Syenite is desired just as much for her contribution to the fictional world's political economy as for sexual reasons. This concept echoes Syenite's value to the empire is in her ability to use her power to protect the said empire and to create new orogenes who can continue to fill that role. In other words, Syenite is desirable only because of how her body can serve the state. In producing young orogenes, Syenite contributes to the political economy of the Sanzed world and stabilizes a status quo that protects and emboldens those in power. Teale's Sable Venus is similar, particularly in light of the intersection of sex and slavery at that time. The enslaved women Teale wrote about were desirable not only for their physical appearance but also, and I would argue primarily, because of their value as commodities.

> That the slave system in the US depended on human beings not just as labor but as reproducible raw material is not part of the story America typically tells itself. That women had a particular currency in this system, prized for their sex or their wombs and often both, and that this uniquely female experience of slavery resonates through history to the present is not generally acknowledged. (Wypijewski)

What Jemisin makes incredibly clear in *The Fifth Season* is that Syenite's reproductive labor is just as important as her orogeny.[26]

SEEN AND UNSEEN

Throughout *The Fifth Season*, Essun/Syenite/Damaya is hypervisible in the world of the Sanzed empire; the Sable Venus experiences a similar hypervisibility. As the previous excerpt suggests, Teale saw the Sable Venus in Black women everywhere he went, across nations and communities. What is also telling is Teale's description of the Sable Venus.

The loveliest limbs her form compose,
Such as her sister Venus chose,
In Florence, where she's seen;
Both just alike, except the white,
No difference, no—none at night,
The beauteous dames between.

Her skin excell'd the ravens plume,
Her breath the fragrant orange bloom,
Her eye the tropic beam:
Soft was her lip as silken down,
And mild her look as ev'ning sun
That gilds the Cobre stream.[27]

In these stanzas, Teale describes the Black Venus as no different from her counterpart, the white Venus, except for her darker skin. His description of her skin, breath, eye, and lips are vague enough to apply to many Black women. This suggests that Teale does not have a specific woman in mind but rather has conjured an imaginary undesirable woman who could be anyone anywhere as the object of his lust. More than this, Teale's descriptions suggest he does not see the Sable Venus (and the real Black women of the poem) as they are, but only as he wishes to see them.

Damaya has a similar problem when she is revealed as an orogene. Her powers were exposed while being bullied on the playground—a typical situation for many children—and she was immediately deemed a threat. Her parents locked her in a cold barn and stood outside, watching and waiting, until Schaffa arrived to take her away. As soon as her identity as an orogene is revealed, she is under surveillance.[28] Her parents watch her. Schaffa watches her. When she arrives at the Fulcrum, a host of people watch her constantly. Syenite is used to the general surveillance that comes with being a Fulcrum orogene. "So for days at a time Syenite and Alabaster encounter only hard-driving merchant caravanners, mailpost-riders, and the local quartent patrol—all of whom give Syenite and Alabaster the eye upon noticing their black Fulcrum uniforms."[29] Syenite is unfazed by people gawking at the uniform that clearly labels her as an orogene. She knows these people might be feeling disgust, fear, and even hate.

Damaya/Syenite/Essun is a Black Venus, with specific connections to the Sable Venus, in part because of her state of hypervisibility. The idea of hypervisibility is not obvious from the word. If being visible is being seen, then hypervisibility would be a state of being extra-seen. Yet, this is not what that concept means here. Instead, hypervisibility is a state of obscured, clouded visibility that in this case is tied to situations of constant surveillance.

The concept of hypervisibility has been developed as an interventionist term for describing the overproduction of visual material that portrays Others in manners that have been so overdetermined and so ever-present that they become of little consequence, thereby rendering that which is hypervisible nearly, or effectively, invisible. Put another way, the overrepresentation of an Othered group can either, or simultaneously, represent, reproduce, and further entrench social and political invisibility for particular populations, effectively disappearing these groups almost entirely from the landscape of hegemonic discourse.[30]

Like the Isaac Teales of our world, the "merchant caravanners, mailpost-riders, and the local quartent patrol" see Syenite as they want to see her, not as she is.[31]

While Damaya and Syenite feel more like the traditional Black Venus, Essun carries some of those characteristics—desired for reproductive labor, a lack of agency on the level of enslavement, hypervisibility—and crucially departs from them: she steals the power to define herself from the Fulcrum. This level of agency is evident in Essun's name. Her parents chose the name Damaya, and Syenite is a name specifically for Fulcrum orogenes (a slave name). However, Essun named herself. After suffering a great tragedy and needing a fresh start, she chose a name that matched the personality she wished for herself. "You could become someone new, maybe. You've done that before; it's surprisingly easy. A new name, a new focus, then try on the sleeves and slacks of a new personality to find the perfect fit."[32] Under this new and final person and under the threat of the apocalypse, Essun is only who she decides to be. Even though the people she meets on her travels make assumptions about her (like the people at Castrima), Essun remains steady and proves their assumptions correct or incorrect just by being herself—unlike the more submissive Damaya and the aggressive Syenite. Essun, as the Afrofuturist Venus, steps into the kind of self-definition that Hortense Spillers talks about concerning Black women—the kind that is such a threat to the status quo it seems monstrous.[33]

IMAGINING THE AFROFUTURIST VENUS

The four kinds of Black Venuses mentioned illuminate different perspectives of Black women throughout history and literature. Saartje Baartman reminds us now of the hypervisibility of Black women. Isaac Teale's Sable Venus is an object of lust, a slave, whose reproductive labor powers an empire. Saidiya Hartman's Black Venus is silent, a ghost. "There is not one extant autobiographical narrative of a female captive who survived the Middle Passage."[34] She is, as Schaffa says, without the right to say no. Now, she exists only in the archive, which is "a death sentence, a tomb, a display of the violated body, an inventory of property, a medical treatise on gonorrhea, a few lines about a whore's life, an asterisk in the grand narrative of history."[35] In N. K. Jemisin's *The Fifth Season*, Essun is an example of the Afrofuturist Venus—the Black Venus who has a voice. Each of these kinds of Black Venuses is connected, and I argue that the Essun's early personas (Damaya and Syenite) were more like Teale's Sable Venus who then gives way to a character with the power of self-definition, the Afrofuturist Venus.

Jemisin's Black Venus is strong and loud. As Damaya turns into Essun, her voice becomes stronger. Her will becomes more resolved, and her rage becomes fiery and productive. What Afrofuturism allows us to do is not only give the Black Venus a voice but also examine her resilience. Jemisin imagines a scenario where a Black woman contributes to the end of the world that enslaved her.

Maybe the Venus is powerful. Maybe the Venus is destructive. Maybe the Venus, if given the right combination of time, opportunity, and rage, can incite a revolution. N. K. Jemisin's work offers room to imagine the Black Venus as neither slave nor ghost but as a force—in some ways a literal rock—that brings the whole system down. This is not at all an attempt to diminish or erase the lives and horrific experiences of the Black Venuses Hartman speaks of. It is also not an attempt to deny the impact of the stereotype Teale imagined. The Black Venus is a contradiction. She is seen and unseen, desirable and undesirable. Hartman asserts, "One cannot ask, 'Who is Venus?' because it would be impossible to answer such a question. There are hundreds of thousands of other girls who share her circumstances and these circumstances have generated few stories."[36] As I have argued here, with Essun, Jemisin offers the reader a Venus in Afrofuturism—a Venus in a story in her voice. She is part of the lineage of Black Venuses that demonstrate the power and resilience that has traversed oceans and centuries.

NOTES

1. N. K. Jemisin, *The Fifth Season*, 1.
2. Hill Collins, *Black Feminist Thought*.
3. Parkinson, "The Significance of Sarah Baartman"; McKittrick, "Science Quarrels Sculpture."
4. Saidiya Hartman, "Venus in Two Acts," *Small Axe: A Caribbean Journal of Criticism* 12, no. 2 (2008): 1–14.
5. Allen, "'The Sable Venus' and Desire for the Undesirable."
6. Ibid., 667.
7. This is not at all to suggest that there are only four types of Black Venuses. Some might suggest that the women marked as Jezebels throughout history would

form another category. I have only concentrated on four kinds that are most relevant for the focus of this chapter.

8. Allen, " 'The Sable Venus' and Desire for the Undesirable," 668.

9. Teale, *The Sable Venus. An Ode Inscribed to Bryan Edwards. [By the Rev. Mr. Teale.]*.

10. Ibid., 670.

11. Wood, "Celebrating the Middle Passage"; Allen, "'The Sable Venus' and Desire for the Undesirable."

12. Lindsey, "'One Time for My Girls'"; Hill Collins, *Black Feminist Thought*; Davis, "Reflections on the Black Woman's Role in the Community of Slaves."

13. Jemisin, *The Fifth Season,* 14.

14. Ibid., 34.

15. Jemisin, "Creating Races."

16. Jemisin, *The Fifth Season*, 86.

17. Ibid., 93.

18. Ibid., 95.

19. Ibid., 97.

20. Ibid., 97.

21. Hartman, "Venus in Two Acts."

22. Jemisin, *The Fifth Season*, 69.

23. Ibid., 70.

24. Ibid., 71.

25. Ibid., 70.

26. My thinking about Syenite's reproductive labor and its connections to slavery are informed by work in the field of Black Feminism that considers how enslavement and other periods of Black oppression have impacted Black women in specific and troubling ways. These works include, "Gendering the General Strike: W. E. B. Du Bois's Black Reconstruction and Black Feminism's 'Propaganda of History,' " McGuire's *At the dark end of the street: black women, rape, and resistance; a new history of the Civil Rights Movement from Rosa Parks to the Rise of Black Power*, and Davis' "Reflections on the Black Woman's Role in the Community of Slaves."

27. Teale, *The Sable Venus. An Ode Inscribed to Bryan Edwards. [By the Rev. Mr. Teale.]*.

28. Simone Browne speaks of surveillance as a "fact of blackness" in *Dark Matters: On the Surveillance of Blackness*. This and related literature on surveillance and race are tangential but related to my argument here.

29. Jemisin, *The Fifth Season*, 118.

30. Medak-Saltzman, "Empire's Haunted Logics."

31. Jemisin, *The Fifth Season*, 118.

32. Ibid., 172

33. See Hortense Spillers, "Mama's Baby, Papa's Maybe: An American Grammar Book," *Diacritics* 17, no. 2 (1987).

34. Hartman, "Venus in Two Acts," 3.

35. Ibid., 2.

36. Ibid.

BIBLIOGRAPHY

Adams, Michael Vannoy. "The Sable Venus on the Middle Passage: Images of the Transatlantic Slave Trade." C.G. Jung and Jungian Analysis: Archetypes, Dreams, Myths, Imagination, August 2007. http://www.jungnewyork.com/venus.shtml.

Allen, Regulus. "'The Sable Venus' and Desire for the Undesirable." *SEL Studies in English Literature 1500-1900* 51, no. 3 (2011): 667–91. doi: 10.1353/sel.2011.0029.

Beale, Frances. "Double Jeopardy: To Be Black and Female." In *Words of Fire: An Anthology of African-American Feminist Thought*, edited by Beverly Guy-Sheftall. New York: New Press : Distributed by W.W. Norton, 1995.

Bridgewater, Pamela D. *Breeding a Nation: Reproductive Slavery, the Thirteenth Amendment, and the Pursuit of Freedom*. South End Press, 2014.

"Danika Medak-Saltzman - 2015 - Empire's Haunted Logics Comparative Colonialisms . Pdf," n.d.

Davis, Angela. "Reflections on the Black Woman's Role in the Community of Slaves." *The Black Scholar* 12, no. 6 (November 1981): 2–15. doi: 10.1080/00064246.1981.11414214.

Hartman, Saidiya. "Venus in Two Acts." *Small Axe: A Caribbean Journal of Criticism* 12, no. 2 (2008): 1–14.

Hill Collins, Patricia. *Black Feminist Thought: Knowledge, Consciousness, and the Politics of Empowerment*. 2nd ed. Routledge Classics. New York: Routledge, 2009.

Ifekwunigwe, Jayne O. "Recasting 'Black Venus' in the New African Diaspora." *Women's Studies International Forum* 27, no. 4 (October 2004): 397–412. doi: 10.1016/j.wsif.2004.10.008.

Jemisin, N. K. *The Fifth Season*. Broken Earth. New York: Orbit, 2018.

Jemisin, N. K. "Creating Races." Epiphany 2.0, August 10, 2015. http://nkjemisin.com/2015/08/creating-races/.

Lindsey, Treva B. "'One Time for My Girls': African-American Girlhood, Empowerment, and Popular Visual Culture." *Journal of African American Studies* 17, no. 1 (March 2013): 22–34. doi: 10.1007/s12111-012-9217-2.

McKittrick, Katherine. "Science Quarrels Sculpture: The Politics of Reading Sarah Baartman." *Mosaic: An Interdisciplinary Critical Journal* 43, no. 2 (2010): 113–30.

Medak-Saltzman, Danika. "Empire's Haunted Logics: Comparative Colonialisms and the Challenges of Incorporating Indigeneity." *Critical Ethnic Studies* 1, no. 2 (2015): 11. doi: 10.5749/jcritethnstud.1.2.0011.

National Maritime Museum. "The Voyage of the Sable Venus from Angola to the West Indies." Accessed November 6, 2018. http://collections.rmg.co.uk/collections/objects/254621.html.

Parkinson, Justin. "The Significance of Sarah Baartman." *BBC News*, January 7, 2016, sec. Magazine. https://www.bbc.com/news/magazine-35240987.

Sharpe, Jenny. *Ghosts of Slavery: A Literary Archaeology of Black Women's Lives*. University of Minnesota Press, n.d.

"Snapshot." Accessed January 7, 2020. http://nkjemisin.com/2015/08/creating-races/

Spillers, Hortense. "Mama's Baby, Papa's Maybe: An American Grammar Book." *Diacritics* 17, no. 2 (1987): 64–81.

Teale, Isaac. *The Sable Venus. An Ode Inscribed to Bryan Edwards. [By the Rev. Mr. Teale.]*. Kingston: Bennett and Woolhead, 1765.

Weinbaum, A. E. "Gendering the General Strike: W. E. B. Du Bois's Black Reconstruction and Black Feminism's 'Propaganda of History.'" *South Atlantic Quarterly* 112, no. 3 (July 1, 2013): 437–63. doi: 10.1215/00382876-2146395.

Wood, Marcus. "Celebrating the Middle Passage." *Atlantic Studies* 1, no. 2 (October 1, 2004): 123–44. doi: 10.1080/1478881042000265518.

Wypijewski, JoAnn. "Reproductive Rights and the Long Hand of Slave Breeding," March 21, 2012. https://www.thenation.com/article/reproductive-rights-and-long-hand-slave-breeding/

Chapter 15

Eco-Justice as Womanist Practice in Contemporary Black Women's Poetry

Marta Werbanowska

In her overview of Black American environmental history, Diane Glave asserts that "long before the birth of the modern environmental movement, African Americans practiced environmentalism through the lenses of religion, agriculture, gardening, and nature study."[1] To illustrate this long tradition, she turns not only to sources from historical, sociological, or agricultural studies but also to literary works, revealing how African American literature has always been rich in ecological and environmental thought. From the topographical instructions that aid the listener of "Follow the Drinking Gourd" in their quest for freedom, to the suggested role of Sandy's root in Frederick Douglass' emancipatory fight with Edward Covey, and the agricultural skill displayed by the Black communities in Zora Neale Hurston's *Their Eyes Were Watching God* and W. E. B. DuBois' *The Quest of the Silver Fleece*, the importance of environmental awareness was underscored in the earliest instances of oral and written African American literary traditions. Later, calls for environmental justice could be heard in landmark works of mid-and late-twentieth-century Black literature, from the descriptions of rat-infested apartments in Richard Wright's *Native Son*, Gwendolyn Brooks' *In the Mecca*, and Gil Scott-Heron's "Whitey on the Moon," to the scheduled bulldozing of the Bottom community in Toni Morrison's *Sula*, and the futuristic catastrophic aftermaths of environmental disaster in Octavia Butler's *Parable* novels.

Today, Black authors continue to address environmental issues with urgency exacerbated by the awareness of the impending global ecological crisis and its impact on Black communities. This chapter focuses on ecological, environmentalist, and environmental justice concerns in the works of four contemporary African American women poets: Camille Dungy, Evie Shockley, Nikki Giovanni, and Wanda Coleman. Guided by an (eco)womanist ethics of responsibility and care, their eco-justice poems constitute part of a larger effort toward social and ecological justice that has been undertaken by Black women activists in the United States and worldwide.

Echoing Alice Walker's now-canonical rumination on how "in search of [her] mother's garden . . . [she] found [her] own,"[2] African American poets today continue to write in the tradition of environmental insight, care, and activism established by earlier generations of Black women authors. Ecological and environmental presences in the works of poets such as Anne Spencer, Lucille Clifton, June Jordan, Jayne Cortez, Audre Lorde, and Walker have seen some critical attention to date.[3] There has, however, been little scholarship so far on the flowering of environmental concern in the poetry of Black women who, writing in the twenty-first century, tend to—and defend—the lyrical "gardens" they have inherited from their predecessors. To fill this gap, this chapter looks at ecopoetry by Dungy, Shockley, Giovanni, and Coleman and discusses their poems as works of environmentalist womanist practice. Spanning issues such as global climate change, biodiversity and species preservation, animal cruelty, toxic waste, air pollution, and unsanitary living conditions, the works of these poets can be classified as "eco-justice poetry," which Melissa Tuckey defines as poetry that recognizes "the environment as home: a source of life, health, and livelihood. It is poetry at the intersection of culture, social justice, and the environment."[4] Importantly, their poems respond to the combined crises of social injustice and environmental destruction in ways that resonate not only with the eco-conscious writings of their literary foremothers but also with environmental activist efforts of Black women that are implicitly or explicitly guided by (eco)womanist ethics.

Although too rarely recognized for this work, Black women have long been at the front lines of environmental and climate justice struggles. Campaigns by Atlanta's Neighborhood Union and the Salisbury Colored Women's Civic League have illustrated how "African-American women attempted to secure reforms and improvements in their urban environments in the early twentieth century."[5] Land justice initiatives from Fannie Lou Hamer's Freedom Farms Cooperative in early 1970s Mississippi to Soul Fire Farm in today's New York have been led and staffed largely by women of color, and some of the most recognizable figures of environmental activism—including the "Mother of the Environmental Justice Movement" Hazel Johnson and the Nobel Peace Prize laureate Wangari Maathai—are Black women. For decades, Black women have been the leaders, organizers, and torchbearers for eco-justice organizations worldwide, from Nigeria and Haiti to the United States.[6]

Importantly, as some scholars have noted, this combined activism for environmental and humanitarian causes is rooted in the tradition of Black women's fight for social justice that dates back at least as early as abolitionist and anticolonial movements. As Valerie Ann Kaalund puts it,

Black women in the environmental justice (EJ) movement use their power and influence to fight against an array of environmental injustices . . . in much the same way their nineteenth-century counterparts" heeded the call "to fight against the enslavement of blacks and for the uplift of women.[7]

Recognizing that the seemingly disparate forms of oppression and exploitation are all rooted in what bell hooks dubs "the politics of domination,"—the dominant ideology of the "white-supremacist, capitalist, patriarchal society" of the United States but also, more generally, much of the global West[8]—Black women have continued to undertake intersectional struggles aiming at immediate political and economic change as well long-term mental and ideological transformation.

In contrast to the white male ideology of domination that fuels anti-Black violence and environmental destruction, both the activist efforts and eco-justice poetry by Black women are often guided by ethical principles aligned with (eco)womanism. I put the prefix "eco" in parentheses because, in many scholars' definitions, the tenets of ecowomanism and womanism overlap to an extent that sometimes makes this prefix hardly necessary. For example, Melanie L. Harris defines ecowomanism as "an approach to environmental ethics that centers on the perspectives, theoretical analysis, and life experiences of woman [sic] of color, specifically the voices of African-descended women as they contribute new attitudes, theories, and ideas about how to face ecological crises."[9] Similarly, Layli Phillips, in her introduction to *The Womanist Reader*, defines womanism as

> a social change perspective rooted in Black women's and other women of color's everyday experiences and everyday methods of problem-solving in everyday spaces, extended to the problem of ending all forms of oppression for all people, restoring the balance between people and the environment/nature, and reconciling human life with the spiritual dimension.[10]

As the latter definition indicates, environmental concern is an integral part of womanist thought and ethics in general; in fact, other definitions of womanism (e.g., by Alice Walker) or Africana womanism (Clenora Hudson-Weems) often implicitly entail the qualities of ecological thinking and environmental care as its core components. Regardless of definitional nuances, eco-justice initiatives by Black women have often aligned with the principles broadly associated with the (eco)womanist ethics of social justice, ecumenical spirituality, focus on the communal and lived experience, and interconnectedness of all (dimensions of) life. These elements can also be traced—although in various iterations and to a various extent—in the eco-justice poetry discussed further.

CAMILLE DUNGY

Author of four collections of environmentally conscious poetry, essays in nature and travel writing, and the editor of *Black Nature* (the first anthology of African American nature poetry), Camille Dungy is surely one of the most recognizable names in contemporary Black ecopoetics. Like the aforementioned activists for racial and environmental justice, she, too, understands that to "separate the concerns of the human world (politics, history, commerce) from those of the many life forms with which humans share this planet" is to engage in "disastrous hubris and folly."[11] Echoing Layli Maparyan's view of *eco-spirituality* as "an inherent dimension of the womanist idea" that recognizes the sacredness of, interconnectedness with, and responsibility for the natural environment,[12] Dungy perceives her writing and gardening efforts as innately spiritual and political at once:

> Thinking about my role in encouraging a sustainable local ecology is not, to me, separate from thinking about social justice . . . . If I am thinking about tending The Creation with conscious attention to balance, I am thinking about social justice as much as I am thinking about the ways flowers help keep me spiritually vibrant.[13]

Consequently, her poems weave together the personal, the political, and the "environmental" in ways that underscore their radical intertwinement and propose an essentially (eco)womanist, maternal ethics of empathy, mutual care, and accountability toward human and nonhuman others alike.

The title poem from her latest poetry book, *Trophic Cascade*, offers a manifesto of such poetics of entanglement. The title refers to the set of interactions that take place when "the impact of a predator on its prey's ecology trickles down one more feeding level to affect the density and/or behavior of the prey's prey";[14] in other words, a trophic cascade is when changes in the population of an ecosystem's top predator trigger changes to other populations down the food chain, effectively shifting the dynamics and shape of the entire ecosystem. The first 26 out of the poem's 31 lines narrate the development of this process in the Yellowstone National Park when in the mid-1990s, a population of gray wolves was reintroduced after several decades of absence from the area:

After the reintroduction of gray wolves
to Yellowstone and, as anticipated, their culling
of deer, trees grew beyond the deer stunt
of the mid-century. [. . .]
Berries

brought bear, while undergrowth and willows, growing
now right down to the river, brought beavers,
who dam. Muskrats came to the dams, and tadpoles.[15]

In this account, the reappearance of a single species sets off a chain of events that rearrange the entire ecological community: as the wolves prey on deer, the trees—no longer stunted by overconsumption—grow taller, providing shelter for birds "who scattered / seed for underbrush, and in that cover / warrened snowshoe hare"; eventually, the increasingly diverse flora and fauna changes the flow of the local river, which, dammed by beavers and shrubbery, is now "compelled to meander, [and] less prone to overrun."[16] Toward the end of the poem, the previously impersonal narration takes an imperative turn: "Don't / you tell me this is not the same as my story," the speaker commands, drawing a parallel between "all this / life" and "new landscape" "born from one hungry animal" and her experience of motherhood that "reintroduced [her]self to [her]self."[17] With this analogy, the "introduction" of the child into the speaker's life rearranges its entire "ecosystem," implicitly restoring to it a (supposedly lost or suppressed) sense of aliveness, heterogeneity, and harmony.

The poem's extended analogy that intertwines the personal experience of motherhood with an ecological process of restoring biodiversity implies an ethics of mothering as a practice of extended, communal care. The assertive, contrapuntal shift that the poem's tone takes with the phrase "Don't / you tell me this is not the same as my story" emphasizes the speaker's sense of connectedness with all the painstakingly listed elements of the Yellowstone ecosystem, from the grey wolves to "falcon, bald eagle, kestrel," bear, willows, tadpoles, American dipper, vulture, coyote, "trees, brush, and berries."[18] The narrative of the trophic cascade is also a litany of names, with the speaker naming individual species of flora and fauna in what Dungy elsewhere terms "a breed of compassion and empathy": "If I know the name of a specific species of bird or tree or grass or flower, I am not lumping those living beings into some generic category that is, by its namelessness, less important than I am."[19] At the same time, these "compassion and empathy" are set within the framework of mothering as a transformational experience that sparks in the speaker a renewed sense of responsiveness to and responsibility for another human being that *cascades* onto the nonhuman world as well. As Patricia Hill Collins observes, the ethics of Black motherhood "challenge prevailing capitalist property relations" by refusing to be limited to the nuclear family and children-as-property models; consequently, African American "women-centered networks of community-based child care [extend] beyond the boundaries of biologically related individuals to include 'fictive kin,' " or extended family made up of unrelated members of the community.[20] In the poem, these boundaries stretch even further to allow kinship with a larger-than-human community of Yellowstone plants, animals, and even inanimate elements of the ecosystem.

This fundamentally inclusive and relational, empathetic, and protective eco-mothering stance of "Trophic Cascade" is a recurring presence in Dungy's poems throughout the volume. In "Characteristics of Life," the speaker continues the practice of naming-as-caring with her repeated assertion of representing the otherwise voiceless, nonhuman life employing poetic imagination and language: "I speak for the damselfly, water skeet, mollusk, / the caterpillar, the beetle, the spider, the ant."[21] The poem "How Great the Gardens When They Thrive" connotes the multiple dimensions of nurture through its juxtaposition of images of garden plants and school buses with reflections on the history of vaccinations:

Yellow as zucchini flowers and, in their season,
as legion, school buses brake and collect...
In the dream the doctors dreamed, no
more
measles, mumps, rubella. Polio put aside.[22]

This seemingly discordant imagery is woven together by the logic of care and cultivation. As the buses stand-in for the children they carry "along the country's subdividing roads," the discoveries in immunology that have led to the "near eradication of microscopic organisms / that have blinded, maddened, paralyzed, and killed"[23] represent the collective nurturing of future generations at the level of an entire population. Both education and health care are crucial for the development of children but the success of these efforts depends precisely on their synchronicity: without herd immunity achieved through vaccinations, gathering sites such as buses and schools can easily become epicenters for lethal contagious diseases; in turn, not only research and development work on vaccines but the very awareness of the need for immunization can hardly be achieved without education. The final stanza of the poem brings this point home with the metaphor of children as plants that need to be cultivated to grow:

Lemons, tomatoes, peaches, zucchini: some crops
are like this. Tended correctly, what fruits
they produce, if they produce any, will seem,
to most of us, like overwhelming plenty.[24]

The thriving gardens in the poem's title are, like Walker's, "mothers' gardens" in the sense that they are literal gardens tended to by Black women and metaphors for the nurturing of the children. Like Walker's mother who, working in her garden, became "radiant, almost to the point of being invisible—except as Creator: hand and eye,"[25] the speaker in Dungy's poem is absent except as a mothering gaze spanning both the departing school buses and the plants in her garden.

While "How Great the Gardens," with its vaccination "praise songs,"[26] can be read as an environmental justice poem (in that it advocates for the creation of a safe, nurturing environment for all children by framing population immunity as an act of care), "A Massive Dying Off" from Dungy's 2011 collection *Smith Blue* is environmentalist in its focus primarily on the well-being of that which is not human. The second-person voice in the poem is as much the speaker's internal monologue as it is a call for the reader to rethink their engagement with the fast-approaching global disaster of species extinction. The poem's opening line—"When the fish began their dying you didn't worry. // You bought new shoes."[27]—is at once a statement of fact and an indictment of passivity and callousness in the face of tragedy that is not one's own—or, at least, not immediately so. The "you" is soon revealed to be not only apathetic but also complicit in various forms of exploitation: the shoes that "look like crocodiles" were manufactured by "someone's tiny, indifferent hands."[28] The you/speaker realizes that, with this purchase, she perpetuates the machinations of global corporate capitalism responsible for the abuse of animals (as signaled by the shoes' "crocodile" quality), workers (perhaps child labor, since the hands are "tiny") and, ultimately, the planet's finite resources. At the same time, however, she marvels almost ecstatically at the "snappy and rich," "beautiful, bejeweled" attributes of "these shoes!"[29] This tension between the satisfaction that comes from participating in the pleasures of consumerism and the sense of guilt and complicity in the impending disaster returns repeatedly in the poem: radio news about the eponymous *"massive dying off"* of *"[s]ea stars, jellies, anemones"* accompany the "you" on the trip to Costco, where "everything comes cheap," and as sea creatures desperately look *"for a place / where they can breathe,"* the human watches "the sunset over the Golden Gate" from her car (emphasis Dungy's).[30]

It is not until the specter of the looming catastrophe assumes a personalized shape that the poem's "you" seriously ponders her accountability toward the planet. Following a dream in which the body of her/"your" father "is the last refuse to wash ashore . . . Stinking. / Swelling." the poem ends in the previously repressed realization returning as a question: "You can't dispose of the rising dead and you're worried. / What can you do?"[31] This final line is at once a meditation on the (in)significance of individual actions and a genuine question on possibilities, with the verb "do" resounding like a wake-up call to take responsibility for the planetary others, contrasting the "you's" apathy in the previous sections of the poem. In a circle-of-life fashion, the death (and return) of the father also becomes the birth of a new consciousness of the poem's "you"—the speaker and reader in one, perhaps—assisted by the dream's image of the "women of the village [who] wept when your father died."[32] If, as Collins asserts, "U.S. Black women's experiences as othermothers provide a foundation for conceptualizing Black women's political activism" and stimulate "a more generalized ethic of caring and personal accountability,"[33] the dream's imagery of a parent's (failed) water burial assisted by a community of othermothers suggests a transition from an over-individualized, capitalist mode of being in the first three parts of the poem into a more-than-human community-oriented womanist stance.

EVIE SHOCKLEY

The radical, programmatic intertwining of the personal and the political—the intimate and large-scale—dimensions of environmental care and environmental justice that characterizes Dungy's poetry is also explicit in the works of Evie Shockley. Describing the importance of making these connections in her poems, Shockley explains that her "exploration of forms and formal structures comes from [her] attempt to juxtapose and suture together figures or scenes or ideas that are normally considered separately"; she then adds that, by "making these interconnections visible," she hopes to "imagine a way of life (a 'blues modality') in which we survive and change—indeed, survive by changing, hopefully becoming freer, fuller, better for ourselves and to each other. In this, the blues are an inspiration, model, and renewable resource."[34] With her sensitivity to the ambiguities, internal contradictions, and the (im)possibilies of language rooted in her literary as well as legal education and practice (she worked as an environmental lawyer for several years), Shockley's verbally and visually innovative poetics explores the "modalities" in which we can respond to the twenty-first-century challenges of political unrest, environmental catastrophe, and the multiple forms of gendered and racialized violence. At the same time, by grounding her poet(h)ics of care in the blues tradition, she situates her work in the longer lineage of Black creative practices of political resistance and spiritual restoration. Formally innovative yet deeply rooted in tradition, Shockley's eco-justice poems follow an essentially womanist paradigm in their fundamentally intersectional approach to exposing and dismantling the "politics of domination" that situates individual cases of violence and injustice in their systemic context.

In "atlantis made easy" from her 2006 collection *a half-red sea*, Shockley draws an analogy between two crimes: the state-sanctioned destruction of New Orleans' Lower Ninth Ward in the wake of the 2005 Hurricane Katrina and a sexual violation of an intoxicated woman. In a fragmentary, dreamlike, associative language that resembles flashes of memory experienced by a victim of either sexual assault or (un)natural disaster, the poem introduces a "she" that is, at the same time, the woman and the submerged area:

> Orange was the color of her address, then blue silt :: whiskey burned brown down the street, then a dangerous drink whirled around a paper umbrella:: intoxication blue across the porch then rose in the attic::[35]

With only a single letter differentiating the word "address" from "dress," the poem's opening phrase brings to mind the misguided arguments regarding survivors' clothing that are regularly brought up in sexual assault cases; at the same time, it may connote the orange "X" marks spray-painted by search-and-rescue teams on the flooded buildings of New Orleans. The "dangerous drink" suggests the use of so-called date rape drugs by the woman's assailant; however, the "whisky" down the street also connotes dirty, brown-colored water flooding the area, and the "intoxication" rising from the porch to the attic further evokes the images of houses flooded by water that, after several days, became putrid and toxic due to the floating debris and bodies. The image of "army corps engineers [running] a 'train on her'"[36] furthers the identification of the woman with the land but also of the perpetrators of both crimes as members of the U.S. Army Corps of Engineers—the military formation responsible, among other things, for devising and overseeing flood protection measures. Shockley's wordplay, however, reveals them to be anything but protective: as "corpse engineers," they design and implement death by intentionally under-developing the infrastructure of low-income, African American areas such as the Lower Ninth Ward, thus violating them through exposure to environmental disasters.

By blending the imagery of sexual, environmental, and structurally racist violence and suggesting the role of government-sanctioned forces and policies as their shared cause, the poem contributes to the crucial environmental justice project aiming to "redefin[e] which issues are considered 'environmental.'"[37] As Dorceta Taylor argues, the human-oriented focus of environmental justice asserts that "if the human environment is poisoned or has been targeted to be poisoned, if there are no opportunities for economic survival or nutritional sustenance, or if there are no possibilities to be sheltered, then these human-environmental issues have to be dealt with before, or in conjunction with, other kinds of environmental issues."[38] The government's delayed and faulty rescue efforts in the wake of the Katrina flooding was another link in a long chain of structural neglect of the Lower Ninth that, as Michael Eric Dyson reminds us, was "one of the last neighborhoods in the city to be developed" and has historically suffered from "concentrated poverty" with inadequate access to transportation, healthcare, and education.[39] In "atlantis," Shockley hints at the roots of these environmental and humanitarian injustices that reach back to the slavery era, bitterly rephrasing the traditional spiritual to "∷ wait in the water, wait in the water, children∷"[40]—a command that reflects the abandonment of Katrina survivors who were forced to wait for FEMA rescue crews for days in unsanitary conditions. By likening the structural environmental injustice plaguing low-income Black neighborhoods to an assault on a woman's body, Shockley's poem also echoes the ecowomanist thought of Delores S. Williams, who argues that the "assault upon the natural environment today is but an extension of the assault upon black women's bodies in the nineteenth century."[41]

Another poem that takes up a specific, singular case as a starting point for exploring the interconnected nature of anti-Black, environmental, imperialist, and ideological violence is "keep your eye on" from Shockley's latest collection, *semiautomatic*. The poem opens with a riff on both "John Brown's Body," a folk hymn for the abolitionist hero, and "John Brown's Ford," a children-friendly take on the song with the lyrics "John Brown's body lies a-moldering in the grave" changed to "John Brown's Ford has a puncture in its tire." In Shockley's repoliticized version, the "body" becomes that of Michael Brown, the Black teenager whose murder by police officer Darren Wilson in 2014 had sparked civil unrest against police brutality in Ferguson, Missouri. The poem opens with the following lines:

michael brown's body has a hole in it(   )
michael brown's murder has a hole in it(   )
michael brown's news coverage has a hole in it(   ).[42]

The verbal and visual "holes" refer at once to the lethal gunshot wounds incurred by Brown and to the gaps in both Wilson's official statement and the mass media coverage of the murder, suggesting that crucial information has been left out of both. The poem proceeds to fill in those gaps not with facts regarding this specific case, but with observations on global current affairs that, at first glance, may seem disconnected from Brown's murder:

through the holes in michael brown's body, i see:
- the fucking fracking chemicals bleeding into the groundwater
- the oil fields of northern africa and the lithium mines of afghanistan
- the flood of black and brown people seeping between prison bars
- the coke brothers controlling the flow
- through the holes in michael brown's murder, i see:
- the GMO CEO of monsanto
- the gazans stripped of ~~dignity~~ property.[43]

By listing the seemingly discrete problems of water pollution, imperialist extraction capitalism, the racially biased prison-industrial complex, organized crime, manufactured food scarcity, and the Israeli occupation of Palestine, the poem unearths their correlations. Michael Brown's murder is, in and of itself, a tragedy that deserves attention and justice; however, the poem suggests, both his murder and the larger problem of state-sanctioned, anti-Black police brutality are embedded in a larger framework of interrelated forms of violence. What connects all of them is the imperialist "politics of domination" enacted globally by the United States against human and non-human actors, whose lives and rights do not matter in the global capitalist scheme of power and profit.

Exposing the large-scale, intricately interwoven web of violence that peeks through the "holes" in the media-spun narrative of Brown's murder, the poem reminds us that "social and ecological justices are not possible without addressing [three kinds of] relationships at once": those among humans, between humans and their environment, and between the human and the spiritual realms.[44] The poem proposes an intersectional vision of environmental and social justice that addresses American imperialism and militarism, systemic racism, police brutality, and environmental destruction at their nexus. Formally, to get its message across, it also interrogates the media discourses that simultaneously perpetuate and obscure the truth about these entanglements. The poem exposes the strategies through which the mass media distracts, confuses, and misinforms its audience by mimicking them: for example, one section of it is composed solely of what looks like headlines and advertising messages ("YOU CAN SKIP THIS AD AFTER 5 SECONDS: EBOLA! EBOLA!"; "'CLIMATE CHANGE IS FOR THE BIRDS' TWEETS HIGH-RANKING SENATOR"; "WILL MILEY CYRUS BECOME THE NEXT LINDSAY LOHAN OR THE NEXT MICHAEL JACKSON?"[45]); while another offers chains of words with "hidden meanings" inserted in barely visible, gray font, forcing the reader to strain their eyes to discover the word "fukushima" (site of a 2011 nuclear disaster in Japan) woven into the sentence "princess di would be proud of anti-bullying charity, say sons," or "imperialism" scattered between the names of victims of police brutality including Trayvon Martin or Renisha McBride.[46] Refusing to separate essential information from gossip and advertising from information, highlighting some events to cover up others, and prioritizing sensationalism over analysis, the media conceals the interconnections whose understanding is necessary to address the root of the problems. Asking the reader to "keep [their] eye on" those complexities and the discursive "holes" designed to hide them from view, the poem reaches back to the Civil Rights Movements' tradition of finding political strength and insight in spiritual practices such as the eponymous gospel music standard. This suggests that, perhaps, an antidote to the mind-numbing, spiritually blind, and deceptive discourses of mass media and mainstream politics can be found in Black spiritual traditions.

Shockley's poems regularly explore the underlying, systemic causes and consequences of particular cases and stories of violence while "keeping their eye" on Black diasporic traditions of spiritual resistance and survival. In one of her poems about the devastating earthquake in Haiti in 2010, Shockley connects that event with another (un)natural catastrophe—the holocaust of the Middle Passage. Commenting on the news story of the "miracle" girl (as the media dubbed her) Darlene Etienne, who survived in the rubble for fifteen days without food or water, the poem speaks in the collective voice of "the survivors / of / t h e m i d d l e p a s s a g e" who "know / how to / live . . . / without water."[47] Bringing the two events together, the poem underlines the continuity of Black resilience but also of violence on and exploitation of Black bodies—after all, Haiti's continued impoverishment is a direct outcome of international policies designed to penalize the country for successfully liberating itself from slavery back in 1804. The *semiautomatic* poem "the way we live now::" likens the 2015 racially motivated massacre of African American churchgoers in Charleston, South Carolina, to a plant grown in a toxic culture. Throughout the poem, imagery of horticulture—where the "the cultivators of corpses" breed the "virile shoots of violence"—implies an analogy and a shared root cause between the (white) American cult of gun violence and the corporate disregard for environmental justice that forces "the disempowered" to breathe "in the ashen traces / of dreams deferred."[48] However, capsulated in the reference to Langston Hughes' famous poem, the inspired and revolutionary violence of the oppressed is suggested as a logical consequence of this aggressive, lethal, and desensitized "way we live now." In the same collection, "weather or not" responds to the 2016 election between the presidential "candid hates" Donald Trump and Hillary Clinton by contextualizing it in the general "climate of indifference [that] was generating maelstormy weather."[49] The poem's closing allusion to Gil Scott-Heron's "Winter in America"—"there was winter all summer in America"[50]—situates its critique of the nation's political apathy and disregard for the environment in the tradition of African American protest songs, once again turning to the poetry of resistance and survival for spiritual consolation and guidance.

Both Dungy and Shockley had their poetic debuts at the turn of the centuries, and belong to a generation that is sometimes referred to as "post-soul"—African Americans who, as Mark Anthony Neal recalls, have "experienced the change from industrialism to deindustrialism, from segregation to desegregation, from essential notions of blackness to metanarratives on blackness" in their formative years.[51] Significantly, this is also a generation that came of age about the same time as the concepts of climate change, ecological disaster, and environmental racism were beginning to emerge in the public discourse; unsurprisingly, much of the eco-justice poetry has come from authors their age and younger.[52] However, as signaled at the beginning of this chapter, the tradition of environmentally or ecologically oriented African American writing and activism reaches much farther back than the current climate change debates, and Dungy and Shockley's spiritual, aesthetic, and thematic indebtedness to literary foremothers such as Lucille Clifton, Alice Walker, June Jordan, and Jayne Cortez clearly illustrates this. Notably, women poets who were affiliated with the Black Arts Movement or came of age during its aesthetic and political height often took up subjects that, in retrospect, can be categorized as environmental justice issues. For example, Nikki Giovanni's "For Saundra" and "Walking Down Park," both published during her BAM period, speak to environmental racism in urban neighborhoods and correlations between settler colonialism and environmental destruction. About a decade later, in "Beaches. Why I Don't Care for Them," Wanda Coleman traces the connections between anti-Black racism and the psychological alienation from the natural environment experienced by African American women in particular. Like their aforementioned contemporaries whose (eco) womanist poetics has already received some critical attention, Giovanni and Coleman, too, have continued their respective brands of eco-justice poetry into the late twentieth and early twenty-first century.

NIKKI GIOVANNI

As Virginia Fowler notes in her introduction to *The Collected Poetry of Nikki Giovanni: 1968–1998*, Giovanni's poems "often speak directly about specific events or people, giving expression to the emotions they provoke and disclosing the realities and truths that underlie them—as she sees them."[53] While this interweaving of the specific and the universal is crucial to all poets discussed in this chapter, Giovanni's work seems to most directly connect "the importance of topicality in poetry to the tradition of the African *griot*," which highlights the oral qualities and community-building functions of poetry.[54] Her environmentally oriented poems are characterized by essentially African ethics according to which "human actions are evaluated morally in terms of the common good—that is, their consequences for the (immediate and extended) community," with the latter being understood as comprising not only living humans and ancestral spirits but also the "nonhuman (animal and natural) world."[55] At the same time, Giovanni's ecological sensibility, like that of many Black women environmental justice activists, stems from personal experience of "surviving within an oppressive society and out of that survival creating the means to be moral agents and arbiters in their communities."[56]

Especially in her later poems, Giovanni's poetic voice assumes the role of an (eco)womanist witness testifying to the social and environmental injustice against her larger-than-human community.

Published in 1999, the collection *Blues: For All the Changes* features a series of prose poems about one R. Kneck Kracker and his Kracker's Pipe and Excavating Company that has, much to the speaker's outrage, been contracted land development near her Virginia home. The first poem in the series, "This Poem Hates," reads almost like a direct continuation of "For Saundra," despite the three decades that separate their writing; the very title may be interpreted as a response to the earlier poem's "neighbor / who thinks i hate" and asks the speaker to write "tree poems."[57] "This Poem Hates," like "For Saundra," illustrates why traditional bucolic or pastoral poetry is impossible—or, at the very least, dishonest—when environmental degradation and pollution threaten neighborhoods inhabited by "us little folks who only purchased a home with the thought of living in it and paying our taxes and growing our tomatoes."[58] True to his identity, thinly veiled by the pun in his name, R. Kneck Kracker embodies the aggressive and destructive essence of white male capitalism: characterized as "a bully" and "a coward," Kracker "does not appear to have ever been told NO in the modern-day" and has no qualms about conducting illegal trash burning that pollutes nearby homes with smoke or, as subsequent poems in the series reveal, "destroying a wetlands" and "diverting a stream onto your backyard."[59] Driven by greed and selfishness, Kracker fails to display ecological thinking that sees the well-being of all life as interconnected but only "wants to bring a small hill down to a smaller size and the fact that other living beings have a home in a small hill has no credit in his bank."[60]

What infuses the poems and the speaker with anger and hate is not so much Kracker's individual behavior as the fact that it is symptomatic of an economic and political system that not merely tolerates but also openly enables and privileges "fat old corrupt white men on their last legs but determined to take everything down with them."[61] From the fire department to the city council, all authorities where the speaker searches protection from "the noise and traffic and garbage"[62] that come with Kracker's development refuse to take her protests seriously; likely, they have their interests in the construction works progressing as planned. Together, these institutions form a hegemonic structure guided by the "Eurocentric, masculinist worldview that . . . tends to only value the parts of reality that can be exploited in the interest of profit, power and control."[63] The violence they sanction and commit harms everyone who is not a part of this structure: from "a small colored woman trying to protect her home" who, in a wording disturbingly similar to that of the infamous 1857 *Dred Scott v. Sandford* decision, has "no rights that anyone is bound to respect," to the nonhuman life destroyed "to build houses which could be built around trees with birds and possums and groundhogs and other things in mind," everything and everyone not profitable enough is relentlessly relegated to what environmental justice terms "sacrifice zones."[64] The speaker's initial helplessness in the face of this overwhelming system is eventually transformed into vengeful action, as the book's closing poem ends on a prophecy: "The Last Poem on the very last day in an act of love and humility . . . will go bang bang bang . . . to try to make it right."[65] This revolutionary violence brings the reader back to Giovanni's militant BAM days (once again echoing "For Saundra," whose speaker considered "clean[ing her] gun / and check[ing her] kerosene supply"[66] as alternatives to writing poetry), implying the unaccomplished transformative potential of the Black Power movement and underscoring the continuity of white supremacist, ecocidal violence that remains unchecked all these years later.

Yet, after the turn of the millennia, the transformative focus of Giovanni's poetry has been moving away from retributive violence and toward restorative ethics of care and respect for all those whose lives are at risk. Rather than responding in kind to the aggressor, her poems often undertake the more challenging task of working out an alternative system of values in which the fragmented, exploitative, and egocentric mode of being in the world becomes ethically and morally untenable. This drive toward ecological thinking that seeks connections across differences is particularly visible in Giovanni's animal poems, in which the speaker's attention is often drawn to small creatures whose lives—like those of Black people under white supremacy—are dismissed as those that do not matter in the anthropocentric Western culture. In poems such as "The Yellow Jacket" or "Allowables," the speaker does not pretend that empathy and care for those who are different from us are easily achieved; in fact, she admits that "We are not friends / The yellow jacket and I," and that, having found a small "papery spider" frightening, she instinctively "smashed her."[67] In both poems, however, the speaker reexamines her learned attitudes toward the insects, eventually coming to admire the "self-possessed / beauty" (106) of the wasp she shares her garden with and to conclude that she is not "allowed // To kill something // because [she is] // frightened."[68] "Possum Crossing," in turn, has the speaker adjust her daily routine to "anticipate a squirrel or a cat or sometimes a little raccoon" while backing out of her driveway; by the end of the poem, her empathy toward the nonhuman extends even to "a big wet leaf / struggling . . . to lift itself into the wind / and live."[69] In Giovanni's latest collection to date, the 2017 *A Good Cry*, the speaker goes as far as to become a nonhuman animal, speaking in the collective voice of "Bears in Spring" who, living in a woods next to a busy road, decide they

need to tell
the cars
and

trucks
and
buses
Not to run
Into
Our children[70]

As Fowler observes, "Giovanni's insistence that aesthetic value emerges from and is dependent upon moral value" causes the poet to embrace interpersonal and larger-than-human empathy over personal experience, thus collapsing in her works "the dualistic structures that polarize our world into 'us' and 'them.' "[71]

The poet's rejection of the dualistic, oppositional Western thinking in favor of a relational and interdependent understanding of life situates her within an (eco)womanist tradition not only via the protective environmental ethics of care and "othermothering" she adopts in her work but also through its embrace of principles characteristic of Africana cosmologies. In "Sanctuary: For Harry Potter the Movie," Giovanni reimagines a piece of American popular culture—which is, arguably, ideologically aligned with the normative "systems of domination"—by relocating the Hollywood blockbuster to an African scenery, enhancing its cast with nonhuman characters, and reinterpreting the film from an Africana perspective:

> The movie should have started with drums. Small drums maybe bongos then trap drums then the full complement of jazz drums. [. . .] Then the Savannah. A community of elephants. The camera moving in on the baby trailing just slightly behind its mother.[72]

The initially confusing connection between the *Harry Potter* franchise and an image of elephants in the Savannah is resolved when, following a massacre of the elephants, its only survivor—the baby—is called upon with a quote from Gwendolyn Brooks' poem "The Second Sermon on the Warpland": "*Live! and have your blooming in the noise of the whirlwind,*" followed by a riff on the opening line of the first *Harry Potter* novel: "Harry Potter was just a boy who lived."[73] By weaving this web of quotations, the poem establishes a universal connection of all stories of suffering and survival across cultures, locations, and species, explaining that Potter's story is also a story of all those who lived on "the forced marches to uninhabitable reservations," in "the stench and starvation of the middle passage," and with the "baby elephants and manatees and the vanishing Savannah and."[74] At the same time acknowledging the uniqueness of each of these events and perceiving them—and their participants—as interrelated, the poem illustrates how "the concepts of person and community arise out of the understanding of being bonded to natural life or the feeling of being in the network of life."[75] This (eco)womanist rewriting of the pop-cultural artifact (which also characterizes Harry as a woman-oriented and possibly biracial man) infuses it with Africana cosmological principles of interdependence and relationality of all life, illustrating that, for Giovanni as for her African ancestors, poetry "is a way of self-understanding in the world, a way of discovering bondedness to other things in life."[76]

WANDA COLEMAN

Compared to the other poets discussed in this chapter, Wanda Coleman's body of work features relatively little overt preoccupation with natural environment or global climate issues. Critics of Coleman's poetry have mostly noted its focus on "pervasive economic inequalities, the overlooked geographies of urban spaces, the heat, and the general grittiness of" Los Angeles.[77] It is, however, precisely this interest in the flawed eco-social systems of the city of "hollywatts"[78] that situates her work as literature of environmental justice—the kind of writing that, in Julie Sze's definition, "places people, especially racialized communities and urban spaces, at the center of what constitutes environment and nature" and offers "a new way of looking at environmental justice, through visual images and metaphors, not solely through the prism of statistics."[79] While not explicitly didactic or activist, some of Coleman's best known early poems—such as "I Live for My Car," "Where I Live," or what Krista Comer terms her "beach poems"[80]—certainly offer a commentary on the environmental aspects of racism that shapes the lives of the predominantly poor and Black residents of inner-city Los Angeles. At the same time, Coleman's visceral poetics situated in daily realities of particular locales reflect Collins' assertion that African American women "use the lived experiences of their daily lives to assess more abstract knowledge claims" and employ "practical images as . . . symbolic vehicles" for such meaning-making.[81] In her later poems, Coleman continues to engage images of Los Angeles environs and the daily lives of its human and nonhuman residents to offer lyrical accounts of social and environmental injustice to which she is both witness and subject.

Published in her 1998 collection *Bathwater Wine*, "Flight of the California Condor (2)" reads like a retrospective prelude to the many texts in which Coleman examines the landscapes and social structures of Los Angeles. The poem's imagery continues that of her 1983 "Flight of the California Condor," where the eponymous bird—described as "wind sistuh blooded eyes/mind full of flesh"—embodies what the Black female speaker must become if she is to live where *"delicate / things do not survive."*[82] Yet, in contrast to that earlier poem's preoccupation with how "the ghetto becomes home" to "the pimp, the pootbutt, the whore, the worker, the blind,"[83] its continuation traces how "the ghetto" became marked as the "ghetto" in the first place; meanwhile, the condor becomes a metaphor for white inhabitants gradually leaving the area in the 1950s and 1960s. Narrating the changing social landscapes of her neighborhood, the speaker describes white flight in a language that is usually associated with the genres of wildlife documentaries and nature writing:

as children, my brother and I watched them
through the thick barrier of morning glory vines
and peach trees
the female always wore an expression of dread
and kept peeking over her shoulders
in our direction
the male seemed less afraid but nevertheless
cautious.[84]

The area's white population, fluctuating throughout the speaker's school years, eventually all but disappears in the aftermath of the 1965 civil unrest against anti-Black police brutality in Watts. As the speaker-witness recounts:

after the Revolt of August 1965
they were rarer still. only a few stubborn
species remained: the blue-coated throat choker,
the red-fisted money grubber, the purple-livered
land snatcher. . .[85]

The poem closes with a mock-scientific meditation on the future of this "carnivorous bird of prey," predicting that it will either "virtually disappear" or, to the contrary, will "persist / not only in our destruction / but in its own."[86]

Blurring boundaries between human history and natural history, sociology, and ecology, the poem draws the reader's attention to the essentially unnatural workings of racial capitalism and its ideologies. By imagining whites as an endangered species, the poem playfully reverses the exoticizing gaze usually reserved for (often white) observers of "others": nonhuman wildlife as well as nonwhite people. On the one hand, the very possibility of such reversal points to the artificiality of categories such as class, race, or perhaps even species; on the other, it is also an act of reclamation of discursive power by the young, Black female speaker and the community she represents. To position white people as objects of observation and analysis is to subvert the power dynamic created and solidified by academic—and, later, mass media—discourses on the inner-cities and their predominantly Black inhabitants. Turning the legacy of, for example, the infamous Moynihan Report on its head, the poem suggests that it is the remaining whites—the "money grubber" and "land snatcher," among others—who are the truly pathological presence in the "black heart of the city."[87] The poem's final stanza takes this hypothesis of the destructive "nature" of whiteness even further, suggesting that not only the organic community of the city (as represented by its "heart") but the entire ecosystem is endangered by this predatory species on its way to harm all life, including "its own."[88] In the light of this concluding warning, the symbol of the eponymous bird acquires an additional meaning for the poem's commentary on racial capitalism: next to the unnatural ghettoization of cities segregated into Black and white neighborhoods, the many consequences of its unsustainable operations include environmental damage that affects nonhuman populations. The California condor, after all, has been brought to near-extinction by "a slew of human-related factors: lead poisoning, habitat destruction, pollution and hunting."[89] Although the poem does not explicitly center on environmental issues, the very choice of its central image signals how the same urban planning and industrial development policies that have segregated human populations have also adversely impacted nonhuman life and the environment.

 This holistic outlook on the larger-than-human environment is also present in "Requiem for a Nest," a poem from *Ostinatio Vamps* that also approaches environmental justice through the figure of a bird. In contrast to the decades-spanning historical narrative of population fluctuations in "Flight," "Requiem" takes an intimate look at just one life: that of a "winged thang [who] built her dream palace / amid the fine green eyes of a sheltering bough" to create "a hatchery for her spawn."[90] The bird, as the speaker-observer notes, is unaware that the seemingly perfect dwelling place she has found for herself and her chicks is, in fact, an "urban turf / disguised as serenely delusional rural," inhabited by "slant-mawed felines and those long-taloned / swoopers of prey," and tainted by "the acidity & oil / that slowly polluted the earth." Not unlike the handful of white "condors" in "Flight" who were "unable to flee due to some / circumstance of age or economy,"[91] the literal bird in "Requiem" does not have the privilege to migrate to a more desirable location. Instead, since "the loss of wilderness in the [Los Angeles] region was accompanied by a thorough fragmentation of remaining wildlands,"[92] the bird has to survive in the only habitat available to her, even if it means exposing her offspring to predators and toxins. Her plight is not only representative of numerous Southern Californian species endangered by human activities but also symbolic of the environmental injustice and limited choices faced by the region's underprivileged human populations. In the tradition forged by Paul Laurence Dunbar and (somewhat ironically, given the 2002 controversy that surrounded Coleman's review of her book) Maya Angelou, the bird in Coleman's poem can be read as a metaphor for the African American experience of inequality and oppression. In particular, referring to the bird as "the winged thang" connotes her with a Black woman (as in "Ms. Thang"), thus expanding the poem's environmentalist concern into a socially oriented reflection on the challenges faced by economically marginalized Black women "doomed" to live and raise their children in harmful environments.[93]

Shedding the bird metaphor in favor of direct identification, several poems in *The World Falls Away*, Coleman's final collection published just two years before her death, adopt voices of women trapped in the matrix of social, economic, and environmental issues that frame their daily lives. Enacting what Collins terms a *Black feminist epistemology*, the poems present concrete, lived experiences of low-income, female, and Black Angelenos as sites of knowledge production. For instance, the socioeconomic situation of the speaker in "Shitworker in General (2)" is made clear through a naturalistic description of her daily activities and environs:

chasing spiders, dust motes, and lint
has become a fulltime occupation
along with preparing meals that
will not poison what's left of our bodies[94]

The litany of daily domestic chores performed by the speaker is concluded by an expression of her "rage / trapped in the desire for a neatness / [she] can't afford,"[95] exposing the conundrum she cannot escape: while she sees taking care of her household and family as her obligations, their economic situation prevents her from performing these duties in a manner that would guarantee not only her satisfaction with her work but even the safety of her loved ones (her criteria for a meal do not mention nutritional value or taste, but only the quality of not being poisonous). Similarly, the speaker in "Yardwork" walks outside to sweep the yard of her house and sees

the remainder of the roof
of the fixer-upper no one could afford to fix up
solid green dumpsters
living without oxygen.[96]

Here, too, the very description of the woman's surroundings is rich in "symbolic representations of a whole wealth of experience."[97] The dilapidated external environment and the repetitive action of sweeping "left to right, left to right" are reflections of her "bungled life and how far / [she has] spun without going very far at all."[98] Likely, the speakers in these and other poems can be identified with Coleman herself, whose lifelong exclusion from elite literary milieus and resulting financial struggles have put her through what she once termed a "brutal existence" of "living close to the bone."[99] Explaining how her writing is a testimony to "what it was like for a young, single black mother to survive in one of the largest cities in America,"[100] Coleman suggests a reading of her poems as acts of witness to experience that is at once her own and representative of many others like her. Implicitly, these lyrical testimonies insist on a holistic understanding of what constitutes environmental issues by asserting that "the human environment [is] intricately linked to the physical environment, and . . . the health of one depends on the health of the other."[101]

The collective historical experience of life at the nexus of multiple systems of oppression and marginalization has afforded African American women "both frustration and creativity" that come with their particular status of what Collins terms the "outsider-within."[102] It is from this multimodal vantage point that Black women poets see the overlapping ideologies of domination and explore the intricate connections between their personal experience, firsthand observation, communal wisdom, spiritual and artistic tradition, scientific knowledge, workings of ideological systems, and global politics. Consequently, their eco-justice poems illuminate the tangled roots and branches of social and environmental injustice and propose holistic, (eco) womanist ways of living in the larger-than-human world as alternatives to the fragmented and exploitative approach to the world imposed by the dominant white male, capitalist civilization. In so doing, these poets both follow in the footsteps of their eco-literary ancestors and contribute to the work of their contemporary eco-activists. In their study of women of color's roles in environmental justice movements, Shirley A. Rainey and Glenn S. Johnson list some of the tactics adopted by women-led organizations: "organizing demonstrations and rallies, educating the public, researching and monitoring toxic sites, preparing and presenting expert testimony to government agencies, reclaiming land through direct action and maintaining traditional agricultural practices, crafts and skills."[103] Eco-justice poetry by authors such as Dungy, Shockley, Giovanni, and Coleman fits into this roster of activities by offering an intellectually stimulating and spiritually nourishing perspective on the multiple modes of environmental injustice as experienced by Black women and their (often larger-than-human) communities.

NOTES

1. Diane D. Glave, *Rooted in the Earth: Reclaiming the African American Environmental Heritage* (Chicago: Lawrence Hill, 2010), 10.

2. Alice Walker, Alice. *In Search of Our Mothers' Gardens: Womanist Prose* (New York: Harcourt, 1983), 198.

3. For ecocritical discussions of Anne Spencer, see, for example, "Protest/Poetry: Anne Spencer's Garden of 'Raceless' Verse" in Evie Shockley's *Renegade Poetics*, and Carlyn E. Ferrari's "Anne Spencer's 'Natural' Poetics"; of Lucille Clifton, "Politics in American Nature Writing: 'Who May Contest for What the Body of Nature Will Be?' " by Gretchen Legler, " 'a responsibility to something besides people': African American Reclamation Ecopoetics" by Katherine R. Lynes, and " 'There Is Hope in Connecting': Black Ecotheology and the Poetry of Lucille Clifton" by Marta Werbanowska; of Alice Walker, "Alice Walker: Poesy and the Earthling Psyche" by Dieke Ikenna; of June Jordan, " 'Moving Towards Home': The Politics and Poetics of Environmental Justice in the Work of June Jordan" by Vermonja R. Alston; for Jayne Cortez, " 'I Got the Blues' Epistemology: Thinking a Way out of Eco-Crisis" in Kimberly N. Ruffin's *Black on Earth*; of Audre Lorde, "Lyric Interiors: The Contemporary Ecological Imagination in American Women's Poetry" by Angela Hume (doctoral dissertation).

4. Melissa Tuckey, "Introduction," in *Ghost Fishing: An Eco-Justice Poetry Anthology*, ed. Melissa Tuckey (Athens: University of Georgia Press, 2018), 1.

5. Shirley A. Rainey and Glenn S. Johnson, "Grassroots Activism: an Exploration of Women of Color's Role in the Environmental Justice Movement," *Race, Gender & Class* 16, no. 3/4 (2009): 156.

6. Sara Mersha, "Black Lives and Climate Justice: Courage and Power in Defending Communities and Mother Earth," *Third World Quarterly* 39, no. 7 (2018): 1431. doi: 10.1080/01436597.2017.1368385.

7. Valerie Ann Kaalund, "Witness to Truth: Black Women Heeding the Call for Environmental Justice," in *New Perspectives on Environmental Justice: Gender, Sexuality, and Activism*, ed. Rachel Stein (New Brunswick: Rutgers University Press, 2004), 78.

8. bell hooks, *Talking Back: Thinking Feminist, Thinking Black* (New York: Routledge, 2015), 20.

9. Melanie L Harris, "An Ecowomanist Vision," in *Ethics That Matters: African, Caribbean, and African American Sources*, eds. Marcia Y. Riggs and James Samuel Logan (Minneapolis: Fortress, 2012), 191.

10. Layli Phillips, "Introduction. Womanism: On Its Own," in *The Womanist Reader*, ed. Layli Phillips (New York: Routledge, 2006), xx.

11. Camille T. Dungy, "Is All Writing Environmental Writing?" *The Georgia Review* (Fall 2018 / Winter 2018), accessed June 5, 2020, https://thegeorgiareview.com/posts/is-all-writing-environmental-writing/.

12. Layli Maparyan, "Seeds of Light, Flowers of Power, Fruits of Change: Ecowomanism as Spiritualized Ecological Praxis," in *Ecowomanism, Religion and Ecology*, ed. Melanie Harris (Boston: BRILL, 2017), 46.

13. Dungy, "Snow Beyond Winter," *Still Harbor*, June 3, 2017, https://www.stillharbor.org/anchormagazine/2017/6/3/snow-beyond-winter.

14. Brian R. Silliman and Christine Angelini, "Trophic Cascades Across Diverse Plant Ecosystems," *Nature Education*, 2012, The Nature Education Knowledge

Project, accessed June 6, 2020, https://www.nature.com/scitable/knowledge/library/trophic-cascades-across-diverse-plant-ecosystems-80060347/.

15. Dungy, "Trophic Cascade," *Trophic Cascade* (Middletown: Wesleyan University Press, 2017), 16.

16. Dungy, "Trophic Cascade," 16.

17. Dungy, "Trophic Cascade," 16.

18. Dungy, "Trophic Cascade," 16.

19. Dungy and Courtney Brown, "Naming is a Breed of Compassion and Empathy: An Interview with Camille T. Dungy," *Nashville Review*, December 13, 2017, https://as.vanderbilt.edu/nashvillereview/archives/14084.

20. Patricia Hill Collins, *Black Feminist Thought: Knowledge, Consciousness, and the Politics of Empowerment* (New York: Routledge, 2000), 182, 179.

21. Dungy, "Characteristics of Life," *Trophic Cascade*, 44.

22. Dungy, "How Great the Gardens When They Thrive," *Trophic Cascade*, 64.

23. Dungy, "How Great the Gardens," 64.

24. Dungy, "How Great the Gardens," 65.

25. Walker, *In Search of Our Mothers' Gardens*, 196.

26. Dungy, "How Great the Gardens," 64.

27. Dungy, "A Massive Dying Off," *Smith Blue* (Carbondale: Southern Illinois University Press, 2011), 7.

28. Dungy, "A Massive Dying Off," 7.

29. Dungy, "A Massive Dying Off," 7.

30. Dungy, "A Massive Dying Off," 7–8.

31. Dungy, "A Massive Dying Off," 8–9.

32. Dungy, "A Massive Dying Off," 9.

33. Collins, 189.

34. Julia Fiedorczuk, *Inne możliwości. O poezji, ekologii i polityce. Rozmowy z amerykańskimi poetami* (Gdansk: WN Katedra, 2019), 44.

35. Evie Shockley, "atlantis made easy," *a half-red sea* (Durham: Carolina Wren Press, 2006), 14.

36. Shockley, "atlantis made easy," 14.

37. Dorceta E Taylor, "Women of Color, Environmental Justice, and Ecofeminism," in *Ecofeminism: Women, Culture, Nature*, ed. Karen J. Warren (Bloomington: Indiana University Press, 1997), 50.

38. Taylor, 54.

39. Michael Eric Dyson, *Come Hell or High Water: Hurricane Katrina and the Color of Disaster* (New York: Basic Books, 2007), 10.

40. Shockley, "Atlantis Made Easy," 14.

41. Delores S. Williams, "Sin, Nature, and Black Women's Bodies," in *Ecofeminism and the Sacred*, ed. Carol J. Adams (New York: Continuum, 1993), 25.

42. Shockley, "keep Your Eye On," *Semiautomatic* (Middletown: Wesleyan University Press, 2017), 46.

43. Shockley, "Keep Your Eye On," 46.

44. Maparyan, 44.

45. Shockley, "Keep Your Eye On," 48.

46. Shockley, "Keep Your Eye On," 48.

47. Shockley, "Haitian Miracle: Girl Survives 15 Days Under Earthquake Rubble," *Callaloo* 34, no. 3 (2011): 769.

48. Shockley, "The Way We Live Now," *Semiautomatic*, 6.

49. Shockley, "Weather or Not," *Semiautomatic*, 5.

50. Shockley, "Weather or Not," 5.

51. Mark Anthony Neal, *Soul Babies: Black Popular Culture and the Post-Soul Aesthetic* (New York: Routledge, 2001), 3.

52. The increasingly urgent issue of global climate change, combined with an accumulation of local eco-disasters from Hurricane Katrina to the water crisis in Flint, Michigan (and numerous other predominantly Black residential areas nationwide and globally), has caused an unprecedented number of African American poets since early 2000s to ponder the fundamental question as aptly formulated by Erica Hunt: "We're going to have to live in a planet that's unlivable. So what does art have to do with that?" (Cruz). Although beyond the scope of this chapter, Tracy K. Smith, Mariahadessa Ekere Tallie, Crystal Good, and Alexis Pauline Gumbs are among poets whose work also grapples with this question and offers creative responses rooted in the tradition of Black (eco)humanism/womanism.

53. Virginia C. Fowler, "Introduction," in *The Collected Poetry of Nikki Giovanni 1968-1998* (New York: HarperCollins, 2003), xx.

54. Fowler, xx.

55. Kai Horsthemke, *Animals and African Ethics* (London: Palgrave Macmillan, 2015), 3.

56. Kaalund, 81.

57. Nikki Giovanni, "For Saundra," *The Collected Poetry of Nikki Giovanni 1968-1998*, 80.

58. Giovanni, "This Poem Hates," *Blues: For All the Changes* (New York: William Morrow, 1999), 19.

59. Giovanni, "This Poem Hates," 19 and "Road Rage," *Blues: For All the Changes*, 48.

60. Giovanni, "The Last Poem," *Blues: For All the Changes*, 99.

61. Giovanni, "In Which Case," *Blues: For All the Changes*, 79.

62. Giovanni, "Road Rage," 47.

63. Shamara Shantu Riley, "Ecology Is A Sistah's Issue Too: The Politics Of Emergent Afrocentric Ecowomanism," in *This Sacred Earth: Religion, Nature, Environment*, ed. Roger S. Gottlieb (New York: Routledge, 2003), 372.

64. Giovanni, "Road Rage," 46, "Me and Mrs. Robin," *Blues: For All the Changes*, 76.

65. Giovanni, "The Last Poem," 100.

66. Giovanni, "For Saundra," 80.

67. Giovanni, "The Yellow Jacket," *Acolytes* (New York: HarperCollins, 2007), 106, "Allowables," *Chasing Utopia: A Hybrid* (New York: HarperCollins, 2013), 109.

68. Giovanni, "The Yellow Jacket" 106, "Allowables," 109.

69. Giovanni, "Possum Crossing," *Quilting the Black-Eyed Pea: Poems and Not Quite Poems* (New York: HarperCollins, 2002), 5.

70. Giovanni, "Bears in Spring," *A Good Cry: What We Learn From Tears and Laughter* (New York: HarperCollins, 2017), 3.

71. Fowler, xxv.

72. Giovanni, "Sanctuary: For Harry Potter the Movie," *Quilting the Black-Eyed Pea*, 88.

73. Giovanni, "Sanctuary: For Harry Potter the Movie," 88–89.

74. Giovanni, "Sanctuary: For Harry Potter the Movie," 89–90.

75. Harvey Sindima, "Community of Life," *The Ecumenical Review* 41, no. 4 (October 1989): 546. doi: 10.1111/j.1758-6623.1989.tb02610.x.

76. Sindima, 544.

77. Jennifer D. Ryan, "'Come. Glory in My Wonder's Will'": An Interview with Wanda Coleman," *MELUS* 40, no. 1 (Spring 2015): 199.

78. Wanda Coleman, "Flight of the California Condor," *Imagoes* (Los Angeles: Black Sparrow, 1983), 93.

79. Julie Sze, "From Environmental Justice Literature to the Literature of Environmental Justice," in *The Environmental Justice Reader: Politics, Poetics, and Pedagogy*, eds. Joni Adamson, Mei Mei Evans, and Rachel Stein (Tucson: University of Arizona Press, 2002), 163.

80. Krista Comer, "Revising Western Criticism through Wanda Coleman," *Western American Literature* 33, no. 4 (Winter 1999): 367.

81. Collins, 259, 258.

82. Coleman, "Flight of the California Condor," 93, 95.

83. Coleman, "Flight of the California Condor," 96.

84. Coleman, "Flight of the California Condor (2)," *Bathwater Wine* (Los Angeles: Black Sparrow, 1998), 31.

85. Coleman, "Flight of the California Condor (2)," 32.

86. Coleman, "Flight of the California Condor (2)," 32.

87. Coleman, "Flight of the California Condor (2)," 32.

88. Coleman, "Flight of the California Condor (2)," 32.

89. Brigit Katz, "The California Condor Nearly Went Extinct. Now, the 1000th Chick of a Recovery Program Has Hatched," *Smithsonian Magazine*, Smithsonian, June 22, 2019, https://www.smithsonianmag.com/smart-news/california-condor-nearly-went-extinct-now-1000th-chick-recovery-program-has-hatched-180972698/.

90. Coleman, "Requiem for a Nest," *Ostinatio Vamps* (Pittsburgh: University of Pittsburgh Press, 2003), 14.

91. Coleman, "Flight of the California Condor (2)," 32.

92. Jennifer Wolch, Stephanie Pincelt, and Laura Pulido, "Urban Nature and the Nature of Urbanism," in *From Chicago to LA: Making Sense of Urban Theory*, ed. Michael Dear (New York: Sage, 2001), 373–374.

93. Coleman, "Requiem for a Nest," 14.

94. Coleman, "Shitworker in General (2)," *The World Falls Away* (Pittsburgh: University of Pittsburgh Press, 2003), 78.

95. Coleman, "Shitworker in General (2)," 78.

96. Coleman, "Yardwork," *The World Falls Away*, 114.

97. Collins, 258.

98. Coleman, "Yardwork," 115, 114.
99. Ryan, 200.
100. Ryan, 200.
101. Taylor, 54.
102. Collins, 268.
103. Rainey and Johnson, 158–159.

BIBLIOGRAPHY

Coleman, Wanda. *Bathwater Wine*. Los Angeles: Black Sparrow, 1998.

———. *Imagoes*. Los Angeles: Black Sparrow, 1983.

———. *Ostinatio Vamps*. Pittsburgh: University of Pittsburgh Press, 2003.

———. *The World Falls Away*. Pittsburgh: University of Pittsburgh Press, 2011.

Comer, Krista. "Revising Western Criticism through Wanda Coleman." *Western American Literature* 33, no. 4 (Winter 1999): 356–383.

Cruz, Angie. "Gardens or Guns: Climate Change, Race and the Future. A Conversation with Angie Cruz, Erica Hunt, Ruth Ellen Kocher, Dawn Lundy Martin and Giovanni singleton." *Aster(ix): A Journal of Literature, Art, Criticism*, April 22, 2019. https://asterixjournal.com/gardens-or-guns/.

Dungy, Camille T. "Is All Writing Environmental Writing?" *The Georgia Review* (Fall 2018/Winter 2018). Accessed June 5, 2020. https://thegeorgiareview.com/posts/is-all-writing-environmental-writing/.

———. *Smith Blue*. Carbondale: Southern Illinois UP, 2011.

———. "Snow Beyond Winter." *Still Harbor*. June 3, 2017. https://www.stillharbor.org/ anchormagazine/2017/6/3/snow-beyond-winter.

———. *Trophic Cascade*. Middletown: Wesleyan UP, 2016.

Dungy, Camille T. and Courtney Brown. "Naming is a Breed of Compassion and Empathy: An Interview with Camille T. Dungy." *Nashville Review. Nashville Review*. December 13, 2017. https://as.vanderbilt.edu/nashvillereview/archives/14084.

Dyson, Michael Eric. *Come Hell or High Water: Hurricane Katrina and the Color of Disaster*. New York: Basic Books, 2007.

Fiedorczuk, Julia. *Inne możliwości. O poezji, ekologii i polityce. Rozmowy z amerykańskimi poetami*. Gdansk: WN Katedra, 2019.

Fowler, Virginia C. "Introduction." *The Collected Poetry of Nikki Giovanni 1968-1998*, xix–xxix. New York: HarperCollins, 2003.

Giovanni, Nikki. *Acolytes*. New York: HarperCollins, 2007.

———. *A Good Cry: What We Learn From Tears and Laughter*. New York: HarperCollins, 2017.

———. *Blues: For All the Changes*. New York: William Morrow, 1999.

———. *Chasing Utopia: A Hybrid*. New York: HarperCollins, 2013.

———. *Quilting the Black-Eyed Pea: Poems and Not Quite Poems*. New York: HarperCollins, 2002.

———. *The Collected Poetry of Nikki Giovanni 1968-1998*. New York: HarperCollins, 2003.

Glave, Diane D. *Rooted in the Earth: Reclaiming the African American Environmental Heritage*. Chicago: Lawrence Hill, 2010.
Harris, Melanie L. "An Ecowomanist Vision." In *Ethics That Matters: African, Caribbean, and African American Sources*, edited by Marcia Y. Riggs and James Samuel Logan, 189–193. Minneapolis: Fortress, 2012.
Hill Collins, Patricia. *Black Feminist Thought: Knowledge, Consciousness, and the Politics of Empowerment*. New York: Routledge, 2000.
hooks, bell. *Talking Back: Thinking Feminist, Thinking Black*. New York: Routledge 2015.
Horsthemke, Kai. *Animals and African Ethics*. London: Palgrave Macmillan, 2015.
Kaalund, Valerie Ann. "Witness to Truth: Black Women Heeding the Call for Environmental Justice." In *New Perspectives on Environmental Justice: Gender, Sexuality, and Activism*, edited by Rachel Stein, 78–92. New Brunswick: Rutgers University Press, 2004.
Katz, Brigit. "The California Condor Nearly Went Extinct. Now, the 1000th Chick of a Recovery Program Has Hatched." *Smithsonian Magazine*. Smithsonian, June 22, 2019. https://www.smithsonianmag.com/smart-news/california-condor-nearly-went-extinct-now-1000th-chick-recovery-program-has-hatched-180972698/.
Maparyan, Layli. "Seeds of Light, Flowers of Power, Fruits of Change: Ecowomanism as Spiritualized Ecological Praxis." In *Ecowomanism, Religion and Ecology*, edited by Melanie Harris, 44–58. Boston: BRILL, 2017.
Mersha, Sara. "Black Lives and Climate Justice: Courage and Power in Defending Communities and Mother Earth." *Third World Quarterly* 39, no. 7 (2018): 1421–1234. doi: 10.1080/01436597.2017.1368385.
Neal, Mark Anthony. *Soul Babies: Black Popular Culture and the Post-Soul Aesthetic*. New York: Routledge, 2001.
Phillips, Layli. "Introduction. Womanism: On Its Own." In *The Womanist Reader*, edited by Layli Phillips, xix–lv. New York: Routledge, 2006.
Rainey Shirley A., and Glenn S. Johnson. "Grassroots Activism: an Exploration of Women of Color's Role in the Environmental Justice Movement." *Race, Gender & Class* 16, no. 3/4 (2009): 144–173.
Riley, Shamara Shantu. "Ecology Is A Sistah's Issue Too: The Politics Of Emergent Afrocentric Ecowomanism." In *This Sacred Earth: Religion, Nature, Environment*, edited by Roger S. Gottlieb, 368–381. New York: Routledge, 2003.
Ryan, Jennifer D. "'Come. Glory in My Wonder's Will": An Interview with Wanda Coleman." *MELUS* 40, no. 1 (Spring 2015): 195–205.
Shockley, Evie. *A Half-red Sea*. Durham: Carolina Wren Press, 2006.
———. "Haitian Miracle: Girl Survives 15 Days Under Earthquake Rubble." *Callaloo* 34, no. 3 (2011): 769..
———. *Semiautomatic*. Middletown: Wesleyan University Press, 2017.
Silliman, Brian R., and Christine Angelini. "Trophic Cascades Across Diverse Plant Ecosystems." *Nature Education*, 2012. The Nature Education Knowledge Project. Accessed June 6, 2020. https://www.nature.com/scitable/knowledge/library/trophic-cascades-across-diverse-plant-ecosystems-80060347/.

Sindima, Harvey. "Community of Life." *The Ecumenical Review* 41, no. 4 (October 1989): 537–51. doi: 10.1111/j.1758-6623.1989.tb02610.x.

Sze, Julie. "From Environmental Justice Literature to the Literature of Environmental Justice." In *The Environmental Justice Reader: Politics, Poetics, and Pedagogy*, edited by Joni Adamson, Mei Mei Evans, and Rachel Stein, 163–180. Tucson: University of Arizona Press, 2002.

Taylor, Dorceta E. "Women of Color, Environmental Justice, and Ecofeminism." In *Ecofeminism: Women, Culture, Nature*, edited by Karen J. Warren, 38-81. Bloomington: Indiana University Press, 1997.

Tuckey, Melissa. "Introduction." In *Ghost Fishing: An Eco-Justice Poetry Anthology*, edited by Melissa Tuckey, 1–12. Athens: University of Georgia Press, 2018.

Walker, Alice. *In Search of Our Mothers' Gardens: Womanist Prose*. New York: Harcourt, 1983.

Williams, Delores S. "Sin, Nature, and Black Women's Bodies." In *Ecofeminism and the Sacred*, edited by Carol J. Adams, 24–29. New York: Continuum, 1993.

Wolch, Jennifer, Stephanie Pincelt, and Laura Pulido. "Urban Nature and the Nature of Urbanism." In *From Chicago to LA: Making Sense of Urban Theory*, edited by Michael Dear, 367–402. New York: Sage, 2001.

Chapter 16

Who Fears Death

Necropolitics, Gender, and Radical Ontology in Africanfuturist Literature

Venise N. Adjibodou

Year 2020 marks ten years since *Who Fears Death*, Nnedi Okorafor's first adult novel, premiered. It has since won the World Fantasy Award for Best Novel and emerged as a finalist for several other prizes. *Who Fears Death* narrates Onyesonwu's mission to save a post-apocalyptic Africa from genocidal violence. Maybe if she was born *either* a light-skinned Nuru *or* a deep-toned Okeke, and perhaps if she were male instead of female, the communities she encounters would embrace her. Alas, she is *ewu*, born from a Nuru man's rape of an Okeke woman, the kind of violence rampant during a war that stems from ethnic tension between the Nuru and the Okeke. Onyesonwu's fate requires her to rewrite the racist and colorist binaries within the Great Book, a sacred text employed to rationalize the Okeke genocide. Her quest raises questions relevant for the second decade in this new millennium: What if racial signifiers did not exist? Through what other perspectives might we humans understand our being? Beneath Okorafor's overt discourse about love's healing powers, about the dangers of tradition, and the complex webs between religion and violence exists a profound ontological theory. Onyesonwu's *eshu*, or shape-shifting, abilities and mystical aptitude suggest the optimized human mode is cosmic. Okorafor envisions a nonreligious, integrated mode of being that unites humans with all of creation and erodes the limitations often used to bind us physically, mentally, and spiritually. In what follows, I examine necropolitics, gender, and cosmology in the novel to uncover Okorafor's Africanfuturist interpretation of embodiment. My methods emerge from the ethnographic study of African religions because, as a subcategory of science fiction per Okorafor's explanation, Africanfuturism decentralizes the West as well as Western methodologies.

Okorafor's Africanfuturist writing requires a hermeneutic anchored in African indigenous worldviews.

The following literary analysis reads for the human through a hermeneutic of the cosmic in what Nnedi Okorafor has called Africanfuturist literature. She explains,

> Africanfuturism is a sub-category of science fiction. [. . .] Africanfuturism is similar to "Afrofuturism" in the way that blacks on the continent and in the Black Diaspora are all connected by blood, spirit, history, and future. The difference is that Africanfuturism is specifically and more directly rooted in African culture, history, mythology, and point-of-view as it then branches into the Black Diaspora, and it does not privilege or center the West.[1]

Who Fears Death is anchored in African indigenous thought. Igbo and Yoruba worldviews provide the forms of knowing, embodiment, cultural context for the novel. It is an interesting choice considering Okorafor's post-apocalyptic Africa is Sudan, in east Africa. As stated in the book's acknowledgments, a *New York Times* article on the genocide in Darfur inspired the novel. Thus, the novel's geographic context is Sudanese, but its epistemology is distinctly Nigerian. Earlier scholars have developed useful interpretive tools based upon Yoruba culture. For example, Henry Louis Gates, Jr.'s seminal work *The Signifying Monkey* argues Caribbean and African American trickster characters such as the signifying monkey originated in the concept of Esu, the Yoruba deity of the crossroads. Importantly, Gates argues the signifying monkey is also a form of narration.[2] Georgene Bess Montgomery's Africana spiritualist literary criticism also claims African American literature has Yoruba influences. Montgomery deploys the Ifa Paradigm, an analytical method informed by Yoruba cosmology, which enables the reader to "examine ways in which the Orisha, the ancestors, colors, numbers, conjurers, conjuring, divination, initiation, ritual, [and] magic are manifested in Caribbean and African American literary texts and demonstrates how to identify and decode signs and symbols central to Ifa located in the text."[3] Montgomery's framework provides a refined tool with which to probe the symbols, colors, numbers, and spiritual practices depicted in Africana literature.[4] What proves most useful about an Africana spiritualist literary method is its capacity to isolate, name, and consider the cosmic in relation to the human experience. Teresa N. Washington also uses Yoruba cosmology to interpret African American literature, and her thinking about the divine feminine in Yoruba thought, as I later discuss, proves essential to interpreting Onyesonwu.[5] To be clear, Gates, Jr., Montgomery, and Washington ground their theories in the *Yoruba* worldview. Nnedi Okorafor, however, employs mostly an Igbo worldview in *Who Fears Death*. Thus, one must implement knowledge of

Igbo cosmology when interpreting this text to best comprehend Igbo culture's hermeneutical value in literature. As a scholar of African indigenous religions, particularly among the Gun-speaking people of southern Benin, I am familiar with the similarities and differences among West African indigenous worldviews. Throughout this essay, I utilize my knowledge as a scholar of religion to address the Igbo and Yoruba references in the novel. I also follow Montgomery's lead and interpret the novel through these worldviews. *Who Fears Death* is an African story envisioning a distinct African future whose potentialities become relevant not only for Africans but for human beings altogether. Whereas other authors have examined the ideas of time and post-coloniality in Okorafor's novel, I examine how African worldviews deployed in the novel introduce a new ontological vision.[6]

In the novel, Okorafor uses the term "the wilderness" to refer to the spirit world, a cosmic terrain full of agential nonhuman beings whose energies can cleanse, heal, or kill. "Wilderness," a neutral term, alludes to an important condition in the novel: the spirit world exists whether or not you believe in the Creator or the earth goddess, Ani. Okorafor's idea of spirituality is not religious, but cosmic. "Cosmic" refers to the spirit world, a dimension sharing a porous border with the terrestrial world. "Cosmic" indicates an ethereal realm, the forces contained therein, and its nonhuman inhabitants. Indigenous African worldviews often feature three distinct realms: "the sky, the earth (land and water), and the ancestral or spirit world, which is located under the earth. . . . Each space dimension is imbued with divinities . . . territorial spirits. . . and a host of minor spirits."[7] The first and third locations comprise the spirit world in Okorafor's novel. Onyesonwu frequently references *Ani*, the earth goddess, when thinking about religion in her post-apocalyptic society. Unsurprisingly, *Ani* is an actual earth goddess among the Igbo, who also call her *Ala* or *Ale*. Victor C. Uchendu explains, "*Ala* is a merciful mother. She intercedes for her children with other spirits. . . . As the custodian of Igbo morality, *ala* must take action to save the community."[8] Similarly, Joseph Thérèse Agbasiere's research reveals, "Igbo belief posits the existence of a complementary vital force to *Chukwu*. This divinity is venerated variously as *Ala*, *Ale*, or *Ani* and is attributed to the creation of the metaphysical or moral universe. Social beliefs and values are centered around *Ala* and not around *Chukwu*. *Ala* is considered female and a mother figure, hence the representation of her nursing a child."[9] As in indigenous Igbo and Yoruba worldviews, the cosmic and the terrestrial interact daily via ritual, prayer, and sacrifice. Spirit beings assist, confound, and otherwise intercede in human affairs. Okorafor's novel portrays a cosmos in which these nonterrestrial bodies sometimes appear invisible to an untrained eye. Nevertheless, cosmic beings affect earthly events. In *Who Fears Death*, the cosmos is as real as the world we taste, touch, hear, see, and smell. "There is nothing that a man must believe that can't be seen or touched or sensed. We are not so dead to the things around and within us."[10] We can know it as well as we know ourselves.

Human beings belong to the cosmic and the terraqueous world. An individual's spiritual knowledge permits access to the celestial world and its supernatural power. Throughout the novel, sorcerers are not mere *juju* artists but skilled herbalists, wise spiritual practitioners whose receptivity to the otherworld circumscribes their ontological experience. Stated simply, they optimize a general rule: human beings consist of cosmic components. In Igbo ontology, the human comprises both *ahu* (flesh) and *mmuo* (spirit).[11] Usually, *ahu* refers to the entire person—flesh and spirit.[12] Among the Igbo, *mmuo* "is considered a kind of separate existence and yet must remain an integral part of the living person . . . the soul of man, notably the *mmuo*, which is identical to the individual's personality, is indestructible."[13] These Igbo principles become the baseline for Okorafor's ontological theory.[14] She combines indigenous African concepts with multispeciesism to construct a radical ontology, which revalorizes the human beyond race, sex, and gender that are known today.

To prioritize the cosmic in an Africanfuturist reading of Onyesonwu's Black, female body is to contrast the precedents set by Molefi Kete Asante and Clenora Hudson-Weems. Molefi Kete Asante's Afrocentrism formulates "a theory and practice of liberation by reinvesting African agency as the fundamental core of our sanity" and aims for the "relocation of a subject place in the African world."[15] Asante prioritizes racial identity and theorizes ontology, religion, class, and gender through an essentialist lens. Similarly, Clenora Hudson-Weems' Africana womanist literary theory assumes race surpasses gender in Black women's liberationist thinking.[16] White patriarchal oppression in any guise remains the constant threat in response to which Asante and Weems develop theoretical paradigms. Sylvia Wynter, however, would suggest Asante and Weems lose sight of the more urgent need to revalorize the human. In "Unsettling the Coloniality of Being/Power/Truth/Freedom: Towards the Human, After Man, Its Overrepresentation," Wynter historicizes contemporary Western ontological perspectives and traces racism, classism, and the resultant overrepresentation of the ethnoclass man—the white, bourgeois male—back to its roots in a local, European worldview. In other words, the racial stratifications governing ontological taxonomies—even names people of color produce for themselves—burgeon within this single ethnocentric gaze. Wynter claims any debate about Black studies or Afrocentrism in response to Eurocentrism fails to escape this European paradigm because it still employs vocabulary whose existence upholds an already overdetermined ontological mode. She finds "the mode of being in which we now are (have socialized/inscribed ourselves to be) is isomorphic with the being of being human itself, in its multiple self-inscripting, auto-instituting modalities."[17]

Scholars in ethnic and cultural studies, she argues, should pursue Aimé Césaire and Franz Fanon's vision and develop "a new science of the Word . . . of our modes/genres of being human."[18] An Afrocentric literary analysis becomes an incomplete methodology for interpreting Okorafor's novel because it presumes race, an inheritance bequeathed by Europeans during their imperialist epoch, supersedes other identifiers when classifying human ontology. Asante's method seems to sublimate the spiritual and it presumes the body supersedes rather than operates *in tandem with* the cosmic element humans contain. To understand Okorafor's radical ontological theory, one must hold both flesh and spirit in balance. African indigenous worldviews operate at the intersection of earth and cosmos, of human, nonhuman, and spirit. *Who Fears Death* offers an ontological theory in which the cosmic threads entwining humanity with human and nonhuman beings, and with visible and invisible bodies, becomes the starting point for any social or political intervention. The interconnectedness between heroine and villain, father and daughter, and between lovers indicates any reparations for the marginalized must begin not with race or gender as its lead, but with an intentional investigation of the invisible bonds uniting self, other, and all creation that enable us to reenvision our possibilities.

Wynter effectually removes racial markers from the body and asks scholars to consider new ways to classify a deracialized *Homo sapien sapien*. Okorafor's novel immediately reaches into the cosmic for new signifiers but Wynter would reject her approach. The Caribbean theorist considers cosmologies that perpetuate oppression to be "ethno-astronomies," perspectives on the cosmic that reiterate what is declared to be true for one particular group but that is disseminated as true for all. In Wynters' view, an Igbo cosmology and its implications for human beings, especially human beings identified as Black, amount to a mere projection of an ethnic group's value system onto the universe, "thereby absolutizing each such criterion; and with this enabling them to be experienced by each order's subjects as if they had been supernaturally (and as such, extrahumanly) determined criteria, their respective truths had necessarily come to function as an "objective set of facts" for the people of that society—seeing that such truths were now the indispensable condition of their existence . . . as such a mode of being human."[19] Okorafor's novel, however, suggests marginalized epistemologies of the south such as African worldviews, make possible liberation, political reformation, and sociocosmic integrity.

NECROPOLITICS

Necropolitics, theorized by Achille Mbembe, exists antithetically to biopower, a Foucaultian concept. Biopower identifies a sovereign power's "administration of bodies and the calculated management of life," "the subjugation of bodies and the control of populations."[20] It stems from the sovereign's preoccupation with fostering life or disallowing it, which results in death.[21] In other words, the state wields biopower over its citizens; a unidirectional flow of power exists between the actor and those upon whom action is taken. Necropower, conversely, involves "those figures of sovereignty whose central project is not the struggle for autonomy but *the generalized instrumentalization of human existence and the material destruction of human bodies and populations.*"[22] For Mbembe, necropower best describes war in the late twentieth and early twenty-first centuries because it acknowledges multiple parties exert control over life and death. Conflicts in African countries, he explains, exemplify the right to kill enacted by parties other than the state. "Urban militias, private armies, armies of regional lords, private security firms, and state armies all claim the right to exercise violence or to kill . . . the vast majority of armies are composed of citizen soldiers, child soldiers, mercenaries, and privateers."[23] In addition, Mbembe's theory encapsulates how multiple controllers of power impact communities: necropower "disaggregates [populations] into rebels, child soldiers, victims or refugees, or civilians incapacitated by mutilation or simply massacred . . . while the 'survivors,' . . . are confined in camps and zones of exception."[24] *Who Fears Death* is a necropolitical novel. Inspired by an Associated Press news article on weaponized rape in Sudan, sexual violence and genocide texture Okorafor's futuristic continent.[25] The Nuru aim to eradicate the Okeke because, according to cosmogonic myth, Ani the earth goddess forsook them and condemned them to slavery. Thus, a Nuru hermeneutic of the Great Book, a sacred text between both ethnic groups, finds divine justification for expunging the Okeke. Similar to the Janjaweed in Darfur, the Nuru militants raid and destroy Okeke villages. Characteristic of necropolitical conflicts, the dispersed communities disintegrate into rebel militias who conscript boy soldiers and bands of survivors who relocate farther east. While the violence in the novel impacts men and women, Okorafor focuses upon gendered necropolitics—the deliberate, multiparty aggression against women. Najeeba's rape by the Nuru leader, Daib Yagoub, which results in Onyesonwu's birth, orients the protagonist's quest for justice.

Mbembe specifies three key traits within necropower: vertical sovereignty, splintering colonial occupation, and infrastructural warfare. Vertical sovereignty, he reasons, involves compartmentalizing occupied territories and sealing off settlements for authorities to maintain control. It works in tandem with the second component, splintering occupation, which references an authorities' ability to seclude communities and also use the urban environment as a surveillance mechanism against its self. Finally, when an authority destroys infrastructure and resources such as highways, edifices, medical equipment, and water supplies, it constitutes infrastructural warfare.[26] The first two components prove most important to necropolitics in Okorafor's revised Africa. Mbembe argues, "Under conditions of vertical sovereignty and splintering occupation, communities are separated across a y-axis. This leads to a proliferation of the sites of violence. The battlegrounds are not located solely at the surface of the earth."[27] In *Who Fears Death*, the protagonist faces three distinct battlegrounds. First, the genocide migrates from the western riverine Nuru communities where the Okeke remain enslaved eastward toward the Okeke-majority desert villages. Because her mission requires confronting Daib in person, Onyesonwu must travel against the tide, from east to west. The mindset of the Nuru and Okeke, however, constitutes a second battleground. Both communities view *ewu* people, those born from rape, as inherently violent and a threat to their community's safety, prosperity, and moral balance. Consequently, Onyesonwu faces sexual assault, attempted murder, and prolific verbal slandering in each village she visits. It is the divisive, disruptive, and pathological philosophies about *ewu* people that need eradication as much as the racist and colorist ideals fueling the war.

Onyesonwu's third battleground is the wilderness, the spirit world. Daib, himself a formidable sorcerer, attacks Onyesonwu within and through this cosmic terrain. For example, he first intimidates her when she enters the wilderness during her circumcision ceremony.[28] Then he attempts to choke his daughter to death via a dream.[29] The dream state brings Onyesonwu into the wilderness' proximity, thus she becomes susceptible to Daib's attack. Last, the final contest between them involves violence against the flesh and the spirit, as both Onyesonwu and Daib wield the mystic points to disable one another, specifically the *uwa* (physical world, the body) and the *mmuo* point (the wilderness).[30] In this way, the y-axis Mbembe describes stretches between the earth and the cosmos, between the body and the spirit. The x-axis extends along the genocide survivors' migratory route from west to east.[31] Placing Onyesonwu at the crux of the conflict also places her at the intersection where the x- and y-axes meet. Significantly, it suggests Onyesonwu finds wholeness by integrating her terrestrial and cosmic identities into one rebalanced being. Okorafor's ontological argument suggests the optimized human achieves balance across multiple inhabitable dimensions. Cosmic balance, therefore, exceeds mere inner peace; it entails a psychic, physical, emotional, and sociopolitical realignment.

GENDER AND SEX IN OKORAFOR'S AFROFUTURISM

Readers may expect a futurist text to propose a radical ontology whose embodiment contrasts the sex and gender constructs characterizing the twenty-first century. "When the constructed status of gender is theorized as radically independent of sex," Judith Butler explains, "gender itself becomes a free-floating artifice, with the consequence that *man* and *masculine* might just as easily signify a female body as a male one, and *woman* and *feminine* a male body as easily as a female one."[32] It would seem plausible, then, for a futuristic interpretation of the human to focus on gender's mutability and theorize the post-gender/post-sex body. What becomes of the body when sex and gender, as discursive acts, no longer circumscribe its possibilities? Yet Okorafor does not invest in this question. While she argues against conventional Igbo gender roles, she leaves the contested equivalence between biology, sex, and gender intact. This does not, however, mitigate Okorafor's ability to theorize sex differently. The key analytical question becomes: *Why* invest in sex as a biological fact? To this end, it becomes crucial to remember *Who Fears Death* as an *African*futurist text.

Like many African indigenous societies, clitoridectomy figures into Igbo cultural history. Joseph Thérèse Agbasiere's extensive research in *Women in Igbo Life and Thought* observes, "the coming of a girl's menses is a signal for the rite of clitoridectomy, which precedes a period of 'fattening' in preparation for marriage."[33] Named the Eleventh Year Rite in the novel, it figures significantly in the plot. Okorafor presents a New Africa in which female circumcision becomes "an old practice" and "no one really remember[s] *why* it was done" yet "the tradition [is] accepted, anticipated, and performed."[34] Onyesonwu, Diti, Luyu, and Binta undergo circumcision because tradition stipulates it is the only means by which eleven-year-old girls in Jwahir attain adult *female* status. The heroine, especially, believes the Eleventh Year Rite will reconstruct her social status by bringing honor to her parents who otherwise are supposed to feel ashamed of her *ewu* identity. Onyesonwu states, "I believed I could be normal. That I could be *made* normal."[35] According to Judith Butler, "Gender is . . . the discursive/cultural means by which 'sexed nature' or a 'natural sex' is produced and established as 'prediscursive,' prior to culture, a politically neutral surface *on which* culture acts."[36] Circumcision is a process through which culture acts upon their clitorides, the "prediscursive." The biological difference, it seems, is the "politically neutral surface" upon which culture scripts femininity. Igbo cultural practices inform the lifeworld depicted in the text, so when Okorafor contests clitoridectomy, she argues against how bodies "matter," in a Butlerian sense, within an African context. To this end, the novelist enables Onyesonwu to use her shape-shifting abilities to replace the bit of flesh taken from her. Later, she heals her friends' incisions and reinstates their capacity to climax. Effectually, Okorafor's futurism envisions a nonviolent "process of materialization that stabilizes over time to produce the effect of boundary, fixity, and surface we call matter."[37]

Undoing the operation, however, does not undo their gender. The theory Okorafor advances in the text argues against gender *roles* but not gender itself. The author establishes a heterosexual relationship in which Onyesonwu's sexuality is strictly normative. Okorafor specifies her protagonist's heterosexuality not only through frequent references to sexual intimacy between Onyesonwu and her male partner, Mwita, but also by articulating her discomfort while laying hands on her friend's *yeye* during healing. "I felt nauseated," Onyesonwu confides, "Not out of fear but more from a deep sense of discomfort. [Diti] would have to spread her legs. But *even worse*, I had to also place my hands on the scar that was left from that swift cut nine years ago."[38] Viewing another woman below the waist seems to transgress the boundaries between female friends. For one woman to touch another woman's pudenda outside, the socially sanctioned ritual context becomes taboo. Even healing lacks enough sacrality to entirely desexualize the contact between Onyesonwu and Diti. This passage in the text, however, also raises productive questions. Why, in an African worldview, is same-sex contact nauseating? Is Onyesonwu's malaise due to the spinning triggered by visual and tactile contact with a wound she once bore? Is the healing process also a matter of reliving the violence from "that swift cut nine years ago"? Why would an older woman's hands on a girl's vagina constitute a rite of passage, but Onyesonwu's healing act upon her age-mate becomes a moment for disgust? The contradiction invites the reader to think carefully about how physical contact between same-sex individuals becomes categorized as permissible or impermissible. Through the ambiguity surrounding Onyesonwu's reaction to touching her friend's *yeye*, Okorafor stirs the pot in the conversation about same-sex loving behavior in African cultures. Perhaps the tension around same-sex loving encounters serves to push to include LGBTQIA+ people within an African cosmization of the human.

Okorafor's inability to move beyond the reification of sex reflects tensions between Western and African feminist theories. Whereas authors like Judith Butler, Joan W. Scott, and Audre Lorde engage gender's constructedness and, thereby, sex's instability, Ifi Amadiume and Onyeronke Olajubu uphold sex as "natural" and "prediscursive" simply by refusing to interrogate how sex emerges in African societies.[39] Amadiume's *Male Daughters, Female Husbands: Gender and Sex in an African Society*, for example, explains how Igbo women often assume male roles within society. An Igbo daughter may become male and become her father's beneficiary in the absences of a male inheritor. Additionally, wealthy women and female merchants may take female husbands, women who would live with them and whose labor would enrich their coffers.[40] To her credit, Amadiume conducts an excellent analysis of how gender impacts women's positionality within Igbo culture. Her research does not, however, probe sex as a discursive act. She states,

"The flexibility of Igbo gender construction meant that gender was separate from biological sex. Daughters could become sons and consequently male."[41] Thus, Amadiume concretizes sex via biology and, inevitably, denies its performativity and citationality. Judith Butler first published three years after Amadiume's landmark text became available, so she would not have been able to address Butler's work. Nevertheless, it is important to notes but Amadiume's work leaves unanswered questions regarding how sex became a biological ("prediscursive") fact among the Igbo. Furthermore, such omissions become a pattern when reading Amadiume alongside more recent African authors such as Onyeronke Olajubu. *Women in the Yoruba Religious Sphere* discusses Yoruba women's participation in various Christian denominations in Nigeria. Women's identities, participation, and movement within institutions become Olajubu's primary concerns. Interestingly, she isolates gender from sex without interrogating the latter:

> For this work . . . gender may be defined as capacities and attributes assigned to persons on the basis of their alleged sexual characteristics. Gender, then, is a construct within a people's living experience, embedded in the base of their philosophy and manifesting at the theoretical and pragmatic levels of their polity . . . it is a process.[42]

Despite the similarities between her definition and Butler's theories, Olajubu never engages the Western theorist. As a result, sex remains a biological fact in Olajubu's analysis. Curiously, Olajubu connects Yoruba gender constructs to their cosmogony. Their engagement with the cosmic, Olajubu concludes, means "The question to ask about the state of the sexes is . . . over which areas do the sexes enjoy prominence?"[43] Notice her leap from gender to sex, suggesting what Judith Butler deems the assumption of sex into gender.[44] It is not this essay's intent to position Butlerian theory as the pinnacle of gender analysis. Neither must Western feminist theory take precedence over its African counterpart. Juxtaposing the two, however, identifies the interstice left unevaluated: *why* might African and Africana writers bypass Butlerian thinking about sex and gender?

When Olajubu defines sex/gender, she notes its enmeshment with indigenous cosmology and ontology. Butlerian ideas about the body counter indigenous cosmological and ontological paradigms by destabilizing the category called "women." All biological bases for understanding sexual difference become subjective and suspect in Western theory. Indigenous Yoruba cosmology, on the other hand, understands the body as a direct correlate to cosmic force. Teresa N. Washington provides an in-depth explanation of *aje*, a divine power and an honored group of women, whose existence in Yoruba cosmology, I argue, explains why it remains difficult to apply Butlerian hypotheses about sex and gender to indigenous African contexts. Anglophone scholars often mistranslate *aje* into "witches," thus demonizing a mystical concept Western worldviews often cannot absorb. Washington concurs with Diedre Badejo's definition: the *aje* are "an embodiment of power and an expression of the matrix of potentiality from which that power emanates."[45] Additionally, Washington finds Henry Drewal and Margret Drewal's explanation insightful. The Drewals ascertain those possessing this mysterious force "possess the secret of life itself."[46] Despite their affiliation with life, women controlling this force can execute others. The belief in power's neutrality enables transforms contradiction into balance. Power is neither positive nor negative; its direction depends on the agent and her objective. Most importantly, *aje* holds a unique relationship with women. According to Washington, it is a "cosmic force" belonging to the Great Mother Deities and manifests as a "naturally occurring property in select human beings."[47] "*Aje* is essential to biological creation" and "female ownership of [it] can be attributed to the life-giving, highly spiritual, and sacred womb."[48] Yoruba cosmogony seems to advance biological essentialism except this worldview has less to do with obligating women to bear life than with explaining *why* "female" and "life-bearer" become synonymous.

Women who hold *aje* bear "divine spiritual vision, divine authority, power of the word, and *age,* the power to bring desires and ideas into being."[49] Washington further explains *Aje* is a critical component Oduduwa, the progenitor of the Yoruba, used to establish Earth; it is an imperative ingredient in biological creation.[50] In sum, *aje* is a cosmic force distinct from women yet carried and controlled by women. Female bodies as sites where creative activity (not just fetal development) transpires, therefore, hold social and cosmic significance.[51] Washington's insights on *aje* suggest sexual difference, especially the category "female," remains immune to deconstruction in African women's theorizing because deconstructing the female means destabilizing a cosmic principle. No discursive act—not even one imbued with *ase*—accomplishes this feat. Judith Butler asserts, "The norm of sex takes hold to the extent that it is 'cited' as such a norm, but also derives its power through the citations that it compels"; this citationality is, in fact, the body's materialization.[52] Indigenous Yoruba cosmogony, on the other hand, upholds Hortense Spiller's conclusion: "before the 'body' there is the 'flesh,' that zero degree of social conceptualization that does not escape concealment under the brush of discourse, or the reflexes of iconography."[53] Spillers nods to the social influences on how communities make meaning out of their ontological experiences but, unlike Butler, she acknowledges an unsurpassable principle, beyond performativity, which informs "flesh." This principle, in African indigenous worldviews like the Igbo and Yoruba, is cosmic.

Nnedi Okorafor maintains an African women's theoretical stance on "female" as a stable category throughout *Who Fears Death*. Knowing both Igbo and Yoruba cosmogonies inform her post-apocalyptic Africa, I argue Okorafor reifies sexual difference to position Onyesonwu as a woman with *aje*. She lacks the "cool, patient, composed, and disciplined" demeanor such women usually possess, but Onyesonwu certainly owns the telltale "spiritual vision" and "holistic healing" this power entails.[54] Women with *aje* control creation, demonstrate compassion, and kill; Okorafor inscribes each capacity into Onyesonwu.[55] The protagonist manipulates creation through healing and restoring life, as evinced when she resurrects a slain goat and when she reverses her companions' genital surgeries. Additionally, her respect for the difference between her birth and Mwita's—his out of love, hers out of violence—exemplifies her compassion for those who suffer oppression and loss. Lastly, Onyesonwu has permission to kill: her father's annihilation remains the primary objective. Women's sacred power, notably, exists within a strict moral code. Washington specifies that an *Aje* may not decimate an individual unless he or she has violated spiritual and earthly laws and a special council agrees to her or his elimination.[56] Okorafor does not incorporate this elite group into the text, however, the morality surrounding the Great Mystic Points aims "to let the eagle and the hawk perch," thereby attaining balance and proceeding with fairness.[57] Effectively, the power of *Aje* is biopower in cosmic mode.

In Okorafor's post-apocalyptic Africa, both the Okeke and the Nuru believe *ewu* children inevitably become violent because, in their view, children born from rape can only perpetuate terror. For this reason, Mwita and Onyesonwu try to commit themselves to nonviolence. In Banza, for instance, Mwita begs his beloved to spare her assailant's lives. Her near-rape experience triggers memories about her mother's rape and Onyesonwu decides to produce a different outcome for herself. Nevertheless, Mwita reminds her, "This is not who we are. No violence! It's what sets us apart."[58] Nonviolence enables the *ewu*-born to negate stereotypes and perhaps whittle a wider social niche for themselves. Yet their mission to end genocide and the oppression of the Okeke requires violence. Okorafor appears to concur with Fanon's arguments about violence's utility for subjugated people. "At the level of individuals," Fanon attests, "violence is a cleansing force. It frees the native from his inferiority complex and from his despair and inaction; it . . . restores his self-respect."[59] In the novel, when Onyesonwu becomes "truly angry, . . . filled with violence, all things are easy and simple."[60] Killing her assailants would avenge her mother's rape and purge that memory's pain from her body. In Onyesonwu's mind, their deaths would exemplify women's boldness and agency in contrast to misogynist beliefs about women's secondary status within society. Vengeance and self-defense tempt her into believing violence would mitigate her low self-esteem. Murder at this moment, however, would reify the pervasive stereotypes about *ewu* people. Consequently, Onyesonwu withholds her *aje pupa*, the red *aje* known to cause "any incident that will result in blood," until she can justify her actions with respect to her mission.[61]

The difference between violence *with permission* and unsanctioned murder such as genocide separates Onyesonwu's actions from necropolitics. First, the protagonist fights Daib with all the earthly and cosmic tools at her disposal. This expedites the interruption of Nuru power. Incapacitating Daib derails his timeline for further genocide. Second, Onyesonwu terminates the Nuru army via biopower. She conceives (permits life) and generates a deadly shockwave, killing all virile men in the town of Durfa. It annihilates Daib's army. Cosmologically, Her *aje* entitles her to creative activity. She holds a divine right to assemble life and exact death simultaneously. To note, Okorafor attributes this decisive action to two agents: Onyesonwu and "something wholly outside of and unconcerned with humanity": the Creator, Ani, whom the author describes as cold and calculating. The Creator facilitates the mass killing, thereby sanctioning violence necessary for social change. Onyesonwu dispenses justice with permission from the Creator.[62] *Aje* as biopower creates and sustains life while simultaneously removing any obstacles to its development. Unlike necropolitics, ensuring life remains its vera causa.

RADICAL ONTOLOGY

Wholeness. Healing. Justice. Onyesonwu's quest pursues not only sociopolitical peace but also right alignment with the world in all its dimensions. By choice, she undergoes circumcision to foment her integration into Jwahir's culture. Her initiation into the Great Mystic Points primes her to live in balance with the spirit world. Finally, she vanquishes Daib's massive Nuru army, causing them to face their due retribution. If Onyesonwu defined herself solely by her ethnicity, race, or gender, these feats would have proven too daunting and too deleterious. Her existence in the eyes of all but her mother and stepfather seemed injurious enough. The trials she undertakes would only decimate her. What, then, surpasses these signifiers and liberates Onyesonwu's consciousness? What relationship reorders her being-in-the-world?

First, the heroine's shape-shifting skills enmesh her embodiment with other species in her environment. For instance, once she transforms into a vulture, she holds the knowledge of its ontology within her body. Familiarity with its wings, beak, and bone never escape her. Onyesonwu reflects, "I was still me, but from a different perspective."[63] Thus, she exists as a vulture and woman in one. This fantastic feature points to the multispeciesism in Okorafor's theory.

The vulture's keen eyesight, flight, and acute hearing enable Onyesonwu to "hear the earth breathing."[64] Theoretically, absorbing an animal's abilities would expand human faculties. More significant for Okorafor, however, is the ideological realignment multispeciesism renders. Observing the earth's breath means Onyesonwu realizes its agency, which effectually disenthrones *Homo sapiens sapiens*. The hierarchical, pyramidal relationship wherein humans dominate the earth becomes an outmoded worldview, an ineffective self-definition.

Second, "the wilderness," or spirit world, contains autonomous mystical flora, which impacts Onyesonwu's terrestrial experience. Wilderness trees attempt to murder her on Daib's behalf, leaving corporeal bruises. Inscribing plants with agency and establishing their place in the cosmic realm relays an African indigenous view that botanical species bear spiritual significance. Humans and plants are siblings born of the same divine force. Notably, when Onyesonwu performs a healing act, she draws from the earth's abundant cosmic energy.[65] What is more, Mwita uses herbal remedies to repair her physical wounds after combat. Okorafor's emphasis upon the natural environment as a pharmacological resource and as a cosmic entity suggests humans must reevaluate their existential purview. We live not only *among* plant species but also *with* them. Learning to balance our engagements with the world, much like how Onyesonwu learns to balances herself among the Great Mystic Points, requires interpreting our ontology as wholly intertwined with the environment. Mbembe explains necropower often involves disputes over labor and minerals, over bodies and earth.[66] Consequently, resisting gendered necropolitics also involves advocating for a sustainable world. Okorafor's ontological theory, in response, promotes an ecofeminist outlook. Sherilyn MacGregor notes, "Ecofeminism undertakes a critical analysis of the underlying *logic of domination* . . . and, hence, has the intellectual potential to problematize all forms of oppression based on dualistic thought."[67] Ecofeminism befits Okorafor's agenda because she invests in blurring the separations between humans and nature, nature and culture, and between the cosmos and earth. Collapsing dualisms seems to be a project Okorafor shares with ecofeminist thinkers.

Third, Onyesonwu's spiritual capabilities require her to search within and beyond her body for self-understanding. She manages to thrive by developing her cosmic being; training with Aro, the strongest sorcerer in Jwahir, is a life or death issue. Lessons on the *mmuo, uwa, okike, and alusi* points equip her with enough offensive and defensive skills to thwart Daib's attacks. Moreover, Onyesonwu understands earth as a borderland and contextualizes her being-ness within the pressurized zone where cosmos and soil meet. Only with a command of "the wilderness" does Onyesonwu find relief from oppressive taxonomies. Okorafor's heroine becomes a powerful liberationist metaphor since she represents how to demote race in African concepts about the human. Okorafor's radical ontological theory argues for the cosmico-terrestrial, a merger of cosmic and bodily identities. This perspective revalorizes the human by claiming the spiritual as an integral component of our species' identity. To clarify, "cosmic" does not equate to "religious." Okorafor suggests something ethereal and consistent exists within human beings; an invisible yet palpable force unites us in a productive sameness by which we can envision new routes toward social and psychological healing. The cosmico-terrestrial differs from Russ Castronovo's *sociocelestial* concept wherein "earthly distinctions no longer exist" but "antipathy to black materiality underlies this promise."[68] A cosmico-terrestrial perspective, on the other hand, concerns itself with factors impacting (Black) bodies. It antagonizes racism, sexism, and classism, while holding spiritual oppression within its frame.

Reading for the human through a hermeneutic of the cosmic in *Who Fears Death* establishes Nnedi Okorafor as an Africana theorist who assumes the revalorization challenge laid out by Sylvia Wynter. If Aimé Césaire speaks the truth when he states, "the West has never been further from being able to live a true humanism—a humanism made to the measure of the world," then Okorafor's vision bears utmost importance for she theorizes a radical ontology informed by a relationship to the universe that differs drastically from European paradigms structuring our sociological and scientific understanding about humankind.[69] The Igbo and Yoruba cosmogonies informing her thinking become significant because they already perceive humans, the earth, and the cosmos as an integrated whole. Essentially, the cosmico-terrestrial has always been with us, embedded deep within autochthonous, non-Western philosophies.

NOTES

1. Nnedi Okorafor, "Africanfuturism Defined," Nnedi's Wahala Zone (Blog), October 19, 2019. http://nnedi.blogspot.com/2019/10/africanfuturism-defined.html. Accessed September 28, 2020.

2. Henry Louis Gates, Jr., *The Signifying Monkey: A Theory of Afro-American Literary Criticism* (New York: Oxford University Press, 1988).

3. Georgene Bess Montgomery, *The Spirit and the Word: A Theory of Spirituality in Africana Literary Criticism* (Trenton: Africa World Press, Inc., 2008), 3–4.

4. Georgene Bess Montgomery, "The Ifa Paradigm: Reading the Spirit in Tina McElroy Ansa's *Baby of the Family*," *August Wilson and Black Aesthetics*, Dana A. Williams and Sandra G. Shannon, eds. (New York: Palgrave Macmillan, 2004), 49–62.

5. Teresa N. Washington, *Our Mothers, Our Powers, Our Texts: Manifestations of Aje in Africana Literature* (Indiana University Press, 2005); Teresa N.

Washington, *Manifestations of Masculine Magnificence: Divinity in Africana Life, Lyrics, and Literature* (Oxford: Oya's Tornado, 2014).

6. See Miriam Pahl, "Time, Progress, and Multidirectionality in Nnedi Okorafor's *Who Fears Death*," *Research in African Literatures* 49, no. 3 (Fall 2018): 207–222; Joshua Yu Burnett, "The Great Change and the Great Book: Nnedi Okorafor's Postcolonial, Post-Apocalyptic Africa and the Promise of Black Speculative Fiction," *Research in African Literatures* 46, no. 4 (Winter 2015): 133–150.

7. Ogbu U. Kalu, "Ancestral Spirituality and Society in Africa," *African Spirituality: Forms, Meanings, and Expressions*, Jacob K. Olupona, ed. (New York: The Crossroad Publishing Company, 2000), 54.

8. Victor C. Uchendu, *The Igbo of Southeast Nigeria* (New York: Holt, Rinehart and Winston, 1965), 96.

9. Joseph Thérèse Agbasiere, *Women in Igbo Life and Thought* (London: Routledge, 2000), 52–53.

10. Nnedi Okorafor, *Who Fears Death* (New York: Daw Books, 2010), 144.

11. Raphael Okechukwu Madu, *African Symbols, Proverbs and Myths: The Hermeneutics of Destiny* (Peter Lang: New York, 1992). Print. Studies in African and African-American Culture Series, 160–161.

12. Ibid.

13. Ibid., 162.

14. Igbo ontological and cosmological concepts also play a more immediate role in the text. *Mmuo* becomes one of the four Great Mystic Points Onyesonwu masters. It represents "the wilderness." The other three points include *uwa* (the physical world), *okike* (the Creator), and *alusi* (cosmic beings). Raphael Okechukwu Madu's research confirms these four concepts are cornerstones in Igbo thought. For more on *mmuo* and *uwa*, see Madu, *African Symbols, Proverbs and Myths*, pages 160–168 and page 177, respectively. Also compare Okorafor's explanation about the Great Mystic Points in *Who Fears Death* (pages 144–145) to the four divisions of Igbo thought in M. A. Onwuejeogwu, "The Igbo Culture Area," *Igbo Language and Culture*, F. Chidozie Ogbalu and E. Nolue Emenanjo, eds. (Ibadan: Oxford University Press, 1975), 1–10.

15. Molefi Kete Asante, "Afrocentricity, Race, and Reason," *Dispatches from the Ebony Tower: Intellectuals Confront the African American Experience*, Manning Marable, ed. (New York: Columbia University Press, 2000), 196–197.

16. See Clenora Hudson-Weems, *Africana Womanist Literary Theory* (Trenton: Africa World Press, Inc., 2004).

17. Sylvia Wynter, "Unsettling the Coloniality of Being/Power/Truth/Freedom: Towards the Human, After Man, Its Overrepresentation," *CR: The New Centennial Review* 3, no. 3(2003): 330.

18. Wynter, 331.

19. Wynter, 271.

20. Michel Foucault, *The History of Sexuality: An Introduction*—Volume I (New York: Vintage Books, 1990), 139–140.

21. ibid, 138.

22. Achille Mbembe, "Necropolitics," *Public Culture* 15, no. 1(2003): 14.

23. ibid, 32.
24. ibid, 34.
25. Okorafor, "Acknowledgements" in *Who Fears Death*.
26. Mbembe, 27–29. Mbembe draws heavily from Eyal Weizman's theories about the Israeli-Palestinian conflict.
27. Mbembe, 29.
28. Okorafor, 41.
29. Okorafor, 70.
30. Okorafor, 365–366.
31. Chapter 14, for example, contains a narrative mapping the violence. The storyteller conveys horrific images to the audience about the genocidal events in the West. Jwahir, where her narration takes place, is in the East. For this reason, when Onyesonwu and her companions set out to confront Daib, they travel west. See pages 90–94 and page 160.
32. Judith Butler, *Gender Trouble: Feminism and the Subversion of Identity* (New York: Routledge, 1999), 10.
33. Joseph Thérèse Agbasiere, *Women in Igbo Life and Thought* (London: Routledge, 2000), 98.
34. Okorafor, 33.
35. Okorafor, 33; original emphasis.
36. Okorafor, 11.
37. Judith Butler, *Bodies that Matter: On the Discursive Limits of Sex* (New York: Routledge, 1993), 9.
38. Okorafor, 229; my emphasis.
39. See Joan W. Scott, "Gender: A Useful Category of Analysis," *The American Historical Review* 91, no. 5(1986): 1053–1075; Audre Lorde, *Zami: A New Spelling of My Name* (Watertown: Persephone Press, 1982).
40. Ifi Amadiume, *Male Daughters, Female Husbands: Gender and Sex in an African Society* (London: Zed Books, 1987), 32, 46–47.
41. Amadiume, 15.
42. Onyeronke Olajubu, *Women in the Yoruba Religious Sphere* (New York: State University of New York Press, 2003), 7.
43. Olajubu, 10.
44. Judith Butler reexamines the relationship between sex and gender in *Bodies That Matter*. She suggests, "If gender consists of the social meanings that sex assumes, then sex does not *accrue* social meanings as additive properties but, rather, *is replaced by* the social meanings it takes on; sex is relinquished in the course of that assumption, and gender emerges, not as a term in a continued relationship of opposition to sex, but as the term which absorbs and displaces sex." Judith Butler, *Bodies that Matter: On the Discursive Limits of Sex* (New York: Routledge, 1993), 5.
45. Diedre Badejo, *Osun Seegesi: The Elegant Deity of Wealth, Power, and Femininity* (Trenton: Africa World Press, 1996), 76.
46. Henry John Drewal and Margret Thompson Drewal, *Gelede: Art and Female Power among the Yoruba* (Bloomington: Indiana University Press, 1990), xxxii.

47. Teresa N. Washington, *Our Mothers, Our Powers, Our Texts: Manifestations of Aje in Africana Literature* (Bloomington: Indiana University Press, 2005), 14.

48. Washington, *Our Mothers, Our Powers, Our Texts*, 15.

49. Ibid., 14.

50. Ibid., 14.

51. Teresa N. Washington elucidates this point when she states, "It is not merely the biological act of giving birth but the entire concept of *creating*, and the mysteries surrounding how to sustain and develop creation that signifies *Aje* Odu [Oduduwa] and her ownership of Oro [power of the word]." Washington, *Our Mothers, Our Powers, Our Texts*, 17.

52. Judith Butler, *Bodies That Matter*, 13 and 15.

53. Hortense J. Spillers, "Mama's Baby, Papa's Maybe: An American Grammar Book," *The Black Feminist Reader*, Joy James and T. Denean Sharpley-Whiting, eds. (Malden: Blackwell Publishers, 2000), 60–61.

54. Washington, *Our Mothers, Our Powers, Our Texts*, 14.

55. Ibid., 21.

56. Ibid., 35.

57. Okorafor, 144.

58. Ibid., 205.

59. Franz Fanon, *Wretched of the Earth*, Constance Farrington, trans. (New York: Grove Press, 1963), 94.

60. Fanon, *Wretched of the Earth*, 94.

61. Washington, *Our Mothers, Our Powers, Our Texts*, 25.

62. According to Washington, "Part of [the *Aje*'s] evolutionary educational and social work involves dispensation of justice. *Aje* are feared for their astral 'outings,' which are undertaken largely to punish trespassers of cosmic and terrestrial laws." Washington, *Our Mothers, Our Powers, Our Texts*, 14.

63. Okorafor, 57.

64. Ibid., 58.

65. Okorafor, *Who Fears Death*, 299.

66. Mbembe states, "Nonstate deployers of violence supply two critical coercive resources: labor and minerals." See *Necropolitics*, page 32.

67. See Sherilyn MacGregor, *Beyond Mothering Earth: Ecological Citizenship and the Politics of Care* (Vancouver: UBC Press, 2006), 34.

68. Russ Castronovo, *Necrocitizenship: Death, Eroticism, and the Public Sphere in the Nineteenth-Century United States* (Durham: Duke University Press, 2001), 171.

69. Aimé Césaire, *Discourse on Colonialism*, Joan Pinkham, trans. (New York: Monthly Review Press, 2000), 73.

BIBLIOGRAPHY

Agbasiere, Joseph Thérèse. *Women in Igbo Life and Thought*. London: Routledge, 2000.

Amadiume, Ifi. *Male Daughters, Female Husbands: Gender and Sex in an African Society*. London: Zed Books, 1987.

Asante, Molefi Kete. "Afrocentricity, Race, and Reason," *Dispatches from the Ebony Tower: Intellectuals Confront the African American Experience*, Manning Marable, ed. New York: Columbia University Press, 2000. 195-203.

Badejo, Diedre. *Osun Seegesi: The Elegant Deity of Wealth, Power, and Femininity.* Trenton: Africa World Press, 1996

Butler, Judith. *Bodies that Matter: On the Discursive Limits of Sex.* New York: Routledge, 1993.

———. *Gender Trouble: Feminism and the Subversion of Identity.* New York: Routledge, 1999.

Castronovo, Russ. *Necrocitizenship: Death, Eroticism, and the Public Sphere in the Nineteenth-Century United States.* Durham: Duke University Press, 2001.

Césaire, Aimé. *Discourse on Colonialism*, Joan Pinkham, trans. New York: Monthly Review Press, 2000.

Dery, Mark. "Black to the Future: Afro-Futurism 1.0," Mark Dery's Pyrotechnic Insanitarium. Web. 5 May 2011.

Drewal, Henry John and Margret Thompson Drewal. *Gelede: Art and Female Power among the Yoruba.* Bloomington: Indiana University Press, 1990.

Fanon, Franz. *Wretched of the Earth*, Constance Farrington, trans. New York: Grove Press, 1963.

Foucault, Michel. *The History of Sexuality: An Introduction* – Volume I. New York: Vintage Books, 1990.

Hudson-Weems, Clenora. *Africana Womanist Literary Theory.* Trenton: Africa World Press, Inc., 2004.

Kalu, Ogbu U. "Ancestral Spirituality and Society in Africa," *African Spirituality: Forms, Meanings, and Expressions*, Jacob K. Olupona, ed. New York: The Crossroad Publishing Company, 2000, 54–86.

Lorde, Audre. *Zami: A New Spelling of My Name.* Watertown: Persephone Press, 1982.

MacGregor, Sherilyn. *Beyond Mothering Earth: Ecological Citizenship and the Politics of Care.* Vancouver: UBC Press, 2006.

Madu, Raphael Okechukwu. *African Symbols, Proverbs and Myths: The Hermeneutics of Destiny.* Peter Lang: New York, 1992.

Mbembe, Achille. "Necropolitics," *Public Culture* 15, no. 1(2003): 11–40.

Montgomery, Georgene Bess. "The Ifa Paradigm: Reading the Spirit in Tina McElroy Ansa's *Baby of the Family*," *August Wilson and Black Aesthetics*, Dana A. Williams and Sandra G. Shannon, eds. New York: Palgrave Macmillan, 2004, 49–62.

———. *The Spirit and the Word: A Theory of Spirituality in Africana Literary Criticism.* Trenton: Africa World Press, Inc., 2008.

Nelson, Alondra. "Introduction: Future Texts," *Social Texts* 71, no. 2 (2002): 1–15.

Okorafor, Nnedi. *Who Fears Death.* New York: Daw Books, 2010.

Olajubu, Onyeronke. *Women in the Yoruba Religious Sphere.* New York: State University of New York Press, 2003.

Onwuejeogwu, M. A. "The Igbo Culture Area," *Igbo Language and Culture*, F. Chidozie Ogbalu and E. Nolue Emenanjo, eds. Ibadan: Oxford University Press, 1975, 1–10.

Scott, Joan W. "Gender: A Useful Category of Analysis," *The American Historical Review* 91, no. 5 (1986): 1053–1075.
Spillers, Hortense J. "Mama's Baby, Papa's Maybe: An American Grammar Book," *The Black Feminist Reader*, Joy James and T. Denean Sharpley-Whiting, eds. Malden: Blackwell Publishers, 2000, 57–87.
Thompson, Robert Farris. *Flash of the Spirit: African and Afro-American Art and Philosophy*. New York: Vintage Press, 1984.
Uchendu, Victor C. *The Igbo of Southeast Nigeria*. New York: Holt, Rinehart and Winston, 1965.
Washington, Teresa N. *Manifestations of Masculine Magnificence: Divinity in Africana Life, Lyrics, and Literature*. Decatur: Oya's Tornado, 2014.
———. *Our Mothers, Our Powers, Our Texts: Manifestations of Aje in Africana Literature*. Bloomington: Indiana University Press, 2005.
Wynter, Sylvia. "Unsettling the Coloniality of Being/Power/Truth/Freedom: Towards the Human, After Man, Its Overrepresentation," *CR: The New Centennial Review* 3, no. 3 (2003): 257–337.

Conclusion

Dear Reader, if I continue to write in the way that I have been writing, I fear that you may challenge my credentials as a competent college composition instructor after reading this conclusion. My former students, if they happen to read this text, are going to recognize the hypocrisy immediately. For in concluding this collection, I find myself introducing a topic not heretofore covered. And this is after I began the introduction in media res rather than with a true beginning! I just used an exclamation mark. That is a punctuation mark not often used in academic writing. As the pastor asks in the Black Baptist/ C.O.G.I.C. churches, please bear with me, Reader, for yet a while longer. In bringing this text to a close, I would like to discuss Ntozake Shange's *For colored girls who have considered suicide when the rainbow is enuf* (1975), Bernice L. McFadden's *Sugar* (2001), and Tayari Jones' *Leaving Atlanta* (2002). I place these texts here in order to demonstrate Black women writers' ongoing commitment to their artistic truths and presenting the humanities of Black characters—even if that humanity is twisted into something horribly monstrous.

When *For colored girls* debuted in 1975, its most vociferous critics were Black men. Because it would be stylistically trite and academically banal to rehash those arguments, even in recapitulation, I am going to bypass them here. Besides, it is my firm belief that is an ultimate waste of effort for Black women (or any other women) to validate these types of attacks with responses. No type of fleshly entity is that fantastically supernal to deserve that type of explanation or energy. The artist is at liberty to present the truth as she sees it. Furthermore, Shange explains her artistic intent better than the author of the essay that you are now consuming, dear Reader. In the preface to a new edition, Shange writes: "*For colored girls* was meant for women of color. The poems address situations that bridged our secret (unspoken) longing. *for colored girls* still is a women's trip, and the connection we can make through it, with each other and for each other, is to empower us all" (11). The women present truths and some of them are uncomfortable: rape, abortion, pregnancy-shaming, poverty, girlhood dreams, parties, music, love, death of children, post-traumatic stress disorder, positive HIV diagnosis, and good sex. Black women, like other women, are vulnerable to rape, desire love, are tired of poverty and underemployment, love their children, have experienced the pain of abortion, enjoy sex, and like to dance. All of these "facts," at some point, have been ostracized and "dirtied" by the white media when the woman was Black.

If Black men were insulted by Shange's play, did any one of them ever stop to think that maybe she was not talking to them or even trying to insult them at all? In fact, who were they talking to when they picketed holding signs that read, "I am a man?" Perhaps the target of their message was also Shange's. For it was that same hegemony that denied Black women the very human emotions of fear of rape in dark alleys (as there was a convenient stereotype created that Black women could not be raped due to her sexual immorality), slave mothers love for their children (as there was the convenient stereotype created that Black slave women did not feel the same affection for their children as white women did, so those children could easily be wrested from her hands and sold away), Black women were not respectable in the first place (as Black men were often lynched for "rape," no one was held accountable for raping Black women and the same lynchers had open sexual relationships with Black women for which they were not punished. They were only alienated if they tried to marry the Black women and give her some kind of legal right to property as that was discouraged legally), Black women were not protected from sexual harassment in the white women's kitchens where they worked (as subservient and "asexual" as Mammy is portrayed, no one ever questions where her children come from), and when Black women are attacked by anyone, none but her own community seemed to care. (After her womb was no longer directly linked to the stock market, she was no longer valued as a commodity and therefore no longer needed what little protection there was available under slavery. Though Black women were not lynched in the numbers that Black men were, Ida B. Wells-Barnett does record the extra-legal murders of Black women, and Black women widows in the North and South had their property legally taken away from them by court action and placed in the hands of white men. Such was the case with Maria W. Stewart, an early Black women political essayist.) *For colored girls* serves a double function: it witnesses to and testifies about the experiences of Black women and women of color in modern, sexists America while speaking truth to a hegemonic structure that perpetuates racism and sexism. In other words, the play validates as it critiques.

However, I want to be careful to avoid reducing *For colored girls* to the protest or naturalist tradition. It is a multilayered piece that, like those pieces presented in the Introduction, does not easily "fit" one critical label, because it spans them. Shange, in presenting women and the burdens they face, places one poem in the series where sexism, racism, poverty, and physical danger collude and interact. The "lady in blue" repeats: "I usedta live in the world/ then I moved to HARLEM/& my universe is now six blocks" (lines 1–3). This is not the Harlem of the Harlem Renaissance. The world of possibility and growth is not open to this speaker. This is the world of Lutie Johnson, the doomed protagonist of Anne Petry's *The Street* (1946). It is restrictive, confining, and filthy as the protagonist reports in the third stanza: "my oceans were life/what waters I have here sit stagnant/circlin ol men's bodies/shit & broken lil whiskey bottles/left to make me bleed" (lines 9–13). Black people were often redlined in Northern cities and restricted to neighborhoods where they did not own the property that they rented for exorbitant prices. There is no growth—as indicated by the word, "stagnant." The danger that she feels in this environment is real and threatens her womanity: "I usedta be in the world/a woman in the world/i hadda right to the world" (lines 66–69). For Harlem is a far cry from the liberatory microcosm of Alain Locke, but it is described as "six blocks of cruelty" (line 72). In fact, the Harlem of this poem mirrors the Harlem of Malcolm X, where the Northern Civil Rights activist described in his speech, "Crime in Harlem," overcrowded, unsanitary conditions and lack of access to quality healthcare that helped spread devastating diseases in the African American community like tuberculosis. Malcolm X, who was formerly a Harlem criminal before his conversion to Islam during a prison sentence, would have been very familiar with the criminal underworld of Harlem, and unfortunately, the speaker's feeling that her womanity is erased once she moved to Harlem is very real, according to the autobiographical experiences of X. Even in the twenty-first century, post–second-wave feminism, women of color, even when they hail from relatively high-profile families, are not safe from the ravages of violence in the city. For example, in 1984, Kimako Baraka, the sister of Amiri Baraka (formerly LeRoi Jones), was found stabbed to death inside her New York apartment. In 2003, according to the *New York Times*, his daughter was shot to death alongside her partner, Rayshon Holmes, by her sister's estranged husband.

Unfortunately, the wretched of humanity are real in Black communities. And why should Black women be prohibited from writing about them when Richard Wright's best-seller featured the bestial, fear-ladened Bigger Thomas? One of the more disturbing spectacles of humanity is the "beau willie brown" cycle. Beau Willie ultimately drops his own children from a balcony and kills them. Yet, Shange refuses to portray him as a two-dimensional villain. Beau Willie is something and someone missing from the larger American conversation: a Black soldier who has returned to American shores with severe post-traumatic stress disorder. In most academic conversations and popular portrayals of America at war, the Black soldier is largely absent. In this poem, Beau Willie's condition is made explicit: "there waznt nothing wrong/with him/p.t.s.d./p.t.s.c./p.t.s./he kept telling crystal/and that social worker/" (lines 14–16). Rather than accept help, Beau Willie turns to alcohol and drugs to ease the trauma of killing "arab children" (line 17). He beats Crystal with a high chair that still held their child, forcing her to take out a restraining order. It is obvious that Willie is not the "norm" for Black men in America. His mind has been traumatized and twisted by war until he abuses his own fiancé and kills their children. Yet, Shange was accused of hating Black men when this play debuted. The reaction to Beau Willie was an over-reaction by Black men. Honestly, it is not beyond white supremacists to take a fictitious character like Beau Willie, whose mind has been warped by war and drugs, and apply him to all Black men. However, holding Shange responsible for what white supremacists may do in response to her honest portrayal of this Black mother's pain after the loss of her children at the hands of her once-fiance and lifelong lover makes about as much sense as blaming a cancer patient for her tumor. The way to cure cancer is to attack the tumor and not blame the patient for her condition. This sequence is about Crystal's pain, and not about how white America may have perceived Beau Willie, for Beau Willie is America's creation. While Beau Willie is certainly a tragedy, how is this woman supposed to pick up the pieces of her life and put it back together after she witnessed the death of her two children? That is the story's focus. The womanist focus of the story reveals the juvenile nature of "social science fiction fiction." Would having the color of the masculine hand dropping the children off the balcony be a white one instead of a Black one ease this mother's pain?

Writing decades later but set decades earlier, *Sugar* asks the same question: How is a woman to pick up the pieces of her life after a child is brutally murdered? This is a pivotal question for Black women writers in the contemporary period when so much literature and "social science fiction fiction" portrays them as emotionally absent, love-starved welfare queens. It is rather remarkable, this turn that Black motherhood has taken: from asexual mammies who love the master's children while castrating her own sons to the jobless food stamp collector who stares absent-mindedly at the television all day while her academically underachieving children go from the schoolhouse to the jailhouse. Black women are everything but good mothers who love their children and struggle to provide them with love, validation, education, and nurturing according to popular culture and "social science fiction fiction."

McFadden opens this narrative with the brutal murder of a little child. The girlchild was discovered by a neighbor, Black John, on the side of the road, beaten beyond recognition, raped, and part of her vagina had been cut out. Since this part of the story was set in rural Arkansas in 1940, the assumption was that a white man had taken sweet little Jude away from her family and there was no need to contact white law enforcement officers who would be indifferent to the rape and murder of a dark-skinned Black girl child. Her mother, Pearl, became a husk of a woman for fifteen years until Sugar Lacey, a prostitute who eerily resembles Jude (she is Jude's half-sister, though Pearl did not know that), moved next door and befriended the aging matron. As the story unfolds, we learn that a Black man, and not a white one, killed Jude.

Lappy Clayton is a reefer-smoking, loud-mouthed, alcoholic, twisted wreck of humanity who feels that women and girls are his objects of sexual pleasure to do with them as he wishes, even if that means killing them. However, Lappy is not the norm for the men of Bigelow and is diametrically opposed to upstanding men like Jude's father, Joe Taylor. The narrator describes Joe: "God-fearing and soft-spoken, all that mattered to Joe was his wife, family and leading a life worthy of entering heaven. Nobody could ever accuse this man of raising his hand or his voice in anger. He understood things about life and women that other men just couldn't" (30). Lappy killed Jude and would have killed Sugar if it were not for Joe, her father. Knowing that Lappy, a Black man killed Jude, and not a white one, would not ease Pearl's grief one bit. In fact, Sugar decides not to tell Joe and Pearl about Lappy, even after Lappy tried to kill her. With a bit of clarity, Sugar knows that Joe, a veteran of World War I, would more than likely exact revenge upon an inhuman wretch like Lappy Clayton and go to the penitentiary. Like Shange, McFadden presents us with a picture of the African American war veteran, but this one does not suffer from post-traumatic stress disorder. Going to war for American has given him a sense of individual pride and Joe does not hesitate to defend his individual rights, though he is soft-spoken. Joe explains the feeling fighting in the army had given him:

> I can't say that I was proud to fight for my country, not say it and be truthful 'bout it. But I can say I felt proud when I looked around and saw the white men fall, bleed and die just like the colored . . . I felt proud because there was the proof right there on the battlefield that we was men just like them. Not monkeys or some ornery creature that hid its tail in its pants. But men that bled the same red blood. (33)

Joe's masculine identity is not based upon conquering women sexually and subduing them physically and financially, but upon his experiences as a soldier that allowed him to witness the parity of death on the battlefield. He had already confronted Lappy in a previous scene and showed absolutely no fear. According to Sugar's estimation, Lappy's homicide would not be worth sacrificing Pearl's newfound happiness and sending her into grief again.

While the story of an unapologetic whore and an aging matron who is cloaked in the politics of respectability in a rural, Southern town is wildly comical and entertaining, there is something else contained in this tale as well: class politics within the African American community. Admittedly, it is sometimes difficult to tease out class politics in any American text, but this is particularly true in African American literature, even during meticulous class preparation. Do we even think class intra-racially? We think politics of respectability as defined by Evelyn Brooks Higginbotham, and we may even point out chromatism, but do we ever point out issues of class explicitly? In the essay, "The Foreigner's Home," Morrison points out why it is very easy for any of us who teach African American literature to miss/dismiss class. She writes about minstrelsy and the function that it served:

> The form worked literally as, and only as, a black façade for whites: whites in black face. The black mask permitted whites to say illegal, unorthodox, seditious, and sexually illicit things in public. In short, it was a kind of public pornography, the main theme of which was sexual rebellion, sexual license, poverty, and criminality .... My point is that African Americans are still being employed in that way: to disappear the white poor and unify all classes and regions, erasing the real lines of conflict. (37–38)

In short, through minstrelsy and the press, the word "poor" became synonymous with Black or African American, and there was a disappearance of poor whites in America's imagination. There is no classism in African Americans throughout the nation, because African Americans are just poor and dispossessed economically, and this is often the direction of social science studies and an inherent danger of "social science fiction fiction."

But Black women writers demonstrate the various stratifications that African Americans demarcate intra-racially. In *Sugar*, this is not based upon her skin color, either. In some texts of the Harlem Renaissance, such as Wallace Thurman's *The Blacker the Berry* (1929), class within the African American community of Harlem is based upon skin color, and this portrayal was not far from the truth. Lighter-skinned African Americans were often allowed to apply for better-paying jobs. African American liberal arts institutions such as Rust College of Holly Springs, Mississippi or the famed Morehouse College of Atlanta, Georgia, that were actually founded and governed by white boards, white presidents, and white faculty members were founded to create a new class within their respective African American communities. African Americans had to protest to be hired by these institutions.

In this text, class is not based upon skin color or pigment. Instead, it is based upon the three women who raised her, the Laceys, who were notorious whores in her hometown of Short Junction, Arkansas. As a little child, Sugar remembers an older woman speaking of her, " 'Don't be talking to the likes of her, Caroline.' The little girl's mother came out and dragged here by the collar away from Sugar. Her bare feet skidded across the dirt, leaving squiggly lines behind. 'She a Lacy and we don't fraternize with those *type of people*" (44, *emphasis mine*). Sugar would meet this little girl again when they are grown women. This time, this little girl is a maid in an upscale home. Sugar pauses to look at the home, and the woman uses the phrase, "the likes of you." This time, Sugar has agency and understands the class implications that this woman hurls at her. She answers: "You live too far South to be so damn uppity. You and me, we the same. The likes of me is the likes of you!' Sugar said, her voice gutted with anger. She threw her bare arm out before the woman's face so that she could see their skin color was nearly identical" (123). A maid is dismissive of Sugar because of suggestive dress and make-up, but not her ebony skin color. The women of Bigelow also do not judge Sugar because of her skin color, but they are jealous because she sleeps with their men or as in the case of Fayline, the local hair dresser, is taking money away from her by encouraging women to wear wigs rather than patronize the local beauty parlor. They want her gone! In *Sugar*, class in the African American community has nothing to do with income, and everything to do with dress and mannerism. Most of these women are not pious (Shirley Brown is a notorious gossip and card cheat), but they try to separate themselves from the juke joint women by dress and mannerism.

Like Sugar, *Leaving Atlanta* hinges around child murder. In fact, it floats upon the Atlanta child murders of the late 1970s, perpetrated by an accused African American serial killer, Wayne Bertram Williams. The book is divided into three sections and though the child murders are tragic enough, by far, the saddest segment features the poorest child, Octavia. First, this child happens to be the darkest skinned child. The other school children in the book refer to her as "Watusi," indicating that her impoverished status and her dark skin are more akin to Africa than African Americans. It is strange that though African Americans have been Othered inside America and do not, in general, tend to view that Othered status as privilege, Black folk tend to find others to Other. Domestically, that other population is always Mississippi: internationally, that population is Africa.

While the children in the previous sections live in two-parent, suburban Atlanta homes, Octavia is the child of a single mother who lives next to the projects. Octavia says of fathers, "I had heard about people's fathers getting rough. And stepfathers supposed to be the worstest one out of all of them. My own daddy never got rough with me because I don't hardly know the man. He stay in South Carolina with his wife and they baby girl" (148–149). As the child of a single mother, this little girl spends nights alone while her mother works at the Sunbeam factory. The children mock Octavia for her poverty and a teacher who helps Octavia's mother: "Every time Mrs. Grier do something for me, kids go around saying its because I can't get somebody to do it for me at home. One time, Mrs. Grier brushed my hair and the next thing I knew, people said, *Octavia so poor she ain't got a brush at home*. Mrs. Grier gave me some banana bread and they said my mama don't feed me" (167, emphasis Jones'). In addition, Octavia's paternal grandmother makes discouraging remarks about her mother. The paternal grandmother refers to everything Octavia's stepmother sends as "quality." Octavia is a precocious child and said, "I was confused at first, until I figured out that she was saying that Gloria was quality. I didn't care if she was quality or not, but I didn't appreciate what Granny was trying to say about my mama" (211). It is the grandmother's remarks about her mother that hurts this child and causes her anger when Octavia learns that for her own safety, she will be going to South Carolina with her father and step mother. The child does not want the nasty implications of "quality." Octavia wants her mother. And that is how the story ends.

Since class issues are difficult in North America, the decision was made to incorporate the Afro Caribbean in this collection. The Francophone Caribbean and the Anglophone write about it with a clarity that is missing from discourse around money in the United States. In "The Occasion for Speaking," George Lamming declares, "To be black, in the West Indies, is to be poor; whereas to be black (rich or poor) in an American context is to be a traditional target for specific punishments. Racism is not just an American problem. It is an element of American culture. No such thing is true of the British West Indies" (33). Writing of the Francophone Caribbean, Edouard Glissant, explains, "As can be seen, there is social progress. The plantation greathouse and the foreman's cabin are replaced by boards, offices, agencies" (36–37). Yet, the inequities of the plantation economy remain the same. And yet, African women experience blackness differently from their Caribbean counterparts. They write their own truths as they see fit.

In concluding this collection, I offer to the you, Reader, that I have not concluded at all. This is merely a beginning or a glimpse into the practices of those in the academy who teach, read, and write about Black women writers in the contemporary era. Black women writers remain committed to telling the truth of humanity—even if that truth is painful. I feel that we owe it to them to see that their truth is kept on our syllabuses and presented to new generations of students and readers beyond our beloved anthologies. Perhaps there will be another edition of this collection soon with even more essays and contributors. Maybe. I am hoping. Black women writers have something to say. And we are listening.

WORKS CITED

Fox, Margalit. "Amari Baraka, Polarizing Poet, and Playwright, Dies at 79." *The New York Times*, January 9, 2014. https://www.nytimes.com/2014/01/10/arts/amiri-baraka-polarizing-poet-and-playwright-dies-at-79.html. Accessed November 15, 2020.

Glissant, Edouard. *Caribbean Discourse: Selected Essays*. Translated by J. Michael Dash. Caraf Books, 1989.

Jones, Tayari. *Leaving Atlanta*, Warner Books, 2002.

Lamming, George. *The Pleasures of Exile*, Allison & Busby, 1960.

McFadden, Bernice. *Sugar*, Plume, 2001.

Morrison, Toni. *The Source of Self-Regard: Selected Essays, Speeches, and Meditations*, Alfred A. Knopf, 2019.

Shange, Ntozake. *For Colored Girls Who Have Considered Suicide When the Rainbow is Enuf*, Scribner, 2010.

Index of Authors and Topics

Achebe, Chinua: *Things Fall Apart*, 159
Adichie, Chimamanda, 147–48; *Americanah*, 147–60
Adjibodou, Venise, 279
African American spirituals, 122
African futurist literature: definition, 280
African Love Stories, 147
Agbasiere, Joseph Thérèse, 281; *Women in Igbo Life and Thought*, 286
Aidoo, Ama Ata, 147
Alabama, Birmingham, 11
Alexander, Margaret Walker, xv *For My People*, xvii; "My Truth and My Flame", xv–xvi, xvi
Amadiume, Ifi: *Male Daughters Female Husbands: Gender and Sex in an African Society*, 287
American Dream, 154–55
American North, 2, 80
American South, 5, 10–11, 218
Anthony, Ronda C. Henry: *The Narrative of William W. Brown, a Fugitive Slave*, 80; *Searching for the New Black Man*, 80

Baartman, Sarah (Hottentot Venus, Sartjie Baartman), 18, 23, 237
Baker, Houston, 121
Baldwin, James: *Another Country*, 5; *The Fire Next Time*, 5, 19; *Giovanni's Room*, 5; *Notes of a Native Son*, 5
Bambara, Toni Cade: *The Black Woman*, 112–13, 118
Banks-Wallace, Joanne, 189
Baraka, Amiri, ix; *Confirmation*, xi, xv
Beale, Fran, 118
Bildungsroman, 186
biomythography, 200
Black Arts Movement (BAM), 117
Black motherhood, 128–32, 168, 255
Black Power Movement, 49, 88, 111, 117
Black Venus literary types: Black Venus, 238, 242–44; Sable Venus, 238–39
Brooks, Gwendolyn: "The Ballad of Chocolate Mabbie", 35; "The Ballad of Pearl May Lee", 34; "The Ballad of Rudolph Lee", 35; "The Boy Died in My Alley", 33–34; "The Children of the Poor", 30; "kitchenette building", 31; "The Life of Lincoln West", 35; "The Lovers of the Poor", 30; *Maud Martha*, xvii–xix, 27, 30, 36–40; *In the Mecca*, 251; "the mother", 32; "An Old Black Woman,

Homeless, and Indistinct", 30; "The Second Sermon in Warpland", 266; "We Real Cool", 27
Butler, Judith, 288
Butler, Octavia: article: "Lost Races in Science Fiction", 175; novels (*Clay's Ark*, 164, 166; *Dawn*, 209; *Fledgling*, 182, 185; *Kindred*, 185; *Mind of My Mind*, 163, 165–66, 169–71; *Parables*, 251; *Patternmaster*, 163, 166–69; *Survivor*, 164); *Wild Seed*, 163, 164–65, 172, 185 (*Xenogenesis*, 175, 210–13)

Call and Response: The Riverside Anthology of the African American Literary Tradition, 115, 118
Chancy, Myriam, 98
Chodorov, Nancy: *The Reproduction of Mothering*, 130–31
Christian, Barbara, 99, 127
City College of New York (CCNY), 51
Civil Rights Movement, xx, 47–49, 122
Clark, Keith: "A Distaff to a Dream Deferred? Ann Petry and the Art of Subversion", 3; *The Radical Fiction of Ann Petry*, 3
Clifton, Lucille: *Blessing the Boats*, 217; "Why Some People Be Mad at Me Sometimes", 217
Coleman, Wanda: *Bathwater Wine*, 267; "Beaches. Why I Don't Care for Them", 263; "Flight of the California Condor", 267; "I Live for My Car", 267; *Ostimatio Vamps*, 269; "Requiem for a Nest", 269; "Shitworker in General", 270; *The World Falls Away*, 270; "Yardwork", 270
Collins, Kathleen, 47–52; films (*The Cruz Brothers and Miss Molloy*, 51; *Losing Ground*, 52); plays: *Remembrance, The Brothers*, 50; posthumous films: *Notes from a Black Woman's Diary, Whatever Happened to Interracial Love*, 47; short stories: "Conference Parts I and II", "The Happy Family", "Whatever Happened to Interracial Love", 48
Collins, Patricia Hill, 128, 258; Black feminist epistemology, 270; *Black Feminist Thought: Knowledge, Consciousness and the Politics of Empowerment* (note), 273; *Black Sexual Politics: African American Gender and the New Racism*, 16
colorism, 34, 48
Critical Race Theory: definition, 29

Dammond, Peggy, 47–48
Danquah, Meri Nana-Ana: *Shaking the Tree: A Collection of New Fiction and Memoir by Black Women*, 12
Davis, Cynthia, 48
decolonial love, 156, 158–59
Dente, Shahara'Tova, 1
Diaz, Junot: *The Brief Wondrous Life of Oscar Wao*, 158
Dixton, Thomas, *The Leopard's Spots*, 187
domestic work, 9–10, 112–13
Dred Scott vs. Sanford, 264
DuBois, W. E. B., 218; double consciousness, 28, 97; *The Quest of the Silver Fleece*, 251; "Talented Tenth", 47
Dungy, Camille: *Black Nature*, 254; "Characteristics of Life", 256; "How Great the Gardens When They Strive", 256; "A Massive Dying Off", 257; *Smith Blue*, 257; "trophic cascade", 254

eco-justice poetry: definition, 252
eco-spirituality: definition, 254
Emecheta, Buchi: *The Joys of Motherhood*, 130
England/UK, 155
environmentalism, 103–4

Fanon, Frantz: *Black Skin, White Masks*, 97
Frost, Elizabeth A.; *The Feminist Avant-garde in American Poetry*, 118

Gates, Jr., Henry Louis: *The Signifying Monkey*, 280
gender discrimination (sexism), 16
Gibson, Ebony, 163
Giovanni, Nikki, 97; "Allowables", 265; "Bears in the Spring", 265; *Blues: For All the Changes*, 264; *The Collected Poetry of Nikki Giovanni, 1968–1998*", 264; *A Good Cry*, 265; "Possum Crossing", 265; "Sanctuary: For Harry Potter the Movie", 266; "For Saundra", 263; "This Poem Hates", 264; "Walking Down the Park", 263; "The Yellow Jackets", 265
Glissant, Edouard, 306

Hansberry, Lorraine: *A Raisin in the Sun*, 32
Higginbotham, Evelyn Brooks: respectability politics, definition, 6; *Righteous Discontent: The Women's Movement in the Black Baptist Church, 1880–1920*, 6
Hirsch, Marianne: *The Mother/Daughter Plot: Narrative, Psychoanalysis, Feminism*, 130
hooks, bell, 129, 212; *Talking Back: Thinking Feminist, Thinking Black* (note), 273; *We Real Cool*, 86
Hudson-Weems, Clenora: Africana Womanism, 253, 281
Hughes, Langston, 18, 49
Hurricane Katrina, 258
Hurston, Zora Neale, xv; *Moses, Man of the Mountain*, xxii; *Their Eyes Were Watching God*, 251

Institute for the Study and Culture of Black People, xv–xvi

Jackson State University, ix, xv
Jemisin, N. K., 237; *The Fifth Season*, 238–43
Jones, Charles, 48
Jones, Gayle: *Corregidora*, 57; *Eva's Man*, 57; "The Women", 57
Jones, Suzanne, 5
Jones, Tayari: *Leaving Atlanta*, 299, 305–6
Jordan, June, xix; *His Own Where*, xix–xx

Kaalund, Valerie Ann, 253
Kelley, Robin D. G., 111; *Freedom Dreams: The Black Radical Imagination*, 114, 121
King Jr., Martin Luther: "Letter from a Birmingham", 173

Lamming, George: "The Occasion for Speaking", 306
lesbian (ism), 59, 168, 200
Lockhart, Lana, 75
Lorde, Audre, 97–98, 209; essays ("Age, Race, Class, and Sex: Women Redefining Difference", 207; "The Master's Tools Will Never Tear Down the Master's House", 206; "Uses of the Erotic", 156); novels: *Zami: A New Spelling of My Name*, 197, 200–201, 206–8

Makeba, Miriam, 104
manhood/masculinity: "Cool Pose", 78; economics and masculinity, 79–81, 90; hegemonic masculinity, 77–79, 82–83, 88–89; manhood redefined, 91–92
Maparyan, Layli Phillips: *The Womanist Reader: The First Quarter Century of Womanist Thought*, 211, 253
Mbembe, Achille: necropolitics, defined, 283
McCray, Carissa, 27

McFadden, Bernice L.; *Sugar*, 299, 302–305
Montessano, Michael C., 111
Montgomery, Georgene Bess, 280; Ifa Paradigm, definition, 280
Morris, Susan M.; "Black Girls Are from the Future: Afrofuture Feminism in Octavia Butler's *Fledgling*" 184, 205
Morrison, Toni, ix; "The Foreigner's Home", 304; *A Mercy* ix; *Paradise*, 132–40; *Playing in the Dark: Whiteness and the Literary Imagination*, 192, 198; "Recitatif" ix; *Sula*, 251
multiracial literature: pedagogical/critical strategy, 27–28
Murray, Albert: "The Clutch of Social Science Fiction", xvii
Mustafa, Linda, 127
Myles, Lynette: *Female Subjectivity in African American Women's Narratives of Enslavement*, 97
Nigeria, 149, 154–55, 157
1963 Alabama Church Bombing, 11

O'Barr, Jean, Deborah Pope, Mary Wyer: *Ties That Bind: Essays on Mothering and Patriarchy*, 120
Okorafor, Nnedi: *Who Fears Death*, 279, 281–85, 290–93
Olajubu, Onyeronke: *Women in the Yoruba Religious Sphere*, 288

Patton, Venetria: *Women in Chains: The Legacy of Slavery in Black Women's Fiction*, 127
"The People Could Fly", 181
Petry, Ann: *The Narrows*, 4; *The Street*, 1, 3–10, 13–17
Phillis Wheatley Festival, xv–xvii
Pillow, Gloria Thomas: *Motherhood in Shades of Black*, 136

Poole, W. Scott, *Monsters in America*, 182
Pratt, Annis, 201–2

racism, 8, 159, 174, 199, 218, 261
Rich, Adrienne: *Of Woman Born: Motherhood as Experience and Institution*, 129, 131–32
Roth, Henry: *The Cruz Chronicles*, 51
Ruddick, Sara: *Maternal Thinking: Towards a Politics of Peace*, 129

Sanchez, Sonia: collected works (*Home Coming*, 119; *Homegirls & Hand Grenades*, 119; *Sacred Ground*, 115; *Shake Loose My Skin: New and Selected Poems*, 115); poems ("For Sweet Honey in the Rock", 115; "Stay on the Battlefield", 111, 115–17); and Sweet Honey in the Rock, 111, 115–17
Sandoval, Chela: *Methodologies of the Oppressed*, 156
Schmidt, Anna, 147
Scott-Heron, Gil: "Whitey on the Moon", 251, 262
sexual violence (gender violence), 13–19, 84, 89, 159, 174
Shange, Ntozake, 57; *For colored girls who have considered suicide when the rainbow is enuf*, 299–302
Shawl, Nisi, xxi; "Pataki" xxi–xxii
Shockley, Evie, 258; "Atlantis Made Easy", 258; "half-red sea", 258; "John Brown's Body", 260
slavery, 182, 237, 261–62, 300
Smart-Grosvenor, xx; "Skillet Blonde", xx–xxi
Smith, Felipe: *American Body Politics*, 183
Smith, Rosalyn Nicole, 197
Smith-Spears, Rashell, 181
speculative fiction: definition, 202–3
storytelling, 189–90

street literature, 2
Student Nonviolent Coordinating Committee (SNCC), 47
Sweet Honey in the Rock, 115

terrorism, 11–12
Thomas, Sheree, *Dark Matter: A Century of Speculative Fiction from the African Diaspora*, 203
Thurman, Wallace: *The Blacker the Berry*, 304
Trethewey, Natasha, 217–18; collected poetry (*Bellocq's Ophelia*, 218, 221–24; *Beyond Katrina: A Meditation on the Gulf Coast*, 230–31; *Congregation*, 233; *Domestic Work*, 218, 219–21; *Native Guard*, 224–30); nonfiction: *Memorial Drive: A Daughter's Memoir*, 233–35

Umbra Writing Workshop, 49

vampires, 182–84, 188–89
violence, 264, 301, 303
voicelessness, 36
Voodoo, xxi–xxii

Wade, Jasmine, 237
Walker, Alice: "Coming Apart", 199; criticism (*Black Women Novelists and the Nationalist Aesthetic*, 84; *In Search of Our Mother's Garden: Womanist Prose*, 95, 113); individual poems ("Before I Leave the Stage", 106; "Democratic Motherism", 102–4; "Democratic Womanism", 99–100; "Turning Madness into Flowers", 100–101); novels (*The Color Purple*, 64; *Meridian*, 130; *Third Life of Grange Copeland*, 75); poetry collections (*Good Night Willy Lee, I'll See You in the Morning*, 95; *Horses Make a Landscape More Beautiful*, 95; *Once*, 95; *Revolutionary Puritans and Other Poems*, 95; *The World Will Follow Joy*, 95, 96, 98); womanism definition, 99, 111, 113–14, 199
Wall, Cheryl: "Nellie–Pioneer of Black Feminist Literary Criticism: Nellie McKay and Black Women's Studies", 4
Warren, Nagueyalti, 217
Warren, Robert Penn: *Segregation: The Inner-Conflict in the South*, 230
Werbanowska, Marta, 251
West African mysticism, 169, 181
Wheatley, Phillis, xii; "To His Excellency General Washington", x; "Liberty and Peace, A Poem", x
Williams, Kimberlé Crenshaw: "Demarginalizing the Intersectioning of Race and Sex", 4; intersectionality definition, 29; "Mapping Margins", 5
Williams, Patricia, 98
Winter, Sylvia: "Unsettling the Coloniality of Being/Power/Truth/Freedom: Towards the Human, After Man, Its Overrepresentation", 282
Wright, Richard: "Blueprint for Negro Writing", 9; *Native Son*, xix, 251

X, Malcolm: "Crime in Harlem", 301

Youngblood, Shay: *Black Girl in Paris*, 1, 5, 8–12, 17–20

About the Editor and Contributors

ABOUT THE EDITOR

LaToya Jefferson-James is from the very small town of Centreville, Mississippi. She is an assistant professor of English at Mississippi Valley State, which is in the very small town of Itta Bena, Mississippi.

ABOUT THE CONTRIBUTORS

Shahara'Tova V. Dente is assistant professor of English and women's studies at Mississippi University for Women (MUW). She is also the graduate director of Women's Leadership. She received her PhD in English with an emphasis on twenty-first-century African-American literature, hip-hop literature, and hip-hop feminism from the University of Alabama. At MUW, Dente teaches a range of courses, including hip-hop literature and feminism and African American literature. Dente's recent publications include "Writing beyond Endings": Toni Morrison's *The Bluest Eye* and Sapphire's *PUSH* in the spring 2018 issue of *POMPA*, and a 2018 encyclopedia entry, "Death Row Records" which appears in the *St. James Encyclopedia of Hip Hop Culture*. Dente is currently revising a book manuscript on hip-hop literature, and she is coediting an anthology on higher learning, the #MeToo Movement, and Trump's America.

Carissa McCray, PhD, is a K–12 instructor in Florida. Her research and teaching philosophy focuses on equitable rural education by including multicultural literature, creating mentor groups, and assisting students in engaging in high impact opportunities. Through theoretical perspectives of critical race theory, intersectionality, and emotional processing theory, Dr. McCray has the ability to include and engage students from diverse backgrounds.

Cynthia Davis is a professor of English at San Jacinto College in Pasadena, Texas. She teaches classes in American Realism, Shakespeare, British Romanticism, and William Blake.

Georgene Bess Montgomery is an associate professor and Interim Chair of the Department of English and Modern Languages at Clark Atlanta University. She received her BA and MA in English from Georgia Southern University and her PhD in English from the University of Maryland. She is the author of *The Spirit and the Word: A Theory of Spirituality in Africana Literary Criticism*, which utilizes a method informed by the ideas and worldview of Ifa, an ancient African spiritual system, to unlock deeper levels of meaning in the writings of African peoples. Bess Montgomery has published extensively on a variety of subjects but also continues to publish scholarly essays that employ the Ifa Paradigm as a lens through which she analyzes Africana literary texts.

Lana N. Lockhart is a lecturer in the English Department at Spelman College. She also teaches African Diaspora and the World. Her areas of research include African American Literature, women's studies, and composition and rhetoric. Most of her publications and presentations explore Black women writers. She has a PhD in English literature and criticism from Indiana University of Pennsylvania.

Michael C. Montesano is a PhD candidate of comparative literature at Indiana University (IU); he is a PhD minor in the African studies program, and he is an affiliate at the IU Center for Research on Race and Ethnicity in Society (CRRES). Michael's work focuses on literary representations of systemic inequality in Nigeria, Peru, and the United States. He has published scholarly work in the *African Conflict and Peacebuilding Review* and the *Journal of Black Studies*. His first book of poems, *We Hailed at the Twilight*, was published in 2016 by *Editorial Palimpsesto, 2.0.*

Linda Mustafa teaches at Ibrahim Badamasi Babandiga University at Lapi, Niger State, in Nigeria. She specializes in African American and Afro Caribbean literature.

Anna E. Schmidt teaches writing and U.S. multiethnic literature at Maryville University. She holds a PhD and an MA in American studies from Saint Louis University. An article on poetry, spirituality, and environmental justice was recently published in *ISLE: Interdisciplinary Studies in Literature and Environment.* Her research interests include comparative multiethnic literature and culture, contemporary poetry, and American religions.

Ebony Gibson is assistant professor of English at Georgia Gwinnett College and teaches first-year writing, creative writing, and African American literature. She has an MA in English from Morgan State University, an MFA in fiction from Columbia University, and an MA in African American studies from Georgia State University (GSU). She is also completing a PhD in English at GSU with a focus in African American literature from the Black Arts Movement to the present. For her dissertation, she plans on using the Butler archives at Huntington Library to analyze the evolution of Lilith Iyapo and Oankali in various drafts of Butler Xenogenesis series.

Rashell Smith-Spears is associate professor and co-chair of English at Jackson State University. In addition to a PhD in English, she has an MFA in creative writing. Her research interests include African American literature, nineteenth-century literature, identity politics, and popular culture.

Roslyn Nicole Smith earned a BA in English from Spelman College and an MA in literature from GSU. She is currently in the dissertation phase of her PhD at GSU. Her primary area of study is contemporary American literature, and her secondary area of study is rhetoric and composition. She is currently a professor at Spelman College where she teaches composition courses and a course on womanist black speculative fiction.

Nicole's literary research centers around Black feminist readings of Black speculative fiction, written by women, as unique responses to intersectional oppression. Her rhetoric and composition interests include translating black feminist theories and speculative stances, such as Afrofuturism, into new media pedagogies in the literature and composition classrooms.

Nagueyalti Warren, professor of pedagogy Emerita African American studies, Emory University, is a poet and academic. Her publications include *Margaret*, winner Naomi Long Madgett Poetry Award; and *Braided Memory*, winner Violet Reed Haas Poetry Award. She is editor of *Temba Tupu! (Walking Naked) The Africana Woman's Poetic Self-Portrait.* Her poetry has appeared in *Essence Magazine, Cave Canem Anthology, The Ringing Ear, Obsession, 44 on 44*, and elsewhere. She is a Cave Canem graduate fellow. Warren also is author of *W.E.B. Du Bois: Grandfather of Black Studies, Critical Insights: Alice Walker*, and *Alice Walker's Metaphysics: Literature of Spirit.*

Jasmine H. Wade is a storyteller, curriculum writer, and PhD student of cultural studies at the University of California, Davis. Her research interests include radical aesthetic practices of contemporary social movements in the Americas. As a writer and scholar, she considers herself a queer time traveler, one who moves, thinks, and imagines in the past, present, and future at once. She has presented her work at several conferences, including the National Women's Studies Association Conference, Critical Ethnic Studies Conference, the Speculative Futures Conference, the Crossings Conference, and the Afrosurrealism Conference. As a storyteller, she is a Pushcart Prize nominee, winner of the Edward P. Jones Short Story Contest, finalist for the Hurston/Wright Founding Members Award for College Writers, and finalist for the Tu Books New Visions Award. Her short stories have appeared in *Drunken Boat*, *TAYO Literary Magazine*, *Lunch Ticket*, *The Copperfield Review*, and others.

Marta Werbanowska is a doctoral candidate and undergraduate instructor at the Department of English at Howard University in Washington, DC. Previously, she received her master's in English studies at the University of Warsaw in Poland, and spent an academic year as a Fulbright scholar/researcher at the University of North Carolina Charlotte. In her dissertation, she traces the presence of the Black Atlantic tradition of ecological thinking and critique of Western humanism in the works of selected contemporary African American poets.

Venise N. Adjibodou earned her doctorate in Africana studies and religious studies from the University of Pennsylvania. Her ethnographic work uses new materialism and affect theory to explore lived religion among Vodun practitioners in southern Bénin. She can be found in *Spirit Service: Vodun and Voodoo in the African Atlantic World* (Indiana University Press).

www.ingramcontent.com/pod-product-compliance
Lightning Source LLC
Chambersburg PA
CBHW021342300426
44114CB00012B/1047